BODY LORE AND LAWS

Body Lore and Laws

Edited by
ANDREW BAINHAM
SHELLEY DAY SCLATER
and
MARTIN RICHARDS

·HART·
PUBLISHING
OXFORD – PORTLAND OREGON
2002

Hart Publishing
Oxford and Portland, Oregon

Published in North America (US and Canada) by
Hart Publishing c/o
International Specialized Book Services
5804 NE Hassalo Street
Portland, Oregon
97213-3644
USA

Distributed in the Netherlands, Belgium and Luxembourg by
Intersentia, Churchillaan 108
B2900 Schoten
Antwerpen
Belgium

Hart Publishing is a specialist legal publisher based in Oxford, England.
To order further copies of this book or to request a list of other
publications please write to:

Hart Publishing, Salter's Boatyard, Folly Bridge,
Abingdon Road, Oxford OX1 4LB
Telephone: +44 (0)1865 245533 or Fax: +44 (0)1865 794882
e-mail: mail@hartpub.co.uk
WEBSITE: http//www.hartpub.co.uk

British Library Cataloguing in Publication Data
Data Available
ISBN 1–84113–197–0 (hardback)
1–84113–196–2 (paperback)

Typeset by Hope Services (Abingdon) Ltd.
Printed and bound in Great Britain on acid-free paper by
Bell & Bain Ltd., Glasgow

Preface

This collection of essays is the product of a series of seminars held by the Cambridge Socio-Legal Group in 2000. As with our first book (*What is a Parent? A Socio-Legal Analysis* (1999)), each chapter was originally presented as a paper for discussion by the Group before it was edited for the book.

Once again the Editors owe their thanks to Jill Brown, Secretary of the Centre for Family Research, for the role she has played in helping in the organisation of the seminars and in the process of preparing the papers for publication. Julie Jessop has played an indispensable role as a copy editor for the book and Sally Roberts has contributed her technical skills. We are very grateful to these three who made the editorial role manageable.

ANDREW BAINHAM
SHELLEY DAY SCLATER
MARTIN RICHARDS
June 2001

Contents

Notes on Contributors

Andrew Bainham is a Fellow of Christ's College, Cambridge and University Lecturer in Law. He has been Editor of the *International Survey of Family Law* (published by Jordans on behalf of the International Society of Family Law) since 1994. He is author of a leading text on children and the law, *Children: The Modern Law* (2nd edn., Jordans, 1998).

Caroline Bridge is a senior lecturer in law at the School of Law, University of Manchester. She is Editor of the *Family Law Reports*, Editor of "Case Comments" for *Family Law*, a member of the research team evaluating Information Meetings under the Family Law Act 1996 for the Lord Chancellor's Department and the author of many articles on family and child law and medical issues concerning children.

Anne Bottomley is a member of the faculty of Kent Law School, University of Kent at Canterbury. She is a founder member of the editorial board of the journal *Feminist Legal Studies* and series co-editor (with Sally Sheldon, University of Keele) of the *Feminist Perspectives on Law* series published by Cavendish. She has published widely in the area of feminist scholarship on law and legal theory.

Belinda Brooks-Gordon is a Lecturer in Forensic Psychology at the University of Leicester where she runs an MSc in applied psychology for practitioners engaged in the assessment and treatment of sex offenders. She completed a PhD at the Institute of Criminology and Churchill College, University of Cambridge under the supervision of Loraine Gelsthorpe. Belinda's research interests encompass the demographics, criminal careers and the subjective accounts and experiences of men who kerb crawl and/or commit street sexual offences.

Elizabeth Chapman is a Research Associate at the Centre for Family Research, University of Cambridge. She is currently a Wellcome Trust Fellow in Biomedical Ethics examining the implications for education and genetic counselling of different ways of conceptualising the body in genetic conditions. Her most recent publication is "Conceptualisation of the Body for People Living with HIV: Issues of Touch and Contamination", in (2000) 20 *Sociology of Health and Illness*.

Richard Collier is Professor of Law and Social Theory at the University of Newcastle Upon Tyne. He has published extensively in the area of law and gender, and is the author of *Masculinity, Law and the Family* (1995) and *Masculinities, Crime and Criminology* (1998). He is presently working on the project "Male Lawyers and Work-Life Balance", funded by the British Academy, and completing a book on heterosexuality, law and family. Richard Collier is a co-editor of *Social and Legal Studies: An International Journal.*

Rachel Cook is a Senior Lecturer in Health Psychology and Field Leader in Psychology at Anglia Polytechnic University, Cambridge. She is a psychologist with research interests in infertility and its consequences. She is currently working on collaborative projects on surrogacy and children conceived by donor insemination.

Shelley Day Sclater is a Reader in Psychosocial Studies at the University of East London and Co-Director of the Centre for Narrative Research. Formerly a lawyer, she has published widely in the field of socio-legal studies. She is currently researching contact disputes in family law, co-editing a book on surrogacy (with Rachel Cook), and writing about subjectivity.

Loraine Gelsthorpe is a Fellow of Pembroke College, University Senior Lecturer in Criminology and Director of the PhD Programme, Institute of Criminology, University of Cambridge. Her particular research interests revolve around discretion and discrimination in the conception and delivery of criminal justice, youth justice issues, and community penalties. Current research includes the criminalisation and detention of asylum seekers, and social exclusion, crime and justice. Her published work includes numerous articles and essays on youth justice, and community penalty issues, *Sexism and the Female Offender* (Gower, 1989), *Feminist Perspectives in Criminology*, co-edited with Allison Morris (Open University Press, 1990) and *Community Penalties: Change and Challenges* (edited with Anthony Bottoms and Sue Rex, Willan, 2001).

Jonathan Herring is a Fellow of Exeter College and University Lecturer in Law at Oxford. He is the author of *Family Law* (Pearson, 2001) and co-author with M. Cremona of *Criminal Law* (2nd edn., Macmillan, 1998). He is also an advisory editor for the *Family Court Reports.*

Julie Jessop has recently completed a PhD at the Centre for Family Research, University of Cambridge researching into parenthood and new partners. She has previously worked on an ESRC funded project on the psychology of divorce and a Joseph Rowntree project on children's definitions of family.

Martin Johnson is Professor of Reproductive Sciences and Fellow of Christ's College at the University of Cambridge. He was a member of the HFEA for six years until 1999, has written over 220 papers on reproduction, bio-ethics and medical education, and is co-author of *Essential Reproduction* (5th edn., Blackwell Science), the major teaching text on Mammalian Reproductive Biology.

Felicity Kaganas is a senior lecturer in law at Brunel University and a co-director of the Centre for the Study of Law, the Child and the Family there. Her writing has focused on feminist issues and on child and family law. She has published both in England and in South Africa, where she was previously a lecturer at the University of Witwatersrand. Her publications include *Family Law, Gender and the State* (with Alison Diduck, Hart, 1999) and "Contact, Conflict and Risk" in Day Sclater and Piper (eds.), *Undercurrents of Divorce* (Ashgate, 1999).

John Keown is Senior Lecturer in the Law and Ethics of Medicine, Faculty of Law, University of Cambridge. He has written widely in his field and his publications include *Abortion, Doctors and the Law* (Cambridge University Press, 1988) and *Euthanasia Examined* (Cambridge University Press, 1995). His next book, *Legalising Voluntary Euthanasia: Evaluating the Case for Reform* will also be published by Cambridge University Press.

Mavis Maclean is Director of the Oxford Centre for Family Law and Policy, a new research group which brings together scholars from family law and social policy. Recent publications include *Family Lawyers* with John Eekelaar, an empirical study of the work of family solicitors and *Making Law for Families*, an edited volume on the legislative process arising from a conference held in Onati (both Oxford, Hart, 2000). She is a member of the Oxford Law Faculty, and Academic Adviser to the Lord Chancellor's Department. She also co-edited *Cross Currents* for Oxford University Press with Sanford Katz and John Eekelaar, an account of family law in the United Kingdom and the USA over the last 50 years.

Derek Morgan is Professor of Health Care Law, Jurisprudence and Bioethics at Cardiff Law School. He is a member of the British Medical Association's Medical Ethics Committee (1995–), was a member of the Chief Medical Officer's Expert Advisory Group on Stem Cell Research (1999–2000) and is co-editor of *Legal Studies*, the Journal of the Society of Public Teachers of Law. The author and editor of numerous essays, articles and books on health and medical law, his most recent book is *Human Fertilisation & Embryology: Regulating the Reproductive Revolution* (Blackstone Press, 2001).

Gregory Radick is a Lecturer in History and Philosophy of Sciences, Leeds University. Publications include J. Hodge and G. Radick (eds.) *The Cambridge Companion to Darwin* (Cambridge University Press, forthcoming)

Martin Richards is Director of the Centre for Family Research and Professor of Family Research at the University of Cambridge. His research interests include marriage, divorce and family life and psychosocial aspects of new genetic technologies. Books include *Sexual Arrangements: Marriage and Affairs* (with Janet Reibstein, Heinemann/Charles Scribners Sons, 1963); *The Troubled Helix: Social and Psychological Implications of the New Human Genetics* (editor with Theresa Marteau, Cambridge University Press, 1996) and *What is a Parent? A Socio-Legal Analysis* (edited with Andrew Bainham and Shelley Day Sclater, Hart, 2000). He is a member of the Human Genetics Commission.

Eileen Richardson is Executive Director of the Centre for Women Leaders and a Fellow of Lucy Cavendish College, University of Cambridge. Her research interests focus on the regulation of new reproductive technologies.

Bryan Turner is Professor of Sociology at the University of Cambridge. He published *The Body and Society* in 1984 and *Regulating Bodies* in 1992. With Mike Featherstone, he is the founding co-editor of *Body and Society*. His current research with Steven Wainwright (University of London) is on injury, the body and retirement among professional ballet dancers.

Jane Weaver is a Research Associate at the Centre for Family Research, University of Cambridge. She is currently working on a three-year project exploring choice and decision making in caesarean section funded by the Nuffield Foundation. Jane trained as a midwife at West Cumberland Hospital in the 1970s and thereafter practised in a variety of hospital and community settings. In 1991 she took a degree in psychology followed by a PhD on control issues in childbirth, both at University College London. Jane's research interests include psychological issues relating to childbirth, women's health and feminist issues in general.

1

Introduction

SHELLEY DAY SCLATER*

"Rationalist legal theory underplays the mundane fact that in order for the law to function at all it must first and foremost have a hold over bodies".[1]

"Once the Cartesian conception of humans as subjective immaterial souls inhabiting, but essentially independent of, physical bodies is rejected, the question of defining the characteristics of bodies becomes inseparable from that of defining persons. So, too, is the *power* to define bodies the *power* to determine persons".[2]

"And 'the body' is never above—or below—history".[3]

THIS BOOK IS about the relationship between law and the human body.[4] As its title suggests, "law" is not seen unambiguously, in isolation, but in its relationships to the diverse range of social discourses that make up "body lore" and which also structure the narratives that rhetorically create law as a body of rational principles and practices. These essays tell tales of inevitable ambiguities—the body is in law, but law is also in the body—and both body and law are necessarily mixed up with our shifting cultural lore. This matrix of relationships points to the mutually constitutive nature of both "body" and "law"; they depend upon each other and there can be no final separation between them. But this is not a marriage made in heaven; on the contrary, body/law intimacies may signify mutual dependencies, but they also signify multiplicities, even antagonisms. Body and law relate to each other in multifarious, sometimes antagonistic, ways; there is no one body of law, but a multiplicity of contingent and provisional bodies, lore and laws.

The purpose of this book is to explore the multiple manifestations of the body in law. This is an enterprise that takes on a new and elevated significance as we stand poised at the beginning of what has been called the "biotech century". Biotechnologies have proliferated apace, and it is now a commonplace that law has

---

* I would like to express grateful thanks to my co-editors for their helpful readings of an earlier version of this chapter, and to Jill Brown and Julie Jessop for editorial support.
[1] Cheah et al. (1996) p. xv.
[2] Fineman and Thomasden (1991) p. 59.
[3] Riley (1988) p. 104.
[4] Of course, as Rose and Valverde (1998) point out, there is no such thing as *the* law; law as a unified phenomenon governed by certain general principles is a fiction that law itself creates.

failed to keep up.[5] The Human Genome Project—what Glasner and Rothman (1998) refer to as the "holy grail of genetics"—has brought into public visibility a whole range of social, legal and ethical issues that remain unresolved, matters for ongoing debate.[6] For example, the legal position concerning property rights[7] in the body, and in body parts, organs, products and fluids, is complex[8] and depends, not on any comprehensive formal legal regulation, but instead on piecemeal contributions from the law of tort, property law, criminal law, family law, commercial law and equity.[9] There are no definitive answers to the fundamental question of who owns DNA[10] or the related issue of whether DNA can be the subject of copyright; the patenting of genes continues to generate controversy and litigation.[11] The extent to which health (including genetic) information may be used, by whom and in what circumstances remains an open question; and where genetic information is to be stored on databases, although the Data Protection Act 1998 offers some protection, there will be concerns about confidentiality and control over disclosure.[12]

Insurance companies and employers clearly have interests in the results of genetic tests (see, for example, Cook (1999)), and these are issues with which the Human Genetics Commission has been concerned.[13] "Genetic privacy" cannot currently be assured in England and Wales, though the coming into force of the Human Rights Act 1998, under which English courts can enforce individual rights

---

[5] See, for example, Brownsword et al. (1998); Fox and McHale (2000). Beck's point that the debate about the course of genetic technology is now occurring as an "obituary" for activities begun long ago, is widely quoted. See Beck (1992) p. 203. See also Morgan and Nielsen (1992).

[6] See, for example, Marteau and Richards (1996); Kevles and Hood (1992); Sloan (2000). The Human Genome Diversity Project similarly raises a number of unresolved ethical issues; see, for example, Dodson and Williamson (1999).

[7] There has been extensive commentary on whether or not bodies and body parts constitute "property", and the related issue of "commodification". For background discussion, see, for example, Scott (1981); Toombs (1999); Smith Jr (1999). Gold (1996) argues that property discourse is not an appropriate framework in which to talk about bodies, body parts and products as it encourages us to make important decisions about the body based on the norms of commercial markets. Beyleveld and Brownsword (2000) would disagree. Hyde (1997) p. 95 considers that the biggest weakness of the "body-as-property" discourse is the risk of making it the property of someone other than the person inside it, as happened in slavery. See also Wilkinson (2000). Discussion of these issues is found in Eileen Richardson and Bryan Turner (ch. 2) and Jonathan Herring (ch. 3).

[8] See, for example, Farsides (1992); Andrews (1986); Campbell (1992); Harris (1996); Bristol Inquiry Interim Report (2000); McHale (2000).

[9] Some specific statutory regulation also exists limiting, for example, commercial dealing in organs; see Human Organ Transplants Act 1989, though the question of commercial benefit from body products is a different matter. See also Human Tissue Act 1961.

[10] It should not be surprising that there is no definitive legal position on the ownership of DNA, since there is also no definitive legal position on the ownership of the body. DNA is therefore not alone in having an anomalous legal status.

[11] Gregory Radick (ch. 4) discusses the complex issues involved in gene patenting.

[12] See Murray (1997) for further discussion of confidentiality issues.

[13] See Human Genetics Commission (HGC) *The Use of Genetic Information in Insurance: Interim Recommendations of the Human Genetics Commission* (2001), and HGC *Whose Hands on Your Genes? A Consultation Document* (2000), both available on www.hgc.gov.uk.

to respect for private life and family life under Article 8 of the European Convention on Human Rights, may make a difference.[14]

Developments in reproductive technologies have renewed debates about the moral and legal status of the embryo[15] and foetus, and the tensions between different areas of law on issues concerning sanctity of life versus quality of life remain unresolved.[16] These are only a few of the most obvious examples of the uncertainties of law regarding some of the fundamental concepts in the wake of biotechnological advance. As Byk (1999) p. 265 reminds us, "today, as elements of the human body, including blood, gametes, and organs, are now distributed outside of the body for transformation or transplantation, we may be in danger of losing many of our legal certainties regarding the human body". It can be seen that these uncertainties are not unique to the issues raised by biomedical advances, but in many ways are uncertainties that bedevil medical law and ethics more generally.[17] It is widely believed that there is a need for comprehensive legal regulation to safeguard the interests of citizens, clinicians and researchers; Gevers (1995) p. 205, for example, has called for "the development of an international set of principles". McGleenan (1999) also expresses concern that the European response appears to be based on pragmatism rather than principle.[18] The coming into force of the Human Rights Act 1998 may provide an impetus for a wider airing of some of these issues in public, and their consideration by the higher courts, though it would seem less than ideal to have a regulatory system based on such ad hoc decision-making, in the absence of a clear legal and ethical framework. The contributors to this volume therefore echo the recent call by Fox and McHale (2000) for an overarching review of the complex issues of ethics, law and policy currently being raised by scientific and technological advances.

At an international level, there have been some attempts to place genetic technologies within frameworks of human rights.[19] At a national level, there are no less than nineteen bodies involved with the regulation of genetic technologies. The

[14] See Sommerville and English (1999). For a discussion of the legal and public policy issues in DNA forensics, see Reilly (2001). See also Nelkin and Andrews (1999) who discuss what they call "surveillance creep" as growing numbers of people have their DNA on file. See also HGC press release *Human Genetics Commission discusses concerns over police forensic DNA database proposals* (2000), available on www.hgc.gov.uk.

[15] See Fox (2000). Derek Morgan (ch. 18) discusses the complexities of defining an "embryo" under the Human Fertilisation and Embryology Act 1990 for the purposes of regulating "cloning".

[16] See Wheale (2000). These issues feature prominently in the euthanasia debate discussed by John Keown (ch. 14).

[17] See, for example, Mason and McCall Smith (1999). For more detailed discussion of the issues raised by the new human genetics see the essays in Brownsword et al. (1998).

[18] McGleenan (1999) p. 18 concludes that: "The procedural model of regulation too readily sacrifices a principled approach in favour of pragmatism while genetic privacy laws may well foster a culture of secrecy and mistrust about genetics which could undermine many of the possible benefits of screening and testing techniques".

[19] See Council of Europe Convention for the Protection of Human Rights and Dignity of the Human Being with regard to the Application of Biology and Medicine: Convention on Human Rights and Biomedicine, Oviedo, 4.IV.1997. The United Kingdom has not yet signed up to this Convention. See also UNESCO Universal Declaration on the Human Genome and Human Rights, 1997.

Human Genetics Commission (HGC)[20] was established to analyse current and
future developments in human genetics and to advise the Government on the ways
in which these developments are likely to impact on people and healthcare, and
their social, ethical, legal and economic implications. The HGC is an "umbrella"
that replaces several other regulatory bodies and is committed to public consultation. It was established following the Government's review of the Advisory and
Regulatory Framework for Biotechnology in May 1999. Three main concerns
emerged from the review, namely: current regulatory arrangements are complex
and difficult for the public to understand; they do not properly reflect the broader
ethical questions and views of potential stakeholders; they are not sufficiently for-
ward-looking for so rapidly developing a technology. The review envisaged that
the establishment of the HGC would make a fundamental contribution to a "system for regulating biotechnology which is rigorous, open and which will effectively safeguard the public interest". The question of how the HGC will function,
and the extent to which its mission will be accomplished, remains an open one. In
addition to official bodies involved in regulating and advising, there are a number
of non-governmental organisations such as the Nuffield Council on Bioethics
whose work is concerned with the impact of technological developments.

There is certainly a pressing need to clarify the boundaries of law in relation to
the new bodies that are currently being constructed in discourses of biotechnologies. But the discourse of the gene is a very powerful one. As Nelkin and Lindee
(1995) point out, the gene has become something of an icon in the developed
world, as scientists and non-scientists alike have talked up its power. Such fantasies
about the unique potency of DNA bear more relation to the metaphors that have
been used to describe it than they do to its biological properties, as Richards (2001)
reminds us. The task of clarifying the boundaries of law in relation to the proliferation of these new bodies is by no means an easy one, for the human body has
always been a problem for law. The advent of biotechnologies has merely brought
to the fore again a whole range of old, yet unresolved, questions about the meanings of life, death and what it is to be human; they force us to confront anew these
old questions of embodiment[21] in new contexts. It is undoubtedly significant that,
as McKenny (1999) p. 354 reminds us, the dominant forms of bioethics have had
little to say about the body, their lexicon instead being populated with terms referring to the obligations and duties of disembodied "persons": "standard forms of
bioethics have failed to address many of the most important issues raised by the
conquest of the body by medicine".

Williamson (1999a) asks a pertinent question that forces us to stop and re-exam-
ine the assumptions that underlie much of the moral indignation with which these
developments are often debated: whether there is anything new in the "new genetics"
from the point of view of ethics and public policy.[22] He suggests three reasons why

[20] See http://www.hgc.gov.uk.
[21] See Bynum (1995).
[22] See also Murray (1997); Richards (2001). Elizabeth Chapman (chap. 17) considers this question
in the context of genetic testing.

genetic knowledge has proved to be so controversial. First, it is knowledge that applies not just to an individual but also to whole families or groups of people. Secondly, the history of atrocities committed in the name of eugenics suggests that genetic knowledge could, in future, be "misused". Thirdly, and most importantly, genetics has been (rightly or wrongly) endowed with a cultural potency that calls forth a deep emotional response;[23] the genetic code has been equated with embodying identity and the very essence of humanity—it appears in the popular mind as a fundamental truth that should not be tampered with. Of course this image of the gene as embodying some fundamental truth about humanity misrepresents what many biologists and geneticists would claim,[24] but such images seem to have taken hold on the popular imagination nevertheless.[25] It is the emotion provoked by these images, and by myths of science as the domain of unlimited possibilities, that have given old questions about the body, about rights and responsibilities, the limits of life and death, and the nature of personhood a new lease of life in the "biotech" century.

Bodies have a material, substantial reality—our flesh, bones and blood, our DNA, are biological facts. But the meanings of the body are facts of culture—partaking of cultural lore—meanings that are provisional, multiple, ambiguous, shifting from context to context. As Eisenstein (1988) has pointed out, the scientific method, with its standpoint of objectivity, has established biology as *the* science of *the* body; the body thus appears as a "natural" entity that seems to stand outside of history, society and culture.[26] What we see reflected, however, in discourses of nature, are cultural concerns embedded in the language of science; science working to negotiate the boundaries of culture. The significances of culture are frequently debated on such scientific terrain. In this context, the body emerges as a contested site: is it nature, or is it culture? Both? Neither?

Law reinforces constructions of "natural" bodies, but it also undermines its own project by its own location in culture, and by its reification of the body as a thing to be regulated in human society. For, primarily, the body appears in culture as a moral entity—it has long been integral to discourses of morality. "It is", argue Friedman and Squire (1998) p. 133, "the apotheosis of immorality, the place where Western culture seeks and finds unnaturalness, depravity and chaos". Thus, discourses and practices designed to civilise, regulate and manage the unruly, unpredictable body proliferate (Foucault (1977)), turning the body into a contested moral terrain. Foucault's disciplined and docile body may be secular and scientific, but what science "knows" about the body is apt to change,[27] and its "truth" can, at

---

[23] Psychoanalyst Christina Wieland (1996) p. 300 states: "Technological culture bears all the marks of a masculine omnipotent creation that includes the substitution of baby, created by the parental couple, by manufactured reality and entails all the destructiveness of an attack on mother and on life".

[24] See, for example, Rose and Rose (2000).

[25] Williamson (1999b) p. 96, for example, argues against cloning and states that "I believe that there is a personal right, ethically based, to individuality, autonomy and identity . . . Reproductive cloning crosses a significant boundary in removing the single most important feature of autonomy: the fact that each of us is genetically unique and individual. Our genetic identity is an essential part of this individuality".

[26] See also Soper (1995) for a detailed discussion of "nature".

[27] This point was amply illustrated at the exhibition "Spectacular Bodies: The Art and Science of the Human Body from Leonardo to now", Hayward Gallery, October 2000–January 2001.

best, be only provisional. In a post-modern world, it is no longer possible unproblematically to appeal to science's truth as the ultimate moral arbiter; rather science itself must struggle to maintain its place among other rhetorical discourses that provide moral frames of reference for different groups (see Friedman and Squire (1998)).

With the advent of new kinds of science and biotechnologies that promise to "know" (and thence, in Foucauldian terms, to discipline) bodies in significant new ways—to make, remake and shape them according to prevailing mores and styles—there is no doubt that we have landed in something of a legal and ethical quagmire. We might hope that science will be the rope to drag us out, but that seems unlikely, as science is increasingly seen as part of the problem—the reason we are in this muddle in the first place. And law, it seems, is as susceptible as the rest of us to the body's moral confusion. Law has not, will not, and probably cannot impose a unifying ethical order; instead, argues McLean (1999), law has been too ready to defer to scientific and medical expertise, opting out of addressing fundamental ethical questions, disenfranchising the citizen and denying her or him moral agency, and foregoing the opportunity to place the issue of biomedical advances firmly within a human rights framework. Law, it seems, is prepared to buy into the fantasy that science has the answers.

But there is another side to law too; it does not always simply co-opt science or rely on science's own (assumed) authority. On the contrary, as King (1991, 1993) and others (e.g. Teubner (1989)) suggest, law is prone to adapt other discourses to its own ends. The powers of law remain not just unsullied but actually enhanced by law's deployment of other authoritative discourses. As Nelken (1996) argues, law deploys its own criteria of significance and creates its own truth. And as Cotterell (1998) reminds us, law's truth is not a unified, distinctive discourse but is an ongoing rhetorical achievement.

Law's "truth", then, may be no more certain than that of science;[28] it too is under siege. As Eisenstein (1988) points out, law establishes regulations and institutes expectations about what is legitimate, acceptable, rational, natural and normal; laws operate as symbols for what is honourable and desirable. The "rule of law" depends upon dominant discourses of law constructing law's processes and truths as fair, neutral, rational and objective. It is this narrative, argues Eisenstein, that that gives law its authority. On this story, law (like science) is a neutral, objective arbiter. The power of law thus depends less on its ability to coerce and more on its ability to persuade people that the world it describes is the only available world.

Law's truth about the human body is no exception. According to Hyde (1997), in law "body" means an inconsistent and incoherent assortment of representations. The law currently constructs a range of different bodies—as property, as machine, as the commodified body of consumer culture, as the bearer of privacy rights, and as the bearer of narratives of all of these things. Law constructs different bodies for different purposes –as inviolable, as sacred, as objects of desire, as a

---

[28] For detailed discussion see Patterson (1996).

threat to society. Such constructs of the body, Hyde argues, are inevitable; they are what make up the democratic citizen as we know it to be. Hyde identifies a close link between the rise of modern market democracy and the rules and practices of manners, civility and bodily control that separate the modern world from the medieval one. Modern democratic citizens are self-controlled and imagine themselves as autonomous and self-determining: "Many of the dances law makes around the body are in the service of a larger mission, law's construction of an autonomous legal self, a self that must be both property and never-property, free and ordered, autonomous and socialised" (Hyde (1997) p. 53). Hyde concludes that law is in the business of constructing a range of multiple and competing discursive bodies; the unifying element is that law's discourse of the body reifies the body—renders it as an object, a thing—separate from the person, but as the bearer of that person as a legal subject, as a citizen in civil society.

Each body is, in a sense, an individuated entity, with distinct boundaries between it and other bodies, with an inside and an outside. The embodied citizen has free will and autonomy, it commands its body and its body obeys. The body of the citizen is private and may not be violated; it signifies the private self, and the public/private division is played out on the surface of the body. Law therefore constructs the personal integrity of the body[29] and the autonomy[30] of the embodied citizen in ways that are consistent with dominant (though unstable) cultural values. The meanings of concepts such as "bodily integrity" and "autonomy" are various and shifting, being constructed and reconstructed anew in broader social discourses as well as in legal decision-making.

The essays in this book address these vexed questions about the multiple manifestations of the human body in law. Contributors bring expertise from a wide range of backgrounds—sociology, law, reproductive medicine, criminology, psychology, philosophy and midwifery. The essays challenge the presuppositions of legal theories that the corporeal body is an object that is external to law and that comes to law already constituted. Liberal law repeats the privileging of mind over body in its portrayal of human subjects and human acts as disembodied. The essays in this book illustrate the ways in which law not only needs the body, but also constitutes the body at the same time as it renders those processes of constitution invisible by an implicit appeal to a discourse of the body as natural. These essays expose the multiple powers of law to constitute and reconstitute human bodies.

Law routinely produces its human subjects, but its task is always necessarily incomplete (if it weren't, there'd be no further need for law). For bodies are material forces as well as sites of discursive relations. If we agree with Butler (1993) that corporeality is active and performative, then it is likely to exceed any discursive representation of it that attempts to tame or contain the feared excesses of the

---

[29] On the "integrity of the body", see McKenny (1999) who argues that the body has been insufficiently present in bioethics.

[30] On the vexed question of autonomy and its genealogy, see Douzinas and McVeigh (1992). For these authors, "autonomy" is an ethico-legal fiction.

body. The bodies that appear in these essays are active and performative, and what we see are instances of law attempting to tame and constrain; there is so much about the body that cannot be discursively represented or brought within the confines of law.

In law's various constructions of the body, "autonomy" has provided a convenient peg upon which to hang the competing claims of, for example, the state, the community and the individual. For Douzinas and McVeigh (1992), autonomy is the privileged site of the encounter between the individual and society, the singular and the general. They show that many manifestations of law's clumsy attempts to process embodiment and to normalise corporeality are to be found in the guise of decisions relating to autonomy. The privileging of this site reveals the fundamental ambiguities of the body, as that which we share and as that which divides us, the locus of both our sameness and our difference. The emphasis on autonomy speaks, ultimately, of our uniqueness and our singularity, our rights and responsibilities as citizens in a community, obscuring, perhaps, the possibility that the value of autonomy might, for some (as Jonathan Herring points out in chapter 3), take second place to a value of human existence with and for others.

These essays locate the body in a dialectical relationship with law. They speak of what bodies do in law, not just what law might do to bodies. They speak of the role of the body in law, in regulating social consensus, and in maintaining law's capacity to allocate rights, responsibilities, blame. The essays suggest strongly that we misrepresent both law and the body if we see them as occupying separate spheres, joined together only by some mutual interaction, one upon the other. The essays suggest a much closer relationship—one of mutual constitution—in which neither law nor the embodied legal subject is capable of independent existence, but rather are interdependent aspects of our social world. The essays offer commentaries on both body lore and laws; the ambiguities of the title illustrate the ambiguities of the topic. Law's truths about the body are multiple and shifting and depend as much upon cultural lore as they do upon the due process of law. Embodied human agents are both subjects of law and subject to law. But law is also subject to the interpretations, negotiations—the resistances—of embodied active subjects. In these essays we are introduced to the determinacy and the indeterminacy of law and the human body.

Several essays in this collection highlight the emotional and symbolic significances of bodies, body parts and bodily products; bodies are highly significant both culturally and personally. What bodies (our own and those of others) mean to us, and the cultural processes whereby we make sense of embodied experience, are absolutely central to our everyday practices. But such processes are only rarely made explicit and visible.

Eileen Richardson and Bryan Turner open the discussion with "Bodies as Property: from Slavery to DNA Maps" in which they set the scene for the chapters that follow by exploring the regulation of the body in historical perspective. The story that they tell takes us from the mid-seventeenth century and Filmer's *Patriarcha*—an exposition of the "natural" rights of kings, and of the notion of self-ownership, through Locke's bourgeois individualism—his affirmation of contractualism and defence of private property, in which labour rather than nature creates property rights, to Foucault's "governmentality"—a view on how the traditional power of kings over the bodies of their subjects has been systematically replaced by an extensive machinery of administrative power over the productive bodies of the subjects of the state. This disciplinary power functions to produce disciplined, docile, bodies through a micro-politics of regimes, technologies, knowledge, practices and regulations.

As we have seen, these regimes have increasingly become bioregimes as the significant new matrices in which contemporary selves are produced and reproduced. The modernisation of the state and the medicalisation of the body has entailed a fragmentation of whole bodies into parts and particles, whilst the Internet further facilitates commodification in a global market. The traditional concerns of law as regards the human body—questions of autonomy and consent—are rapidly being eclipsed by new scientific and technological developments and commercial opportunities that raise new questions for science and for law. One such question concerns the law and ethics of the sale and donation of organs and other body parts, discussed by Jonathan Herring in his chapter "Giving, Selling and Sharing Bodies". As Johnson (2000) reminds us, trading by some in body parts weakens the rights of others not to be regarded as commodities or to be instrumentalised. Another such question concerns the control by corporations of genetic codes via patenting, as Greg Radick discusses in his chapter.

Herring's starting point is the supposition that the body, at least since the abolition of slavery, has not been, strictly, "property", and therefore could not be owned, bought or sold. Others have taken a contrary view. Beyleveld and Brownsword (2000), for example, argue that regarding the body as property can usefully enhance conceptions of human dignity. But, whatever stance is taken on the property issue, it is undeniable that, as technologies have developed, and bodies have become increasingly valuable resources—commodities even—courts are being asked to resolve increasingly complex disputes, and law is being forced to develop a more sophisticated stance in relation to the body.

The continuing tensions between an autonomy-based approach—people should be free to do with their bodies (including sale) as they wish—and an approach based on the body as assuming a special, even unique, status—the law must regulate dealings with the body, including commercial ones, and must restrict extreme "misuses" of the body—are well illustrated in a number of chapters in this book. The English courts' refusal to condone certain sado-masochistic sexual practices;[31] the controversy that has long surrounded the medicalisation of childbirth and, most recently, the issue of forced caesarean sections;[32] the deeply divided opinion concerning the legalisation of euthanasia;[33] the need for contemporary law and practice to take full account of religious and cultural difference in

[31] See, for example, the case of *Brown*, discussed by Andrew Bainham (chap. 10).
[32] Discussed by Jane Weaver (chap. 13).
[33] See John Keown (chap. 14).

a pluralistic society;[34] and the revelation that body parts had been stored or disposed of without proper consent at Bristol[35] and Alder Hey, are all cases in point that are readily visible in public debates.

Herring begins with the question "is my body my own?". But he cannot answer in the affirmative; to say that "my body is mine" reveals only a partial understanding. There is clearly a sense in which my body *is* me but, at the same time, my body is what mediates my relationships with others and the world around me. The body is a constantly changing entity, engaged in continual exchanges with others and with the world, in which mutual dependence and interconnectedness, rather than autonomy, are its defining features. On this basis, Herring builds an argument that donation or exchange of body parts and products, far from being bizarre activities requiring close regulation by law, could be regarded as a mere extension of the ordinary interchange and interdependence of bodies that characterise our everyday lives. These questions of interconnectedness and our responsibility to others have, as Somerville and English (1999) point out, been brought to the fore in new ways by the advent of genetic testing.

The commodification of what Richardson and Turner call "body particles", in the form of patents over DNA, is discussed by Greg Radick in his chapter. Patents make the global sale of genetic information commercially viable but, as Turner and Richardson point out, they also promote a range of inequalities between the developed and the developing worlds. To put it bluntly, patenting reduces genes—some would say the stuff of human life—to marketable commodities. Radick highlights a further tension provoked by genomic research, that between the institutionalised co-operation and sharing of knowledge within a scientific community, and the desire to keep knowledge private, so that commercial possibilities may be exploited and patents owned. The old lore, by which patents on human genes were an impossibility, has given way to a new law that cloaks patents in an air of inevitability, albeit controversially. Radick shows us that it is becoming increasingly difficult to imagine a world without gene patents.

The chapters in this book address some of these complexities of embodiment in relation to law. Another aspect of this complexity is a new visibility currently being accorded to the emotional and symbolic aspects of embodiment, evident, for example, in the recent media exposure of the retention of organs after post mortem in Bristol and Alder Hey. Mavis Maclean sat for two years on the Inquiry into the management and care of children receiving complex heart surgery at the Bristol Royal Infirmary. She begins her chapter "Letting Go: Parents, Professionals and the Law in the Retention of Human Material After Post Mortem" with a discussion of the profound distress felt by parents who discovered that they had buried their children without some of their vital organs. Maclean refers to her experience on the Inquiry as "sad but inspiring", reminding us that our encounters with the body, even as lawyers or researchers, are never neutral, dispassionate,

[34] See Caroline Bridge (chap. 15).
[35] Discussed by Mavis Maclean (chap. 5).

but are more likely to be deeply emotional. Particularly, perhaps, the bodies of children carry a symbolic significance that is difficult to explain in wholly rational terms.[36]

Similarly, Martin Johnson in "Male Medical Students and the Male Body" illustrates the profound anxieties that can attach to bodily practices. Doctors must deal professionally with many situations that, in ordinary social life, are subject to complex rules and taboos; one example is their physical access to (often intimate parts of) the body of another person. Medical practitioners, like most of us, have absorbed this cultural lore about the body, but good practice often requires the application of different rules and values; for instance, they may engage in visual and tactile exploration of areas of others' bodies usually considered private, and to do so within an accepted legal and ethical framework. Here, the imperatives of law and lore may collide, requiring complex adjustments (including emotional ones) on the part of doctors, and complex rules about appropriate behaviours and standards, on the part of the professional bodies and the law. Importantly, legal and ethical issues are routinely addressed in medical training, but matters of body lore are not. Johnson's essay illustrates the importance of dealing openly and constructively with emotional processes that are set in play by the fact that bodies are not just flesh, but are mediators of deep-set emotions and bearers of our culture's most potent symbols.

In "Domestic Homicide, Gender and the Expert", Felicity Kaganas illustrates the ways in which body lore and laws intersect; she shows how implicit gendered ideas have become embedded in the conceptual frameworks and practices of the criminal justice system at a number of levels. Examining cases of women who have killed their abusive male partners, she exposes the gendered and embodied nature of the crime and, crucially, its consequences. Social and emotional reactions to women who kill are complex (Fox (1996)) and likely to be deeply rooted. Kaganas illustrates the ways in which the salience of embodied gender is rendered invisible in a criminal justice system that cannot take cognisance of the social context in which offences are committed, insists on constructing legal subjects as gender-less, race-less, class-less, disembodied abstractions, and maintains an appearance of neutrality on all these dimensions, but perpetuates an implicit masculinity in the type of defences that are permissible, and in the evidential rules that apply (O'Donovan 1991, 1993).

In domestic violence we find the embodied power of men being used to subjugate and control (and sometimes to maim and to kill) the bodies of women. When women fight back, they do so in similarly gendered and embodied ways—for example, they may wait until the partner is drunk or asleep before striking. The point emphasised by Kaganas is that law cannot take account of embodied gender in such a way that the killing becomes comprehensible or excusable. Women who kill, it seems, are so anomalous that they are best explained as aberrant, as abnormal. As Raitt and Zeedyk (2000) have argued, only when women's experiences of

---

[36] For further discussion of this point, see Day Sclater and Piper (2001).

and responses to abuse are framed within medical discourse—"battered woman syndrome" (BWS)—do they become comprehensible; courts are showing an increasing willingness to accept expert evidence of such syndromes to support pleas of diminished responsibility. For individual women, invoking this defence may mean the difference between incarceration and freedom, but each case must further entrench an image of woman-as-victim of both men and biology, their behaviour explicable not with reference to real conditions of existence but to expert medical discourse and, only then, excusable in law.

What we are seeing in Kaganas's discussion of battered woman syndrome is an alignment, to paraphrase Derek Morgan, of naming, taming and constraining in an alliance of law with medical experts. Together, they produce a new truth about the body, indicating the limits of the truth that law is prepared to tolerate, eclipsing the phenomenological truths of the embodied experiences of "battered" women.

The embodiment of gender appears as a significant theme in several other essays in this collection. In "The Many Appearances of the Body in Feminist Scholarship" Anne Bottomley sets out the background and conditions for a critical reading of bodies of law. Like Richard Collier (Chapter 9) she reminds us that bodies are both flesh and flesh-to-be-represented; we need to hold in mind both the materiality of the body—the fact of our embodiment—alongside a nuanced understanding of the multiple significations and shifting meanings of the body. Importantly, too, for any discussion of the relations between law and the human body, is a recognition that there is no one body, and no one law. Rather, as Hyde (1997) reminds us, in law, "body" is an incoherent assortment of representations; bodies of law are contingent and provisional, constructed and reconstructed for different purposes, with different consequences flowing from these constructions. But it is also crucial, argues Bottomley, that we resist scholarship in which bodies are portrayed as passive sites of exploitation or the inscription of power relations; persons are too often reduced to passive bodies, whilst law is amplified as a powerful and active agentic force. The body is a contested domain and the body of law no less so.

Implicit in Bottomley's argument is an invitation to discover more about the two-way, mutually constitutive relations[37] between law and the body; a focus on possibilties rather than inevitabilties, an invitation to create open-ended and multiple narratives that might begin to dislodge the traditional certainties that leave so much unsaid and unsayable. As Bottomley shows, feminist work on the body has

[37] Judith Butler (1993) p. 30 similarly talks about the mutually constitutive relations between the body and its linguistic representation as follows: "The body posited as prior to the sign, is always *posited* or *signified* as *prior*. This signification produces as an *effect* of its own procedure the very body that it . . . simultaneously claims to discover as that which *precedes* its own action. If the body signified as prior to signification is an effect of signification, then the . . . mimetic status of language, which claims that signs follow bodies as their necessary mirrors, is not mimetic at all. On the contrary, it is productive, constitutive, one might even argue *performative*, inasmuch as this signifying act delimits and contours the body that it then claims to find prior to any and all signification. This is not to say that the materiality of the body is simply . . . a linguistic effect . . . Such a distinction overlooks the materiality of the signifier itself".

been instrumental in undermining the traditional fixities of positivist thinking; in particular, feminist scholarship has pointed a way towards challenging a range of binaries and dualisms (such as mind/body, nature/culture, public/private) that have long been implicit in Western thought, including in both law and legal analysis. Both the body and the law, Bottomley concludes on an optimistic note, are sites of multiplicity and instability and, therefore, of potential for positive change.

Richard Collier, in his essay on "Male Bodies, Family Practices" connects with many of the themes raised by Bottomley. His starting point is a recognition that specific engagements with the bodies of men are curiously rare in socio-legal scholarship and he sets out to render visible the bodies of men in family life and family law. Like Bottomley, he is intent on shifting the terms of the debate—challenging the epistemological framework that has been structured around binaries, particularly the distinction between (biological) sex and (socially constructed) gender.[38] Such dualistic thinking assumes that, if we could peel off all the layers of culture, we could find underneath a natural, biological body; the error of this thinking lies in the fact that discourses of nature, and of biology, are themselves human constructions.

A desire to break down this old binary is not simultaneously a desire to deny the materiality of embodiment—quite the contrary. Both Bottomley and Collier are at pains to rescue the materiality of the gendered body from the discursive and semiotic quagmire that has, in recent years, threatened to engulf it. Collier's constant reminders about the fundamental importance of human practices, too, are a useful corrective. They remind us that, ultimately, embodiment is about lived experience—law is clearly engaged in multiple constructions of corporeality, in persuasion, but its "hold" over bodies (Cheah *et al* (1996)) can happen whether citizens are persuaded or not. It is through our everyday practices that we take up, negotiate or resist the discursive positions on offer to us, it is through such mundane practices that we "perform" our gendered subjectivities every day of our lives.

Collier discusses the vexed question of law's gender-neutrality, a question that surfaces also in some of the other essays in this book.[39] As a feminist scholar, I have often been challenged to defend my opposition to any blanket policy of gender-neutrality in law. It seems that those outside the feminist circle regard such opposition as paradoxical, to say the least. To reply that it is a complex issue, that we cannot assume a unified law, that we would need to think more locally, take account of the situatedness of gendered discourses and practices, and so on, all sounds to the sceptics like too much of a cop-out. Law is now routinely *written* as gender-neutral but, for me, the problem lies in the fact that it is not *read* in the same way; rather, what men and women do continues to be interpreted through the discursive lens of what is deemed appropriate for men and women to be doing. At root, the problem is one of the relationship between law and lore, where the latter is not usually explicit and sometimes not even consciously accessible.

---

[38] For an interesting discussion of the whole issue of dualisms in law, see Murphy (1996).
[39] See, in particular, Andrew Bainham (chap. 10)

At another level, law's gender-neutrality too easily translates into an assumption that legal actors come to law as un-gendered beings. I find such an assumption preposterous; it flies in the face of a consistent body of social scientific evidence that most human practices, at least in our society, remain gendered in significant ways. Gender remains a significant organising principle in society and, in this context, law's gender-neutral stance amounts to little more than a denial of that state of affairs. For me, gender-equality is a preferable goal; law's gender-neutrality is an obstacle in the way of achieving that goal, and not a means towards it. As Martha Fineman (1991) argued long ago in relation to family law, a useful distinction may be made between "equality of rules" and "equality of results"—the former can only perpetuate existing inequalities, whilst the latter could take us towards a more substantive equality.

We also cannot ignore the argument made by many feminist legal scholars (and amply illustrated, for example, in relation to criminal law in Felicity Kaganas's essay in this book) that law's discourse is a "masculine" one that not only cannot take account of the realities of women's lives but also, more fundamentally, positions woman as Other.[40] I am continually forced to the conclusion that the social, cultural and personal significance of gender is such that it cannot simply be obliterated by a decision to use gender-neutral language and to act as though gender difference did not exist. Collier and Bottomley reach similar conclusions about how a more liberatory politics of gender might be fashioned in relation to law—a need to understand and respect embodied gender practices (for instance, in the family, in relation to sexualities, crime, and so on) as they are played out in concrete contexts, and a need to think about both the body and law as sites of multiplicity and potential.

Andrew Bainham's essay "Sexualities, Sexual Relations and the Law", like much of Collier's work, challenges the heterosexual paradigm as normative. Consistent with Bottomley's calls for more fluid readings of both bodies and law, Bainham documents important shifts in both family law and criminal law whereby the Othering of same sex relationships is being challenged and the dominance of the heterosexual paradigm is being disrupted. He shows how new constructions of heterosexual bodies are emerging alongside a new visibility of homosexual bodies. Of course, there remain pockets of resistance (witness, for example, the controversy in recent years over attempts to alter the age of consent for gay sex), but there are also new areas of freedom that are opening up. Bainham's analysis further illustrates the complexities of embodied gender: the question of whether it is gender or heterosexuality that is more fundamental for law admits of no easy answer; rather, gender and sexuality remain closely tied together in legal discourse. But Bainham's analysis is also an optimistic one that points to the multiple potentials of both law and the body.

The shift, observed by Bainham, in law's increasing willingness to consign decisions concerning sexualities and consensual sexual relations to each individual is,

---

[40] See Anne Bottomley (chap. 8)

according to McCall Smith (1999),[41] one more manifestation of the elevation of the principle of "autonomy" in relation to the body. Increasing secularisation,[42] accompanied by scientific and technological advance, has paved the way for a belief that nature and biology can be controlled to suit our needs. In parallel, argues McCall Smith, the principle of autonomy—a liberal vision of an autonomous self, free to choose, and unrestrained by the expectations of others—has become central in public debate and has led, as Bainham shows, to a gradual retreat of law from matters sexual. On this view, under the influence of the premium placed on autonomy, the body became less of a public object and more of a private one, the focus not of a broader social vision of human dignity but of individual expression.

Richardson and Turner remind us that the notion that the body can function as economic property was characteristic of slavery, but its legacy remains in contemporary practices, such as prostitution. This issue is explored by Belinda Brooks-Gordon and Loraine Gelsthorpe in their chapter "Hiring Bodies: Male Clients and Prostitution". As their title suggests, "hiring" of a body for the purposes of sexual gratification must be differentiated from "ownership" of another's body for production, as in slavery, or reproduction, as in patriarchal marriage; modern consumption of sexual services more precisely involves renting or hiring rather than ownership, where control over the transaction rests more with the sex worker than with the "client". These authors outline the social and legal construction of men who hire women's bodies for sexual gratification. They pursue an historical narrative of the development of a punitive attitude towards male clients, and an alignment of the punter alongside the pimp as an abusive character from whom the public as well as individual women should be protected. In Victorian times, men who went to prostitutes were normalised in the discourses of masculinity, medicine and law. But a shift has now taken place and their practices are now more likely to be regarded as deviant, calling forth legal sanctions. In the past two decades, the male client has been criminalised to the extent that buying sexual access to a woman's body is perceived as criminally and sexually deviant; punters, as legal objects, are now being constructed as a danger to the public at large. Thus these authors suggest that only within certain limits does autonomy prevail, and women are free to hire out their bodies for sexual purposes and for men to buy them; laws reflect changing lore, but they also create it.

Rachel Cook in "Villain, Hero or Masked Stranger: Ambivalence in Transactions with Human Gametes" examines the mixed messages in law, policy and popular images of gamete "donation". Cook, notably, prefers to talk about "provision", pointing to a fundamental ambivalence: are gametes given, or are they bought and

---

[41] See also McCall Smith (1997).

[42] It should be noted that arguments that rest on claims of an "increasing secularisation" of society are prone to overlook the fact that substantial sections of our multicultural society would claim some adherence to values based on religion and community. If this is borne in mind, the "autonomous" subject of law appears as a very particular kind of construction. For a discussion of the relations among law, religion and culture, see Caroline Bridge (chap. 15).

sold? "Donation" would suggest a discourse of gift, of altruism, whilst "sale" suggests one of commercial transaction, of contract, of commodification. Cook resists both; gametes, she says, are "incomplete commodities". She is of course referring to the commercial language (sperm is "banked", eggs are "harvested") that describe infertility practices, but she is also making reference to the disdain with which such commercial transactions are commonly held, at least in the United Kingdom.

The nature of gametes is ambiguous, argues O'Donnell (2000); they blur the distinction between persons and property, and the current regulatory framework for gamete manipulations and transactions owes more to a desire to preserve traditional family ideologies than it does to any coherent construction of the status of gametes. Thus, these very basic ambiguities open the door for "lore" to come in. Murphy (2000), for example, shows how discussions of assisted reproduction are cross-cut by wider forces, dilemmas and debates, including contestations around kinship, family, globalisation and sexual difference. We should, she argues, be wary of the rhetoric that renders contemporary reproduction as either "familiar" on the one hand, or "novel" on the other. On the contrary, reproductive technologies are probably both more familiar and more novel than is usually thought.

As Cook shows, the Human Fertilisation and Embryology (HFE) Act 1990, likewise, is ambivalent as regards the question of payment for eggs and sperm. On the one hand, there is a clear intention that providers should not be paid—a commitment to altruistic "donation", reflecting a widely held belief that gamete provision should be the consequence of consent, free from inducement and pressure. On the other hand, exchange of money can be and has been condoned under the Act; financial inducement may or may not be helpful, useful, beneficial or moral, depending on your perspective. And this is the crux of Cook's argument; we have no idea about the long-term consequences of either strategy, since research is lacking—it is anyone's guess. The vast majority of heterosexual parents who use donated gametes do not tell their children about their genetic origins and, what is more, they never intend to. Whether this will, ultimately, be held to contravene human rights provisions remains to be seen.

Clearly, what is going on here is very much a product of our time and our culture; in the case of gamete donation, we can see the massive impact of "lore" and its contradictory and controversial manifestation in "law". This is what lies at the root of Cook's "ambivalence". At the very simplest of levels, gamete donation has profound consequences for how we think about kinship and family. Perhaps these consequences are what underlie the ambivalences of the HFE Act—it assures donor anonymity, but also ensures that information about donors is kept on a register. What we see here is at least a partial disappearance of the gamete provider which, given the current preoccupation with genetics and with the supposed psychological significance of "origins" (usually posed in genetic discourse), is anomalous to say the least. Cook refers to the gamete provider as the "masked stranger", conjuring up images of highwaymen who are only after the innocent traveller's purse, but not discounting the possibility that the masked stranger might just have altruistic motives, like Robin Hood.

Cook has pointed to the ambivalence of law when it comes to gametes as body products. But what this ambivalence signifies is an inability to resolve the contradictions between the idealisation of altruism and the denigration of commercial corporeal transactions. Both positions, though, seem to rely upon a fetishisation of gametes—gametes are constructed as "standing in" for the person and thus, at once, signify both corporeal mortality and a denial of it. In her chapter on "Court-Ordered Caesarean Sections" Jane Weaver examines a not dissimilar conundrum. Women who refuse to follow obstetric advice are women who resist the dominant discourses of medical and, ultimately, legal dominance. They resist, too, the crucial fetishisation of the foetus, as something apart from their own bodies, that Western medicine has created.

Weaver's chapter is about the application by doctors and hospitals to courts to obtain the legal right to impose caesarean operations upon pregnant women who refuse to follow obstetric advice. Statistics in industrialised countries indicate an increasing rate of caesarean section over the last twenty years or so, though the reasons for this are not yet entirely clear. The problem at the crux of Weaver's chapter is whether the mother and foetus should or should not be managed as a single body, or two separate bodies. In the former case the mother, as a competent adult, has the capacity to consent, or withhold consent, to medical treatment. On this view, a caesarean-section performed without consent would amount to an actionable tort. In the latter case, although the foetus has no strict legal right of action until birth and, indeed, is not even a "person" legally-speaking until birth, courts in the USA and United Kingdom have concerned themselves with the well-being of the foetus, sometimes in contravention of the strict rights of the mother. These operations have been justified with reference to physicians' professional judgements as being necessary to save the life of mother and child, though there has been some disquiet about the apparent tendency of judges to abrogate their own, specifically legal, responsibility in favour of the privileging of medical opinion (see, for example, McLean (1999)). Crucially, though, had the woman in question not been pregnant, her right to refuse treatment would have been far less contentious.

At the heart of the problem lies a fundamental dilemma of women's embodiment: is the foetus part of a woman's body, or is it a separate entity? Implicit in the enforced caesarean-section cases is the idea that the foetus can be managed as though it were independent of the mother, not part of her body at all. The legal difficulty lies in the fact that the foetus has no legal status as a "person" unless and until it is born alive. Weaver makes a very important point at this stage in her argument, namely that this dualistic thinking not only flies in the face of reality (since there is an important sense in which the life of the foetus is entirely dependent upon its location in the mother's body) but, significantly, it reflects the language and technologies of obstetrics. This "lore" that derives from the discourses and practices of Western medicine and, in turn, makes an appeal to broader cultural symbols, has implicitly informed law to the detriment of women. The image is one of maternal-foetal "conflict" with the foetus positioned as the helpless innocent victim of the mother's selfish insistence on her own autonomy and bodily integrity.

But, as Weaver shows, we are mistaken if we regard law as little more than medicine's sidekick. Neither is law just the unwitting purveyor of culture's dominant values. In *St George's Healthcare Trust* v. *S* [1998] 3 All ER 673 a pre-enclamptic mother, who refused treatment and had a history of moderate depression, was detained under the Mental Health Act 1983 (although she received no treatment for any mental disorder) and her baby was born by caesarean-section after the court ordered the operation. The Court of Appeal ruled that the use of the Mental Health Act to effect forced obstetric intervention had been unlawful, and it reiterated a competent adult's right to autonomy and self-determination. Damages were awarded. In future, it was said, these kinds of cases should only occur where the woman is deemed incompetent, when it is incumbent upon the doctors to make a specific assessment and inform the judge, accurately, of all relevant matters. As the Lord Chancellor (1999) has recently argued, the right to refuse medical treatment may be bolstered, in some cases, by reliance on Article 9 of the European Convention on Human Rights.

Autonomy, competence, and capacity to consent are, however, potentially problematic concepts as they do not only have meaning within a specifically legal, or even a medical discourse. Rather, as the enforced caesarean-section cases show, these concepts also derive meanings from broader cultural discourses such as those about femaleness in general and motherhood in particular. Implicit ideas about women's reproductive bodies permeate culture, medicine and law, constituting a body of lore that, at some level, seems self-evident. Worryingly, as Weaver points out, so powerful is the idea that it is in the nature of motherhood that the child's interests have priority above all else—good mothers are selfless—that constructions of "competence" may be made, by doctors and lawyers alike, with reference to these kinds of invisible criteria.

The essays in this book illustrate the point that, in a complex, pluralistic and fast-changing society such as ours, law has the difficult task of negotiating a growing number of competing claims within a complex network of shifting values, changing discourses and new practices. Perhaps it is small wonder that law's responses to social and technological change are often confused and muddled. Like Weaver, John Keown, in "Dehydrating Bodies: the *Bland* Case, the Winterton Bill and the Importance of Intention in Evaluating End-of-Life Decision-making" is concerned with one aspect of an increasing number of cases[43] concerning the right to life and the right to terminate life. His chapter is about a debate that shows little sign of abating—the question of whether voluntary euthanasia should be permitted by law.[44] The starting point for Keown's analysis is that the decision in *Bland*[45] left the law, in the words of Lord Mustill, in a "morally and intellectually

---

[43] See the Rt Hon the Lord Irving of Lairg (1999).

[44] For a contrary view, see Morris (2000). For a defence of the law as it is on euthanasia, see McCall Smith (1999).

[45] *Airedale NHS Trust* v. *Bland* [1993] AC 789.

misshapen" state, prohibiting doctors from intentionally terminating life by an act but permitting them intentionally to terminate life by omission. In 1999, a Bill introduced by Ann Winterton MP sought to repair this inconsistency in the law; it would have made it unlawful to withold or withdraw medical treatment (including tube-feeding) with the purpose of hastening death.

Keown shows how the Bill failed, having encountered fierce opposition from both the British Medical Association and the Government. Crucially, for the themes of this book, Keown's analysis reveals that the decision in *Bland* rests on a blurring of the distinction between "intention" and "foresight"; in subverting this historic distinction, the Law Lords have, Keown argues, invented an arbitrary category of patients who are living bodies but not persons—doctors may be permitted to end the lives of the former, but not the latter. The euthanasia debate, like that over the new human genetics, illustrates the problems for law and ethics that follow in the wake of scientific and technological advance. Technologies have increasingly provided us with the means to create and manipulate bodies, and to shift the boundaries of life and death; as Lord Browne-Wilkinson put it in *Bland*, in the past "death in the traditional sense was beyond human control . . . it occurred automatically in the course of nature",[46] whereas now there is, as Lord Lowry pointed out, a gap between "old law" and "new medicine" and perhaps also "new ethics".[47]

But there are other gaps too, ones that have been opened up by an increasing social recognition of the need to respect difference. Issues of the significance of embodied difference are raised in several essays in this book, most notably those of Caroline Bridge, Martin Richards and Elizabeth Chapman.

Caroline Bridge begins her chapter on "Religion, Culture and the Body of the Child" with an observation that one of the great challenges currently facing law is the task of recognising and embracing religious and cultural diversity. She explores the ways in which law approaches such diversity in the context of the child's body (more specifically, her focus is on practices of circumcision); is the law, she asks, bound by its own traditional concepts and by dominant ideologies in defining the "welfare of the child", or has it begun to develop a notion of religious or cultural welfare? What is the law's approach to cultural pluralism in relation to medical decisions involving children?

The welfare of the child has long been a constraint upon the exercise of the powers of parents. It is clear that courts will overrule parents in life and death situations, and that judges will not hamper doctors by restrictive anticipatory declarations. It is also clear that a consultative approach, between doctors and parents, is the favoured model but, ultimately, the views of parents count for little in the face of opposition by doctors or the court. Bridge concludes that English law balances "risk" against "benefit" and comes down firmly in favour of the individual child rather than the family, community, religion or culture; diversity can be acknowledged only to the extent that it fits with dominant discourses of welfare,

---

[46] *Ibid.* at 878.
[47] *Ibid.* at 877. See also McLean (1999).

in which ideas like "risk" and "benefit" take on particular meanings. Law will endorse those practices that accord with dominant norms; Otherness that falls outside of this model must remain on the outside.

In his essay "Future Bodies: Some History and Future Prospects for Human Genetic Selection" Martin Richards considers what kind of bodies might populate our planet as the "biotech century" proceeds. He critically examines the argument that we will increasingly have societies divided into those who can afford to access technologies to reduce the burden of inherited disadvantage and those who can't. Silver (1998) has produced a vision of a future society, deeply divided, consisting of the "GenRich" and the "naturals", depicting a truly nightmarish scenario of technologies used, not for common benefit, but to consolidate power and privilege. Such images, like those of Frankenstein, have immense appeal. But Richards refuses to be seduced and, instead, dispassionately evaluates the gloomy predictions with reference to what we already know about people's reproductive choices and aspirations. Contextualising his argument with a reminder of our eugenic past, he argues that the evidence suggests that "selective breeding", of the sort envisaged by Silver, is not a likely outcome of current biotech capabilities, not least for the reason that many of the characteristics (such as intelligence, talent, looks) that parents might want to choose for their "designer" babies are actually the products of complex biosocial systems, impossible to achieve by genetic manipulations alone.

On this argument, difference and diversity have a future, but nevertheless there are those who remain concerned about the potential of genetic technologies to enable us to undervalue diversity or even to erase certain types of difference. As Castro-Rios (1999) p. 26 puts it: "The Biotechnological Revolution provides enormous possibilities to human development (nutrition, medicine, industry), while at the same time, creates social-ethical apprehensions due to the dangers to Human Rights that an improper use could generate". He advocates, with reference to the Universal Declaration on Human Rights, that there should be continuing social debate to ensure that human rights principles are not eclipsed by the rapid adoption of new techniques. Sociologist Tom Shakespeare (1998/9) is not alone in fearing that genetic testing and screening sets us on a slippery slope, as genetics becomes "blurred" with eugenics, to the ultimate detriment of people with disabilities (see also King (1999)). Lippman (1991) expresses a wider concern with the consequences of "geneticization", particularly when coupled with the new reproductive technologies. "Individual good", she reminds us, does not necessarily equate to the "common good" (p. 47) and "[T]here are choices to be made and the choices will reflect our values and ideology. How we choose our culture (by the routes we take) is no less problematic than how we choose our children, and the consequences from both will be among our legacies" (p. 48). It seems that, at best, critics see the coming together of genetic and reproductive technologies as reproducing existing structures of race, class, gender and heterosexuality (see, for example, Steinberg (1997)).

In the "risk society" (Beck (1992)), risk has become an important aspect of how we think about and manage our bodies. With this background, Elizabeth

Chapman in her chapter "Perceptions of the Body and Genetic Risk" asks whether the advent of genetic testing has consequences for how we envisage our bodies and how we construct our identities: does genetic testing give rise to unique perceptions of the body? Clearly, genetic tests have the power to make us think differently about ourselves—they have the capacity to interrupt, even disrupt, our autobiographical narratives—as our evolving sense of self becomes bound up with the risk of future illness and disability. Chapman compares the experiences of people whose body image has been potentially affected by testing for three conditions: Huntingdon's disease, cystic fibrosis and HIV. From a comparison of these three conditions (the first two are genetically determined, the last is viral) it is clear that positive genetic testing does not always result in a unique sense of a risky body. Rather, feelings about risk and their impact on body image vary within each of these conditions. To what extent, then, should we consider genetic tests to be unique? For Chapman, the differentiating factor is that genetic knowledge and practices affect not only the present but also future generations; present decisions potentially alter future life courses. But others would argue (see, for example, Zimmerman (1999)) that there is little in the nature of gene tests that justifies a special approach to regulation; regulation needs to take account of those morally relevant features that justify regulation.

In "Science, Medicine and Ethical Change" Derek Morgan examines the question of whether cell nuclear replacement (CNR) techniques (commonly called "cloning") result in a new kind of embryo, and what is the legal status of such a creation. The Human Fertilisation and Embryology Act 1990 provided that a licence be required for the creation of an embryo outside the human body. Such licences cannot authorise the cloning of human tissue where the technique involves replacing the nucleus of a cell of an embryo with a nucleus taken from elsewhere. But, Morgan points out, the technique that created Dolly the cloned sheep involves a different type of cloning from that envisaged by the Act—it involves the nucleus substitution into an egg, not an embryo. The question therefore arises as to whether the creation of a human embryo by the Dolly technique is actually lawful as falling outside the scope of the 1990 Act. The situation is further complicated by the definition of "embryo" that appears in section 1 of the Act. It refers to the necessity of "fertilisation", but CNR techniques do not involve fertilisation as such. It may therefore be argued that an "embryo" created by the Dolly technique is not an "embryo" for the purposes of the Act, and so its creation is not covered by that Act.

This is the legal and ethical conundrum that Morgan confronts: when is an embryo not an embryo? The answer to the question about the moral and legal status of CNR embryos depends upon whether a "purposive" or "literal" view is taken; on a purposive reading, the moral status of the embryo is given from what results, so the means of its creation are irrelevant. Not so on a literal view. If the matter comes before the courts, Morgan anticipates that the outcome will depend, at least in part, on the context of the legal proceedings (for example, is it a criminal prosecution, or an application for judicial review?).

Like Rachel Cook's concern with the ambiguous status of gametes, and the societal ambivalence underlying it, both Weaver and Morgan highlight the ambiguities and ambivalences in relation to embryos. As Fox (2000) points out, one discourse constructs the embryo as a person, whilst an opposing one dismisses the embryo as a commodifiable object. The former discourse has taken hold, not only in abortion debates, but also in popular culture in, for example, films such as "Look Who's Talking" (see Petchesky (1987)). It is this kind of fundamental ambiguity as regards the legal status of the embryo that underlies controversies over cryo-preserved embryos. The essays in this book suggest that the present debate over the status of the embryo is unresolvable unless the terms of that debate are altered. Here we are faced with another instance where, as with gametes, polarisations are unhelpful. As Fox (2000) argues, we need to find ways of thinking that allow us to overcome the old dichotomy; now that we can create embryos by technological means perhaps we should find a new language in which to conceptualise them, instead of trying to squeeze them into old legal categories of either persons or property that are both woefully inadequate.

Importantly, though, debates seem to be characterised by an emotivism that brutally shunts rational appraisal aside.[48] The result is unresolvable arguments between those who think that advances in biotechnologies will be our salvation and those who believe the opposite, that they will take us down a road that can only lead to our destruction. Polarised fantasies these may be, but there can be no doubt that it is such fantasies that are setting the terms of the debate –"science as redeemer" versus "science as destroyer" is the trope that occupies the popular imagination of today, nowhere more than in the realm of the body.

The force of these fantasies could be seen as requiring a "third way", or at least the opening up of a space where the rationality of law might usefully step in and decide once and for all, within an agreed ethical frame, what ought to be done. But any appeal to the (supposed) rationality of law has to take account of the forces that produce the fantasies in the first place, as well as the difficulties, in an acknowledged pluralistic society, of finding any general consensus on ethical principles.

Embodied subjects are, as Freud reminded us, of necessity emotional subjects. And embodied subjects have a finite existence. Turner (1992), for example, draws our attention to the inevitable frailty of the human body. Paradoxically, bodies signify both sameness and difference, but the sameness, what unites us as human beings despite a whole range of other differences that divides us, is the knowledge that our bodies will age and will eventually die. Death remains problematic in our society (Seale (1998, 2000)), the final taboo, managed by means of elaborate rituals; death is as unknown to us, as threatening to us, as it is inevitable. In marshalling science, and now biomedical technologies, to "know" and manage the body, we are attempting to ward off the inevitable, attempting to deny the uncomfortable fact of our own mortality (Craib (1994)).

---

[48] For an elaboration of this argument in the context of genetically modified crops see Yates and Day Sclater (2000).

In these vain attempts to deny the uncomfortable fact of our own mortality, lie hidden enormous psychological investments that not only spawn the idealised "science-as-redeemer" versus the denigrated "science-as-destroyer" fantasies that have dominated popular debate, but also lend their cruel power to images of the bodies of the old, the sick, the dying and the dead. We look on with fear, horror, disgust, loathing and fascination at those bodies we have come to see as "abject",[49] where we are confronted with the parts of ourselves we have cast out, come back to haunt us.

Our construction of certain bodies as "abjected" reflects our vain search for the unattainable pure body, a body that has been purified by the expulsion of the polluting Other. Hyde (1997) argues that law facilitates the construction and abjection of hated Others whenever it permits the classification of sameness and difference. In her classic work *Purity and Danger*, anthropologist Mary Douglas argued that there was a correspondence between the establishment of bodily limits (taking place through expressions of disgust and fear of "filth") and the establishment and maintenance of social order. Thus the personal struggle against "filth" is also a social struggle against those who seem to threaten the social order. There are clear parallels between this argument and our more psychological argument utilising Kristeva's concept of abjection.[50] It is, in the end, as Friedman and Squire (1998) p. 140 remind us, such abject bodies that discourses of the body try to regulate. But despite the proliferation of discourses and technologies, these bodies cannot be silenced, because they speak to us from inside ourselves, from the very limits of our capacity to bear our own mortality.

We can see, therefore, that what law regulates is no longer just "the body" but is increasingly the "biotech body", a body variously constructed within the discourses and practices of medical, genetic and reproductive technologies and, moreover, a body in which we all make deep emotional investments. Questions about "so what's new?" in the age of technology have provoked endless debates, and it is perhaps most comfortable to conclude, as many have done, that nothing much is truly new after all; the implicit message is that there is nothing to worry about. Genetic testing, based on DNA profiling, we are told, is not that different from what went on before without much comment—vague predictions made on the basis of patients' stories about family histories of particular conditions; even pre-implantation genetic diagnosis has been equated with pre-natal diagnosis (plus termination of affected pregnancies), and infertility resolved by gamete donation may be closer than we like to think to supposedly "natural" conceptions. It is, indeed, fashionable—even politically correct—to bridge the gap between the polarised fantasies and to appear, at least, to take it all in one's stride; science equals progress, after all, and there is nothing much we can do about it anyway.

But, and here is the ruse, what *is* new is the emergence of what might be called a secular fundamentalism, the proliferation of discourses that position embodied

---

[49] See Kristeva (1982).
[50] See also the essays in Terry and Urla (1995).

subjects as "essentially" biological, as the inevitable outcomes of particular genetic constellations. What *is* new is a resurgence of discourses that position the biological as fundamental. That a good deal of body lore is at work in this process is indicated, first, by the panic reactions that set in when remote science (e.g. human cloning) is made to seem imminent (see, for example, Jonsen (1998)) and, secondly, the fact that prominent biological and genetic scientists regularly dismiss what is claimed by those less in-the-know as the determinative power of biology and genes as preposterous. Thirdly, and most crucially, we are daily faced with the paradoxical situation whereby we seem to need an ever-increasing battery of scientific practice and technological equipment to reveal biology's secrets and to create ever-more variants of the biological template. What *is* new in our current situation is the new meanings for "biology" that are being created by technological practice.

So, questions of what is new about "biotech bodies", and what law should do about them, will not be answered until we begin to address these new bodies in new terms that adequately address the ways they depart from bodies of the past as well as the ways they remain the same. If law is effectively to regulate biotech bodies, then it also needs to rethink regulation. Perhaps the bodies we can now and will, in future, create are no longer Foucault's "docile" and "disciplined" bodies but are, instead, transgressive bodies, disruptive of old certainties. If this is so, then law will need to rethink regulation in the light, not only of new science and new technologies, but also in the light of new ethics and the rapidly shifting cultural lore of bodies, biologies and selves.

REFERENCES

ANDREWS, L., "My Body, My Property" (1986) 16 *Hastings Center Report* 28.
BECK, U., *Risk Society: Toward a New Modernity* (London, Sage, trans. M. Ritter, 1992).
BEYLEVELD, D. and BROWNSWORD, R., "My Body, My Body Parts, My Property?" (2000) 8 *Health Care Analysis* 87.
BRISTOL INQUIRY INTERIM REPORT *Removal and retention of Human Material* http://www.bristol-inquiry.org.uk (2000).
BROWNSWORD, R., CORNISH, W.R. and LLEWELLYN, M. (eds.), *Law and Human Genetics: Regulating a Revolution* (Oxford, Hart, 1998).
BUTLER, J., *Bodies that Matter: On the Discursive Limits of "Sex"* (London, Routledge, 1993).
BYK, C., "The Impact of Biomedical Developments on the Legal Theory of the Mind-Body Relationship" in M Cherry (ed.), *Persons and Their Bodies: Rights, Responsibilities, Relationships* (London, Kluwer Academic Publishers, 1999).
BYNUM, C., "Why All the Fuss about the Body? A Medievalist's Perspective" (1995) 22 *Critical Inquiry*.
CAMPBELL, C., "Body, Self and the Property Paradigm" (1992) *22 Hastings Center Report* 34.
CASTRO-RIOS, A., "Human Rights in the World of the Genetic Revolution" (1999) 5 *Human Reproduction and Genetic Ethics* 26.

CHEAH, P., FRASER, D. and GRBICH, J. (eds.), *Thinking Through the Body of the Law* (St Leonards, NSW; Allen and Unwin, 1996).

COOK, E.D., "Genetics and the British Insurance Industry" (1999), 25 *Journal of Medical Ethics* 157.

COTTERELL, R., "Why Must Legal Ideas be Interpreted Sociologically?" (1998) 25 *Journal of Law and Society* 171.

CRAIB, I., *The Importance of Disappointment* (London, Routledge, 1994).

DAY SCLATER, S. and PIPER, C., "Social Exclusion and the Welfare of the Child", (2001) 28(3) *Journal of Law and Society* 409.

DODSON, M. and WILLIAMSON, R., "Indigenous Peoples and the Morality of the Human Genome Diversity Project" (1999), 25 *Journal of Medical Ethics* 204.

DOUGLAS, M., *Purity and Danger: An Analysis of Concepts of Pollution and Taboo* (Harmondsworth, Penguin, 1970).

DOUZINAS, C. and MCVEIGH, S., "The Tragic Body: the Inscription of Autonomy in Medical Ethics and Law" in S. Wheeler and S. McVeigh (eds.), *Law, Health and Medical Regulation* (Aldershot, Dartmouth, 1992).

EISENSTEIN, Z.R., *The Female Body and the Law* (Berkeley, University of California Press, 1988).

FARSIDES, C., "Body Ownership" in S. Wheeler and S. McVeigh (eds.), *Law, Health and Medical Regulation* (Aldershot, Dartmouth, 1992).

FINEMAN, M.A. and THOMASDEN, N.S. (eds.), *At the Boundaries of Law: Feminism and Legal Theory* (New York, Routledge, 1991).

FOUCAULT, M., *Discipline and Punish: The Birth of the Prison* (London, Allen Lane, trans. A Sheridan, 1977).

FOX, M., "Crime and Punishment: Representations of Female Killers in Law and Literature" in J. Morison and C. Bell (eds.), *Tall Stories? Reading Law and Literature* (Aldershot, Dartmouth, 1996).

—— , "Pre-persons, Commodities or Cyborgs: the Legal Construction and Representation of the Embryo" (2000), 8 *Health Care Analysis* 171.

FOX, M. and MCHALE, J. (eds.), *Regulating Human Body Parts and Products* (Special issue of (2000) *Health Care Analysis* 8).

FOX KELLNER, E., *The Century of the Gene* (Cambridge MA, Harvard University Press, 2000).

FRIEDMAN, E. and SQUIRE, C., *Morality USA* (Minneapolis, University of Minnesota Press, 1998).

GEVERS, J.K.M., "Response of the Law to Developments in Genetics" (1995) 14 *Medicine and Law* 199.

GLASNER, P. and ROTHMAN, H. (eds.), *Genetic Imaginations: Ethical, Legal and Social Issues in Human Genome Research* (Aldershot, Ashgate, 1998).

GOLD, E.R., *Property Rights and the Ownership of Human Biological Materials* (Washington, DC; Georgetown University Press, 1996).

HARRIS, J., "Who Owns My Body?" (1996), 16 *Oxford Journal of Legal Studies* 55.

HYDE, A., *Bodies of Law* (Princeton, NJ, Princeton University Press, 1997).

THE RIGHT HONOURABLE THE LORD IRVINE OF LAIRG, "The Patient, the Doctor, their Lawyers and the Judge: Rights and Duties" (1999) 7 *Medical Law Review* 255.

JOHNSON, M., (2000), "The Medical Ethics of Paid Egg Sharing in the UK", paper presented to the Cambridge Biomedical Ethics Forum.

JONSEN, A. R. The Birth of Bioethics (New York; Oxford, Oxford University Press, 1998).

KEVLES, D.J. and HOOD, L. (eds.), *The Code of Codes: Scientific and Social Issues in the Human Genome Project* (Cambridge, MA; Harvard University Press, 1992).

KING, D.S., "Preimplantation Genetic Diagnosis and the 'New' Eugenics" (1999), 25 *Journal of Medical Ethics* 176.

KING, M., "Child Welfare Within Law: the Emergence of a Hybrid Discourse" (1991) *Journal of Law and Society* 303.

—— , "The Truth About Autopoesis" (1993) 20 *Journal of Law and Society* 1–19.

KRISTEVA, J., *Powers of Horror: An Essay on Abjection* (New York, Columbia University Press, trans. L.S.Roudiez, 1982).

LIPPMAN, A. (1991), "Prenatal Genetic Testing and Screening: Constructing Needs and Reinforcing Inequities" (1991) XV11 *American Journal of Law and Medicine* 15.

MARTEAU, T. and RICHARDS, M. (eds.), *The Troubled Helix: Social and Psychological Implications of the New Human Genetics* (Cambridge, Cambridge University Press, 1996).

MASON, J.K. and MCCALL SMITH, A., *Law and Medical Ethics* (London, Butterworths, 1999).

MCCALL SMITH, A.), "Beyond Autonomy" (1997) 14 *Journal of Contemporary Health Law and Policy* 23.

—— , "Euthanasia: the Strength of the Middle Ground" (1997) 7 *Medical Law Review* 194.

MCGLEENAN, T., "Genetic Testing and Screening: the Developing European Jurisprudence" (1999) 5 *Human Reproduction and Genetic Ethics* 11.

MCHALE, J., "Waste, Ownership and Bodily Products" (2000), 8 *Health Care Analysis* 123.

MCKENNY, G.P., "The Integrity of the Body: Critical Remarks on a Persistent Theme in Bioethics" in M. Cherry (ed.), *Persons and their Bodies: Rights, Responsibilities, Relationships* (London, Kluwer Academic Publishers, 1999).

MCLEAN, S., *Old Law, New Medicine: Medical Ethics and Human Rights* (London, Pandora, 1999).

MORGAN, D. and NIELSEN, L., "Dangerous Liasons: Law, Technology, Reproduction and European Ethics" in S. McVeigh and S. Wheeler (eds.), *Law, Health and Medical Regulation* (Aldershot, Dartmouth 1992).

MORRIS, A., "Easing the Passing: End of Life Decisions and the Medical Treatment (Prevention of Euthanasia) Bill" (2000) 8 *Medical Law Review* 300.

MURPHY, T., "Bursting Binary Bubbles: Law, Literature and the Sexed Body" in J. Morison and C. Bell (eds.), *Tall Stories? Reading Law and Literature* (Aldershot, Dartmouth, 1996).

—— , "Gametes, Law and Modern Preoccupations" (2000) 8 *Health Care Analysis* 155.

MURRAY, T.H., "Genetic Exceptionalism and 'Future Diaries': is Genetics Different from Other Medical Information?" in M.A. Rothstein (ed.), *Genetic Secrets: Protecting Privacy and Confidentiality in the Genetic Era* (Yale University Press, 1997).

NELKEN, D., "Can There be a Sociology of Legal Meaning?" in D. Nelken (ed.), *Law as Communication* (Aldershot, Dartmouth, 1996).

NELKIN, D. and LINDEE, M., *The DNA Mystique: The Gene as Cultural Icon* (New York, Freeman, 1995).

NELKIN, D. and ANDREWS, L., "DNA Identification and Surveillance Creep" (1999) 21 *Sociology of Health and Illness* 689.

O'DONNELL, K., "Legal Conceptions: Regulating Gametes and Gamete Donation" (2000) 8 *Health Care Analysis* 137.

O'DONOVAN, K., "Defences for Battered Women who Kill" (1991) 18 *Journal of Law and Society* 219.

—— , "Law's Knowledge: the Judge, the Expert, the Battered Woman and her Syndrome" (1993) 20 *Journal of Law and Society* 427.

PATTERSON, D., *Law and Truth* (Oxford, Oxford University Press, 1996).

PETCHESKY, R., "Foetal Images: the Power of Visual Culture in the Politics of Reproduction" in M. Stanworth (ed.), *Reproductive Technologies: Gender, Motherhood and Medicine* (Cambridge, Polity Press, 1987).

RAITT, F. E. and ZEEDYK, M. S., The Implicit Relation of Psychology and Law: Women and Syndrome Evidence (London, Routledge, 2000).

REILLY, P., "Legal and Public Policy Issues in DNA Forensics" (2001) 2 *Genetics* 313–17.

RICHARDS, M., "How Distinctive is Genetic Information?" *Studies in the History and Philosophy of Biological and Biomedical Sciences* (2001).

RILEY, D., *Am I That Name? Feminism and the Category of "Women" in History* (Basingstoke, Macmillan, 1988).

ROSE, H. and ROSE, S. (eds.), *Alas Poor Darwin: Arguments Against Evolutionary Psychology* (London, Jonathan Cape, 2000).

ROSE, N. and VALVERDE, M., "Governed by Law?" (1998) 7 *Social and Legal Studies* 541.

SCOTT, R., *The Body as Property* (New York, Viking, 1981).

SEALE, C. (1998), *Constructing Death: The Sociology of Dying and Bereavement* (Cambridge, Cambridge University Press, 1998).

—— , "Resurrective Practice and Narrative" in M. Andrews, S. Day Sclater, C. Squire and A. Treacher (eds.) *Lines of Narrative: Psychosocial Perspectives* (London, Routledge, 2000).

SHAKESPEARE, T., "Eugenics? Slipping Down the Slope" (1998/9) 5 *The Splice of Life.* http://www.geneticsforum.org.uk/eugenic.htm

SILVER, L. (1998) Remaking Eden: Cloning, Genetic Engineering and the Future of Human kind (London, Weidenfeld & Nicolson, 1998).

SLOAN, P.R. (ed.) (2000), *Controlling Our Destinies: Historical, Philosophical, Ethical and Theological Perspectives on the Human Genome Project* (Notre Dame, Indiana; University of Notre Dame Press, 2000).

SOMMERVILLE, A. and ENGLISH, V. (1999), "Genetic Privacy: Orthodoxy or Oxymoron?" (1999) 25 *Journal of Medical Ethics* 144–50.

SOPER, K. (1995), *What is Nature?* (Oxford, Blackwell, 1995).

SMITH, A. L. JNR, "An Orthodox Christian View of Persons and their Bodies" in M. J. Cherry (ed.) *Persons and their Bodies: Rights, Responsibilities, Relationships* (London, Kluwer Academic Publishers, 1999).

STEINBERG, D.L., *Bodies in Glass: Genetics, Eugenics and Embryo Ethics* (Manchester, Manchester University Press, 1997).

TERRY, J. and URLA, J. (eds.), *Deviant Bodies: Critical Perspectives on Difference in Science and Popular Culture* (Bloomington, Indiana University Press, 1995).

TEUBNER, G., "How the Law Thinks: Towards a Constructivist Epistemology of Law" (1989) 22 *Law and Society Review* 727.

TOOMBS, S.K., "What Does it Mean to be Some*body*? Pheomenological Reflections and Ethical Quandries" in M. J. Cherry (ed.), *Persons and their Bodies: Rights, Responsibilities, Relationships* (London, Kluwer Academic Publishers, 1999).

TURNER, B.S., *Regulating Bodies: Essays in Medical Sociology* (London, Routledge, 1992).

WHEALE, P., "Moral and Legal Consequences for the Fetus/Unborn Child of Medical Technologies Derived from Human Genome Research" in P. Glaser and H. Rothman (eds.), *Genetic Imaginations* (Aldershot, Ashgate, 2000).

WIELAND, C., "Matricide and Destructiveness: Infantile Anxieties and Technological Culture" (1996) 12 *British Journal of Psychotherapy* 300.

WILKINSON, S., "Commodification Arguments for the Legal Prohibition of Organ Sale" (2000) 8 *Health Care Analysis* 189.

WILLIAMSON, R., "What's 'New' About Genetics?" (1999) 25 *Journal of Medical Ethics* 75.

—— , "Human Reproductive Cloning is Unethical Because it Undermines Autonomy: Commentary on Savulescu" (1999) 25 *Journal of Medical Ethics* 96.

YATES, C. and DAY SCLATER, S, "Culture, Psychology and Transitional Space: the Case of GM Foods" in C. Squire (ed.), *Culture in Psychology* (London, Routledge, 2000).

ZIMMERMAN, R.L., "Genetic Testing: a Conceptual Exploration" (1999) 25 *Journal of Medical Ethics* 151.

2

Bodies as Property:
from Slavery to DNA Maps

EILEEN H. RICHARDSON and BRYAN S. TURNER

1. INTRODUCTION: REPRESENTATION AND CONSTRUCTION

THE RECENT SOCIOLOGY of the body evolved through a critique of the prevailing rationalist and cognitive assumptions that are the legacy of Cartesianism; its analytical intention has been to place the notion of embodiment at the centre of any theory of social action (Turner (1984)). This interest in the body is also paradoxically a consequence of the influence of new theories of language and culture that are generally referred to as "the cultural turn", in which the body is presented as a text from which the political structures of society can be interpreted. In the last twenty years, the focus of theoretical interest has shifted from the anthropology of the body as a site of classification of pollution and risk (Douglas (1966)) to studies of sexuality from the perspective of knowledge and power (Foucault (1979)).

The body now enjoys some prominence in sociology and cultural studies, but this revival has often been narrow and one-sided. Contemporary writing has often been dominated either by arguments about social representation or about social construction. The first line of inquiry suggests correctly that the body is a rich system of metaphors about social and political relations (for example the Body of Christ as a metaphor of ecclesiastical relationships). The second line of inquiry argues that we cannot take the body for granted and that its "naturalness" is an ideological smoke screen. The body is historical rather than natural in the sense that it has a variable meaning depending on place and custom. For example, the "facticity" of the body (its unchangeable character) has been employed to support repressive social and political arrangements. The very anatomy of the reproductive organs has often been interpreted historically to justify the subordination of women to men (Laquer (1990)). However, it is increasingly clear that sweeping assertions that the body is socially constructed do not in themselves produce creative or valuable social research programmes (Hacking (1999)).

The future of the sociology of the body requires less rehearsal of arguments about representation and construction, and more exploration of different empirical research issues. For example, the relationships between the legal and social aspects of the body have not been a prominent issue in the social science literature, but these relationships are clearly crucial to any understanding of how society functions. Recent research on gay and lesbian rights has raised important issues about the law in relation to the body (Cheah, Fraser and Grbich (1996); Stychin and Herman (2000)). Issues about the legal framework of the body provoke a fundamental question—who owns the body?

2. GOVERNING THE BODY

In this attempt to extend the sociological debate into fresh terrain, we open up a discussion about the body as property via the concept of governmentality (Foucault (1991)). This term emerged in Michel Foucault's later writing on the state and administration, namely that the modern state is no longer primarily concerned with the torture of the criminal body but with its moral productivity. The concept of population size was originally an important indicator of the state's administrative interest in making populations fully productive. Hence, the notions of generation, regeneration and population became important in the development of political institutions.

The question of the ownership of the body cannot be disconnected from the problem of sovereignty. The notion that the body as a whole can function as economic property was characteristic of slavery, and played an important part in the growth of patriarchal power. In traditional political systems, women, children and servants generally were conceptualised as part of the household over which (male) heads of households had (absolute) rights. An economy was simply the management of a household within which a woman was an essential asset. This doctrine, when applied to kingship, supported absolutism, but it was challenged by individualistic notions of private property and the limited rights of kings to rulership under a social contract. Where property was defined by the investment of labour, this bourgeois theory of property depended on a distinction between ownership and control of property and rights to its use.

There are important differences surrounding for example the exploitation of the sexual labour power of another (prostitution), ownership of other persons' bodies for the sake of economic production (slavery), and sale of parts of a body for commercial gain (the organ market). At the core of the contemporary legal debate about bodies are the notions of self-ownership and consent, but scientific developments have opened up new economic opportunities for the commercial exploitation of the human body. In particular, modern genetic sciences have stimulated another set of possibilities, namely the development of patents over genetic innovations.

Our argument explores the social ambiguities of the body through a historical sketch of the changing legal framework: from ownership of persons (whole bodies) under slavery; the emergence of individualism and the notion of possessive individualism; the development of a market through medical specialisation in body parts; the commercialisation of what we call body particles (including the sale of genetic codes); and the emergence of a medical market that is global, competitive and largely unregulated. This history traces the fragmentation of the body into systems of information and its commercial applications. The legal and political regulation of this process by either the state or the professions is virtually impossible, given the globalisation of body markets.

3. POWER AND THE BODY

The problem of the body needs to be made more explicit in any reading of social and political theory. The body is central to any theory of power, and to any modern vision of citizenship and human rights. Our discussion presumes a historical context within which the human body is differentiated into the whole body (persons), its parts and particles. The patrimonial state in the form of a sovereign naturally assumed rights over the whole bodies of persons. Under conditions of chattel slavery, bodies were typically the property of the state in a system of absolute power. The modern state encounters a range of very different issues. With advances in medical science (particularly anatomy and anaesthetics), it became possible for a global market to emerge in the sale and exchange of parts of bodies, for example kidneys. With the further differentiation of the body into what we will term "particles", there are new possibilities for the commercialisation of the body through the sale of patents of the genetic code. While our contribution to the debate about law and the body is to problematise the notion of the body through a discussion of its differentiation and fragmentation, there are equally important differences between the notions of ownership, control and use of the body. A more complete exploration of these issues would have to note the difference, for example, between outright ownership of another's body for sexual reproduction in slavery and the sexual hire of a body in a modern society for personal gratification (see Belinda Brooks-Gordon and Loraine Gelsthorpe (chapter 11)). The growth of individualism and norms of social equality has made the unconditional ownership of another's body unlikely. Modern consumption of sexual services more precisely involves a rental charge rather than ownership.

The ownership of the body starts therefore with the historical origins of patriarchal powers. Patriarchy was an ancient philosophy of power that, through a primitive notion of generation, justified the power of gods over men, kings over their subjects, and fathers over their households. Indeed, the private household was a model of the public domain. Aristotle's *Politics* assumed both domestic and public slavery, and that women, children and slaves would remain within the private sphere, that is in the world of privation which characterised the domestic labour of animals and dependent human beings. The growth of chattel slavery followed the economic and military expansion of Greece, and the paradoxical dependence of freemen on the institution of slavery was not lost on the Greek citizens of the ancient world (Bryant (1996)). Women constituted the most significant component of domestic slavery and were the basis of small-scale production.

The sexual division of political space in the ancient world was further elaborated by the development of Christianity in late antiquity. In Pauline theology for example, women are a necessary evil, that is necessary for the reproduction of the human species but through an act that is the ultimate folly. Augustine laid the foundations of Christian sympathy as non-sexual *agape* and saw the City of God as the arena wherein "amorous sympathy" could unite men and women in communal harmony. Where a negative view of women as secondary and irrational creations persisted, women's spirituality was often deviant and secretive (Bynum (1991)). The dominant Christian view of humanity remained critical, because this world is one fallen from grace. Thus, Luther and Calvin developed Christian political philosophy further in the notion that the state as an institution is a necessary evil for the subordination and control of sinful men.

All of these theories might be said to be "patriarchal", because the state and fatherhood were required to regulate the sinful passions of men. The original formulation of these notions is to be found in Robert Filmer's *Patriarcha: a Defence of the Natural Power of Kings Against the Unnatural Liberty of the People* (written around 1640 and published posthumously in 1680). As the subtitle indicates, Filmer attempted to develop a critique of early "possessive individualism" by arguing that there was a "natural" (creative/generative) right of kings to rule which was parallel to the creative power of God. The household power of husbands was based on the same natural right. In the seventeenth century, traditional medical notions were still important in justifying patriarchy, because medical philosophy argued that the male seed produced the child where the woman's uterus was merely a vehicle or vessel of male creative powers. Robert Burton's analysis of female hysteria as a consequence of idleness (for example failure to reproduce) in *The Anatomy of Melancholy* in 1621 was representative of medico-legal opinion (Burton (1927)). Filmeristic patriarchalism went into decline in the late seventeenth century, because the Stuart Restoration was constitutionally an affirmation of contractualism rather than of natural law theory. John Locke's individualistic defence of private property in his *Two Treatises of Government* (published in 1680) became the dominant mode of explaining property as legal alienation.

Locke is important in laying the foundations of a (bourgeois) theory of labour power. Recognising that in a state of nature things are held in common, Locke (1956) p. 15 argued that, "the labour of his body and the work of his hands we may say are properly his. Whatsoever, then, he removes out of the state that nature hath provided and left it in, he hath mixed his labour with, and joined to it something that is his own, and thereby makes it his property".

The view that labour creates property rights might be easily extended to the ownership of bodies through reproductive labour. Do we, following Lockean principles, own our children? Locke as a liberal philosopher rejects such a proposition, which could be used to justify the absolute powers of a generative God—the fundamental problem of Milton's *Paradise Lost*. The power of parents can only be temporary: "the power, then, that parents have over their children arises from that duty which is, incumbent on them, to take care of their offspring during the imperfect state of childhood" (Locke (1956) p. 29).

Parental power exists for as long as the child lacks the powers of reason to direct his or her own actions. However, Locke's argument was problematic, because it assumed implicitly the power of landowners over the landless serf who in this sense remained childlike. Locke casually noted that "the turfs my servant has cut . . . become my property without the assignation or consent of anybody" (Locke (1956)). In early capitalism, the individual achieved personal sovereignty and liberal theorists such as J. S. Mill declared that the individual enjoyed sovereignty over their own minds and bodies. This tradition gave rise to the "sovereign individual of capitalism" (Abercrombie et al. (1986)) and to "possessive individualism" (Macpherson (1962)). Sovereignty over one's body has become a fundamental assumption of modern theories of social development. The theory of liberal individualism presupposed the continuity of class relations and the exploitation of the labour power of servants and subordinates.

While Filmer has been eclipsed by the legacy of Locke's liberalism, he is still important for any discussion of law and the body, because he is the *locus classicus* of the legal notion of "self-ownership" (Steiner (1994)). God created the earth, and gave Adam sole dominion over this creation. Being the owner of Eve, Adam has ownership of their offspring and their offspring's offspring. Through primogeniture, there is only one person at a time that is a self-owner. Everyone else is owned. This doctrine, while resting on bizarre pre-suppositions, provided the legal foundation for American slavery within which slave owners also had ownership of the offspring of their slaves, and thus female slaves had a status very similar to cattle. It was their reproductive capacities that contributed to accumulation in agrarian slavery, since they reproduced labour through reproducing themselves.

4. GOVERNMENTALITY

In order to develop a view of how the state came to regulate human bodies in a rational system of administration, it will be useful to outline and discuss Foucault's theory of governmentality. The analysis of governmentality rests more generally on his historical commentaries on the body in Western society. In *The History of Sexuality* the relationship between power, body and government is explicit. The regulation of the human body was first ensured by:

> "the procedures of power that characterized the *disciplines: an anatomo-politics of the human body* . . . The second, formed somewhat later, focused on the species body, the body imbued with the mechanics of life and serving as the basis of the biological processes: propagation, births and mortality, the level of health, life expectancy and longevity . . . Their supervision was effected through an entire series of interventions and *regulatory controls: a bio-politics of the population*"[1] (Foucault (1979) pp. 139–40).

---

[1] Emphasis added by the present authors.

The traditional power of kings over the bodies of their subjects, expressed historically by the power of death, was now replaced by a powerful machinery of administrative power over the productive bodies of the subjects of the state. Foucault's analysis of power can be briefly summarised in the following arguments. Disciplinary power, such as panopticism, functions to produce servile, disciplined and effective bodies through a micro-politics of disciplinary regimes, practices and regulations. Docile but productive bodies are functional for the modern state, as part of a general apparatus of control that can be termed "governmentality". The modern self arises from these bio-regimes that control the body to produce "truths" such as the truth of the self that, originally a product of torture, is now an effect of a confessional culture. Power that is typically local, diffuse, practical and normative means ultimately the power to produce different types of bodies, that is, power over life.

Foucault's concept of "governmentality" is a useful paradigm for understanding the micro-processes of administration and control within which self-regulation and social regulation are united. The concept of "governmentality" provides an integrating theme that was concerned with the socio-political practices or technologies by which the self is constructed. "Governance" or "governmentality" refers to the administrative structures of the state, the patterns of self-government of individuals and the regulatory principles of modern society. For Foucault, governmentality had three aspects:

> "(1) The ensemble formed by the institutions, procedures, analyses and reflections, the calculations and tactics that allow the exercise of this very specific albeit complex form of power, which has as its target population, as its principal form of knowledge political economy, and as its essential technical means apparatuses of security (2) . . . the formulation of a whole series of specific government apparatuses, and , on the other, in the development of a whole complex of *savoirs* (3) The process . . . through which the state of justice of the Middle Ages, transformed into the administrative state during the fifteenth and sixteenth centuries, gradually becomes 'governmentality' " (Foucault (1991) pp. 102–3).

Foucault argues that governmentality has become the common foundation of modern forms of political rationality. The administrative systems of the state have been extended in order to maximise the state's productive control over the processes of the population. More specifically, it was the conceptualisation of "population" that marked the origins of the administrative sciences. With the demographic upswing in Europe, it was necessary to produce systems of measurement, surveillance and control. As a consequence:

> "(t)he project of a technology of population begins to be sketched: demographic estimates, the calculation of pyramid of ages, different life expectations and levels of mortality, studies of the reciprocal relations of growth of wealth and growth of population, various measures of incitement to marriage and procreation, the development of forms of education and professional training. Within this set of problems, the 'body'—the body of individuals and the body of populations—appears as the bearer of new variables". (Foucault (1980) pp. 171–2).

This extension of administrative rationality was first concerned with demographic processes of birth, morbidity and death, and later with the psychological health of the population. Medical practice in the eighteenth century recognised an important connection between the government of the body through dietary management and the government of society through effective political management (Turner (1992)). Political theory saw the necessary connections between the ownership and control of bodies and the sovereignty of the state.

Foucault's historical inquiries gave rise to a distinctive notion of power, in which he emphasised the importance of its local or micro manifestations, the role of professional knowledge and expertise in the legitimation of such power relationships and the productive rather than negative characteristics of the effects of power. His approach can be contrasted usefully with the concept of power in traditional Marxist sociology, where power is visible in terms of the police and army, concentrated in the state and ultimately explained by the ownership of the economic means of production. In the Marxist perspective, power is typically negative and signifies a system of institutions that contain, prohibit and control. Foucault's view of power is more subtle, with an emphasis on the importance of knowledge and information in modern means of surveillance.

Governmentality is the generic term for these power relations. The importance of this definition is that historically the power of the state is less concerned with sovereignty over things (land and wealth) and more concerned with maximising the productive power of administration over population and reproduction. We might also note here that one implication of Foucault's theory of power is that over time power relations tend to become more refined, detailed and specific. Whereas simple forms of patriarchal power took the whole body as its site of operation, the modernisation of the state has involved an increasing focus on parts of the body. Medical power itself becomes specialised through the differentiation of the body into its respective parts. The body of modern medicine was differentiated into the specialised sites of the medical gaze and medical science. Hospitals consequently specialised not only in particular bodies (such as the children's hospital) but in specific parts of the body (the eye hospital, or the ear, nose and throat clinic).

These specialised and differentiated forms of medicine are not punitive divisions. They are to make the body more productive by, as Foucault would argue, forcing the body to reveal its secrets. Foucault interprets the exercise of administrative power in productive terms, that is enhancing population potential through for example state support for the family. The state's involvement in and regulation of reproductive technology is an important example of governmentality, in which the desire of couples to reproduce is enhanced through the state's support of new technologies. The existence of a demand for fertility is supported by a pro-familial ideology that regards the normal household as a reproductive social space.

5. REPRODUCTIVE CITIZENSHIP

The growth of modern citizenship is closely associated with the idea of governmentality in terms of a disciplining of the subject. Because gender is crucially important in the production of modern subjectivities, we need to consider the relationship between body, sexuality, reproduction and the state. Recent writing in the field of citizenship studies has underlined the neglect of gender in the analysis of the national development of citizen entitlements and obligations in the nation state. We need to extend the discussion of citizenship, nationalism and gender by examining the relationship between parenthood and entitlement. Reproducing the next generation of citizens through marriage and household formation is a central means of acquiring comprehensive entitlements of citizenship and fulfilling its corresponding obligations.

Contemporary government policies on new reproductive technologies demonstrate implicitly the general importance of eugenics, or at least reproductive control, for the modern state. Because the majority of Western societies in demographic terms enjoy only modest rates of successful reproduction, the state promotes the desirability of fertility as a foundation of social participation. Recent debates about the decline of the birth rate in post-communist Russia are instructive about the state's relationship to population stagnation in a society in crisis. The Russian birth rate has declined from 1.89 in 1990 to 1.17 children per woman in 2000, and it is predicted that the population of the Russian Federation will decline from 146,934,000 to 123 million by 2015. Alcoholism and drug abuse have had a dramatic impact on the health of young men, while poverty and the collapse of public health institutions are associated with the rise in tuberculosis and AIDS. While President Vladimir Putin has promised to reverse these trends by, for example, the repatriation of ethnic Russians, Vladimir Zhirinovsky, an ultra-nationalist politician, has proposed that the family code be amended to legitimise polygamy.

Although the Russian dilemma (an increasing death rate and a declining birth rate) is almost unique in a technologically sophisticated society, it underlines the important relationship between the state, governmentality and demography. With an ageing population and a declining birth rate, Britain is no exception to this rule. Population growth in the United Kingdom has been since the 1980s increasingly dependent on net migration. The privileged position that is given to heterosexuality is a function of the manner in which public policies seek to normalise reproduction as the desired outcome of marriage. Indeed, within a broader context, the Church under the influence of Pauline theology has typically regarded reproduction as the principal justification for marriage as an institution that can harness the irrational force of sex to some rational purpose.

The liberal regime of modern citizenship regards parenthood in "normal" families, rather than heterosexuality as such, as the defining characteristic of the "average" citizen and as the basis of social entitlement. Reproduction through heterosexual sexual intercourse has simply been, until recently, the only means to achieve the social, cultural and biological goals of parenthood. The introduction of technologies of artificial human reproduction in the late 1970s served to underline the manner in which reproduction plays a foundational role in citizenship, because they provide the potential for reproduction without heterosexual sexual intercourse. Despite their widespread acceptance as a treatment for infertility, new reproductive technologies remain controversial medical procedures. Since their inception in the late 1970s, methods of human artificial reproduction have prompted considerable public debate, because they promise new means of human fertilisation and provide unanticipated options for family formation. The more significant issues which the technologies raise explicitly concern mothering, parenthood and conception, and implicitly the nature of the self in modern society. The manner in which governments respond to these technical and social challenges reveals the moral assumptions of the state towards parents and families, namely the system of reproductive values prevalent in society. The concept of "sexual citizenship" (Richardson (2000)) which has been promoted by some sociologists does not adequately describe the relationship between sexuality, reproduction and citizenship.

Gay and lesbian movements have claimed that sexual liberation, especially the right of individuals to decide on their own sexual orientation and sexual pleasures, is an important component of a civilised and egalitarian society. These arguments have promoted the idea of "sexual rights" as an important extension of T.H. Marshall's model of the three stages of citizenship (Evans (1993)). The growth of such rights has been described elsewhere as the early formation of "intimate citizenship" (Plummer (2000)). In sociological terms, these changes in social attitudes form part of a larger "transformation of intimacy" (Giddens (1992)). These accounts of sexual citizenship run into a number of traditional problems relating to individual rights. There are two fundamental issues which theories of sexual or intimate citizenship must confront. First, critics of modern consumerism might argue that rights to personal sexual activity are merely consequences of hedonistic consumption that have little to do in reality with freedom or individuality. Such rights to sexual pleasure might be better described as "consumer rights". Secondly, "sexual rights" appears to cover two rather separate issues, namely the demand of gay and lesbian persons to enjoy the same rights as heterosexuals (sexual citizenship proper), and the expectation of increased sexual pleasure in a more open and liberal society (intimate citizenship).

While the rights of gay and lesbian individuals to equality under the law can be readily characterised as a citizenship claim, intimate citizenship at best looks like a form of negative liberty (to enjoy a right provided it does not inhibit the freedoms of other individuals) and at worst it could entail an infringement of the rights of others such as children. A negative liberty is "the area within which a man can act unobstructed by others" (Berlin (1979) p. 122). While Berlin's gendered terminology may be ironic in this context, negative liberty does raise the question of how far our wish to expand our sexual pleasures may be unobstructed (see Andrew Bainham (chapter 10)). Does it recognise the existing protection of minors from sexual exploitation or interference? Does it accept existing constraints on pornography?

The state's interest in sexuality and sexual identity is secondary and subordinate to its demographic objective of securing and sustaining the connection between reproduction and citizenship. Against the idea of sexual citizenship, we want to defend the idea of reproductive citizenship as a concept that is sociologically more adequate. Reproductive citizenship recognises that state's interest in population within the framework of governmentality. The notion that state-building, nationalism and reproductive citizenship describe a set of necessary connections is supported by traditional theories of patriarchy and by the history of the modern state. The nation state presupposed a continuing pattern of patriarchy and patriotism as the dual legacy of monarchy and state-building. The modern matrix of nation, citizenship and masculinity has been changed by the global challenge to national sovereignty, by the transformations of work and warfare in modern societies, and by the transformation of sexuality and parenthood associated with the development of reproductive technology. Despite these fundamental social and political transformations, the foundations of national citizenship and the basis of individual entitlement remain legally and socially connected with reproduction and hence with the family and heterosexuality. A familial ideology of procreation has been a major legitimating support of the contemporary ensemble of entitlements that constitute the social rights of citizenship.

6. LAW AND THE MODERN BODY: PERSONS, PARTS AND PARTICLES

The conflict between legal regulation as systems of values and markets as systems of demand and supply is particularly problematic in the domain of the scientific dismemberment of human bodies. The potential marketisation of women's bodies by means of reproductive technologies was readily recognised by feminists. In 1985, Gena Corea observed that such technologies are:

> "something created in the interests of the patriarchy, reducing women to Matter. Just as the patriarchal state now finds it acceptable to market parts of a woman's body (breast, vagina, buttocks) for sexual purposes in prostitution and the larger sex industry, so it will soon find it reasonable to market other parts of a woman (womb, ovaries, egg) for reproductive purposes". (Corea (1985) p. 2)

This diagnosis was prescient. Internet marketing of surrogate mothers and human gametes is now established on a global scale (see Martin Richards (chapter 16)). The technology of the Internet promotes the globalisation of the human body market, which in turn was made possible through new reproductive technologies, and presents the greatest challenge to attempts to regulate the market through the imposition of moral standards upheld by law. The next regulatory problem arising in this field is the control by corporations of genetic codes via patenting (see Gregory Radick (chapter 4)). Patents are important because they make the global sale of genetic information commercially viable, but they also insure the economic inequalities between the developed and developing world.

It is clear that, historically, legal theory has often had difficulty understanding the complexity of the body. However, the revolution in micro-biology and the potential application of genetic engineering to the body in contemporary society have raised new questions for the law. Changes in contemporary biological sciences and their commercial application invite us to make a distinction between three levels of law and embodiment. In modern societies, law will in principle have to distinguish between:

(1) rights to whole bodies (in practice therefore to persons);
(2) rights to buy or to sell or to store parts of bodies (as in organ transplants, organ donations and organ sales);
(3) rights over "particles" of bodies (such as DNA codes, genetic material and material relevant to human reproduction, for example, eggs and sperm), that is to phenomena below the whole organism.

The collapse of slavery in Western societies and changes in the legal status of women have made the notion of the outright ownership of a person obsolete, but self-possession is still fundamental to liberal theory. The tradition of possessive individualism (from Locke onwards) never envisioned the prospect that a (rational) person might sell a part of their body (a kidney for example) for profit. Globalisation and commercialisation have also had important consequences for this debate. It is now possible, for example, for foreigners to buy the kidneys of executed convicts in China. *The Observer*, 10 December 2000, reported that rich customers from Malacca were paying $10,000 cash for kidneys from the People's Liberation Army hospital in the provincial city of Chongqing, where it is alleged that condemned prisoners are allowed to die once their organs have been removed.

The commercial use of body parts or particles raises serious ethical questions that do not have neat solutions. The creation of human embryos *in vitro* and their storage in fertility clinics has made latent human bodies potentially available for experimentation and purchase. These technological developments of the late twentieth century compelled many states to attempt to impose legal regulations that attempted to protect incipient human life from technological hazard (Warnock (1985); Mulkay (1997)). Whether a "pre-embryo" is a body is contestable, but the delineation of its embodiment in principle is crucial to its treatment in practice. Similarly, organ transplant sales are not like the sale of other body parts such as hair. The practice of selling one's hair for a profit was not regarded as reprehensible in an era of wigs. Prostitution might be better regarded, within a Marxist framework of the alienation of labour, as the sale of the use of a body for commercial purposes, but, since prostitutes are themselves typically controlled by pimps, the issue of ownership and control is more complex. The real test of the notion of ownership may well be to consider how the law manages what we have referred to as body particles (for example reproductive material such as sperm or gametes). Because these transactions are typically regarded as having profound implications for the nature and meaning of life itself, many governments have not been content to allow the market (or the professions) to determine their character. One can speculate that given the potential danger of the unintended consequences of new reproductive technologies, cloning, organ sales and genetic interventions, the state will impose governmentality or indeed a new pattern of patriarchy.

These three levels (persons, parts and particles of bodies) are increasingly the subject of legal intervention and regulation. Who owns, controls or manages human bodies can be regarded as the most recent stage in a process of social change that sociologists have referred to, following Max Weber, as rationalisation and secularisation, that is the application of science to everyday life to achieve greater levels of prediction and control. The rationalisation of human reproduction is an important aspect of this general rationalisation of the human body. The medical rationalisation of childbirth is a case in point (Ritzer (2000) p. 153). We can refer to this specific component of social change as "reproductive citizenship", namely the rights and obligations that surround human reproduction that determine the legal limits of who can reproduce and under what socio-legal arrangements. We have distinguished this concept from the related notion of "sexual citizenship". New reproductive technology thus raises a specific question about a more general problem—who can own or control bodies (persons, parts and particles)? The globalisation of science, especially medical innovation, makes the regulation of medical practice increasingly problematic. How is this ownership/control exercised? This question suggests several answers, but one that may be of interest to sociology would be what we might call the "new patriarchy".

7. CONCLUSION: IRONIES OF DE-COMPOSITION AND REIFICATION

In this chapter, we have explored law relating to the body through a historical narrative from Filmer's patriarchy to Locke's bourgeois individualism to Foucault's governmentality. We have suggested that the traditional understanding of law in relation to the body has been rendered largely obsolete by the growth of medical sciences that first made possible the sale of parts of bodies, then the sale of reproductive material, and eventually the sale of genetic maps. The globalisation of medical or body markets has meant that there is now little regulation of the use and purchase of the body. Within the global system, we now have the sale of whole bodies into a criminal sexual market. There is also the sale of organs, such as kidneys from the third world to affluent patients, and this market is also largely unregulated. There is a global market in reproductive materials, and finally there is the competitive economic scramble to own and control genetic codes through patents.

In conclusion, there is an interesting paradox that returns us to Karl Marx's theory of alienated labour power and nature (Schmidt (1971)). The body through specialisation, differentiation and fragmentation has become a fiction, because the human body has been de-composed into genetic cartography; it is dissected into information systems. At the same time, the body has been reified by becoming a commodity in a global system of capitalist exchange relationships. The sensuous lived body of the everyday world has become a thing that is exchanged as a commodity on the world market where demand and supply cannot be easily controlled by existing legal conventions. The paradoxical fictionalisation and reification of the human body is an effect of the current intersection of medicine and markets.

REFERENCES

ABERCROMBIE, S., HILL, S. and TURNER, B.S. (eds.), *Sovereign Individuals of Capitalism* (London, Allen & Unwin, 1986).

BERLIN, I., *Four Essays on Liberty* (Oxford, Oxford University Press, 1979).

BRYANT, J.M., *Moral Codes and Social Structure in Ancient Greece. A Sociology of Greek Ethics from Homer to the Epicureans and Stoics* (Albany, State University of New York Press, 1996).

BURTON, R., *The Anatomy of Melancholy* (London, Chatto & Windus, 1927).

BYNUM, C.W., *Fragmentation and Redemption. Essays on Gender and the Human Body in Medieval Religion* (New York, Zone Books, 1991).

CHEAH, P., FRASER, D. and GRBICH, J. (eds.), *Thinking Through the Body of Law* (St. Leonards, Allen and Unwin, 1996).

COREA, G., *The Mother Machine: Reproductive Technologies from Artificial Insemination to Artificial Wombs* (New York, Harper & Row, 1985).

DOUGLAS, M., *Purity and Danger. An Analysis of Concepts of Pollution and Taboo* (London, Routledge & Kegan Paul, 1966).

EVANS, D., *Sexual Citizenship. The Material Construction of Sexualitie* (London, Routledge, 1993).

FOUCAULT, M., *The History of Sexuality* (London, Tavistock, 1979).

——— , *Power/Knowledge. Selected Interviews and Other Writings 1972–1977* (Brighton, Wheatsheaf, 1980).

——— , "Governmentality" in G. Burchell, C. Gordon and P. Miller (eds.), *The Foucault Effect. Studies in Governmentality* (London, Harvester Wheatsheaf, 1991) 87.

GIDDENS, A., *The Transformation of Intimacy. Sexuality, Love and Eroticism in Modern Societies* (Cambridge, Polity Press, 1992).

HACKING, I., *The Social Construction of What?* (Cambridge, Mass, Harvard University Press, 1999).

LAQUER, T., *Making Sex. Body and Gender from the Greeks to Freud* (Cambridge, Mass, Harvard University Press, 1990).

LOCKE, J., *The Second Treatise on Government and a Letter concerning Toleration* (Oxford, Basil Blackwell, 1956).

MACPHERSON, C.B., *The Political Theory of Possessive Individualism* (Oxford, Oxford University Press, 1962).

MULKAY, M., *The Embryo Research Debate: Science and the Politics of Reproduction* (Cambridge, Cambridge University Press, 1997).

PLUMMER, K., "Intimate Citizenship" in D. Richardson and S. Seidman (eds.), *Handbook of Gay and Lesbian Studies* (London, Sage, 2000).

RICHARDSON, D., *Rethinking Sexuality* (London, Sage, 2000).

RITZER, G., *The McDonaldization of Society* (Thousand Oaks, Pine Forge Press, 2000).

SCHMIDT, A., *The Concept of Nature in Marx* (London, New Left Books, 1971).
STEINER, H., *An Essay on Rights* (Oxford, Blackwell, 1994).
STYCHIN, C. and HERMAN, D. (eds.), *Sexuality in the Legal Arena* (London, The Athlone Press, 2000).
TURNER, B. S., *The Body and Society. Explorations in Social Theory* (Oxford, Blackwell, 1984).
—— , *Regulating Bodies. Essays in Medical Sociology* (London, Routledge, 1992).
WARNOCK, M., *A Question of Life: The Warnock Report on Human Fertilization and Embryology* (Oxford, Blackwell, 1985).

3

Giving, Selling and Sharing Bodies

JONATHAN HERRING*

1. INTRODUCTION

F OR CENTURIES THE law has been able to respond to most legal disputes over
bodies by the simple proposition that the body is not property and therefore
cannot be owned, bought or sold. But as technologies develop and bodies become
potentially valuable resources courts are being asked to resolve increasingly complex disputes over the body. The law is being forced to develop a more sophisticated
response to the body than simply a statement about what the body is not. This
chapter will consider specifically the sale and donation of organs and other body
parts.[1] At a very simple level legal commentators tend to divide into two camps.
There are those who argue that the principle of autonomy is a fundamental one in
our law and that people should be free to donate or sell their bodies or parts of their
bodies as they wish (Engleheart (1999)). On the other hand, there are those who
argue that the body should not be commercialised and the law must restrict
extreme misuse of the body in order to uphold its unique status. Recent news items
have demonstrated the tension between these approaches. In the last year the media
have highlighted desperate appeals from parents pleading for donors of hearts for
their sick children, who required transplants to escape death.[2] But also great shock
greeted the revelation that children's body parts have been stored or disposed of
(allegedly without parental consent) at Alder Hey,[3] Bristol Royal Infirmary and
other hospitals.[4] On the one hand, the parents' heart-breaking pleas for donated
hearts reminded the public of how many people are dying due to the lack of organs
available for transplantation. Enthusiasts for organ donation argue that the shortage of donated organs reveals that our society is privileging the interests of the dead
over the interests of the living. But by contrast, the Alder Hay and Bristol scandals
reveal a distressing lack of respect shown to the bodies of dead babies.

* I have greatly benefited from the comments on this chapter of the editors and other members of
the Group, especially John Keown. I am grateful to Dr P.-L. Chau of New Hall, Cambridge for his useful insights on some of the medical issues.

[1] See www.uktransplant.org.uk for current figures on the number of transplants performed and the
number of people awaiting transplants.

[2] For example, the public appeals of the parents of Sally Slater. A donor was eventually found and
the transplant appears to have been successful (*The Times*, 18 April 2000).

[3] There is to be a government investigation into what happened at Alder Hey.

[4] See the Royal Bristol Infirmary Inquiry (2000) and Mavis Maclean (chap. 5).

This chapter will start by examining the idea that our bodies are our own. It will propose that a core element of understanding the role of our bodies is that they are interconnected with other bodies and the world around us. It will be argued that seen in this light, organ donation should be regarded as a reflection of the natural interdependence between our bodies. The law on donation and selling of organs and body parts will then be discussed (see Norrie (1985) and Price (2000)) and the chapter will consider the implications for the law if it were to take on board the proposed understanding of the interconnectedness of bodies.[5]

2. IS MY BODY MY OWN?

The argument of this chapter is that to say "my body is mine" is but only part of a proper understanding of the body. It claims too much and too little. Too much because the body is more than just "mine", something I own; in some sense it *is* me. As Justice Mosk explains, the body is "the physical and temporal expression of the unique human persona".[6] To regard our bodies as simply something that we own and use in order to achieve our goals fails to capture the core differences between our bodies and other objects that we use to achieve our ends. For many people their bodies and their aims in life are intimately connected. Our bodies are not merely objects to reach goals but are integral to our goals. Without our bodies many of the plans we have for our lives would be unattainable. Not only that, to other people our bodies represent what we are: what they see identifies us and can determine how they treat us.[7] In these senses our bodies are not just "ours"; they, in part, capture the essence of us.

Saying, "my body is mine" claims too little in that it fails to capture the inter-connectedness of our bodies with other people's bodies and with the world around us (see Leder (1999)). Our bodies begin and develop in a relationship of connectedness with another body. In pregnancy, the foetus and the mother share fluids and space. Even following birth the baby is dependent on the mother's body for food and nurturance. Without the body of the mother (or some other carer) the body of the baby would not survive. The mother must perform the acts for the baby that the baby would need to perform for herself if she were capable.[8] In illness, old age or disability again the body of one person may be dependent on the bodies of others.[9] The body of a person caring for a dependant can be directed to carry out the functions the dependant would wish to carry out with her own body. So, if the carer breaks an arm this could restrict the lifestyle of the dependant as if

---

[5] Steps are being taken to harmonise the law in this area at a European level (Council of Europe Resolution (78) 29).

[6] Mosk J dissenting in *Moore* v. *Regents of the University of California* (1990) 271 Cal Rept 146 at 182.

[7] See Anne Bottomley (ch. 8).

[8] An extreme, although rare, example of interconnection is conjoined twins (see *Re A (Conjoined Twins: Medical Treatment)* [2001] I FLR 1.

[9] This is not meant to suggest that this is a one-way process. In a sense, the carer's body is dependent on the dependant's (the greater the dependant's disability the more will be required of the carer).

she herself had broken her arm. In a wider sense, it is in sharing our bodies with others that our bodies acquire meaning. A whole range of human actions, which we value highly, involves the interconnection of bodies. In activities ranging from sexual relations to handshakes; from sports to massage, many of the pleasures of the body are found in interacting with other bodies. Therefore, to describe our bodies simply as "ours" fails to capture the significance that for part of our lives our bodies are inevitably dependent upon and connected to other bodies and that even if not essential many of the pleasures of life involve interrelating bodies.

The argument can be taken further. Our bodies are also interconnected with the world around us. The body takes in food, which in due course is removed as excreta and urine and which is returned to the earth. Air is inhaled and exhaled. Inside our bodies bacteria play crucial roles in the working of the body, being replenished with new bacteria from outside. The body is therefore not a single static organism by any means: it is constantly changing and interacting with the world around it. It gives to the world and receives from the world. Even our genetic material, which is unique to us, is shared to a large extent with other animals and, of course, comes from our parents, and may be passed on to any children we have. Hence, it has been claimed "genetic information about any individuals should not be regarded as personal to that individual, but as the common property of other people who may share those genes" (Royal College of Physicians (1991)).

Further, to see the body as a given, non-changing entity that is inviolate is artificial. To give three examples: first, the limits of our bodies are constantly changing, as cells die and fall off, and new cells are created. By the time we die there is little of us biologically that is the same as when we were born. Secondly, at birth the exact place where the umbilical cord is cut and falls off is a matter of chance and so exactly the shape of the tummy button[10] is arbitrary. Thirdly, some wheelchair users record that, to them, their wheelchairs become as parts of their body such that, for example, touching their wheelchair can be felt as an invasion of the person (Toombs (1999)). All of these demonstrate that the body is not a static entity; it is a complex constantly changing entity.

So far it has been suggested that crucial to our understanding of bodies should be the following: that the interconnection of our body with other bodies and the world around us is both natural and indeed necessary for life; further that it is a false picture to see our bodies as inviolate entities, rather their substance is constantly changing. In the light of these arguments the transplanting of organs from one body to another can be seen as a reflection of the normal part of the interchange and interdependence of our bodies with others and the reception of an organ from another person can be seen as just an example of the mutable nature of the body. Donation of body parts and products should not be seen as a bizarre activity which the law should reluctantly permit people to do only if it is convinced they really want to and there is good reason to permit them to do so. The consequences if this approach is accepted will be addressed shortly.

---

[10] A common term for the umbilicus.

3. LIVING DONORS

The law on live organ donation is governed by the Human Organ Transplants Act 1989 (Garwood-Gowers (1999)). However, to understand the law in this area it is important to have an overview of the law on when and whether a living person can, while alive, have parts or products of her or his body removed. First, the law will be explained and discussion of it will follow. It is necessary to distinguish the following five situations.

(a) Removal of body parts or products against the wishes of a competent patient

The prospect of live organ donation contrary to the competent donor's wishes is shocking[11] and contrary to fundamental human rights.[12] It is therefore not surprising that the law states that if a competent patient opposes the removal of a body part, the removal will constitute a criminal offence, unless there is a special legal defence.[13] The charge could range from murder to battery, depending on the level of harm caused and whether or not a pure consequentialist approach be taken (Harris (1986), *cf.* Maclean (1993)).[14] Even if it would save several people's lives it would be illegal to remove forcibly organs from a competent person against his or her will. For example, the Court of Appeal in *St George's* v. *S* (Herring (2000); Bailey-Harris (2000))[15] confirmed that it would be wrong to perform a caesarean section on a pregnant woman without her consent, even if the operation were necessary to save her life and that of her foetus (see Jane Weaver (chapter 13) for a full discussion of the issue).

(b) Removal of body parts or products where the patient is unable to consent

It is necessary to distinguish between children and incompetent adults. It is very rare for live donors to be children (Price and Garwood-Gowers (1995)).

---

[11] *McFall* v. *Shimp* (1978) 10 Pa D&C 3d 90 at 92.

[12] Arts. 3 and 8 of the European Convention on Human Rights (now incorporated in the Human Rights Act 1998) protect people from inhuman and degrading treatment and lack of respect for their private life.

[13] For example, if it could be regarded as an act of self-defence or is permitted under s. 65 of the Police and Criminal Evidence Act 1984.

[14] For support of a pure consequentialist approach see Harris (1986). For fierce criticism of this view see Maclean (1993).

[15] [1998] 3 All ER 673.

(i) Children

The regulations under the Human Organ Transplant Act 1989 governing live transplants to a person unrelated to the donor require that the donor is able to understand the nature of the medical procedures and the risks involved.[16] This suggests that unless the child is very mature it would be illegal for a child to donate to an unrelated person.[17] The Act does not deal with a case where the donation is to a relative, or the removal, is not of an organ. In such cases the matter is one of common law,[18] although the common law is not clear. Even if both the child and parents consent to the removal, the safest course of action for a doctor seeking to remove a part of a body from a child for transplant purposes is to bring the matter before the court and request the court to declare the proposed treatment lawful.[19] If the matter is brought before the court, it must decide whether the donation would be in the child's best interests.[20] For example, the court may well approve a donation to a sibling to whom the child is close on the basis that the maintenance of the relationship with the sibling was in the child's interests.[21]

(ii) Incompetent adults

As explained above, organ donations to unrelated people are only lawful if the donor understands the procedure and risks. It will therefore never be permissible to remove an organ for donation to an unrelated person if the donor is an incompetent adult. If the donation is to a relative (as defined by the Human Organ Transplant Act) or if the donation involves a body part which is not an organ, then the donation can be carried out only if the court's authorisation is obtained.[22] The court may authorise the donation if it is in the donor's best interests.[23] If the donor has a strong relationship with the recipient and so will benefit from the recipient's continued relationship then the donation will be in the incompetent adult's interests. The law might also be willing to find a benefit to the donor in other cases. In *Re Y*,[24] for example, bone marrow removal from Y to be given to her sister was

---

[16] Human Organ Transplants (Unrelated Persons) Regulations 1989, SI 1989/2480, reg. 3(2)(b).

[17] Reference could be made to the *Gillick* competence test (*Gillick* v. *West Norfolk and Wisbech AHA* [1986] AC 112).

[18] For examples of American cases see *Hart* v. *Brown* (1972) 289 A 2d 386 and *Strunk* v. *Strunk* (1969) 445 SW 2d 145 (Ky CA).

[19] A child between sixteen and eighteen may be able to consent effectively to treatment under s. 8 of the Family Law Reform Act 1969. There is, however, doubt over whether donation of body parts may be "treatment". In *Re W* [1992] 3 WLR 758 Lord Donaldson seemed to apply the reasoning in *Gillick* (that a competent child under sixteen can effectively consent to medical treatment) to organ donation ([1992] 3 WLR 758, at 767 and 772) but then suggested that it would be inconceivable that a doctor would rely on the child's consent alone (at 676) without bringing the matter to court.

[20] Children Act 1989, s. 1.

[21] *Hart* v. *Brown* (1972) 289 A 2d. 386. Art. 20 of the European Convention on Human Rights and Biomedicine accepts that exceptionally an organ can be removed from an incompetent adult or child.

[22] *Re F (Mental Patient: Sterilisation)* [1989] 2 All ER 376.

[23] *Ibid.* at 390–1, 404, 413.

[24] *Re Y (Mental Incapacity: Bone Marrow Transplant)* [1997] 2 WLR 556.

authorised on the basis that were the sister to die Y's mother would suffer and this would damage the mother's relationship with Y which would be contrary to Y's well-being.

(c) Removal of body parts or products not for medical purposes, with the patient's consent

The crucial question here is whether the removal is carried out by the "victim" or by a third party. If a third party removes any part of another person, it is prima facie a criminal offence. The charge could range from battery to murder depending on the severity of the injury caused.[25] However if the "victim" consented, this would be a defence if the injury was less than "actual bodily harm".[26] If the injury constitutes actual bodily harm or a greater injury then the removal will constitute an offence unless it falls into a few exceptional categories in which it is thought to be in the public interest to allow a person to cause such injuries (Simester and Sullivan (2000)). These exceptional circumstances include, for example: medical treatment; regulated sporting activities; dangerous exhibitions; tattooing; body piercing; and decorative branding.[27]

If the case involves someone injuring him or herself then the law is different. It seems that you may cause yourself actual bodily harm, but it can be an offence intentionally to cause yourself grievous bodily harm.[28] Recently in *Greatorex* v. *Greatorex*[29] it was held that a person who negligently injured himself did not owe a duty of care to friends and relatives who had witnessed the injury (and so was not liable to pay damages to them for distress they suffered). The justification given was that otherwise there would be a danger of infringing the right of self-determination; the liberty of the individual; and the freedom of autonomy. This suggests the law may even recognise a right to injure oneself.[30]

(d) Removal of body parts or products as part of a medical operation for therapeutic purposes with the patient's consent

If the operation promotes the best interests of the patient (i.e. it will be therapeutic) then the operation will be lawful if the patient is competent and consents. So,

---

[25] In *Wright's* case 1 *Coke on Littleton* para. 194 at 126.6, severing a hand so that a defendant might beg more effectively was held to be a crime.

[26] *R* v. *Brown* [1993] 2 All ER 75.

[27] For example, *R* v. *Wilson* [1996] QB 47.

[28] Offences Against the Person Act 1861, s.18 forbids intentionally causing grievous bodily harm "to any person"; by contrast other sections within the Act forbid harm "to any other person". There is also the ancient offence of maim, but it is far from clear what the extent of the offence is.

[29] *The Times*, 6 June 2000.

[30] This could even be said to be an aspect of the right to respect for private life, protected under the Human Rights Act 1998.

obviously, removal of a cancerous cyst would be lawful. Even removal of a patient's organ for the purpose of transplantation could be permitted if the removal of the organ was necessary for the patient's own health.

(e) Removal of body parts or products for non-therapeutic purposes with the patient's consent

This section will discuss the removal of a patient's parts or products not for the patient's medical well-being, but for use of another patient. The law distinguishes the removal of organs and the removal of other body parts or products.

(i) Removal of organs

The law is governed by the Human Organ Transplants Act 1989. The Act only covers "organ" donations. An organ is defined as "any part of a human body consisting of a structured arrangement of tissues, which, if wholly removed, cannot be replicated, by the body". There is, however, debate over whether the statute covers removal of parts of an organ (Kennedy and Grubb (2000)). It obviously includes hearts, lungs and kidneys and excludes regenerative parts, such as blood or hair. According to section 2 of the Human Organ Transplants Act 1989:

> "(1) Subject to subsection (3) below, a person is guilty of an offence if in Great Britain he
> (a) removes from a living person an organ intended to be transplanted into another person; or
> (b) transplants an organ removed from a living person into another person, unless the person into whom the organ is to be or, as the case may be, is transplanted is genetically related to the person from whom the organ is removed".

Section 2(3) permits the Secretary of State to make regulations permitting the donation of organs by those unrelated to the donor. These regulations have been made, allowing donations to unrelated persons to be made if permitted by a government agency, the Unrelated Live Transplant Regulation Authority. The Authority will grant permission where it is satisfied *inter alia* that no unauthorised payment has been made and the donor fully understood the nature of the treatment.[31]

So, the law draws a sharp distinction between donations to people genetically related to the donor and donations to those who are not genetically related. If the parties are not related it is a criminal offence for such removals if the consent of the Authority has not been obtained.[32] Permission can be granted if the Authority is satisfied that no wrongful payments have been made and that full and informed

---

[31] The detailed provisions are found in the Human Organ Transplants (Unrelated Persons) Regulations, SI 1989/2480.

[32] Human Organ Transplants Act 1989, s. 7(2).

consent has been given. For those donors and recipients who are related the permission of the Authority is not required.

(ii) Removal of parts and products other than organs

This is an important area because bone marrow and blood are not organs, but are commonly transferred from one person to another. If it is a non-organ which is removed the issue is one of common law. Professor Dworkin has suggested four conditions that need to be satisfied if the removal of a non-organ is to be lawful (Dworkin (1970)): the patient must give full consent; the operation must be therapeutic (that is it must be expressly for the patient's benefit); there must be lawful justification; and finally, the operation must be performed with appropriate medical skills. There is some dispute whether it is possible to consent to non-therapeutic operations and what is meant by a "lawful justification" in this case. The most popular view appears to be that the donation is justified if it could be shown not to be contrary to the patient's best interests, even if it cannot be shown to be positively in the patient's best interests (Mason and McCall Smith (1999)). A more radical view is that it would be open to a court to go even further than this and permit consent to removal of non-organs unless the procedure threatened the patient's life (Law Commission (1995)).

4. COMMERCIAL DEALINGS IN BODY PARTS

Section 1 of the Human Organ Transplants Act 1989 clearly prohibits the making or receiving of payment for the supply of an organ or offering to supply an organ.[33] However, there is provision to allow the recipient to pay the donor's legitimate expenses.[34] It is generally accepted that any contract to donate an organ would be unenforceable (Kennedy and Grubb (2000)). The law on commercial dealing with body parts and products which are not organs is a little unclear. The Human Fertilisation and Embryology Act 1990 forbids the sale of gametes.[35] The fact that Parliament has thought it necessary specifically to forbid sale in these cases might suggest that if there is no specific statutory prohibition on sale, then sale of non-organ body parts and products would be permitted. For example, no doubt had David Beckham decided to sell his fine golden locks before removing them there would have been people willing to pay good money for them. It seems highly unlikely the law would not give legal effect to such a sale.

The key discussion here is over whether the body can be regarded as property (Dworkin and Kennedy (1993)). It is necessary to distinguish dead and live bod-

[33] The Act also forbids initiating or negotiating for payments for supply of organs.
[34] Human Organ Transplants Act 1989, s. 1(1); SI 1989/2480, reg. 1(3)(b).
[35] Section 12(e) of the 1990 Act forbids selling gametes except in the exceptional circumstances set out in the Human Fertilisation and Embryology (Special Exemptions) regulations. 1991 (SI 1991/1588).

ies. The traditional approach of the law is that a body cannot be owned, it is *res nullius*.[36] The historical explanation is that dead bodies were seen as issues for the ecclesiastical courts (Skegg (1998)) and so outside the common law courts' jurisdiction (Myers (1990)). Recently the law was thrown into doubt in *R v. Kelly*,[37] where an artist who arranged with a technician to take bodies from a hospital for use in a piece of modern art was convicted of theft of the bodies. The Court of Appeal accepted that corpses could be property if "they have acquired different attributes by virtue of the application of skill, such as dissection or preservation techniques, for exhibition or teaching purposes".[38] Further, Rose LJ stated that "the common law does not stand still. It may be that if, on some future occasion, the question arises, the courts will hold that human body parts are capable of being property for the purposes of s.4, even without the acquisition of different attributes, if they have a use or significance beyond their mere existence. This may be if, for example, they are intended for use in an organ transplant operation, for the extraction of DNA, or for that matter as an exhibit in a trial".[39] This case suggests that the law does now recognise that body parts *can* be regarded as property. What is far from clear is exactly when body parts are property. There is some evidence that patients do not regard themselves as donors of bodily products removed from them during an operation (Start et al. (1996)). The position taken in *Kelly* appears to be that a body part is transformed from being *res nullius* to property by the exercise of some skill. The Court of Appeal gave dissection as an example of an exercise of skill and, if that is correct, then that would seem to mean that all severed body parts could be owned. Grubb has suggested that what makes a part of a corpse property is that it has been turned into a new item with a value of its own (Grubb (1998)). The difficulty with that approach is in deciding who is to determine what is "value" for these purposes. For example, a severed body part may be regarded as having artistic value of its own to one artist, but not be so regarded by another (Matthews (1995); Magnusson (1998)).

In relation to live body parts there have been few cases. The criminal law has been able to avoid questions about the ownership of the body by distinguishing offences against the person and offences against property. So for example, if a person were to approach their favourite pop star from behind and cut off a piece of hair, this conduct could readily be regarded as a battery. The question of whether the hair was property that could be stolen could therefore be easily avoided. However, in cases where the orthodox view that a body cannot be property was liable to mean that blameworthy conduct might go unpunished, then the courts have been willing to treat the body and its products as property. For example, when defendants suspected of drink driving took away samples of blood[40] and

---

[36] The Court of Appeal has recently accepted that the authority for the position is limited, but held that it has become such a well accepted proposition within the legal community that it should be accepted: *Dobson v. North Tyneside Health Authority* [1996] 4 All ER 474; *R v. Kelly* [1998] 3 All ER 741.

[37] [1998] 3 All ER 741.

[38] *R v. Kelly* [1998] 3 All ER 741 at 749–50.

[39] *Ibid.* at 750.

[40] *R v. Rothery* [1976] RTR 550.

urine[41] that had been provided to the police they were convicted of theft of samples. It therefore seems open to a court to develop the law so as to recognise a property interest in pieces of the body, even if the law has not yet reached that stage.

5. DISCUSSION OF THE LAW

Some specific aspects of the law will now be discussed:

(a) Should competent people be permitted to donate organs?

First, it is argued that the law on organ donations is not consistent with the law's general approach in this area. Normally the law permits one person to injure another with their consent if that is in the public interest.[42] There should therefore be no need to show that the operation was in the patient's own interest, nor even not contrary to their interests. Dangerous sports or displays are exempt from criminal liability on the basis that they promote the public interest rather than specifically promoting the injured person's best interests. Similarly, society permits citizens to volunteer to be fire-fighters and soldiers, running risks of serious injury or death, not on the basis of their own interests, but rather the public interest. So, to be in line with the general law on offences against the person the law on live organ donation should be whether the patient consents and the operation is in the public interest. If it is, and most organ donations will be, then the removal should be permitted.

Even if the test is whether the operation is in the patient's best interests, it is argued that donation of body parts would be. The saving of another's life, with limited injury to her or himself, may, quite properly, be regarded as a proper pursuance of a person's own vision of the "good life" and be for them in their own interests, as *they* would define them to be. Indeed it could be argued that even if the removal of an organ would lead to the donor's death, such an act (if genuinely consented to) would be seen as heroic (analogous to those willing to fight in a war for a greater good) and so should be permitted.[43] This argument could be further supported by reference to the fact that it is no longer an offence to commit suicide.[44] Of course, this does not mean that such a person could force a doctor to carry out the operation.

These arguments, it is submitted, are even stronger in the light of the argument made at the start of this chapter about the interconnectedness of bodies. The desire to transfer body parts to another person is but one aspect of the interrelationship of all bodies. Where consented to, far from the law seeking to impede it, organ donation should be encouraged.

---

[41] *R* v. *Welsh* [1974] RTR 478.
[42] *R* v. *Brown* [1993] 2 All ER 75.
[43] The argument against this may be that the principle of sanctity of life would be infringed.
[44] Suicide Act 1961.

(b) The incompetent organ donor

As outlined above the law discourages donations of body parts from children and incompetent adults unless the removal can be said to be in the interests of the donor. It might be argued that donation can benefit a donor, because it is to some-one's benefit to live an altruistic life. One reply to this argument is that altruism only has value if a person is competent and chooses to be altruistic; "compelled altruism" is not true altruism (Price (2000); Keown (1997)). A more compelling argument in favour of permitting donation from incompetent people is that dona-tion may be permitted if the donation is a fair sacrifice in the light of the ongoing relationship between the donor and donee, where that relationship as a whole benefits the donee. This argument may also be developed in relation to children (Herring (1999)).

(c) Should we restrict donations to situations where there is no commercial motive?

The concern over commercial transplants came to public attention when evidence arose that impoverished people in Turkey were selling kidneys which were transplanted to rich clients in London (Brahams (1989); Harvey (1990)). It is important to distinguish two reasons for wanting to forbid sale of organs: first it might be thought that where there are commercial motives there might not be genuine consent; secondly there are objections to the commercialisation of the body.

The first argument is that where someone is willing to sell his or her organs, this indicates such desperation that it cannot be the result of free choice. This argu-ment is not convincing for various reasons. First, financial pressures are not the circumstances which may threaten genuine consent. For example, the donation to a much loved relative may involve even more pressure (albeit emotional pressure) than the need for money. Secondly, in contract law it has become accepted that asking whether there was a free choice is a vacuous question. Many choices are made under pressure and distinguishing free choice and impelled choice is arguably impossible (Atiyah (1982)). It is far more fruitful to consider whether the pressure placed on the individual was legitimate or not.[45] This approach rephrases the question to ask whether offering payment to donate organs constitutes improper pressure. If this is asked, it is hard to see how an *offer* of money could constitute illegitimate "pressure". The pressure here results from the would-be donor's financial situation not the offer (Radcliffe-Richards et al. (1998)). It is therefore submitted that the question should not be regarded as one of freedom of choice, but rather one of whether there is any public policy objection to treating the body as property which can be sold.

---

[45] *Atlas Express* v. *Kafko* [1989] QB 833.

There is much debate over whether a body has the necessary attributes to constitute property (Litman (1997)). This chapter will not directly address this issue, partly because the question has been dealt with in great detail elsewhere (Harris (1996)) but also because even if the body is not regarded as property this would not necessarily mean that there would be no commercialisation of the body (Gold (1996)). It would, for example, be possible to regard organ donation as a service. The chapter will therefore focus on the policy arguments for or against the commercialisation of the body.

There is a notable international consensus on opposition to a market in organs: (Transplantation Society Council (1985); UNESCO (1989); the World Health Organisation (1991); Nuffield Council on Bioethics (1995) and United States Task Force on Organ Transplantation (1986)). However, it may be that in fact the general public do not share this abhorrence at selling body parts. Research has in fact found that 40 to 50 per cent of those questioned find selling organs acceptable (Guttman and Guttman (1993)). So what might be the policy issues that would weigh in favour or against the body being seen as property?

The key argument against treating the body as a commodity is that it would be wrong to value a body in the same way as we value other pieces of property. It has been argued that the body cannot be valued in terms of market in the market economy. However this particular objection is not strong. Wedding rings have value beyond the physical, but we have no difficulty buying and selling them. Similarly libel law gives damages for lost reputation and tort law for lost limbs, even though here monetary value is being placed on the incalculable. The point can be made that in one of the Turkish kidney selling cases it appears the organ was sold in order to fund medical treatment for the seller's daughter. It may be that the father's body was not capable of valuation but, in our world, his daughter's treatment was given a commercial value. To deny him treatment for his daughter because he could not afford to pay for it could be said, if anything, to show less respect for bodies than allowing the sale of a kidney. Perhaps the true position is that adopted by Gold who states: "My argument . . . is not that the human body or human health can never be appropriately valued in terms of economic modes of valuation; it is simply that economic modes of valuation do not exhaust the ways in which we value the body and health. The conclusion that I reach is not that we should not allocate rights of control over human biological materials, but, rather, that we must construct a method of allocating right of control over these materials that takes all modes of valuation, both economic and non-economic, into account" (Harvey (1990); Erin and Harris (1994)). This suggests that it might be possible to accept the body being property as long as there were suitable controls to counteract the possible disadvantageous side-effects.[46]

There are also more practical concerns in treating the body as property which can be bought and sold. If organs can be bought and sold as property the concern

---

[46] European Convention on Human Rights and Bioethics 1996 states: "The human body and its parts shall not, as such, give rise to financial gain".

is that, at the receiving end of the transplant, the richer people would be more able to purchase the organs. This might lead to organs being distributed not according to need or fairness, but wealth (Lamb (1996)). In short, this could result in a market in which organs would be received by the rich and donated by the poor. On the other hand Dickens has argued that only permitting relations to donate organs works unequally towards the friendless or those without families (Dickens (1997)). If we are to ensure that transplantation does not discriminate between rich and poor recipients it may be necessary to have a state controlled transplantation scheme. Lord Hunt, the government minister on transplantation, has stated: "Donated organs are a national resource which are available to people regardless of race, religion and other circumstances" (Department of Health Press Release, 2000a). To give effect to this, it would be quite possible for the state to be willing to pay for donation but not require recipients to pay for any organs.

The point made at the start of this chapter was that there is continuous interaction between our bodies and the world around us. This is in a sense part of the "natural order". To require payment for this interchange may seem so at odds with the free exchange that does and should take place between our bodies and between our bodies and the world. That said, there are many circumstances where medicine assists nature and medicine is now commercialised. Infertility treatment where medicine seeks to mimic reproduction is paid for. Similarly the provision of tax benefits to those who give money to charity reinforces the good of monetary donation and does not deprive donation of its goodness. That is not to say that is how it should be. It should be that organs are donated as part of the great give and take between humankind recognising our interconnectedness. But where commerce can aid and reinforce that it should be permitted (Price (2000)).

(d) Distinguishing different body parts

It is notable that people react to different parts of the body in different ways. Those which are most visible are those which are most treasured, with the possible exception of hearts. It is notable that even among those willing to donate organs there is a reluctance to donate corneas (Kounougeri-Manoledaki (2000) and Rachel Cook (chapter 12)). Sperm and eggs are often treated very differently from other bodily fluids with states creating special regulations over the storage of such materials (Jones (2000)). In part, the different attitudes to different bodily parts and fluids reflect different symbolic means that attach to these parts. The English and Welsh law places much weight on the distinction between organs and non-organs that seems based on a distinction between those parts of the body that regenerate and those that do not. As noted above, the body is constantly changing and evolving with new cells being created and old cells lost. The distinction between regenerative and non-regenerative parts therefore seems arbitary.

6. DEAD DONORS

The transfer of body parts and tissues from someone who has died will now be considered. This is governed by the Human Tissue Act 1961. In summary then, the Act states that a registered medical practitioner[47] can remove organs after death for therapeutic purposes, such as donation, if either:

(a) the deceased gave consent to the use by:
　(i) executing a written request while alive, which has not been withdrawn; or
　(ii) orally giving consent during his last illness;[48] or
(b) the person in lawful possession of the body after reasonable enquiries believes neither the deceased, nor spouse, nor relations have objected.

　Many of the Act's detailed provisions are unclear. There has been much debate over who is "lawfully in possession of" the body; what "reasonable enquiries" are (Skegg (1998)); what "death" is (see John Keown (chapter 14)); who are "relatives"; or what the penalties are for breaching the Act (Kennedy (1991)). Enough has been written on the ambiguities of the exact wording of the Act and here it is intended to focus on the thrust of the policy behind the Act (Jones (2000)).

　The law could, in theory, take the following starting points (Kennedy (1991)):

(a) organs could be removed regardless of the views of the deceased and relatives;
(b) only the wishes of the deceased would be relevant; the law could then create a presumption to deal with the situations where the deceased expresses no view;
(c) only the wishes of the deceased's relatives would be relevant; again a presumption would deal with the position if the relatives express no view;
(d) the wishes of both the deceased and the relatives matter; a presumption would be needed to deal with the position where the views of the deceased and the relatives diverge or where no views are expressed;
(e) organs could not be removed regardless of the deceased or relative's opinions.

　A core question is what weight should be placed on the views of the deceased? Some argue that the deceased's views should be regarded as irrelevant. One approach would be to argue that the dead have no interests (Callahan (1987); Feinberg (1984); Jones (2000)). Harris has argued that: "The dead person cannot be wronged or harmed by the transplant of their organs 'against their will' for they have no will—they are not there to be harmed" (Harris (1984) p. 119). This, it is argued, is wrong. Our lives are part of a story and our death, and the manner of our death, is a crucial last chapter of our biography. Many people make careful directions for their funerals or the disposal of their bodies. They wish their bodies to be treated with dignity. They clearly feel they have an interest in what happens to their bodies after their death, and how they are remembered.[49] Dworkin (1993)

[47] Human Tissue Act 1961, s. 1(4), (4A).
[48] The consent must be in the presence of two or more witnesses.
[49] Chadwick (1994).

p. 211 has argued, "There is no doubt that most people treat the manner of their death as of special, symbolic importance: they want their deaths if possible to express and, in that way, vividly to confirm the values they believe most important to their lives". To respect the views of the deceased is, then, an aspect of respecting their autonomy: permitting people to determine how to live their lives.

If the deceased's views as to disposal of his or her body and its organs are accepted, the next issue to clarify is what the presumption should be if the deceased expresses no such views about use of her body after her death (Caplan (1984)). It is submitted that if the deceased leaves no directions then we should assume that the deceased has consented to the transplant for three main reasons. The first and most important is that normally, where a patient is unable to express an opinion, the action which best promotes the patient's interests should be performed. It is submitted that donation is in the patient's best interests on their death. Donation on death leads to the saving of life—accepted as a good in our society. The deceased will, in death, have provided a benefit to society and this will, by the majority of people, be recognised as a good way to end a life. Our society praises those who, in death, save others: "Greater love hath no man than this, that a man lay down his life for his friends"[50] is often quoted. To end a life with such a gift of life to others is in a person's interests. To back this argument further, as was argued at the start of this chapter, the interaction, intermingling and sharing of bodies is an important and indeed essential aspect of every person's life. To continue this interconnection after death will be to continue the way the body was used during life. Secondly, the statistics suggest (Price (2000)) that 75 per cent[51] of people do wish to donate on their death (even if the majority do not actually hold donor cards or otherwise express this wish). It is therefore a reasonable guess that the deceased would wish to donate if there is no evidence to the contrary. True, there is a serious risk that the deceased did not wish the donation and that we could be "wronging" the deceased. However, the wrong is not quite an infringement of the right to bodily integrity, which involves harming a person against his or her wishes. Against this risk must be weighed the argument that the deceased will be wronged and denied the opportunity of making provision as he or she would have wanted at his death (Cohen (1992)). If a person is unconscious the law makes assumptions about how they would wish to be treated, namely that he or she be given the treatment that best promotes their interests and wishes (Hallam, Hockey and Howarth (1999)). Here, to treat the deceased's body as participating with the interconnection and sharing with other bodies as it did during its life would promote the interests of the patient as most likely understood by the patient and by our community at large. Thirdly, it is arguable that morally the donation should be made. It might be thought that a "contracting out" system would lead to a higher number of organs available for transplant, but this is debated (Price (2000)). As the Health Department insists: "If you are prepared to

[50] *The Bible*, John 15,13 KJV.
[51] In the United Kingdom only 20 per cent of those willing to donate carry an organ donor card ((1998) *The Lancet* 70).

consider accepting a transplant for yourself or your family, it seems only fair to play your part in being willing to be a donor" (Department of Health (1999)). There are huge dangers in arguing from the fact that the decision was morally right to argue the decision is the one that the patient would have made, but it is a relevant factor in deciding what to do where no view is expressed. Opponents of this argument would suggest that this approach is promoting "presumed consent" which is a fiction: "Without the actual consent of the individual, there is no consent" (Erin and Harris (1999)). But here we do not have either true consent or a true lack of consent. The law may therefore presume that the deceased is happy for his or her body to be shared with others, as he or she has done throughout his or her life.

Then it is necessary to consider what weight should be attached to the views of relatives. It is important to distinguish the role that the relative might play. Relatives may argue that the deceased did not really consent to the donation. This kind of argument, as contended above, is important. Relatives may also argue against donation based on their own feelings about what should happen to the body. These arguments, it is contended, should carry little weight. First, if the deceased has expressed a view as to how they wish their life to end, this should override the wishes of relatives. We do not permit the executors of a will to change its terms on the basis that the terms of the will distress the relatives. If the deceased's wishes as regards her money cannot be overridden owing to the distress of the relatives, surely the wishes of the deceased in relation to her body, an even more intimate aspect of her person, should not be overridden. An even stronger analogy is that we do not allow the grief of the relatives to prevent an autopsy, proper burial or other disposal of the body (although these can be justified on the basis of protecting the deceased's interests). Secondly, the relatives' wishes are outweighed by the claims of the person seeking the transplant. Unless the relatives can claim an especially strong right to the corpse, it is unclear why their sensibilities should carry any more weight than the presumed consent of the deceased, the interests of the person who will die without the transplant, and their relatives (see Mavis Maclean (chapter 5)). As well as considering the interests of the deceased, her relatives and the would-be recipient, the interests of the state could also be given weight. The cost, both economic and social, of the unnecessary loss or the continued expense of treatment of the would-be recipient, all argue in favour of permitting donation in the absence of opposition from the deceased.

It is therefore argued that out of respect for the autonomy of the deceased, her wishes should determine the issue. However, where the wishes of the deceased are unknown then the law should authorise the donation. The interests of the state, of the would-be recipient of the organ, and the fact that the donation will reflect the interconnection between bodies which will have inevitably been an aspect of the life that the deceased enjoyed, join together to justify this approach.

7. CONCLUSION

This chapter has stressed the importance of appreciating the interconnection between bodies, and between bodies and the world. Our bodies are constantly changing, receiving and giving to the world at large and other bodies. Without the interaction of our bodies with each other and the world, bodies would lose much of their significance. In this light organ donation should be regarded as a natural reflection of that process. The law should therefore readily accept the permissibility of voluntary organ donation. The autonomy of the person requires emphasising respect for the choice of the person wishing to donate, as a legitimate and worthy decision. As these donations are in the public interest they should be permitted. Although commercial dealing with organs does not sit comfortably with free transfers between bodies, commercial payment for organs (especially if the distribution of organs can be free of charge to the recipient) is less objectionable. In relation to donations from the dead, if the deceased has not expressed a view then the law should authorise the donation of organs as a reflection of the way bodies operate. Appreciating the natural interrelation between bodies provides us with a way of encouraging donation, while at the same time respecting the value and status of bodies.

REFERENCES

ATIYAH, P, "Economic Duress and the 'Overborne Will' " (1982) 98 *Law Quarterly Review* 197.

BAILEY HARRIS, R., "Patient Autonomy—A Turn in the Tide" in M. Freeman and A. Lewis (eds.), *Law and Medicine* (Oxford, Oxford University Press, 2000).

BRAHAMS, D., "Kidney for Sale by Live Donor" (1989) *The Lancet* 285.

CALLAHAN, J., "On Harming the Dead" (1987) 97 *Ethics* 341.

CAPLAN, A., "Ethical and Policy Issues in the Procurement of Cadaver Organs for Transplantation" (1984) 311 *New England Journal of Medicine* 981.

CHADWICK, R., "Corpses, Recycling and Therapeutic Purposes" in R. Lee and D. Morgan (eds.), *Death Rites* (London, Routledge, 1994).

COHEN, C., "The Case for Presumed Consent to Transplant Human Organs After Death" (1992) 24 *Transplantation Proceedings* 2168.

DEPARTMENT OF HEALTH, *Organ Donation. Everything You Need to Know* (London, Department of Health, 1999).

—— , Press Release, 22 February 2000 (London, Department of Health, 2000a).

—— , Press Release, 23 March 2000 (London, Department of Health, 2000b).

DICKENS, B., "The Control of Living Body Materials" (1997) 27 *University of Toronto Law Journal* 142.

DWORKIN, G., "The Law Relating to Organ Transplantation in England" (1970) 33 *Modern Law Review* 353.

DWORKIN, G. and KENNEDY, I., "Human Tissue: Rights in the Body and its Parts" (1993) 1 *Medical Law Review* 29.

DWORKIN, R., *Life's Dominion* (London, Harper Collins, 1993).

ENGLEHEART, H.T., "The Body for Fun, Beneficence, and Profit: A Variation on a Post-Modern Theme" in M. Cherry (ed.), *Persons and Their Bodies* (Dordrecht, Kluwer, 1999).

ERIN, C. and HARRIS, J., "A Monopsonistic Market" in I. Robinson (ed.), *Life and Death under High Technology Medicine* (Manchester, Manchester University Press 1994).

——, "Presumed Consent or Contracting Out" (1999) 25 *Journal of Medical Ethics* 365.

FEINBERG, J., *The Moral Limits of the Criminal Law* (Vol. 1) *Harm to Others* (New York, Oxford University Press, 1984).

GARWOOD-GOWERS, A., *Living Donor Organ Transplantation* (Dartmouth, Ashgate, 1999).

GOLD, E. R., *Body Parts: Property Rights and the Ownership of Human Biological Material* (Washington, Georgetown University Press, 1996).

GRUBB, A., "'I, Me, Mine': Bodies, Parts and Property" (1998) 3 *Medical Law International* 299.

GUTTMAN, A. and GUTTMAN, R., "Attitudes of Health Care Professionals and the Public Towards the Sale of Kidneys for Transplantation" (1993) 19 *Journal of Medical Ethics* 148.

HALLAM, E., Hockey, J., Howarth, G., *Beyond the Body: Death and Social Identity* (London, Routledge, 1999).

HARRIS, J., *The Value of Law* (Oxford, Oxford University Press, 1984).

——, "The Survival Lottery" in P. Singer (ed.), *Applied Ethics* (Oxford, Oxford University Press, 1986).

HARRIS, J. W., *Property and Justice* (Oxford, Oxford University Press, 1996a).

——, "Who Owns My Body?" (1996b) 16 *Oxford Journal of Legal Studies* 55.

HARVEY, J., "Paying Organ Donors" (1990) 16 *Journal of Medical Ethics* 167.

HERRING, J., "The Welfare Principle and Parents' Rights" in A. Bainham, S. Day Sclater and M. Richards (eds.), *What is a Parent? A Socio-legal Analysis* (Oxford, Hart, 1999).

——, "The Caesarean Section Cases and the Supremacy of Autonomy" in M. Freeman and A. Lewis, *Law and Medicine* (Oxford, Oxford University Press, 2000).

JONES, D. G., *Speaking for the Dead* (Dartmouth, Ashgate, 2000).

KENNEDY, I., "Further Thoughts on Liability for Non-Observance of the Provisions of the Human Tissue Act 1961" in *Treat Me Right* (Oxford, Oxford University Press, 1991).

KENNEDY, I. and GRUBB, A., *Medical Law* (London, Butterworths, 2000).

KEOWN, J., "The Gift of Blood in Europe" (1997) 23 *Journal of Medical Ethics* 96.

KOUNOUGERI-MANOLEDAKI, E., "Sperm, Ovum, and Fertilised Ovum Outside the Human Body" in A. Bainham (ed.), *The International Survey of Family Law* (Bristol, Family Law, 2000).

LAMB, D., *Organ Transplantation and Ethics* (Aldershot, Avebury, 1996).

LAW COMMISSION, *Consultation Paper no. 139: Consent in the Criminal Law* (London, HMSO, 1995).

LEDER, D., "Whose Body? What Body?" in M. Cherry (ed.), *Persons and Their Bodies* (Dordrecht, Kluwer, 1999).

LITMAN, M., "The Legal Status of Genetic Material", in B. Knoppers, C. Laberge and M. Hirtle, *Human DNA: Law and Policy* (The Hague, Kluwer, 1997).

MACLEAN, A., *The Elimination of Morality* (London, Routledge, 1993).

MAGNUSSON, R., "Property Rights in Human Tissue" in N. Palmer and E. McKendrick (eds.), *Interests in Goods* (Oxford, Oxford University Press, 1998).

MASON, J. and MCCALL SMITH, A., *Law and Medical Ethics* (London, Butterworths, 1999).

MATTHEWS, P., "The Man of Property" (1995) 3 *Medical Law Review* 251.

MYERS, D., *The Human Body and the Law* (Edinburgh, Edinburgh University Press, 1990).

NORRIE, K., "Human Tissue Transplants: Legal Liabilities in Different Jurisdictions" (1985) 34 *International and Comparative Law Quarterly* 442.

NUFFIELD COUNCIL ON BIOETHICS, *Human Tissue: Ethical and Legal Issues* (London, 1995).

PRICE, D., *Legal and Ethical Aspects of Organ Transplantation* (Cambridge, Cambridge University Press, 2000).

PRICE, D. and GARWOOD-GOWERS, A., "Transplantation From Minors" (1995) 1 *Contemporary Issues in Law*.

RADCLIFFE-RICHARDS, J. et al., "The Case for Allowing Kidney Sales" (1998) 351 *The Lancet* 1950.

ROYAL BRISTOL INFIRMARY INQUIRY, *Interim Report* (London, Department of Health, 2000).

ROYAL COLLEGE OF PHYSICIANS, *Ethical Issues in Clinical Genetics: A Report of Working Group of the Royal College of Physicians Committees on Ethical Issues in Medicine and Clinical Genetics* (London, RCP, 1991).

SIMESTER, A. and SULLIVAN, G., *Criminal Law* (Oxford, Hart, 2000).

SKEGG, P., *Law, Ethics and Medicine* (Oxford, Clarendon, 1998).

START, R., BROWN, W., BRYANT, R., REED, M., CROSS, S., KENT, G. and UNDERWOOD, J., "Ownership and Uses of Human Tissue: Does the Nuffield Bioethics Report Accord with Opinions of Surgical Inpatients?" (1996) 313 *British Medical Journal* 1366.

TOOMBS, K., "What Does it Mean to be Somebody?" in M. Cherry (ed.), *Persons and Their Bodies* (Dordrecht, Kluwer, 1999).

TRANSPLANTATION SOCIETY COUNCIL, "Commercialisation in Transplantation: The Problem and Some Guidelines for Practice" (1985) *The Lancet* 715.

UNESCO, *Human Rights Aspects of Traffic in Body Parts and Human Fetuses for Research and/or Therapeutic Purposes* (UNESCO, 1989).

UNITED STATES TASK FORCE ON ORGAN TRANSPLANTATION, *Organ Transplantation: Issues and Recommendations*, (Washington, US Government Printing Office, 1986).

WORLD HEALTH ORGANISATION, "Human Organ Transplantation, A Report on the Developments under the Auspices of the WHO", reprinted in *International Digest of Health Legislation: Transplantation* (Dordrecht, Martinus Nijhoff, 1991).

4

Discovering and Patenting Human Genes

GREGORY RADICK*

"I COMPARE THIS INFORMATION to the discovery of celestial galaxies. I would patent the moon!" Those are the words of the French geneticist Axel Kahn, on learning, in the summer of 1991, about an attempt to patent DNA sequences for molecules active in the human brain (quoted in Davies (2001) p. 62). Patents on human genes were nothing new in 1991. Now, ten years later, hundreds of partial and complete human genes have been patented, with thousands of applications awaiting judgement at patent offices around the world (see, e.g., "Patenting Life" (2000); Regalado (2000)). Yet the startled indignation that Kahn expressed has proved hard to shake. In this chapter I aim not to dispel that indignation but to diagnose one of its sources.

What follows is a preliminary study of the changing nature of gene discovery in the age of gene patenting. I claim that Kahn's remark resonates not because there is something fundamentally amiss about the patenting of discovered genes, but because gene discovery has changed in ways that have made it increasingly unlike patent-worthy invention. In the first section of the chapter I motivate this claim by way of some general reflections on embodied genes, patent lore and patent law. The remainder of the chapter chronicles the events surrounding the discovery and patenting of four human genes or parts of genes. The second section concerns the gene for the human hormone erythropoeitin. This gene was discovered and patented in the 1980s, and represents something of a parade case for the appropriateness of granting patents on human genes. Much less straightforward are the cases discussed in the third and fourth sections. These concern, respectively, the patent application that aroused Kahn's indignation, and the subsequent discovery and patenting of a gene for a human cell-surface receptor.

Note that Kahn's remark dates from 1991, one year after the official launch of the Human Genome Project, the large-scale, public initiative to map and sequence all the genes in the human genome and in several non-human genomes. It is widely acknowledged that the Human Genome Project accelerated the rate of gene discovery, in large part by stimulating advances in the automation of the process

* For helpful comments on earlier drafts, I am grateful to Thomas Dixon, Lindsay Gledhill, Jon Hodge, Fu-Kuen Lin, Margaret Llewelyn, and the editors of this volume.

of discovery. But, as we shall see, automation involved more than acceleration. The conclusion I draw from the cases examined in the second, third and fourth sections is that gene discovery after automation was not just a faster version of what came before, but a different kind of activity altogether, with different, and less plausible, claims to producing patentable results. I go on to qualify this conclusion in the fifth section, however, with a look at the mid-1990s discovery and patenting of a breast cancer susceptibility gene. That discovery was made using techniques from the pre-automation era, but the patent has proved highly controversial nonetheless.

1. KAHN'S REMARK

Diverse anxieties cluster around human gene patenting. The commodification of life; the commercialisation of scientific research; the chaos of litigation that can stifle research; the chasm between patent-rich developed countries and gene-rich developing countries: I shall touch on most of these in what follows. But my chief concern is with the argument gestured toward in Kahn's remark: that patents on human genes are fundamentally amiss because genes, like moons and galaxies, are not invented but discovered. It is natural enough to gloss this argument along the following lines. The point of the patenting system, after all, is to spur technological innovation. In exchange for putting in the time, money and labour needed to invent something, and then making the design of the new invention public, an inventor receives a right to prevent others from duplicating and profiting from the invention for up to twenty years. Not all inventions merit a patent, of course. The inventor must show that the invention is new, useful and, in the standard phrase, "non-obvious", that is, not just an obvious variation on the state of the art (see, for example Zweiger (2001); Caulfield, Gold and Cho (2000); Black (1998) and Eisenberg (1992)).

The genes and associated proteins found in human or other bodies seem to fail on all three counts. Far from being new, most have been around for millennia. Bodies function by virtue of their genes, and in that sense genes are "useful". But we do not use embodied genes in anything like the way we use can-openers and computers. As for "non-obviousness", it is hard to know what it could mean in this context. Of course, one could invent genes never found in bodies. Since the early 1980s, it has been possible to combine the nucleotides that constitute genes in new sequences in the laboratory. One might also use knowledge about discovered genes to invent new, useful and non-obvious things, such as treatments for diseases, or ways of generating treatments for diseases; and these inventions could be patented. But not the genes themselves.

There is a time-honoured riposte. Genes in bodies are not, strictly speaking, the objects that feature in patent applications. What are patented are genes isolated from bodies, and genes just do not exist in isolation in nature, neither in their entirety, nor in the pared-down forms that geneticists often create. When, through human ingenuity, a gene is isolated and purified thus for the first time, something new and potentially useful and non-obvious is brought into being. To alter Kahn's remark a little, we should compare the discovery of a DNA sequence of a natural gene to the discovery of the composition of a natural chemical in its pure state. Patents have long been awarded to those who succeed at purifying natural chemicals; and, so the argument goes, patents on isolated genes are no different (Haseltine (2000); Barton (1991); *cf.* Bobrow and Thomas (2001)).

Something like this argument underwrites the willingness of patent examiners, from the 1980s onwards, to approve patents on naturally occurring human genes. I raise the argument now to put it to one side. Not because it is invalid, but, on the contrary, because it suggests that human gene patents per se are not ruled out in advance as incompatible with common assumptions about the patent system and its purpose. This abstract lesson takes concrete form, up to a point, in the following section, about the gene for the human hormone erythropoeitin (EPO). If ever a gene discovery deserved a patent of some kind, this was it. "Up to a point", I say, because the real-life patent has remained under constant legal challenge. Never mind: what interests me is the conceptual contour of the discovery, not the contested details of the patent application made in its wake.

2. PATENTING EPO

The patent for the gene encoding EPO was one of the earliest patents on a human gene. Long known to stimulate the production of red blood cells, EPO has had a bad press of late, due to its growing popularity among athletes. Some of them take the genetically engineered version of the hormone to boost performance, since red blood cells transport oxygen to energy-needy tissues throughout the body, and more red blood cells make for greater endurance. Widespread use of engineered EPO among cyclists in the 1998 Tour de France created a scandal. At the start of the 2000 Olympic Games, new blood and urine tests forced the withdrawal of a large number of EPO-enhanced competitors (Campbell (2000)).

But before engineered EPO became the bane of the sports establishment, it was hailed as a medical boon. In adult humans, EPO is made in the kidneys. When these are damaged, anaemia often results, because poorly functioning kidneys make too little EPO to sustain production of red blood cells at high enough levels. Too fatigued to work or do much else, patients already encumbered with lifelong dialysis had turned to periodic blood transfusions and other treatments for relief. The gains were modest, the risks associated with blood-borne diseases significant. Then, in the mid-1980s, the American biotech firm Amgen began clinical trials of engineered EPO, bringing it to market in 1989. Engineered EPO has since become a drug on which millions depend. It has also made a fortune for Amgen, whose scientists worked out how to make it, and whose managers, by securing and defending a patent on the human EPO gene, worked out how to monopolise it. Though far from uncontentious, the Amgen patent on the gene for EPO is nevertheless good to think with, as it shows just how closely the discovery of a naturally occurring gene can conform to patent-worthy invention (Erslev (1987); "Erythropoietin" (1987); Flynn (1987); Abbott (1994); Wadman (2000)).

Started in California in 1980, Amgen was one of a small number of young firms aiming to transmute new techniques of gene discovery and manipulation into biomedical gold. After two years of searching for the EPO gene, a group of researchers at Amgen, led by Fu-Kuen Lin, succeeded roughly as follows (Lin et al. (1985)). At the time, the sequence of amino acids making up the protein encoded by the EPO gene was unknown. (The EPO hormone is the EPO protein further elaborated with small sugars that are nonetheless crucial to its functioning as a hormone.) Even under the best of circumstances, finding out which amino acid followed which in a protein was, and remains, a difficult business. In the case of EPO, the usual difficulties were compounded, because EPO occurs naturally in such small quantities, and researchers as a result had so little of it with which to work. Nevertheless, Lin's group managed to sequence two short stretches of the protein, one of them seven amino acids long, and one of them six. The researchers then set about synthesising short nucleotide chains that would encode these two short amino acid chains. Due to redundancy in the genetic code relating nucleotides and amino acids, the number of possible nucleotide chains was large—128 for each amino acid sequence.

The next step was to use these two sets of 128 nucleotide chains as probes to find the gene for EPO. Nucleotide chains can serve as probes because they selectively match up or "hybridise", according to the simple rules of nucleotide pairing (adenine to thymine, cytosine to guanine), with nucleotide chains of a precisely opposite, or complementary, sequence. Using a collection or "library" of recombinant phages—viruses that infect bacteria—Lin's group proceeded to probe the human genome, introducing the two sets of probes into each of the one and a half million phages making up the library (each phage containing in its own genome a small stretch of human DNA). In the end, there were only three random stretches of human genome where probes in both sets hybridised, and where DNA sequencing confirmed the presence of nucleotide chains encoding the specified sequences of amino acids.

To discover which of the candidate stretches of genome contained the gene for EPO, the Amgen researchers turned from examining gene structure to examining gene function. They introduced the candidate DNA into animal cells, since only these kinds of cells add the sugars that transform EPO into a functioning hormone. Next, the group injected mice with material collected from the cell cultures. The number of red blood cells shot up in some of the mice, showing the presence in the mice of functional EPO, and thus the presence in the relevant cells of the gene for EPO.

Lin's group also collected the mRNA transcripts issuing from this gene. mRNA transcripts mediate between a gene and the cell machinery needed to make the encoded protein. They are basically edited versions of a gene, representing only those regions of DNA that encode amino acids (genes include much non-coding

DNA as well). By virtue of their truncated structure, mRNA transcripts can be used, again via the nucleotide pairing rules, as templates for the creation of edited-down versions of a gene, full of DNA complementary to RNA in the transcript. Comparing the sequence of this complementary DNA or "cDNA" with the sequence of the full genomic DNA, the Amgen researchers were able both to check their results, and also to see better how the EPO gene was organised into coding and non-coding regions.

From first laboratory fumblings to clinical success, it was a hard, expensive slog. Amgen was awarded a patent in 1987. For what, precisely? That was a matter of dispute. Another research group at a rival biotech start-up, the Massachusetts-based Genetic Institute, had done similar work at roughly the same time, and was also awarded a patent. The two companies have been in almost constant litigation ever since over just who has patent rights, and where those rights end. The complicated and continuing history of legal tangles over the patent on the gene for EPO does not, however, throw light on the nature of the discovery that led to the patent, and so should not concern us here (but see, for example, Andrews (1990); Warshofsky (1994); Abbott (1994); Wadman (2000); Bobrow and Thomas (2001)).

For present purposes, there are three related points to note about the discovery and patenting of the human EPO gene. First, the principle of human gene patenting has not been much at issue, not in the wider worlds of research and medicine where engineered EPO has had its impact, and not in the courtrooms where Amgen has fought off its rivals. What has been disputed is whether Amgen deserves the patent on the EPO gene, and what the scope of that patent is. Secondly, the biochemical, functional characterisation of the gene came right at the beginning. The immediate process of discovery started from knowledge of biochemical function—"there exists a gene whose function is to direct the formation of a protein that, suitably elaborated, stimulates the production of red blood cells"—and proceeded to knowledge of molecular structure—"there exists a gene whose sequence is AAGCTTC . . .". Thirdly, because EPO is a hormone, the mere presence of which causes bodies to behave in predictable and, under certain circumstances (anaemia, world-class athletics competitions), beneficial ways, the route to commercialising knowledge of the EPO gene, to turning biology into therapy, was more or less direct. No more needed to be known about how, precisely, EPO stimulated the production of red blood cells, or how to manipulate the EPO gene in humans. It was enough to know that EPO functioned as it did, and that animal cells containing the human EPO gene made functional EPO. Patenting the EPO gene was like patenting the chemical recipe for a new drug. Recombinant EPO basically was a new drug.

3. PATENTING ESTS

The first public and professional expressions of consternation about the patenting of human genes came in 1991–92, in response to developments at one of the main

US governmental genome research centres, the National Institutes of Health (NIH). Following the lead of others, a molecular geneticist at one of the institutes, Craig Venter, had begun to speed up the sequencing process, in part by automating it, and in part by streamlining it. Rather than sequence stretches of DNA that might not contain any genes at all, Venter's group concentrated on the most immediate products of switched-on genes, mRNA transcripts. Working with the DNA complements of transcripts collected from human brain tissue, Venter's group had DNA certain to belong to genes, though they had no idea how those genes functioned. Breaking this cDNA into fragments, the group proceeded to sequence a more or less random sample of fragments (Davies (2001); *cf.* Schimmel (2000)). Since the fragments derived from genes that had been expressed in cells, the fragments could be used as probes to "tag", or locate, the genes from which they derived (through selective hybridisation). The sequenced fragments thus came to be called "expressed sequence tags", or ESTs (Anderson (1992a); Anderson (1992b); Carey (1995)).

Venter's group had begun generating ESTs by the hundreds when a patent attorney at a large biotech firm, Genentech, raised a new worry. If published before a patent application had been filed, he advised, the sequences might become commercial poison. The patent office could well rule that, because parts of their sequences were public knowledge, the fully characterised genes were unpatentable, since full characterisation at that point required little more than obvious extensions of the genetical "prior art" (Roberts (1991); *cf.* Warshofsky (1994) pp. 209–10). If NIH patented the sequence, however, commercial protection for later work on the genes could be preserved, with the patent-holding NIH acting as licensor. Persuaded, NIH officials quietly applied for patents on 357 of the Venter group's ESTs in June 1991, just before the group published them. Another application, covering even more ESTs, was already in preparation.

When news of these applications began to circulate, a number of prominent molecular geneticists were stirred to protest. Among them was Axel Kahn, and also James Watson, co-discoverer of the double helical structure of DNA, and then head of NIH's branch of the Human Genome Project. In what has proved an enduring quip, Watson was reported as saying that, since "virtually any monkey" could run an automated sequencing machine, it made no sense to reward those who generated sequence data in this way with patents (Roberts (1991); *cf.* Carey (1995); Macilwain (2000)). Watson and the other opponents of the EST patent applications emphasised that there was nothing wrong with patenting human genes in principle. Their concerns were two-fold: first, how little work it took to create ESTs; and secondly, how little genetic knowledge was gained. ESTs were just parts of genes, the functions of which were altogether unknown, or known only by analogy with genes catalogued in a public database. In Watson's view, gene patents should be awarded later in the day, to those who put in the hard work of puzzling out the structure and function of a whole gene, thus enabling its biomedical exploitation. Outside the USA, meanwhile, genomic researchers in other nations struck back with patent applications of their own. With European researchers calling for new rules for human gene patenting, and

Japanese researchers defiantly publishing their own EST data without seeking patent protection, NIH went ahead with a second patent application, now on 2,375 of the Venter group's ESTs (Roberts (1991); "Free Trade" (1991); Coghlan (1992); Charles and Coghlan (1992); Swinbanks (1992); see especially Cook-Deegan (1994)).

It was well known that Watson disagreed with NIH director Bernadine Healy on the issue of EST patents; and, though conflicts of interest were cited (Watson held shares in several biotechnology firms), Watson's resignation from the Human Genome Project in April 1992 prompted wide speculation that he was pushed out to smooth the way for the new patenting regime. Several months later, Venter announced his personal opposition to the patenting of mere sequences—he claimed his own patents of this sort were intended only to force clarity on the issue—and promptly left NIH to head up a private genomics research institute, fabulously well-funded by a venture capital group eager for lucrative gene patents (Anderson (1992b)). Venter's institute, called The Institute for Genomic Research, soon attracted a number of deep-pocketed clients, including the pharmaceuticals firm SmithKline Beecham. (Amgen had tried and failed to woo Venter to work for them along similar lines.) In short order, the new institute's commercial counterpart, Human Genome Sciences, was filing applications for patents on vast numbers of ESTs. But doubts remained about the commercial wisdom of this strategy (Carey (1995) p. 76).

"Don't Patent Human Genes" was the verdict of the editors of the London *Financial Times*—meaning, much less surprisingly, don't patent human genes of indeterminate structure, function and use. "It will be in the interests of all parties—even the US taxpayers whose interests NIH claims to protect—to agree that mass-produced genes cannot be patented" ("Don't Patent" (1992)). In August 1992, NIH director Healy published a lengthy defence of the NIH position (Healy (1992)). But the following month, the US patent office rejected its applications on the ESTs. This decision brought little clarity to the larger issues, however, as the ruling skirted these altogether. NIH lost not because gene fragments of unknown function were unpatentable, but because some of the fragments in the Venter application had sequences already publicly available. Ironically, the same "prior art" worry that prompted the NIH applications in the first place caused their demise. Healy and Venter vowed to fight on (Anderson (1992c)). The editors of *Nature* lamented the technical grounds of the decision, but welcomed it nevertheless. "The whole business has served to heighten public anxiety about the supposedly innate wickedness of geneticists" ("Gene patents" (1992)). Eventually NIH stopped seeking patents on ESTs, and the US patent office started granting them (Dickson (1995); O'Brien (1997); Grubb (1999), pp. 248–9).

4. PATENTING CCR5

During the 1980s and early 1990s, the catalogues of known genes began to swell with ever more sequences, from human and non-human genomes, while the computers managing the catalogues grew more powerful (see Zweiger (2001)). It turned out that genes were much of a muchness: within and across species, genes performing similar functions had similar sequences. Technological innovation and evolutionary conservatism thus combined to make possible a new and highly effective method of gene discovery. The main idea was to match like with like. By comparing freshly sequenced stretches of the human genome to sequences already catalogued, computers helped to pick out likely gene candidates in those new sequences. When genes of similar or "homologous" sequence were matched up in this way, and when the function of the formerly catalogued gene had been established (easier to do with genes from non-human species), researchers could even guess at the function of the newly sequenced gene, on the assumption that structure and function went together. Thus it became possible, with a few keystrokes, not just to find genes, but to know, to a first approximation, what effects those genes had on bodies.

Not all catalogues were equal, however (Zweiger (2001)). In 1994, amid wide publicity, the EST database at Craig Venter's new institute yielded up one of the genetic culprits behind colon cancer. Unlike searches of public databases such as GenBank, searches of the institute's database came with strings attached. First shot at patent rights went to Human Genome Sciences (Carey (1995)). Under the direction of its chief executive officer, the Harvard molecular geneticist William Haseltine, Human Genome Sciences was mounting a patenting drive as aggressive as Venter's sequencing drive. But for all the power of homology searches to reveal the functions of just-discovered genes, Haseltine judged that, for patent purposes, computers were not enough, or at least not always. Their role at Human Genome Sciences was the somewhat more circumscribed one of nominating promising candidates for patenting, and thus worthy recipients of laboratory investigations to characterise function more fully (Marshall (2000)).

How complete did a characterisation of gene function need to be for a patent to be granted? The question remained hotly debated. To its critics, Human Genome Sciences' patent applications fell far short of the required standard. One of the most vociferous critics was Thomas Caskey, research scientist at the pharmaceuticals giant Merck, and president of the body charged with overseeing the sequencing of the human genome, the Human Genome Organization (HUGO). Merck had decided its interests lay in ensuring that gene sequences were available to all, for use as research tools, and that patents went only to those who had made the potential utility of a gene manifest. As backer of an important sequencing centre at Washington University in St. Louis, Merck was in a position to make at least some of the sequences public, and thus (it was hoped) unpatentable. (Zweiger (2001); Carey (1995); *cf.* Poste (1995)).

In his role as HUGO president, Caskey took a similar line on gene patents. At a meeting about gene patenting held in Paris in January 1995, Caskey warned of how patents on uncharacterised bits of sequence "would reward those who make routine discoveries, but penalize those who determine biological function or application". According to another participant, the director general of the Pasteur Institute, Maxine Schwartz, the gathered scientists, lawyers, and business people all agreed that "genes can be patented when we know their function" (Butler (1995)). A few months later, Caskey explicitly criticised Human Genome Sciences for its patent policy. The criticisms came with the release of a HUGO policy statement affirming, again, that the "task of identifying biological functions of a gene is by far the most important step in terms of its difficulty and its social benefit". With respect to the granting of patents, it was this step towards full determination of function that "therefore merits the most incentive and protection". Included in the statement were predictions of trouble further down the line, when researchers would find they had no commercial rights to hard-won physiological or biomedical discoveries, because firms such as Human Genome Sciences had quietly secured pre-emptive patents (Dickson (1995)).

Five years later, the prediction appeared to be borne out. At issue was the cell-surface receptor CCR5. In 1995, Human Genome Sciences had filed an application for patents on a number of ESTs, among them one associated with a gene that, according to homology computer searches and some laboratory studies, encoded a protein belonging to a well-known family of cell-surface receptors. These receptors were often targets of drug action, in combating allergies, ulcers and other conditions. In its application, the firm characterised possible therapies based on the new gene accordingly, noting as well the possibility of therapies that interfered with viruses docking at the receptor. Though Haseltine was himself a distinguished HIV researcher, no mention was made of HIV. By the time the US patent office granted the patent on the receptor gene in February 2000, however, other research groups, in the course of laborious experimental and epidemiological work, had revealed the role of the encoded protein as a docking point for HIV. With lucrative licences for AIDS treatments in the offing, CCR5 became the centre of another flaring up of debate over the whole system of gene patenting, and in particular about how much needed to be known about a gene before it could be patented (Marshall (2000); Davies (2001)).

Even as it awarded the CCR5 patent, the US patent office was preparing to raise the bar. In December 1999, it had released new draft guidelines, advising firms and universities that examiners would award patents only where claims about gene utility were, as the new mantra soon had it, "specific, substantial and credible" (Smaglik (2000a, 2000b); Grisham (2000)). Did that rule out patents for genes whose function has been explored only *in silico* (from Brown (2000); Howard (2000); Zweiger (2001))? Apparently not—a possibility that drew heavy criticism, from NIH and other institutions.

Craig Venter, who broke with Human Genome Sciences in the late 1990s to start Celera Genomics, also criticised the lax patent criteria. Though he now spoke up for responsible gene patenting, Venter at this point was fast becoming a symbol of the new biotechnology at its most rapacious. As leader of Celera's bid to beat the Human Genome Project to the "rough draft" of the full sequence of the human genome, he managed to stoke popular and professional fears about a privatised genome to new levels. In March 2000, President Bill Clinton and Prime Minister Tony Blair issued a joint statement about the need to keep access to genomic data open and free. Biotech stocks tumbled (briefly) (Davies (2001)). Following Clinton and Blair's example, Bruce Alberts and Sir Aaron Klug, the leaders of the most prestigious American and British scientific societies respectively, issued a statement of their own, calling for open access, and also for an end to CCR5-style patents. "It is a trivial matter today—using a computer search of public databases—to use DNA sequences to identify new genes with particular types of biochemical functions. In our opinion, such a discovery should not be rewarded with a broad patent for future therapies or diagnostics using these genes when the actual applications are merely being guessed at" (Alberts and Klug (2000); *cf.* "Intellectual Propriety" (2000)).

5. PATENTING BRCA1

We have seen how increasing automation and associated changes in the 1990s affected the discovery and patenting of human genes. It is time now to sharpen the contrast between 1990s-style and 1980s-style paths of discovery, but also to see that the former cannot bear all the blame for unease about gene patenting. Let me begin with a term much bandied about: "reverse genetics" (see, for example, Zweiger (2001); Eisenberg (1992); Judson (1992)). It well describes the path of discovery along which researchers at Human Genome Sciences travelled in characterising CCR5 in the 1990s, roughly:

molecular structure → biochemical function → organismic trait

I say "reverse genetics" fits, because this path neatly reverses the one along which researchers at Amgen travelled in characterising EPO in the 1980s, roughly:

organismic trait → biochemical function → molecular structure

As it happens, however, "reverse genetics" was introduced to pick out, not the 1990s-style, CCR5 path of discovery, but a quite different path, roughly:

organismic trait → chromosomal location → molecular structure →
biochemical function

This complicated discovery path turns out to have complicated patenting consequences. Notice for now that it is the only one of the three paths that includes the discovery of the chromosomal location of a gene as an essential step. Chromosomal location was irrelevant to discovering the structure and function of the EPO and CCR5 genes. But it was essential to discovering the structure and function of the breast cancer susceptibility gene BRCA1, and a number of other genes associated with heritable diseases, beginning most famously with the discovery of the gene for Huntington's disease in 1983. Notice too that this third or BRCA1 discovery path is the "reverse" of the EPO path mainly so far as knowledge of molecular structure comes before knowledge of biochemical function.

More generally, the BRCA1 path is intermediate between the EPO path and its true reverse, the CCR5 path, in three respects. First, the BRCA1 path partakes of the character of both of the others. Like the EPO path, and unlike the CCR5 path, the BRCA1 path begins with knowledge of an organismic trait ("people are suffering from such and such a condition"). But like the CCR5 path, and unlike the EPO path, the BRCA1 path passes to knowledge of biochemical function from knowledge of molecular structure ("this gene has such and such a DNA sequence, so it will encode that protein, with those properties"). Secondly, the BRCA1 path does not belong as comfortably as the others to a single decade. It spans the temporal divide I have so far worked to make conspicuous. Thirdly, the gene discoveries made along the BRCA1 path tend to be more or less immediately useful, but in a problematic way: as the basis, not for drugs, but for tests.

The explanation of this last intermediate feature is not far to seek. It is mainly to do with the costs and benefits of travel along a discovery path that takes a chromosomal detour around knowledge of biochemical function, enabling passage straight from knowledge of an organismic trait ("people are suffering from this condition") to knowledge of molecular structure ("because they bear a gene with that DNA sequence"). On the benefit side, the BRCA1 path enables discovery of the molecular structure of genes with effects we are interested in combating—heritable disease—even when those effects are achieved through biochemical interactions so fiendishly complex that they defeat present understanding. Indeed, the genes discovered along the BRCA1 path tend to be precisely of this sort. On the cost side, however, the leap to molecular structure often brings enough knowledge to detect the presence of a "disease" gene, but not enough to predict with certainty the onset of disease, or to intervene effectively to prevent or ameliorate disease. Prediction and intervention ultimately require knowledge of biochemical function. Of course, the disease in question could turn out to be due to a simple protein deficiency, in which case intervention will be just a matter of engineering and supplying the gene-encoded protein, along EPO lines. But the biochemical causal chains often turn out to be as complex as suspected, and intervention a matter of finding a suitable link to cut in the chains, with drugs perhaps still undreamt of. That is why patenting genes discovered in this way is *not* like patenting the chemical recipes for new drugs, and the justification of these gene patents much less straightforward than the justification of patents for genes such as EPO.

The details of the BRCA1 discovery make vivid these points about benefits and costs. Doubts about the existence of a breast cancer susceptibility gene persisted until 1990, when the population geneticist Mary-Claire King (then at Berkeley) presented data from several stricken families, suggesting a strong link between early-onset breast cancer and inheritance of a particular version of a marker on chromosome 17. This marker was one of many revealed throughout the human genome in the 1980s through assiduous use of new molecular techniques (see Judson (1992)). On the assumption that the gene for breast cancer susceptibility lay on the same chromosome as the marker (since they were inherited together, as a unit), the search narrowed to the DNA in the neighbourhood of the marker.

Further narrowing of the search area depended on continued analysis of ever more refined familial marker data, coupled with nucleotide-by-nucleotide comparisons of potential genes (see especially Waldholz (1997)).

There is no doubt about the hard work and large funds expended on the search for BRCA1. Still, the patent awarded to the University of Utah and Myriad Genetics, the Salt Lake City firm whose researchers found the gene first, in the autumn of 1994, aroused controversy on a much larger scale than Venter's EST applications of 1991–92 (Gershon (1994)). Myriad's successful bid for the patent on BRCA1 at least delighted its shareholders. University of Utah geneticist Mark Skolnick founded the firm in 1991, after NIH had turned down his application for funds to do research on breast cancer genetics (Waldholz (1997)). When Myriad went public, a year or so after the discovery of BRCA1, a test for mutations in the gene was still in development. But the prospect of millions of women soon paying large sums to find out whether they had the mutation meant that Myriad's stock sold high and climbed still higher (Smith (1995)). The test finally became available in late 1996, selling in one version for over 2,000 dollars (Waldholz (1997)).

Whatever its level around the time of the EST debacle (see Macer (1992)), public anxiety climbed far higher, and grew far more widespread, after the discovery and patenting of BRCA1. Part of the problem was that Myriad appeared to have thrown private funds at a problem nearly solved. Public and charitable funds had enabled essential earlier steps—the assembling of families for marker-disease linkage studies, and the carrying out of those studies. Within the scientific community, the Myriad patent occasioned, in addition to the inevitable patent disputes (in this case, with NIH, Gavaghan (1995)), open debate about whether patents on human genes served the public interest at all, even when the genes were of known function and structure ("Genes and Patent Law" (1994); Stewart (1995)).

As for the BRCA1 test, it became an object of concern and contention even before its arrival. Perhaps because breast cancer was so pervasive a threat, or because no test for an adult-onset disease had anything like the potential number of test-takers as did the BRCA1 test, worries about Myriad's patent on BRCA1 became entangled in more general worries about the test, and genetic testing as such. In May 1996, the biotechnology critic Jeremy Rifkin organised a coalition of women's rights groups and their allies to challenge Myriad's patent, described as an "assault on women" (Charatan (1995); "US Coalition" (1996)). Once the test emerged, the controversies only accumulated. Not long after the discovery of BRCA1, it became clear that the mutations turning it into a cancer susceptibility gene were legion—at one point, it seemed, nearly every family had a different mutation. Concerns about expense and possible inaccuracy aside, no-one was sure just how to interpret test results, or even who should take the test. More research made the link between mutant BRCA1 and breast cancer ever more tenuous. As the risk of breast cancer associated with possessing mutant BRCA1 began to fall, the difficulty of making decisions on the basis of the test began to rise. Voluntary removal of healthy breasts, or sometimes ovaries (to reduce tumour-promoting oestrogen, and also the risk of ovarian cancer), began to seem less than obviously rational responses to a positive result. There was also disagreement over the desirability of testing when there was no history of breast cancer in the family. (Smith (1995); Waldholz (1997)).

Myriad's aggressive enforcement of its patent rights over BRCA1, and over a second breast cancer susceptibility gene, BRCA2, has kept the patenting of these genes controversial (see, e.g. Borger (1999)). In January 2000, there were revelations of threats to shut down labs in Britain using other, protein-based tests that cost half as much as Myriad's own (Meek (2000)). In response, the *Guardian* called for full-scale repeal of patents on genes as such, in favour of patents on specific applications of genetic knowledge. "The gold rush for genes" did not serve the public interest, according to the editors. "It must be stopped: they belong to us" ("Gold rush" (2000)). Meanwhile, there is little indication that knowledge of the chromosomal location, molecular structure and even, increasingly, broad biochemical function (DNA repair) of BRCA1 is leading toward a therapeutic breakthrough (Zweiger (2001), pp. 128–9).

6. CONCLUSION

The discovery and patenting of EPO shows that patents on gene discoveries do not always prompt outraged comparisons with patents on celestial discoveries. There is a sharp contrast between the directed, craft-like research that led to the EPO patent application and the mass filtration of genes and data that led to the EST and CCR5 patent applications. Automation has enabled the rapid discovery of large numbers of genes, most of which their discoverers are in no position to exploit immediately. On traditional patenting criteria, these genes seem to lack demonstrable usefulness. As such, their being discovered is indeed much like moons and galaxies being discovered. Such discoveries add to knowledge about what is in the world, but not to knowledge about how to change the world for the better. There is a second, related source of difficulty. Patents traditionally reward investment and ingenuity. But there just is not enough of either when discoverers merely switch on the sequencer and run the database searching programmes. To return to the question of hard-to-shake indignation about human gene patenting: what has troubled is not so much the idea of gene patenting, as the idea that patents are being awarded for genes that no-one can use, and that no-one worked hard to discover. At bottom Axel Kahn's complaint still resonates because gene discovery has changed in ways that have made it increasingly unlike activities traditionally deemed patent-worthy.

But this is not the whole story. The history of gene discovery is a history of accumulation, not replacement. The discovery and patenting of a breast cancer susceptibility gene, BRCA1, forces some qualification of the above. Though the gene was found in the mid-1990s, its discovery depended on techniques forged in the pre-automation era. The discovery was as hard-won as the discovery of EPO. The BRCA1 discovery was expected to be useful, and has so proved. But the patent on the gene has been hugely controversial, over and above the challenges of rivals pipped at the post, and concerns expressed about corporate power over women's health. The root problem is that the gene discovery is of use in a limited and fraught direction. The gene cannot be used to produce a therapy for breast cancer, at least not directly, in the way EPO can be used to produce a therapy for anaemia. BRCA1 can merely be tested for cancer-predisposing mutations. Awarding a patent in this case seems uncomfortably close to awarding a patent on a heavenly body, just because its discoverer can reliably find it over and over again.

Needless to say, the four snapshots offered here fall far short of the history we still do not have of the patenting of human genes. That history will notice, for example, how gene patents have come to matter in agribusiness as well as bio-medicine, and will take account of controversies in the patenting of non-human genes. It will show in detail how opponents to human gene patenting in Europe, notably among the "Greens", were outmanoeuvred. It will tell of a debate that now scarcely exists, about the sharing of patent rights between those who find genes and those who contribute tissue to genetic research (see, e.g., Dickson (1996); Smaglik (2000c)). Perhaps this future history will even venture to judge whether the patent rush of the 1990s stimulated or blocked innovation, or stimulated it in certain directions rather than others (*cf.* Heller and Eisenberg (1998); Shulman (2000); Caulfield, Gold and Cho (2000); Zweiger (2001); Llewelyn (forth-coming)). In the meantime, we can do worse than attend to the recent changes in gene discovery, and the role of these changes in sustaining stubborn, perhaps permanent, unease about the patenting of human genes.

REFERENCES

ABBOTT, A., "Protein Gene Patent Faces Challenge in Court" (1994) 371 *Nature* 645.
ALBERTS, B. and KLUG, A., "The Human Genome Itself Must be Freely Available to All Humankind" (2000) 404 *Nature* 325.
ANDERSON, C., "Watson Resigns, Genome Project Open to Change" (1992a) 356 *Nature* 549.
——, "Controversial NIH Genome Researcher Leaves for New $70-Million Institute" (1992b) 58 *Nature* 95.
——, 'NIH cDNA Patent Rejected; Backers Want to Amend Law" (1992c) 359 *Nature* 263.
ANDREWS, E. L., "Mad Scientists" (1990) 135 *Business Month* 54.
BARTON, J. H., "Patenting Life" (1991) 264 *Scientific American* 18.
BLACK, J., "Regulation as Facilitation: Negotiating the Genetic Revolution", in R. Brownsword, W. R. Cornish, and M. Llewelyn (eds.), *Law and Human Genetics* (Oxford, Hart, 1998) p. 29.
BOBROW, M. and THOMAS, S., "Patents in a Genetic Age" (2001) 409 *Nature* 763.
BORGER, J., "Rush to Patent Genes Stalls Cures for Disease", *The Guardian*, 15 December 1999.
BROWN, K., "The Human Genome Business Today" (2000) 283 *Scientific American* 40.
BUTLER, D., "Patent System Gets Vote of Support from Gene Workers" (1995) 373 *Nature* 376.
CAMPBELL, D., "Doping in Athletics: Growth Drug that will Put Out Olympic Flame" *The Observer*, 10 September 2000.

CAREY, J., "The Gene Kings", *Business Week*, 8 May 1995, p. 72.

CAULFIELD, T., GOLD, E. R. and CHO, M. K. (2000), "Patenting Human Genetic Material: Refocusing the Debate" (2000) 1 *Nature Reviews: Genetics* 227.

CHARATAN, F., "US Religious Groups Oppose Gene Patents" (1995) 310 *British Medical Journal* 1351.

CHARLES, D. and COGHLAN, A., "Ministers Move to Limit Genome Patents", *New Scientist*, 14 March 1992, p. 9.

COGHLAN, A., "US Gene Plan 'Makes a Mockery of Patents'", *New Scientist*, 22 February 1992, p. 10.

COOK-DEEGAN, R., *The Gene Wars* (London, W. W. Norton, 1994).

DAVIES, K., *Cracking the Genome* (New York, Free Press, 2001).

DICKSON, D., "HUGO and HGS Clash Over 'Utility' of Gene Sequences in US Patent Law" (1995) 374 *Nature* 751.

——— , "Whose Genes are They Anyway?" (1996) 381 *Nature* 11.

"Don't Patent Human Genes", *Financial Times*, 24 April 1992, p. 16.

EISENBERG, R. S., "Patent Rights in the Human Genome Project", in G. J. Annas and S. Elias (eds.), *Gene Mapping: Using Law and Ethics as Guides* (Oxford, Oxford University Press, 1992) p. 226.

ERSLEV, A., "Erythropoietin Coming of Age" (1987) 316 *New England Journal of Medicine* 101.

"Erythropoietin", *Lancet*, 4 April 1987, p. 781.

FLYNN, J., "The Hormone that's Making Amgen Grow", *Business Week*, 16 March 1987, p. 96.

"Free Trade in Human Sequence Data?" (1991) 354 *Nature* 171.

GAVAGHAN, H., "NIH Resolves Dispute on Cancer Gene Patent" (1995) 373 *Nature* 649.

"Gene Patents" (1992) 359 *Nature* 348.

"Genes and Patent Law" (1994) 371 *Nature* 270.

GERSHON, D., "Breast Cancer Discovery Sparks New Debate on Patenting Human Genes" (1994) 371 *Nature* 271.

"Gold Rush for Genes", *The Guardian*, 18 January 2000.

GRISHAM, J., "New Rules for Gene Patents" (2000) 18 *Nature Biotechnology* 921.

GRUBB, P. W., *Patents for Chemicals, Pharmaceuticals and Biotechnology: Fundamentals of Global Law, Practice and Strategy* (Oxford, Clarendon Press, 1999).

HASELTINE, W., "The Case for Gene Patents" (2000) September/October *Technology Review*, online version (www.techreview.com).

HEALY, B., "Special Report on Gene Patenting" (1992) 327 *New England Journal of Medicine* 664.

HELLER, M. A. and EISENBERG, R. S., "Can Patents Deter Innovation? The Anticommons in Biomedical Research" (1998) 280 *Science* 698.

HOWARD, K., "The Bioinformatics Gold Rush" (2000) 283 *Scientific American* 46–51.

"Intellectual Propriety" (2000) 18 *Nature Biotechnology* 469.

JUDSON, H. F., "A History of the Science and Technology Behind Gene Mapping and Sequencing" in D. J. Kevles and L. Hood, *The Code of Codes* (London, Harvard University Press, 1992).

LIN, F. K. et al., "Cloning and Expression of the Human Erythropoietin Gene" (1985) 82 *Proceedings of the National Academy of Sciences USA* 7580.

LLEWELYN, M., "The UK Patents Regulations 2000: a Hostage to Fortune" *Genetics Law Monitor* (forthcoming).

78   *Gregory Radick*

MACER, D., "Public Opinion on Gene Patents" (1992) 358 *Nature* 272.
MACILWAIN, C., "World Leaders Heap Praise on Human Genome Landmark" (2000) 405 *Nature* 983.
MARSHALL, E., "Patents on HIV Receptor Provokes an Outcry" (2000) 287 *Science* 1375.
MEEK, J., "US Firm May Double Cost of UK Cancer Checks", *The Guardian*, 17 January 2000.
O'BRIEN, C., "US Decision 'Will Not Limit Gene Patents'" (1997) 385 *Nature* 755.
"Patenting life" (2000), *The Guardian*, Special Report, 15 November 2000.
POSTE, G., "The Case for Genomic Patenting" (1995) 378 *Nature* 534.
REGALADO, A., "The Great Gene Grab", September/October 2000, *Technology Review*, web version (www.techreview.com).
ROBERTS, L., "Genome Patent Fight Erupts" (1991) 254 *Science* 184.
SCHIMMEL, P., "Industry Benefits from the Public Funding of Intellectual Curiosity" (2000) 406 *Nature* 826.
SHULMAN, S., "Toward Sharing the Genome", September/October 2000, *Technology Review*, web version (www.techreview.com).
SMAGLIK, P., ". . . as US Tightens up on 'Speculative' Claims" (2000a) 403 *Nature* 3.
——, "Could AIDS Treatments Slip Through Patents Loophole?" (2000b) 404 *Nature* 322.
——, "Tissue Donors Use their Influence in Deal over Gene Patent Terms" (2000c) 407 *Nature* 821.
SMITH, G., "A Key Test for Genetic Testing", *Business Week*, 4 December 1995, p. 109.
STEWART, A. D., "Patenting of Human Genes" (1995) 373 *Science* 185.
SWINBANKS, D., "Japanese Researchers Rule out Gene Patents" (1992) 356 *Nature* 181.
"US Coalition Counters Breast Gene Patents" (1996) 381 *Nature* 265.
WADMAN, M., "US Court Tests the Breadth of Patent Protection on Proteins" (2000) 404 *Nature* 532.
WALDHOLZ, M., *Curing Cancer* (New York, Simon and Schuster, 1997).
WARSHOFSKY, F., *The Patent Wars* (New York, John Wiley, 1994).
ZWEIGER, G., *Transducing the Genome* (London, McGraw-Hill, 2001).

5

Letting Go . . . Parents, Professionals and the Law in the Retention of Human Material after Post Mortem

MAVIS MACLEAN

> *On an Infant Dying as Soon as Born*
> "I saw where in the shroud did lurk
> A curious frame of Nature's work;
> A flow'ret crushed in the bud,
> A nameless piece of Babyhood,
> Was in her cradle-coffin lying;
> Extinct, with scarce the sense of dying:
> So soon to exchange the imprisoning womb
> For darker closets of the tomb!"
> Charles Lamb, *Palgrave's Golden Treasury*,
>   (Oxford University Press, 1933)

1. INTRODUCTION

F ROM AUGUST 1998 until July 2001 I have had the sad but inspiring duty of sitting with Professor Ian Kennedy, Professor Sir Brian Jarman and Mrs. Rebecca Howard on the Inquiry into the management and care of children receiving complex heart surgery at the Bristol Royal Infirmary. The sadness requires no explanation—the loss of a child cannot be other than a tragedy, and may be even harder to bear when there is any possibility that things might have been otherwise. The inspiration lies in the commitment of all concerned to understand what happened, to learn from this understanding, and to develop ways of helping to secure high quality care across the National Health Service.

During the hearing of oral evidence by the Inquiry it became clear that it was common practice among hospital pathologists to retain material removed from the body during post mortem examination. It also became clear that a number of the parents of children who had died in Bristol and elsewhere were not aware of this practice and had not been asked for their agreement. They were very distressed by this knowledge. When the Inquiry sought legal advice on the matter it became clear that the legal position was confused, and not well understood by those professionally involved in post mortem work.

The Inquiry published an Interim Report in May 2000 entitled *Removal and Retention of Human Material*[1] (Central Office of Information, BRROJOO–5418/IK). This chapter draws on that Interim Report and on the evidence to the Inquiry which is available on the Inquiry website (www.bristol-inquiry.org.uk). It will examine the place of law within the tangled web of professional science-based arguments and the emotional needs of the families.

On 25 January 2000 Professor Robert Anderson, Professor of Paediatric Cardiac Morphology at University College London, wrote to the Inquiry after giving oral evidence, setting out the scale of current retention of congenitally malformed hearts in this country. He estimated that the largest collection was at Alder Hey Children's Hospital with approximately 2,500 hearts, he himself had built up a collection at the Royal Brompton Hospital of 2,000 hearts, there was a similar collection at Great Ormond Street and other smaller collections in Birmingham, Leeds, Bristol, Southampton, Newcastle and Manchester. A "Panorama" documentary programme followed, and also press stories referring to the scandal of stolen hearts (see, for example, Polly Toynbee in *The Guardian*, 2 February 2000).

2. PARENTAL DISTRESS

Many parents who gave evidence to the Inquiry in Bristol (BRII) were acutely distressed by this information, both by the fact of the retention and because they believed that they had not been informed or consulted. Mr. Paul Bradley who gave evidence on day 53, speaking about his daughter Bethan, said:

> "I think what distressed us was the extent of the retention, that it was not just limited to the heart but also her lungs, as we understand, a part of her brain, a part of her kidney, and the extent of it extenuated the stress, and I just cannot explain . . . the reactions we have felt. It might be considered over the top, but we cannot help how we feel . . . we felt it was criminal, what was done. It is how we felt, that it was very contemptuous what was done, to the dignity of our child that her body has been, as we see it, invaded and body parts stolen and that is how we see it".

Mr. Bradley describes clearly the elements involved in compounding the distress of the bereavement which this new knowledge brought to him and his wife; the lack of respect shown to his daughter after her death, the special nature of the parts retained, and the impact of such large-scale retention which he saw as theft. Mrs. Rex, mother of Steven, who spoke on the same day, echoed his views, saying, "Heart and soul are emotive". Mr. Bradley went on to describe how a parent feels in control of his child's life, and that "with the operation you lose that control, but then to further lose control in this way after the death, it is so upsetting". Although

[1] The term "human material" is a general term developed by the Inquiry, not a legal term, and refers to tissue in its various forms, organs, parts of organs, and other materials such as amputated limbs.

the terms "theft" and "stolen" were used by several parents this took place in the context of the continuation of parental responsibility and caring after death. The only immediate form of care which a parent can offer their child after death is to arrange the funeral. When this event is based on lack of information about the physical state of the child, this final act of care may for some families seem to be somehow devalued and damaged. We heard not about parental rights to the body of their child as property (see Eileen Richardson and Bryan Turner (chapter 2)), but about the central concept on which the Children Act 1989 is founded, that of parental responsibility which not only transcends the legal relationship of the parents but also continues after death.

Mrs. Rex spoke about the question of consent for retention, saying, "If only people had been honest and open with parents. I realize that doctors have to be trained and only see organs as specimens. The distress which we have all felt could have been alleviated by treating parents and patients as human beings rather than an extension of specimens" (see Martin Johnson (chapter 6)). Mr. Bradley said

> "If they had asked us I know how I would have reacted. If they had asked us the night before Bethan's operation I would have . . . been affronted that they would have been seemingly dismissive, even before the operation that she was going to die, so I would not have liked that . . . my feeling is that well before the operation, a low key appointment, an interview, would help to put the seed in a person's mind and even if it was not a case of deciding then it would have helped to put the seeds in the mind of the parent . . . if we had been told well before the operation we would have had a better judgement to have perhaps come and say yes, okay, they can have the heart".

The direct nature of the distress experienced, in some cases years after the death of the child, can be heard in the words of Mrs. Sharon Tarantino mother of Corinna: "It is the thought of having to go through another funeral again", and of Helen Rickard, mother of Samantha, who told us:

> "I have held my daughter's heart in my hand and I feel highly privileged to have been able to do that because of who my daughter was. It is a situation I did not want to be in. And I do not think it is fair for people to be put in that situation, to deepen the distress that is already there" (day 52).

The loss of a child due to a congenital heart defect compromises many elements which combine to exacerbate the distress of bereavement. The congenital factor adds to the bereaved parents' feeling of having failed the child in that they have directly contributed to the cause. The surgical intervention requires that the parents have given consent, and in some cases the parents physically carried their child down to theatre and handed the child over for the procedure which preceded death. In many cases, after successful early crisis intervention, the child may have appeared relatively well up to the time of surgery, so that although parents are generally aware that the condition is serious and that surgery carries a risk, they have not experienced the slow and gradual decline of some other illnesses, such as the cancers of childhood. It may feel as if a well child has been handed over for surgery from which the child did not return.

In the course of the Bristol Inquiry proceedings this potent combination of factors led some parents to feel great anger as well as distress at the discovery of the retention of their children's organs.

3. THE RESPONSE OF THE MEDICAL PROFESSION

The purpose of post mortem examination was described to the Inquiry by the doctors involved in the procedures. Professor Alan Green of the University of Sheffield and consultant to the Home Office described autopsy as the "gold standard" for identifying the impact of new medical techniques, for identifying new conditions, and for noting patterns of outcomes for a particular hospital. He described, as examples, the contribution of autopsy to establishing the relationship between deep vein thrombosis and the contraceptive pill, and in identifying the new strain of Creutzfeldt-Jakob Disease. He confirmed that in the past the prevailing culture was not to go into details with the family of the deceased about precisely what was involved in a post mortem in order to avoid causing further distress. He said:

> "I qualified in 1960 . . . the general lesson drilled into me as a medical student was: be courteous, be polite, explain that you are asking for this autopsy because it will help others both in learning and in the treatment of disease, but do not go into any more detail; it will upset the relatives and they might refuse consent" (day 42).

Professor Berry, Consultant Paediatric Pathologist at the Bristol Royal Infirmary since 1983 and Professor of Paediatric Pathology at Bristol since 1990, saw a range of purposes and alternative procedures for post mortem, and in particular saw it as:

> "part of formal audit and review, fed back as appropriate to parents, providing information, and the autopsy should be carried out according to the parents needs and giving them choice and information including, if the coroner is not involved their right not to have a post mortem examination and if they choose the right not to know what goes on" (day 55).

Mr. Janardan Dhasmana, Consultant Cardiac surgeon at Bristol from 1986 to 1998 described in a written statement how the post mortem helped the surgeon, saying it is "a necessary requirement to improve one's knowledge and also to check on one's technique and learn from post mortem examinations" (WIT 0084 0105).

The post mortem was particularly important to the learning process in paediatric cardiac surgery as this was a high risk and relatively new specialty, where the range of defects to be corrected was wide, and the caseload for each surgeon was small, and therefore to have the opportunity to see an example of the condition to be treated in the next operation was of great value. The primary purpose served by the retained hearts seems to have been of direct value to practising surgeons rather than academic research where any benefit to patients would be potential and in the future, without immediate impact.

Professor Berry said:

"many of these conditions are rare and no two hearts with a given condition are quite the same. So by keeping quite a large number (a very large number to people who are not pathologists) it is possible to provide somebody who wishes to study a particular anomaly a range of examples that would take them many years to see in their own practice" (day 55).

4. THE PLACE OF THE LAW

We have heard from angry and anguished parents who felt that their children's bodies had been violated without their knowledge or consent, and body parts referred to as stolen.

We have heard pathologists and surgeons describing the part played by these retained materials in the improvement of mortality rates in the rapidly developing high-risk low incidence practice of paediatric cardiac surgery.

What is the legal framework and what part does it play in regulating these conflicting interests?

The law differentiates between two kinds of post mortem, that which is carried out at the request of the coroner and that which is carried out at the wish of the hospital. The coroner's purpose in requesting this examination is to determine identity, and the cause of death, originally in the sense of checking for any irregularity of practice or unlawful factors. The aim of a hospital post mortem was also to determine the cause of death, but from a more scientific perspective, looking for any new patterns of disease, co-morbidities, and checking for the impact of the various medical interventions not only to check adequacy of care but also to evaluate new procedures and other developments. For example, Professor Berry's article (Russell and Berry (1989)) indicated the value of the post mortem examination in identifying a number of abnormalities in children with congenital heart defects which had not been diagnosed pre-operatively despite extensive cardiological investigation. The hospital post mortem traditionally tended to be more extensive and take longer, and to be associated with a wish by the hospital to keep specimens for further analysis and for teaching purposes.

The coroners' examinations now constitute the vast majority of post mortems. For hospital deaths occurring in 1998 the Office of National Statistics found that 304,350 deaths took place in hospital, of which 59,264 were followed by post mortem examination, in 55,929 cases at the request of the coroner. (See Interim Report, p. 5, reporting unpublished information provided by the Office for National Statistics). The number of post mortems following death in hospital carried out not at the request of the coroner has fallen from 19,367 in 1984 to 11,199 in 1990 to only 3,335 in 1998.

How is it decided whether an autopsy should take place and if so under which heading? As a matter of law a registrar is obliged to refer to the coroner deaths which fall into a number of categories, including those where the cause of death appears to be unknown or where death appears to have occurred during an operation. In practice it is often the doctor who asks the coroner's office whether a post mortem may be carried out. With increasing pressure on hospital resources, and the desire of the clinicians to learn from autopsy, there may be institutional pressures involved in this changing balance towards the examinations which must by law be carried out, and where the cost does not fall on the hospital.

Under the Coroners Act 1988 and the Coroners rules which date from 1984, there is no statutory requirement for the coroner or his officers to obtain consent, nor is there any requirement to desist if relatives object before holding an inquest or seeking a post mortem, although there are provisions for relatives to be notified of the date and time of such an examination. Nor is there any statutory duty to provide the family with a copy of any report. In order to establish the cause of death it would be both lawful under Rule 9 and common practice to remove tissue for analysis. The difficulty in interpretation of the law arises when the post mortem examination is complete, and the coroner is satisfied concerning the cause of death and the death certificate issued. The coroner has then discharged his function and is "functus officio". At this stage, what is the legal status of any human materials removed and what should the pathologist do?

Professor Green told the Inquiry on day 42 that the prevailing view among the medical profession during the 1980s and early 1990s was that, when the analysis required by the coroner had been completed, material which had been removed by the hospital pathologist in his capacity as agent of the coroner reverted to being the property of the pathologists and the department which had processed it. As the materials had already been processed, and changed, it was therefore held to be perfectly licit to use such materials for research purposes, and he stressed that "it is perfectly licit to use that organ for teaching purposes". In 1996 the Royal College of Physicians advised on the use of "discarded tissue" that "the anonymous use for research of tissues removed at surgery or at autopsy is a traditional and ethically acceptable practice that does not need consent from patients or relatives . . . there may be legal constraints and it remains unclear to whom such samples belong in terms of beneficial ownership". In practice the length of time for which such materials could be kept by the hospital was not defined, nor whether these guidelines referred to histological slides or whether the term was meant to include entire organs. But when the coroner had finished with the case and his powers ceased, there would be no formal communication from his office to the pathology department instructing the hospital to dispose of the materials. As Professor Green said "They can tell you for how long you can keep it but they tend not to tell you that you must dispose of it. There is no disposal order" (day 42). Mr. Burgess, Secretary of the Coroner's Society (which has 140 members, all but six of whom are lawyers and of these all but eight are solicitors, paid but not employed by the local authority) commented that "The Coroner will expect the pathologist to clear his laboratory out periodically . . ." (day 43). A full review of the legal position at the time can be found in the Inquiry Interim Report, pp. 20–28).

In the case of hospital post mortems the procedure is quite different, and is governed by the Human Tissue Act 1961. Section 1 of the act is concerned not with post mortems but with the removal of parts of bodies for certain specified purposes, and the Act states at section (2) that:

> "the person lawfully in possession of the body of a deceased person may authorise the removal of any part from the body for therapeutic purposes, medical education or research if, having made such enquiry as may be practicable he has no reason to believe that the deceased had expressed an objection to his body being so dealt with or that any surviving relative objects".

This means there is no obligation on the hospital to seek a positive consent, but only to discover any objection by reasonable efforts. In practice the main difference between the two requirements is that the latter enables the procedure to be carried out in cases where no-one could be found to give consent. A similar procedure is required before a hospital post mortem is carried out under section 2(2) of the Human Tissue Act 1961.

5. RESOLVING THE CONFLICT BETWEEN EMOTION AND SCIENCE

The feelings expressed by the parents who gave evidence to the Bristol Inquiry are clearly at variance with the existing legal position. There was some disagreement over whether they would or would not have given permission for post mortem examination and the retention of materials, IF they had been asked. But there was unanimity over their concern for the necessity to seek that consent.

Practice in Bristol, however, had moved on at least some way from the minimum requirements of the 1961 Act and the Coroners Rules of 1984. For hospital post mortems the legal need to ensure the lack of objection was widely talked of as the need for gaining consent from relatives. Professor Berry had begun to develop more sympathetic forms for paediatric use, but had had to work hard to try to secure the support of his clinical colleagues. By the early 1990s he was becoming increasingly uncomfortable about the lack of clarity on the duties of pathologists concerning retention of tissue, especially as public sensitivity about the use of foetal tissue developed. He told the Inquiry that he was concerned about colleagues taking tissue in the course of work for the coroner which was necessary for establishing the cause of death, such as valves from the heart which could be used for other purposes, but he held to the view that tissue which had been lawfully taken could be used for the greater good. He also explained the confusion, which can arise, about the term "retention" with respect to human material. To the parent such a term sounds like taking and keeping a part of the body of their child for some length of time. To the pathologist the term was more limited in meaning, and referred to taking and keeping back some material for the clinico pathological discussion on the case. But the same term tends also to be used for long term retention for teaching and study by surgeons about to undertake a similar case, and for trainees.

Professor Berry described how post mortems were designed for establishing the cause of death in simpler times, when such causes would include falling off a horse—not deaths following complex medical procedures carried out by teams rather than an individual, and where there is a series of events which may result in a death. Marc de Leval, consultant paediatric cardiac surgeon at Great Ormond Street Hospital gave an account to the Inquiry of the research being carried out by Professor James Reason into the human factors involved in mortality in paediatric cardiac surgery. Reason and de Leval suggest that mortality in complex paediatric cardiac surgery tends to follow on not from a major adverse incident, as such a major event will be noted by all members of the team who will co-operate to counter the impact of the problem. Far more dangerous for the child were cases where a number of more minor problems developed, none of which were suffi-cient to alert the whole team to respond, but where the cumulative effect proved fatal. Professor Berry was of the view that the consent procedures for hospital post mortems should be more specific about the purpose of retention especially of entire organs, and should discuss eventual disposal.

The Interim Report of the BRII recommended a new code of practice, based on the principles of respect for parents and their dead child, and also the value of continued access to human material for the advancement of medical care and treatment. This code of practice could be incorporated into the medical profes-sional's terms of employment and could be overseen by a national regulatory body. It is suggested that although consent is not a requirement in law for a coro-ner's post mortem that parents should be informed, and, where they do object, that the coroner should provide an explanation as to why the examination is nec-essary. The parents' circumstances should be taken into account and the eventual disposal of any material not reunited with the body before burial or cremation should be agreed. Finally, any material to be kept after the completion of work for the coroner must be kept only with the parents' consent. The purposes for which it is to be kept should be defined, and procedures for final disposal agreed. For hos-pital post mortem, even though all that the law requires is the absence of objection, nevertheless the proposed new code of practice recommends that consent is sought.

The recommendations can be seen in full in the Interim Report and will not be discussed in further detail here. It is not the purpose of this chapter to discuss solu-tions, but rather to focus on the nature of the ongoing lack of congruence between the views of the parents, of the professionals and of the law. Parents felt betrayed, robbed and deceived. Pathologists believed that they were simply doing their job. The legal framework lay in between: complex, lacking in clarity and hard to access.

Two questions arise for the socio-legal scholar. First, what mechanism could be brought into play to enable a regulatory framework for the removal and retention of human material after death, to avoid these pitfalls and achieve clarity and acces-sibility for all those affected, both professionals and families, as well as acceptabil-ity and compliance? Secondly, what information and materials would facilitate the task of informing and updating outdated regulatory procedures?

Concerning the first question, the mechanism chosen by the BRII in its Interim Report has been briefly referred to as a code of practice but it is a code with a difference. It is not designed to be a professional code, at risk of capture by the professional group concerned, but to offer a national framework which could be incorporated into the terms and conditions of employment of those coming into contact with this kind of work. This would include the surgeons and physicians treating children who may not survive, as well as the pathologists themselves. The format of a regulatory code is not selected in preference to legislative change but was chosen as being a more accessible and immediate adjunct to legislation which might be required in the long term to shore up such provision.

As to the content of these regulations, given the conflicting views and expectations of parents and doctors, a valuable source of information lay in the work of the Confidential Enquiry into Stillbirths and Death in Infancy (CESDI), whose guidance offered to those needing to seek permission from recently bereaved parents to carry out post mortem examination leading to retention of material reads as if based on experience reflected upon with sensitivity. The CESDI guidance (see *The Fetal and Infant Post Mortem: Brief Notes for the Professional* (April 1999)) starts from trying to understand the experience of the parents, bearing in mind that, for some, this will be the loss of their first child while others will have other children to care for, and for some the experience will come after a long illness and for others after a brief emergency. But for all there will be a strong need to know where the baby is being taken, how the baby will be transported and by whom, and when the child will be returned. Parents need to know what to expect visually, and whether they will be able to dress or hold the child, and whether they or other family members would be able to spend time with the child afterwards. There may also be religious or cultural needs to be met, for example the Jewish need to hold a funeral before the Sabbath. For members of other religions a post mortem is believed to be an unacceptable invasion of bodily integrity. There may be implications arising from the Human Rights Act 1998, which has incorporated the European Convention on Human Rights into the law of the United Kingdom from 2 October 2000. Article 8 deals with the right to respect for private life and family life except where intervention is in accordance with the law and necessary in a democratic society for a number of reasons including the protection of health.

These recommendations have been presented to the Chief Medical Officer for England, and are under consideration. The process of changing the regulatory framework for paediatric post mortem was expedited by the nature of the Inquiry into the management and care of children receiving complex heart surgery at the Bristol Royal Infirmary. But it would be wrong to characterise the process of development as purely externally driven. Before any question of setting up external review arose, there was already the beginning of an iterative process, stimulated by pathologists at the forefront of the profession. In Bristol itself, Professor Berry was beginning to pay more attention to the need to take greater care over seeking more specific consent for the retention of entire organs as opposed to slides and microscopic specimens, and to specify the purpose and time period for which the materials were needed. There was also growing awareness of the need to make arrangements for disposal to comply with the wishes of the family, and to understand the special needs of the bereaved parents of a young baby. Professor Berry was involved in the preparation of guidelines by the Royal College of Pathologists published in 2000.

6. OBSERVATIONS

These ideas for change were coming from a variety of sources. There was a general increase in the attention paid proactively to the needs of the individual patient seen as an active consumer of medical care, rather than as a passive recipient, and also a recognition of the higher levels of knowledge and expectations among those in contact with the healthcare system. From a more critical perspective, we see also a questioning of the omnipotence of all professionals, not only the medical profession but also lawyers and teachers, which demanded that professional mystiques should be challenged and that their working methods should be more open and accountable. And there was also a need to control a potentially unacceptable development of scientific market-factors. The increase in the potential value of human materials for research and in treatment led to the development of a market in such items, in particular the possibility of using veins for vein grafting, and the use of fetal material in the treatment of Parkinson's disease (see Jonathan Herring (chapter 3)).

At the extreme end of this continuum we have seen the sale of gametes, and even the organs of healthy donors for transplantation. New institutions to cope with the resulting concerns and in particular the Nuffield Council for Bioethics have been established and are considering and reporting on these issues. (See, for example, the Nuffield Report on Human Tissue, Ethical and Legal Issues (April 1995)). The Home Office issued a circular letter concerning harvesting of venous materials in 1993. Controls were not only being discussed but also gradually being put into effect to deal with the commodification of human material. At the same time the pressure for some hospitals post 1991 after achieving Trust status, to balance budgets and to offer services for which there was a purchaser, resulted in the lack of demand for hospital post mortems which were not a high purchasing authority priority. The reduction in hospital post mortem work, before which family objections needed to be checked, and the increase in autopsy work for the coroner for which even objection was not a ground for holding back, led quite understandably to confusion for both the clinicians and the families. In the Bristol case, completed consent forms were available for almost every case of hospital post mortem, and the clinicians claimed that they had not proceeded without consent. But these hospital cases were in the minority, and for the majority of cases autopsy had been carried out for the coroner and no such consent had been required, with the result that the parents rightly claimed that they had not been asked for their permission before post mortem.

The matter became even more confusing when material quite correctly taken for work for the coroner was simply retained after the work for the coroner had been completed. This work in itself takes a period of time; for example, analysis of the heart must await proper perfusion, though this procedure is now being done more quickly. At the point of determination of cause of death such material ceased to be covered by the Coroner's rules but reverted to the requirements of the Human Tissue Act 1961 which covers work carried out for the hospital and requires the pathologist to check for any objection from the family. The pathologists were moving towards talking to the family about the reasons for autopsy, what would be done, with respect for any particular wishes of the family, even when working within the requirements of the coronial jurisdiction. But it is clear that at this stage in the transition process, when a number of factors were working for change, the law was not providing a helpful framework, and to seek a change in the law is a lengthy and fraught process in a matter of such sensitivity. Reliance on professional reflection, sensitivity and capacity for change would require either a triumph of hope over experience or a profession which has the time and space to develop the necessary capacity for reflection and development. The third way, of seeking a regulatory framework devised as a code of professional practice nationally agreed, but given enforceability through incorporation in the contract of employment, offers not only the possibility of rapid change but also a flexible procedure for revising and updating at a time of rapid change in both the needs of the scientists and of the norms and values of a culturally diverse society. But whatever the mechanism, there can be no easy way around the moment at which the responsibility of the parent for her child becomes shared with the responsibility of the scientists and doctors who need to learn from the study of what has become redefined as human material.

REFERENCES

RUSSELL, G.R. and BERRY, P.J., "Post-Mortem Audit in a Paediatric Cardiology Unit" (1989) 49 *Journal of Clinical Pathology* 912.

6

Male Medical Students and the Male Body

MARTIN H JOHNSON*

1. INTRODUCTION

Doctors are required by society to engage in the visual and tactile exploration of areas of our bodies usually considered private and intimate, such as our genitalia, breasts and rectums, and, for some patients and religions, any body part. They undertake these examinations as men or women, with their own internally absorbed social and cultural body lore, but also as professionals within a legal and ethical framework of respect for patient autonomy. The imperatives of lore and law may collide. How do they cope? Is their coping appropriate? Can different coping mechanisms be developed? This chapter explores these questions in respect of male medical students and examination of the male genitalia.

There is an implicit "contract" between doctor and patient that bodily access is granted exclusively for professional purposes, and there is a strictly enforced policing (both preventative and retributive) of transgressions by either party (General Medical Council (1998)). The general framework of patient consent may operate at an implied or an explicit level. Thus, consent to straightforward clinical investigation is implied by the visit of a patient to a doctor or in a medical emergency. However, the sensitive doctor will none the less ask permission to proceed to a physical examination, especially if this involves investigation of sexual body parts, during which doctors are advised always to have a chaperone present for their own as much as their patient's welfare. Should, however, a doctor exceed or stray from what would be considered professional standard practice during a genital examination, or undertake for example genital examination where this was unnecessary, he or she would be transgressing patient autonomy by abusing their consent (implied or explicit), and would be guilty of a sexual assault, since any consent would no longer be valid. At least in theory this could lead to criminal prosecution.

Although legal and ethical issues surrounding the examination of the body are addressed during medical training, issues to do with body lore are by and large not

* I wish to thank former students for the work they did with us. I also thank Penny Henderson, Simon Christmas and Martin Richards for their critical and constructive readings of an early draft of this chapter.

addressed. Medical students are given remarkably little opportunity to address explicitly the emotional and attitudinal issues raised, their personal concerns, or possible strategies for coping successfully. How the students feel about a clinical procedure or body type or part will affect how they act as doctors. The Education Committee of the General Medical Council (GMC (1993)) has raised the general issue of training doctors to have "appropriate attitudes", but gave rather general guidance on how this educational aim might be translated into objectives, and no guidance on how, in practice, any identified objectives might be achieved (see Johnson and Henderson (2000) for discussion). Over the past ten years, Cambridge University Anatomy Department has been evolving a course which attempts to address attitudinal issues as part of its aims. A central objective has been to develop reflective skills in students as a tool to help them understand and integrate personal and professional attitudes and, thereby, achieve appropriate professional behaviours. The approach has generated interest in other professions, such as law and the priesthood, in which personal and professional conflict may affect professional behaviour such that, for example, the "legal body" or the "religious body" may become sites of potential conflict for the professional.

In this chapter, material generated by students on the course is used to address the issues raised for the doctor by his privileged professional access to the patient's body and to explain how the actual process of generating this material can itself aid a constructive approach to resolving many of the issues. These issues are neither simple nor homogenous. Key variables are the genders of doctor and patient, their relative ages, their culture and religious beliefs, and their sexualities. The focus of this chapter is on access by male doctors to male bodies and, specifically, male genitalia. First, however, the wider literature is briefly reviewed to give this narrower focus a context.

2. THE DOCTOR AND THE BODY

Traditionally medical students have encountered the dilemma of the "body" in the first week or two of their training when they enter the dissecting room. This "rite of passage" is stressful for most and traumatic for some. Students confront the internal dilemma that here lies a body that was recently a person. The body is usually that of an old person and may evoke associations with grandparents, but other associations around relationships, loss by death of peers or family or so on can be triggered (Druce and Johnson (1994)). The students are then required to touch and dissect this body. The available evidence suggests that most do so by separating thoughts and feelings about the body as "person" from those about the body as "object to aid the learning of anatomy" (Druce and Johnson (1994); Evans and Fitzgibbon (1992)), and that men are more likely to do this consciously than women (Dickinson et al. (1997)). This is a form of denial by mental segregation, which in a small minority of students may be difficult to achieve (Evans and Fitzgibbon (1992)); Finkelstein and Mathers (1999)). For other students, the achievement may be vulnerable to events. For example, the dissection of specific body parts such as the eye or the palm of the hand or the genitalia may breach the barrier temporarily. There is also evidence that the variety of personal strategies used by different students to maintain the segregation may lead to mutual difficulty among peers. For example, humour may be used by some to reinforce denial, in for example how body parts are handled or in the "naming" of the body: while releasing emotional concerns in some students this approach may elicit them in others who wish to maintain respect for the person who was the body (Druce and Johnson (1994)).

Denial may be an appropriate response to help achieve an immediate and essentially unavoidable objective, in this case the learning of human anatomy. However, if this experience provides a highly formative model for trainee doctors on how to deal later with living bodies (patients), then in the long run it may be inappropriate (Gustavson (1988); Weeks, Harris and Kinzey (1995)). Learning, particularly from emotive situations, can produce recurring behavioural responses in a context-dependent manner (Jolly et al. (1985)). The initiation into the dissecting room has characteristics likely to make it highly formative, being emotionally charged (Pillemer (1998)), coming early in their training in an alien and new environment, binding students together and separating them from their non-medical peers, and being generally inadequately prepared for and processed by their teachers. Students are "expected to deal with it" as part of their own personal development, although surveys of their attitudes show that most want more help to do so (Druce and Johnson (1994); Penney (1985)). Courses can be structured to be helpful (Marks, Bertman and Penney (1997)). The fact that many students deal with the immediate situation by denial, and that this works, plausibly sets a paradigm for their interactions with living bodies, in which the doctors' traditional approach has indeed been criticised as too focused on the body and its disease and inadequately on the person and their illness (Balint (1986); Kurtz, Silverman and Draper (1998); Lupton (1994)). Indeed, it is possible to understand the actions of doctors in removing and retaining without parental consent post mortem samples from children as representing a failure to properly understand or use this artificially imposed mental segregation of the living and the dead body (see Mavis Maclean (chapter 5)). Thus, the mechanism of denial may have less appeal as a way of dealing with living bodies if the boundary between the two mental and emotional domains comes to be navigated inappropriately.

Similar concerns arise over the narrower issue of access by doctors to the patient's genitalia. There is some literature on issues raised by the access by doctors to female bodies, although this is largely from the perspective of the patient. However, there is evidence that if students are taught in ways that do not respect their own sensitivities, then they are less likely to examine patients sensitively, or may avoid performing examinations at all, leading to potential misdiagnosis. Patients are adept at picking up discomfort in doctors, and this may lead to implicit collusion in avoidance or delay of necessary physical examinations (vaginal, rectal, testicular, breast), which may lead to delayed diagnosis and less effective therapy.

Thus, addressing the student's own concerns early in training is likely to have major beneficial effects on the attitudes, clinical skills and therapeutic effectiveness of doctors (Billings and Stoekle (1977); Robinson (1985)). Teaching the pelvic exam- ination of women to medical students has been a very sensitive area for patients (Bewley (1992)), and a few studies have addressed the concerns of students and staff and how they cope (Buchwald (1979)), as well as reporting on experimental learning strategies designed to reduce concern, such as use of "trained" professional patients (Beckman, Barzansky, Sharf et al. (1988); Shain, Crouch and Weinberg (1990)) and undertaking examinations on one another (Metcalf, Prentice, Metcalf et al. (1982)).

3. AN APPROACH TO LEARNING

Against this background, the more specific issue of male medical students and male bodies will now be considered. The chapter is based around an exercise that we have developed for use with third year pre-clinical students at Cambridge University. A group of about eighteen to twenty-four students meets once a week for sixteen weeks. Each week different issues are explored, largely experientially, under the guidance of two or three facilitators. A key element in the learning process is that students either experience a situation in an exercise devised by the facilitators or formally draw on their own past experiences in a structured way. These activities are then "processed" by the students in a way that encourages learning and develops useful strategies (see Henderson et al. (2001); Johnson and Henderson (2000) for discussion in more detail of the general conditions required to make this learning effective). For most of the time, male and female students work together, but for two exercises males and females work separately. I use the experience of developing one of these exercises both to illustrate the nature of the issues raised by the students and to offer a process for constructive education about them. Because process is important, the conduct of the exercise is described in some detail.

4. THE EXERCISE

The exercise is experienced by male students with one or two male facilitators. The specific objective of the exercise is for each student to identify his attitude towards the male genitalia and to explore how this attitude might affect his behaviour pro- fessionally. The exercise is performed as described below.

(1) A group of six to twelve male students is shown a silent two minute clip from the video "Private Dick" by one or two male facilitators. This video shows a sequence of brief (three to five seconds) shots of the genital region (penis, testes, loins and upper thighs) of a range of men of different ages and races.

The students are asked to remain silent throughout.

(2) Each student is then given a card and, without discussion, they are asked to record on the card their *feelings* about what they have just seen. It is explained that what they write will *not* be identifiable to them and will be seen by one other person (a facilitator) only. If they wish, they may print what they write. They are given one minute only.

(3) The cards are placed face down on the floor, shuffled, and collected by a facilitator, who then reads out the recorded feelings whilst two of the students write them on a flip chart.

(4) The students then look at the recorded words before group processing begins as described in the text.

After the students have looked in silence at the material generated (Table 6.1), they are then asked for any reactions to what they see. Characteristic responses are "Its all mostly pretty negative/awful/disrespectful/not very proud", while some may respond more dismissively "this is a waste of time/what do you expect/this is daft". On one occasion, an "out" gay student commented that he really could not relate to the words he saw and he was amazed by it. It can then be helpful for the facilitator to suggest that the students might like to try and group the material, e.g. positive-negative-neutral, or celebrating-discussing-ignoring-denying, or nasty-humorous-affectionate. This process of sorting can start to elicit and explore some of the reasons behind the reactions.

When the students are broadly satisfied with their sorting, the facilitator can then ask: "So overall, does this material provide an accurate representation of how each of you feels about your own genitalia?". This question can be quite difficult for the students. Usually, there are immediate protestations that their feelings about their own genitalia are quite different. It is usually not useful to pursue responses to this question at this point beyond simply drawing their attention to the fact that some of them at least seem to be holding two apparently conflicting models in their minds: men's genitalia are not very nice, but my male genitalia are.

Table 6.1: List of feelings recorded (drawn from several sessions)

Note: where the word on the card was not a "feeling" it was wherever possible converted to one by the facilitator, e.g. disgusted for disgusting, foolish for "made a fool of". Terms which appeared frequently are marked (c).

Disgusted (c)	Amused	Hurt	Empty
Bored	Sick/Pukey	Foolish (c)	Ill
Nothing* (c)	Excited/ Aroused**	Offended	Negative
Dirty	Ridiculous	Sheepish	Put-Off
Embarrassed (c)	Angry (c)	Assaulted	Upset/Distressed

*   In discussion it emerged this could mean either numb or uninterested.
** Later "owned" by gay students.

This can then be followed by a second question: "Given that you as a group have such a negative view of other men's genitalia, how will this influence how you perform examinations and/or manipulations (e.g. penile catheterisation) on the genitalia of your male patients?". The responses to this second question tend to be slower and more reflective. "I guess I am not looking forward to doing it . . . I'll try and avoid it . . . I'll get the nurse to do as much as possible. . . . I'll be very formal, with minimal contact, physically or eye to eye . . . I won't linger over it . . . It's part of any professional work, so I'll treat it just like examining a hand or any other body part . . . it's not an issue in the consulting room, is it?" Almost all these responses rely on denial, avoidance or authority, responses that would disconnect the doctor from the patient, and profoundly affect the doctor–patient interaction. Not surprisingly, therefore, few responses go beyond the doctor's dilemma to the patient's likely experience. So we then ask explicitly how they think the man being examined might be feeling and whether their approaches are likely to be helpful to him? More specifically, are their attitudes going to impair or delay the chances of an accurate diagnosis or reliable treatment? Two main points generally emerge in the discussion that follows: (1) the patients will have difficulties with the examination, as do the doctors, and (2) the doctors are probably not going to do it very effectively.

At this point, it is useful to suggest that the students work in pairs or threes to discuss a couple of questions (see below) in turn. We explain that their discussion on specifics will be confidential to them, but they will be asked to bring back some general points for plenary discussion. Then the first question for discussion is flip-charted and followed, after ten to twenty minutes depending on time constraints and the level of intensity of work being done, by the second question. Ten to twenty minutes after this, they are called back to plenary with the facilitator(s). It is useful to give them some advance warning (say three to five minutes) of when question 2 and the return to plenary are coming. The reason for going into small groups without a facilitator present at this point is that by this stage the students have already been taken sufficiently far into territory perceived as potentially dangerous personally to open up the issue, but have also been shown the professional context of the issue and the potential difficulties it poses. Going into small groups provides a safer place for personal disclosure of fears, experiences, worries that can then be drawn upon to prepare solutions. Experience shows that small group work followed by plenary work is successful in moving the students' work forwards. The plenary sessions can then draw out themes from the two questions, and the students can be asked to continue this process when reflecting on the day's work and writing their evaluations of it. Some general points that emerge in respect of each of the questions are summarised below, but it should be stressed that not all apply to all men. These are themes that tend to recur.

Question 1: "Can you identify what lies behind your reactions to the videos of men's genitalia?"

From their shared discussions it seems that men are particularly worried about inappropriate genital arousal (or lack of it), potentially stigmatising them as gay or non-masculine. Some men are, or have been, worried that their own genitalia are in some way inadequate or abnormal and will be demonstrated as such in comparison to other men, but are unsure how to find out—interestingly, their experiences with doctors have not been good by and large. Although they are both curious and ignorant about other men's genitalia in relation to their own, "looking" is described as furtive and is discouraged as "poofterish" or "perverted", and so routes to resolving curiosity and ignorance tend to be oblique. Men associate their genitalia with excretory functions and therefore as being smelly or dirty in some way. This is both a useful "defensive" view to keep other men away, but equally makes other men aversive for them. Finally, it is clear that men do not talk seriously amongst themselves about their own genitalia: it is usually done by boasting or joking. It should be noted that for some men male genitalia may be associated with sexual abuse or rape, and the facilitators should be prepared to be very sensitive to this issue if it arises.

This list is not exhaustive. It would be interesting to know whether the same list would derive from equivalent work with women about their genitalia or with a group of gay male medical students about male genitalia. What does seem to be uniquely valuable to these men is that they have been able to share the discussion. This value is the single strongest recurrent theme that runs through their evaluations. It is almost as though they have been liberated by the process. There appears to be substantial male denial about the reality of their "shared genitalia", and medical students are not an exception despite what will be expected of them. We then use their analysis and experience of the process that they have gone through to help them move on productively with the second question.

> *Question 2*: "Does an understanding of what lies behind your reactions help you to devise possible strategies for coping more effectively with male genital examination and/or manipulation clinically?"

A number of suggestions emerges. Since this exercise has helped them to talk about this issue by "defusing it" , perhaps by identifying and providing the conditions that have made this discussion possible for them, they might in turn be able to apply them to their patients. They then do some identifying and generalise from it. They also suggest expanding the serious discussion of male genitalia with other male peers not on the course to (1) ease their own concerns, (2) experiment and practice to see what helps them and others to achieve a serious discussion. Identifying and confronting their own individual "hang-ups" rather than denying them is considered, as is identifying the support they might need to do that. Sometimes it is suggested (or can be suggested by the facilitator) that if talking about genital examination among themselves helps, could actually doing it with each other under controlled supervision help? This suggestion usually provokes an immediate negative reaction, which always then moderates as they attempt to identify and then consider how to provide conditions that might make the approach both acceptable and useful. There is a general awareness that being honest with their patients at a level that seems appropriate might be helpful, as might even asking for feedback on whether they are examining/manipulating sensitively. The facilitator can interpolate that this may need to be done cautiously at first and developed through experience. These general points can be fleshed out more specifically in discussion, with practical strategies. Most importantly, they provide a framework which gives the students confidence that they *can* go forward, take risks and learn productively. They also now have each other to call on for support when doing so.

The qualitative outcomes derived both from the discussions and from written student evaluations suggest that the specific objective of the exercise ("for each student to identify his attitude towards the male genitalia and how this might affect his behaviour professionally") is substantially achieved.

5. DISCUSSION

The exercise described is effective at achieving two important outcomes, which might be classified broadly as personal and professional learning. In achieving these outcomes, it also helps to integrate both types of learning into a more coherent framework.

(a) Personal learning outcomes

The exercise seems to liberate young men to reflect and talk about an issue that they normally do not seem to discuss seriously. By being explicit, thinking and discussing the unthinkable and/or unspeakable, the students articulate concerns, confront fears, discover that some are common, but also understand how individual males differ from one another. This reflection is continued in their written evaluations. This personal learning process accesses areas that may have been denied or suppressed through lack of any effective safe protocol for otherwise reaching them. The exercise achieves progress in addressing this deficit through its three step structure. First, the exercise extracts from the students themselves a set of responses, which they are then unable easily to disown and so must engage with, a structure which subverts their defences and denial. Secondly, it demonstrates the professional relevance of the engagement, thereby providing "an authorisation" to explore a dangerous area further and to do so productively (Johnson and Henderson (2000)). Thirdly, it encourages fruitful mutual exploration by providing small groups in which discussion can be risked. This process is then summarised in a final plenary session, which focuses on practical ways to take the understanding forward through the development of strategies for experimental learning professionally.

An effective mechanism for addressing taboo issues such as that raised in this exercise is needed more widely and not just in professional education. Other studies have found that young men generally talk less (or differently) than women about intimate and emotional issues both with one another (Cheng and Chan

(1999); Floyd (1995); Johnson (2001); Nardi (1992); Roy, Benenson and Lilly (2000)) and to support organisations (MacLeod and Barter (1996)), and tend to delegate sexual health concerns to women and be ignorant or denying about aspects of their own bodies other than as a means to assert their masculinity (Barker (2000); Forrest (2000). A problem with sex education with young men has been a group tendency to subvert and joke so as to impress peers and girls and not reveal vulnerability or ignorance in front of peers (Forrest (2000); Measor, Tiffin and Fry (1996)). Such inter-male group discussion about sexual matters as does occur seems to be predominantly about boosting sexual status (Gorgen et al. (1998); Holland, Ramazanoglu, Sharpe et al. (2000); Marsiglio (1988)). Richard Collier (chapter 9) has pointed out the legal and social consequences that may derive from social collusion with this denial of the reality of how men behave, especially when attempting to change men's behaviour. In medical education, there has traditionally been a use of "black humour" as a way of coping with situations that otherwise are denied and not discussed, for example, jokes about a person's facility at rectal examination and homosexuality, or about penis size or tumescence in dissected cadavers. These types of group male behaviours deny individual men's needs, concerns and vulnerabilities (Forrest (2000)), which can be revealed and shared if men are given, or circumstances compel them to take, the opportunities for personal reflection and secure group discussion (Barker (2000)). All men are not the same. Yet, despite the fact that the men worked with here are a self-selected group of students who are highly intelligent, embarking on a caring profession and have knowingly selected a course that confronts emotionally difficult issues, even most of them clearly have not reflected deeply on the matters raised nor shared their reflections with other men. In the process of doing this, they begin to realise that many of their socially expressed attitudes towards genitalia derive from fears about not being thought fully male, and the serious consequences for them of being seen to have such an identity. The body is a major danger zone for their betrayal with both women (performance anxiety; Holland et al. (2000)) and with men (inappropriate contact and, worse, arousal; Nardi (1992)). In addition, it is useful for them to articulate other emotional responses to the body, such as revulsion or disgust. The explicit awareness of their socially absorbed concepts of the "masculine role" in our society (Formaini (1999)) and their personal concerns about and behaviours towards the male body that this exercise raises is a first step to confronting and understanding the concerns in a constructive way, something they need to do if they are to behave professionally.

(b) Professional learning outcomes

In education generally, and professional education such as medicine and law in particular, there has perhaps been too little emphasis on the role that emotions can play in conditioning intellectual and behavioural activities. Thus, the expression of emotion professionally is generally disapproved of, and this disapproval has translated somewhat illogically into training and educational regimes that encourage suppression of emotion and thereby denial of its importance. Perhaps a more logical response to teaching how to arrive at sound professional decision-making and behaviours is to encourage students to identify how important emotions are and to offer them containment or management strategies. In making this suggestion, it is not being suggested that denial is always an inappropriate response to a situation. In many medical situations, the ability to focus on a task without distraction may only be achievable through emotional shut down by denial. It is suggested, however, that a permanent state of denial is likely to be harmful to both the doctor and his patients. The capacity to switch denial on and off as appropriate to task or situation is a key skill that doctors could usefully be encouraged to develop. The General Medical Council has emphasised the ethical dimension to caring and considerate treatment of both patients and colleagues (GMC (1993, 1998)). If medical education does not help doctors to achieve this effectively, it will fail them and may lay them open to legal challenge for negligent practice.

The exercise described uncovers two sorts of denial. First, there is the professed belief that "my genitalia are good whereas those of other men are bad", and secondly there is the belief that "personal genitalia" are different from "professional genitalia". The exercise works to make explicit these contradictions and explores where they might come from. It thus provides professional learning by helping to defuse, in advance of their entry to the wards, concerns the man has about physical contacts between him and his male patient's genitalia. It does so by offering a platform for discussion and understanding of the range of reactions of the men present, from which then to explore strategies for dealing with the concerns raised, with a risk-based learning process to test them. The advantage of not having to deal with these difficult issues in front of patients or even on the wards is considerable, because professional performance anxiety is avoided. The students can give their full attention to the personal issues raised and then move to consider professional implications and how to address them. One might regard the first part as diagnostic and the second part as therapeutic, to capture a clinical analogy. Moreover, as a group of students has embarked on this process together, there is a learning and support group for continuing work and the pooling of experiences and strategies.

(c) Personal-professional integration

The structured exercise described here, together with the subsequent reflection as the students write their evaluations, offers a route to the breaking down of conscious or unconscious barriers between different parts of the student's experiences as men. They confront the incongruity of their views on their own and other men's genitalia, and begin to understand its origins. The men reflect on how their emotions can affect profoundly their thoughts and actions to undermine their professional effectiveness, and how (and why) personal strategies developed for one context might conflict with social and professional expectations in a different context. Understanding that this is the case may enable them to accept the conflict and manage it more effectively in their own and the patients' interests. It may even allow them to start resolving conflicts between different parts of their experience and to start assembling a more integrated view in which professional and personal coherence of attitudes and behaviours is more possible. Whilst segregation and denial may be a useful short-term device for getting through a difficult situation, there is increasingly a view that integrating experience within a coherent conceptual framework gives greater personal robustness, for example approaches to bereavement that accommodate the dead within a framework for continued living (Walter (1996)), to recovery from traumatic shock disorder by integrating the trauma effectively into continuing life (Herman (1992)), to acquiring an integrated adult attachment pattern (Rosenberg (1997)) by integrating childhood images into a mature adult narrative (Spence (1982)), and by reconciling the personal and the social selves (Harter (1997)).

In the context of the physical relationship between doctor and patient, it may well seem possible for male doctors to contain unresolved personal attitudes to the male body in a discrete compartment of their experience, and behave responsibly. However, it seems likely that such a fragmented state will result in attitudes spilling over this barrier either subtly in the way the doctor signals his inner feelings through body language, or explicitly when he is under pressure. A non-integrated approach to practice is also likely to generate internal tensions that undermine the doctor's own health. It is well established, for example, that doctors are very bad at recognising (or admitting) ill health in themselves (Bolsover (2000); Mandell and Spiro (1987)), another example perhaps of compartmentalisation of one's own body and that of "the patient"? An understanding of his own feelings and attitudes and where they come from is a first step to then incorporating them constructively into a personal and professional framework. A similar approach, tailored appropriately, to address the more general issue of integrating the medical students' attitudes to the dissected cadaver in relation to the living body might likewise be adopted through a death studies learning module. The medical body might thereby cease to be a site of lore-law conflict. Since there must be a presumption that we would prefer to be treated by doctors who have made some progress in integrating their own personal and professional lives effectively, this exercise, and others like it, may offer possibly fruitful educational routes for doctors and patients alike. Might a similar approach for legal education also render the legal body less of a lore-law battle ground?

REFERENCES

BALINT, M., *The Doctor, his Patient and the Illness* (Edinburgh, Churchill Livingstone, 1986).
BARKER, G., 'Gender Equitable Boys in a Gender Inequitable World: Reflections from Qualitative Research and Programme Development in Rio de Janeiro' (2000) 15 *Sexual and Relationship Therapy* 263.

BECKMAN, C., BARZANSKY, B., SHARF, B. et al., "Training Gynaecological Teaching Associates" (1988) 22 *Medical Education* 124.

BEWLEY, S., "The Law, Medical Students and Assault" (1992) 13 *British Medical Journal* 6.

BILLINGS, A. and STOEKLE, J., "Pelvic Examination Instruction and the Doctor-Patient Relationship" (1977) 52 *Journal of Medical Education* 10.

BOLSOVER, G., "Doctors who are Unsympathetic to Colleagues who are Psychologically Vulnerable" (2000) 321 *British Medical Journal* 635.

BUCHWALD, J., "The First Pelvic Examination—helping Students Cope with their Emotional Reactions" (1979) 54 *Journal of Medical Education* 9.

CHENG, S. and CHAN, A., "Sex, Competitiveness, and Intimacy in Same-Sex Friendship in Hong Kong Adolescents" (1999) 84 *Psychological Reports* 45.

DICKINSON, G. E., LANCASTER, C. J., WINFIELD, I. C. et al., "Detached Concern and Death Anxiety of First Year Medical Students: Before and After the Gross Anatomy Course" (1997) 10 *Clinical Anatomy* 201.

DRUCE, M. and JOHNSON, M. H., "Human Dissection and Attitudes of Pre-Clinical Students to Death and Bereavement" (1994) 7 *Clinical Anatomy* 42.

EVANS, E. J. and FITZGIBBON, G. H., "The Dissecting Room: Reactions of First Year Medical Students" (1992) 5 *Clinical Anatomy* 10.

FINKELSTEIN, P. and MATHERS, L., "Post-Traumatic Stress Among Medical Students in the Anatomy Dissection Laboratory" (1990) 3 *Clinical Anatomy* 219.

FLOYD, K., "Gender and Closeness among Friends and Siblings" (1995) 129 *Journal of Psychology* 193.

FORMAINI, A., *Men: the Darker Continent* (London, Heinemann, 1990).

FORREST, S., " 'Big and Tough': Boys Learning About Sexuality and Manhood" (2000) 15 *Sexual and Relationship Therapy* 248.

GMC, *Tomorrow's Doctors* (London, General Medical Council, 1993).

——, *Good Medical Practice* (2nd edn., London, General Medical Council of the United Kingdom, 1998).

GORGEN, R., YANSANE, M., MARX, M. et al., "Sexual Behaviours and Attitudes Among Unmarried Youth in Guinea" (1998) 24 *International Family Planning Perspectives* 65.

GUSTAVSON, N., "The Effect of Human Dissection on First-Year Students and Implications for the Doctor–Patient Relationship" (1988) 63 *Journal of Medical Education* 62.

HARTER, S., "The Personal Self in Social Context: Barriers to Authenticity" in R. D. Ashmore and L. Jussim (eds.), *Self and Identity: Fundamental Issues* (New York and Oxford, Oxford University Press, 1997) p. 81.

HENDERSON, P., JOHNSON, M., BARNETT, M. et al., "Supporting Medical Students to Take Responsibility for Developing their Communication Skills" (2001) 23 *Medical Teacher* 86.

HERMAN, J. L., *Trauma and Recovery* (New York, Basic Books, 1992).

HOLLAND, J., RAMAZANOGLU, C., SHARPE, S. et al., "Deconstructing Virginity—Young People's Accounts of First Sex" (2000) 15 *Sexual and Relationship Therapy* 221.

JOHNSON, M., "Exploring Masculinity with Male Medical Students" (2001) 16 *Sexual and Relationship Therapy* 165.

JOHNSON, M. H. and HENDERSON, P., "Acquiring and Demonstrating Attitudes in Medical Education: Attitudes to Homosexuality as a Case Study" (2000) 22 *Medical Teacher* 586.

JOLLY, B., COLES, C., NORMAN, G. et al., "The Generalisability of Knowledge and the Assessment of Clinical Performance" in *Directions in Clinical Assessment* (Cambridge, Office of the Regius Professor of Physic, 1985) p. 42.

KURTZ, S., SILVERMAN, J. and DRAPER, J., *Teaching and Learning Communication Skills in Medicine* (Oxford, Radcliffe Medical Press, 1998).

LUPTON, D., *Medicine as Culture: Illness, Disease, and the Body in Western Societies* (London, Sage, 1994).

MACLEOD, M. and BARTER, C., *We Know its Tough to Talk: Boys in Need of Help* (London, Childline, 1996).

MANDELL, H. and SPIRO, H., *When Doctors Get Sick* (New York, Pleum Medical Book Co, 1987).

MARKS, S. C., BERTMAN, S. L. and PENNEY, J. C., "Human Anatomy: a Foundation for Education about Death and Dying in Medicine" (1997) 10 *Clinical Anatomy* 118.

MARSIGLIO, W., "Adolescent Male Sexuality and Heterosexual Masculinity: a Conceptual Model and Review" (1988) 3 *Journal of Adolescent Research* 285.

MEASOR, L., TIFFIN, C. and FRY, K., "Gender and Sex Education: a Study of Adolescent Responses" (1996) 8 *Gender and Education* 275.

METCALF, N., PRENTICE, E., METCALF, W. et al., "Peer Group Models in Examination Instruction as an Integral Part of Medical Gross Anatomy" (1982) 57 *Journal of Medical Education* 8.

NARDI, P., *Men's Friendships* (London, Sage Publications, 1992).

PENNEY, J. C., "Reactions of Medical Students to Dissection" (1985) 60 *Journal of Medical Education* 58.

PILLEMER, D. B., *Momentous Events, Vivid Memories* (Cambridge, Mass., Harvard University Press, 1998).

ROBINSON, J., "Are We Teaching Students that Patients Don't Matter?" (1985) 11 *Journal of Medical Ethics* 15.

ROSENBERG, S., "Multiplicity of Selves" in R. D. Ashmore and L. Jussim (eds.), *Self and Identity: Fundamental Issues* (New York and Oxford, Oxford University Press, 1997) p. 23.

ROY, R., BENENSON, J. and LILLY, F., "Beyond Intimacy: Conceptualising Sex Differences in Same-Sex Friendships" (2000) 134 *Journal of Psychology* 93.

SHAIN, R., CROUCH, S. and WEINBERG, P., "Acquisition of Pelvic Examination Skills: Evaluation of Student Feelings about a Surrogate Patient Programme" (1990) 162 *Journal of Psychosomatic Obstetrics and Gynaecology* 4.

SPENCE, D. P., *Narrative Truth and Historical Truth* (New York, Norton, 1982).

WALTER, T., "A New Model of Grief: Bereavement and Biography" (1996) 1 *Mortality* 7.

WEEKS, S. E ., HARRIS, E. E. and KINZEY, W. G., "Human Gross Anatomy: a Crucial Time to Encourage Respect and Compassion" (1995) 8 *Clinical Anatomy* 69.

7

Domestic Homicide, Gender and the Expert

FELICITY KAGANAS*

1. INTRODUCTION

"ON MATTERS IN which the legal system is accused of being draconian . . ., it is often the case that the motivation is a fear of reckless precedent . . . There are women who kill their male partners in genuine terror for their lives; but courts are often hard on such cases because of the danger of encouraging murder as an alternative to divorce" (Mark Lawson, "Topsy-Turvey Logic of the Terminator", *The Guardian*, 22 April 2000, p. 16).

For that journalist, the solution to an abused woman's predicament is generally simple: divorce. And in many cases this is undoubtedly correct. However, his views reflect a popular failure to appreciate the reality of the lives of those women driven by fear or despair to kill, a failure which extends, to some degree, also to the legal system. That domestic violence is gendered in nature and that the responses of victims of abuse too are gendered are factors to which the criminal law has remained largely impervious. Unless they fall within the narrow parameters of the defences of self-defence or provocation, the actions of these women can be categorised by the criminal law only as either bad or mad; they do not qualify as reasonable responses to unreasonable situations. Unless these women behave as the reasonable man would, by fighting back or by walking out, the law has shown itself unwilling to excuse or exonerate their behaviour. Their principal recourse has been to seek to show that they suffer from some abnormality of mind.

Part of the problem facing abused women who kill lies in the reluctance of the criminal law to take cognisance of the social context within which offences are committed: "the legal subject is constructed as a gender-less, race-less, class-less individual abstracted from its social situation" (Lacey and Wells (1998)). As a result, embodied gender is rendered invisible. The embodied power of men who abuse women and the effects of the exercise of that power on victims disappear in the face of apparently commonsensical and neutrally applied legal rules. And the actions of women whose bodies are constantly threatened or attacked, who have

* I would like to thank William Wilson, Andrew Choo and Alison Diduck for their helpful comments on earlier drafts.

learned that resistance or retaliation are fruitless or even dangerous, are judged as the acts of autonomous, freely choosing agents unconstrained by their circum-stances.

Another, and more important, factor in relation to domestic homicide is the "implicit masculinity" (*ibid.*) discernible in the law. Even where it does acknow-ledge the salience of context, as it seems to do in respect of the defences of provo-cation and self-defence, the law has tended to evaluate the actions of the defendant within that context against a standard that reflects typically male behaviour. Rendered "gender-less", women who kill have been judged against an implicitly male template and many simply do not measure up; the reasonable person of law is embodied as male (O'Donovan (1993) p. 428). Their difficulties have been com-pounded by the fact that it has not been easy to counter the adverse inferences drawn from the nature and timing of their actions; that some wait until their assailants are physically most vulnerable before striking condemns them.

Gender-blind, the law has shown itself oblivious of the gendered power rela-tions that characterise abusive relationships and the actions of abused women who kill have been scrutinised through the lens of common sense. That stock of common-sense knowledge deployed by law does not encompass the growing body of knowledge about domestic violence emanating from research produced by the "psy" professions and by social scientists. Moreover, such knowledge cannot, scholars assert, easily be brought to law's attention; since courts are thought to need no help in understanding the "normal" world, generalised expert evidence about domestic violence is hard to introduce (Lacey and Wells (1998) p. 591). It is suggested that it is only when women's experiences of and responses to abuse are couched in medicalised terms suggesting abnormality, such as "battered woman syndrome", that they have readily been admitted in the form of expert evidence (*ibid.*). In that event, battered women's actions become explicable through science and excusable in law. But the price of this is the marginalisation of the women's experiences and their designation as "mad" (Lacey and Wells (1998) p. 591; Raitt and Zeedyk (2000) ch. 4).

By locating the problem within the woman who kills rather than in the mater-ial conditions of her life, the law has failed to address fully the relevance of the more intractable problem of domestic violence and the deficiencies in the services available to protect victims of it. By ignoring the available evidence of the nature and effects of abuse, the law has misinterpreted and so, arguably, has not judged fairly the actions of its victims. However, recent developments point to the begin-nings of change.

Increasingly, the issue of domestic violence has been attracting the attention of the media and increasingly it is being portrayed as a serious social problem. Government has clearly felt a need to demonstrate its concern and has announced the launch of initiatives to provide better protection and improved resources for vic-tims (Home Office (2000)).The law too has responded to the greater visibility of the risks and the difficulties faced by abused women and their children. And although this response has hitherto been confined principally to the sphere of family law, there appears to be greater readiness within criminal law too to take cognisance of domestic violence. In particular, the recent decision of the House of Lords in *Smith*[1] is likely to prove a significant one for the law's approach in future to domestic homicide in the context of abuse. First, the case extends the boundaries of the defence of provocation. Secondly, it demonstrates a receptiveness to expert evidence that belies the assumptions and expectations expressed in the legal literature.

This chapter will accordingly seek to argue that, despite the many criticisms made of expert evidence in relation to domestic homicide, it is, for the moment, with the experts that women's best hope lies. In addition, it will be argued that not only might expert evidence, by exposing the real conditions of the lives of women subjected to domestic violence and their embodied experiences of it, open the way to a successful provocation defence, it also has the potential to make a plea of self-defence more easily available to abused women who kill.

2. DOMESTIC VIOLENCE

Domestic violence is, overwhelmingly, violence directed by men at women's gendered/sexed bodies.[2] While many explanations have tended to centre on individual pathology, stress, alcohol[3] or "family violence" suggesting mutual combat,[4] increasingly the phenomenon is being explained in terms of male power, control and possessiveness over women's bodies. Dobash and Dobash (1979) say that their findings show that abusive husbands demonstrate a sense of "possessiveness, domination and 'rightful' control" over their wives; arguments that led up to violent incidents tended to be associated with husbands' possessiveness, sexual jealousy or wives' perceived shortcomings in carrying out domestic duties. Campbell (1992) also focuses on men's proprietariness and dominance and Polk (1994), in his Australian study, found that this could take a lethal form; women were killed because of their suspected infidelity or pursuant to terminating the relationship.

Polk's study highlights the fact that, for some women, ending the relationship does not free them of violence. According to Wilson and Daly (1992) the risk of being killed escalates when the woman leaves, and Mahoney (1994) states that violence may be used as a means to re-assert control over a woman who seeks to go; it cannot be assumed that leaving is always possible or that to do so will bring safety.

[1] *R* v. *Smith* [2000] 4 All ER 289.
[2] See Mirrlees-Black et al. (1996); Kershaw et al. (2000); Law Commission (1992). See also the discussion of Mirrlees-Black (1999) in Diduck and Kaganas (1999); Stanko (2000).
[3] See e.g. Borkowski et al. (1983).
[4] See e.g. Straus (1993). See, for a discussion of the research, Dobash and Dobash (1992) ch. 8. These authors, amongst others, criticise the basis of the "family violence" studies which tend to rely on the Conflict Tactics Scale (CTS). This method fails to explore the context in which acts of violence take place and does not distinguish between acts of aggression and self-defence. Nor does it discriminate between different acts or levels of violence. It ignores the severity or otherwise of injuries. Finally, it excludes acts of sexual violence which are almost invariably perpetrated against women. Mirrlees-Black (1999) reports that it is overwhelmingly women who suffer serious abuse, injury and sexual violence.

Women who turn to the police for protection, may still, it seems, be disappointed. In spite of the creation of specialist domestic violence units and the existence of guidelines directing officers to arrest offenders and support victims, it appears that the police still do not treat domestic violence like other crimes. Stanko et al. (1998), for instance, found that few recorded cases ended in arrest.[5] In any event, says Hoyle (2000), the law is too blunt an instrument for dealing with abuse. It has been argued, for example, that if the pro-arrest policies were to be translated from the realm of rhetoric into action, this could have the effect of further endangering victims; arrest could lead to reprisals from an angry partner (Morley and Mullender (1992)). Morley and Mullender argue that what is needed is "a criminal justice response which is both internally co-ordinated (between police, prosecution and sentencing) *and* integrated within a broader community response" including support networks and housing.

Those integrated responses have not yet been forthcoming. Only a minority of perpetrators are charged, fewer are convicted and only a very small proportion are jailed.[6] Moreover, victims receive little support in negotiating the prosecution process and many drop charges (Cretney and Davis (1997b)). Civil injunctions were found by Barron (1990)[7] to be largely ineffective and, in any event, courts remain reluctant to eject men from their homes, declaring that to do so is "Draconian" and justifiable only in "exceptional circumstances".[8] Victims may find it difficult to obtain alternative housing (Diduck and Kaganas (1999)) and refuges are overstretched (Stanko (2000)).

For those women driven to kill their assailants, the killing may appear to them the only way to prevent their own deaths or at least serious injury to themselves or their children.[9] McColgan (1993) suggests that in the context of police ineffectiveness and the fact that women who are injured or killed are often those attempting to exit the relationship, "viewed from the woman's perspective, her use of force might be the only way to escape an escalating spiral of violence which she believes will end with her death". Certainly, in some of the reported cases, the defendants had either tried to leave[10] or had turned to the police and to the courts before resorting to killing.[11] That some women kill men who are drunk or asleep points not so much to revenge but rather to the level of their fear and their physical inability to defend themselves against attack. Yet the criminal law offers little acknowledgment of these gendered differences.

---

[5] See also Stanko (2000); McColgan (2000).

[6] See McColgan (2000). See also Peacock (1998); Cretney and Davis (1996, 1997a).

[7] See also McGee (2000). It appears however that powers of arrest are being attached more frequently to injunctions as a result of the implementation of Part IV of the Family Law Act 1996 (Edwards (2000)).

[8] *Chalmers* v. *Johns* [1999] 1 FLR 392, 397.

[9] Home Office (1993) statistics report that 41 per cent of homicides recorded in 1991 were killings of women perpetrated by their husbands or lovers. 8 per cent of men killed were killed by wives or lovers.

[10] *Janet Susan Gardner* (1993) 14 Cr App R(S) 364, 367.

[11] R v. *Thornton* [1992] 1 All ER 306, 309; *Kathleen Hobson* (1998) 1 Cr App R 31, 33; R v. *Ahluwalia* [1992] 4 All ER 889, 892.

3. DEFENCES TO A CHARGE OF MURDER

A charge of murder in the context of domestic homicide can be met with the justificatory defence of self-defence, leading to an acquittal, or either of two mitigatory, partial defences which will reduce the conviction to one of manslaughter. The latter two defences, provocation and diminished responsibility, were developed to circumvent the rigidity of the law and, it is said, to avoid imposing the mandatory life sentence for murder.[12]

(a) Self-defence

Self-defence has proved to be largely unavailable as a defence to women who kill their abusers. To fall within the parameters of self-defence, a use of force must be reasonable, and this means that it must have been necessary and proportionate to the harm which the defendant was attempting to prevent (Ashworth (1975)). A killing does not qualify as a reasonable use of force unless it is necessary to avert an imminent threat (Wilson (1999)). And while pre-emptive action is permitted,[13] the defendant must believe herself to be in imminent danger.[14]

McColgan (1993) contends for a less rigid application of the proximity requirement. Examining the leading case of *Palmer*, she argues that it did not lay down "inflexible rules about imminence"; it established merely that the proximity of the anticipated harm is an indicator of whether the defendant was acting in self-defence, was simply being aggressive or was acting to settle an old score. Certainly, the court stated that where "the attack is over and no sort of peril remains",[15] the requirement of necessity may not be satisfied. However, as McColgan points out, a victim of abuse may find herself in a position where she cannot escape or where escape would be dangerous and this inability to escape may extend to a situation where a threat is less than immediate. "The victim of ongoing violence" she says, "may have to strike when the chance arises, rather than waiting until it is too late" (McColgan (2000)). It may thus be necessary to attack an abuser who is asleep or drunk, but who has threatened violence when he awakes (*idem*). In the same way that a hostage threatened with death, albeit not imminent death, should be justified in killing to avoid that fate before it became unavoidable, so too should the abused woman be justified if, should she wait, the harm will become unavoidable.[16] To expect her to remain passive until the next, potentially fatal, attack

---

[12] See Lacey and Wells (1998).
[13] *Beckford* v. *R* [1988] AC 130, 144.
[14] See *Devlin* v. *Armstrong* [1971] NI 13, 33.
[15] *Palmer* v. *R* [1971] AC 814, 831.
[16] See McColgan (1993); McColgan (2000).

110   *Felicity Kaganas*

would, in the words of a judge in the Canadian case of *Lavallee*, "be tantamount to sentencing her to 'murder by installment' ".[17]

In addition to the requirement of necessity, there is a requirement that the degree of force used must be proportionate to the threat. It was held in *Williams*[18] and affirmed in *Owino*[19] that the test is: "a person may use such force as is (objectively) reasonable in the circumstances as he (subjectively) believes them to be". The degree of force used is taken as an indicator of the defendant's state of mind; increasingly, it has been said, the reasonableness of the force used is coming close to being treated as evidence of "whether the accused was genuinely motivated by self-defence or whether he was acting with some other illegitimate motive" like angry retaliation (Blackstone (2000)).

The difficulty faced by women who kill, even if they believe their lives to be in danger, is that their use of force may be regarded as excessive. Normally, the courts require comparable degrees of force; an armed defence against an unarmed assailant may not be reasonable. This approach might be justifiable, says McColgan (1993), when attacker and defender are comparable in strength. But it may be inappropriate where an abusing man and his victim are involved. In particular, it would operate unfairly where the woman "knows from experience that unarmed resistance by her to an unarmed attack by him may result in an escalation of that attack".

It has been suggested that excessive force should, provided the defendant honestly believed the degree of force used to be reasonable in the circumstances, form the basis of a partial excuse. A successful plea of excessive self-defence should, its proponents say, result in a conviction for manslaughter instead of one for murder. The possibility of such a defence was discussed, but the point left open, in *Clegg*,[20] but it has been recommended by scholars as a potentially useful innovation. However, a defence of this kind, while appearing attractive on the face of it, may not benefit women who kill unless the court has a clear understanding of the nature of the threat to severely abused women and the risks they face in attempting to escape. Its availability, say Lacey and Wells, may lead courts to convict of manslaughter instead of accepting the complete defence of self-defence.[21]

(b) Provocation

Provocation was defined in 1949 as something that "would cause in any reasonable person, and actually caused in the accused, a sudden and temporary loss of self-control, rendering the accused so subject to passion as to make him or her for the moment not master of his mind".[22] Section 3 of the Homicide Act 1957 has

---

[17] *Lavallee* v. *The Queen* (1990) 1 SCR 852, 883.
[18] [1987] 3 All ER 411.
[19] [1995] Crim LR 743, 744.
[20] [1995] 2 WLR 80.
[21] See, for a brief discussion, Lacey and Wells (1998).
[22] *R* v. *Duffy* [1949] 1 All ER 932.

expanded the defence to cover provocative words as well as acts and it requires the jury to take into account, in determining whether the provocation was enough to make a reasonable person react as the accused did, "everything both done and said according to the effect which . . . it would have on a reasonable man". Nevertheless the 1949 definition has remained basically intact. It is the loss of control that distinguishes a response to provocation from a considered act of revenge and it is important, therefore, to decide whether there was time "for passion to cool and reason to regain dominion over the mind".[23]

The first question, then, is whether the defendant lost self-control as a result of the provocative conduct. There has to be a sudden and temporary loss of self-control in order for what has been termed the "subjective" element of the defence to be satisfied; those who act out of illegitimate motives like revenge do not qualify. The second question, directed at establishing the "objective" element, is whether the provocative act would have caused a reasonable person to lose her self-control and behave as the defendant has, taking into account all the circumstances. So, not only must the court decide whether the provocation would have caused a reasonable person to lose self-control, but also whether the reasonable person would have reacted in the way that the accused did.[24] In *Camplin*,[25] Lord Diplock said that a reasonable person "means an ordinary person of either sex, not exceptionally excitable or pugnacious, but possessed of such powers of self-control as everyone is entitled to expect that his fellow citizens will exercise in society as it is".[26] It is, therefore, not enough to claim to be quick tempered, for example, as this would fail to take sufficient account of the ordinary or reasonable man standard. The reasonable person can, however, be someone who shares "such of the accused's characteristics as [the jury] think would affect the gravity of the provocation to him".[27] There must be a connection between the provocation and the characteristic. For example a court can take into account a defendant's disability where the provocation took the form of a taunt alluding to it.[28] In addition, the courts appear willing to take into account circumstances affecting the gravity of the provocation that are not strictly speaking characteristics, such as the defendant's history.[29] Yet an examination of the reported cases dealing with domestic homicide reveals that provocation based on a history of abuse has tended to fail as a defence. Abused women who kill have been found wanting on both the subjective and the objective criteria.

Thornton was such a case. The Court of Appeal upheld a decision which designated the defendant's act as neither the product of a loss of control nor as reasonable. First, she had left the room and sharpened the knife with which she had then

---

[23] *Ibid.* at 932–3.
[24] *Phillips* v. *The Queen* [1969] 2 AC 130, 137.
[25] *DPP* v. *Camplin* [1978] AC 705.
[26] *Ibid.* at 717; *Thornton, supra* n. 11, 310.
[27] *Camplin, supra* n. 25, 718.
[28] *R* v. *McGregor* [1962] NZLR 1069, 1081–2, cited with approval in *R* v. *Humphreys* [1995] 4 All ER 1008, 1017–18.
[29] See *R* v. *Morhall* [1995] 3 WLR 330, 336.

stabbed her husband. Secondly, said the trial judge, it would be difficult to describe as reasonable the act of stabbing the husband "as he lay defenceless on that settee ... There are ... many unhappy, indeed miserable, husbands and wives ... But on the whole it is hardly reasonable, you may think, to stab them fatally when there are other alternatives available, like walking out or going upstairs".[30]

Some movement towards accommodating a less masculine response to provocative conduct or words occurred in *Ahluwalia*, where the court accepted, *obiter*, the possibility of a "slow-burn" reaction to ongoing abuse rather than an instantaneous loss of control.[31] However, while the subjective element of provocation was not, said the court, negatived as a matter of law by the fact that there was delay in reacting, it nevertheless had to be shown that there was a "sudden and temporary loss of control" at the time of the killing; "the longer the delay and the stronger the evidence of deliberation" the less likely it would be that the defence would succeed.[32] McColgan (1993) suggests that this interpretation of the sudden and temporary rule is useful for abused women in that it links the suddenness to the loss of control rather than demanding temporal proximity between the provocation and loss of control.

As regards the objective element, the appeal court in *Ahluwalia* was asked to consider the argument that the defendant suffered from "battered woman syndrome" (BWS) leading to "learned helplessness",[33] and that this was a characteristic that the judge should have taken into account. This argument was rejected because there was no evidence before the judge to suggest that the accused suffered from post-traumatic stress or BWS or any other condition that could amount to a characteristic in terms of Lord Diplock's formulation in *Camplin*. There had been evidence of "grievous ill-treatment" but nothing to suggest its effect was to make her different from the ordinary run of women.[34] Had such evidence been put to the trial judge, different considerations might have applied, the court said.

Even if there is evidence of BWS, this will not suffice on its own. As the court in *Thornton (No. 2)*[35] indicated, it is still necessary to show a sudden and temporary loss of self-control. However, it said *obiter*, BWS might be relevant in two ways. First, a background of abuse might go to show a loss of control "on a 'last-straw' basis" despite the apparently minor significance of the immediate trigger to the killing.[36] Secondly, the syndrome might be shown to have affected the defendant's personality so as to constitute a relevant characteristic.[37] BWS, like other characteristics such as anorexia, obsessiveness and mental disorder, might be thought

[30] *Thornton, supra* n. 11, 312.
[31] *Ahluwalia, supra* n. 11, 896.
[32] *Idem.*
[33] It is thought that repeated violence renders a woman likely to become immobilised, passive and to feel that she is trapped and unable to escape (see Lacey and Wells (1998); Raitt and Zeedyk (2000)).
[34] *Ahluwalia, supra* n. 11, 898.
[35] [1996] 2 All ER 1023.
[36] *Ibid.* at 1030.
[37] *Idem.*

to reduce or deprive one of the capacity for rational thought but is nevertheless consistent with the concept of the reasonable person.[38]

It appears, then, from these reported decisions, that evidence of BWS or some equally distinct and diagnosable condition might help to bring the defendant's conduct within the confines of the defence of provocation. However, it seems that it may now be possible for battered women to raise the defence in circumstances that fall outside these narrow boundaries. Surprisingly, the case that has opened up this prospect involved neither domestic homicide nor domestic violence.

The House of Lords in *Smith*[39] was asked to decide whether the characteristics of an accused can be taken into account not only in determining the gravity of the provocation, namely how provocative something might be to a particular defendant, but also in setting the standard of self-control to be expected of him or her.[40] The majority of the Lords answered this question in the affirmative.

Lord Hoffmann, reviewing the *Camplin* case, confirmed that "for the purpose of considering the gravity of the provocation, the reasonable man should normally be assumed to share the relevant characteristics of the accused".[41] Furthermore, he said, Lord Diplock's judgment left the way open to taking personal characteristics into account also for the purposes of determining the level of self-control that could reasonably be expected of the accused. Indeed, said Lord Hoffmann, the question of the gravity of the provocation is difficult to separate from the question of the degree of self-control to be expected, and so the characteristics of the accused must be relevant to both.[42]. He accordingly held that an abnormality of mind[43] in the form of depression, which affected the defendant's powers of self-control, could be taken into consideration.

This approach appears to go further than both *Ahluwalia* and *Thornton (No. 2)*. First, it is now clear that characteristics are relevant to both the gravity of the provocation and to the requisite degree of self-control.[44] Secondly, while Lord Taylor in *Ahluwalia* appears to have confined his remarks to characteristics in the form of an abnormal condition such as BWS or PTSD,[45] Lord Hoffmann did not restrict the defence in this way. He went on to observe, *obiter*, that mental characteristics short

---

[38] See the discussion in *Humphreys, supra* n. 28, 119–22. However, the court in *Gardner* (1993) 14 Cr App (S) 364, while it accepted evidence of BWS, stated that the case might be akin to one of diminished responsibility rather than one of provocation. The defendant stabbed the man who was coming at her after holding her by the neck and banging her head against a door frame. In the past, he had brutally assaulted and raped her. He pursued her whenever she tried to leave the relationship so that she came to feel it was "futile" to hide (367). The night of the killing, he had mounted what the doctor called "a frenzied life threatening assault" (368). Self-defence was not pleaded.

[39] *Supra* n. 1.

[40] See, for an explanation of these concepts, Ashworth (1976).

[41] *Supra* n. 1, 298.

[42] *Ibid.*, 307.

[43] The judge found that the wording of s. 3 of the Homicide Act 1957 meant that the defences of diminished responsibility and provocation are not mutually exclusive.

[44] The jury in *Ahluwalia* were instructed to take into account the whole history of the marriage but only, it seems, in assessing the gravity of the provocation: "in order to decide whether the defendant may have been provoked" (307). See also *Thornton (No. 2), supra* n. 35 and *Humphreys, supra* n. 28.

[45] *Supra* n. 11, 898.

of some abnormality of mind would be relevant for the purposes of provocation and, turning specifically to the issue of domestic violence, said:

> "There are people (such as battered wives) who would reject any suggestion that they were "different from ordinary human beings" but have undergone experiences which, without any fault or defect of character on their part, have affected their powers of self-control. In such cases the law now recognises that the emotions which may cause loss of self-control are not confined to anger but may include fear and despair".[46]

Lord Clyde in turn said:

> "I would not regard it as just for a plea of provocation made by a battered wife whose condition falls short of mental abnormality to be rejected on the ground that a reasonable person would not have reacted to the provocation as she did. The reasonable person in such a case should be one who is exercising a reasonable level of self control for someone with her history, her experience and her state of mind".[47]

These analyses may well release victims of domestic violence from the burden of presenting themselves to the court as suffering from a medicalised syndrome or disorder. Not only does medicalisation of the defendant's state of mind have a stigmatising effect, it is a strategy that may well fail to reflect the reality of the experiences of many women who have been abused. In many cases it is terror and the knowledge that they are trapped, rather than mental abnormality, that leads to the loss of self-control. The House of Lords, in recognising this, and in entertaining the idea of the ordinariness or reasonableness of this response appears to have widened the scope of provocation as a defence.

However, Lord Hoffmann made it clear that, although subjective characteristics should be taken into account in evaluating the degree of self-control demanded, this did not entail jettisoning all objective standards. He cautioned that not all mental characteristics should be treated as relevant to the issue of self-control; male possessiveness and jealousy for example do not qualify, he said. The purpose of the objective element in provocation "is to mark the distinction between (partially) excusable and inexcusable loss of self control".[48] If there are no limits, the fact that a person is liable to lose self-control would excuse loss of self-control. Nevertheless, domestic violence was clearly regarded by the judge as a potentially exculpatory factor.

It is the notion of excusable as opposed to inexcusable loss of self-control that lies at the heart of Lord Hoffmann's judgment. Rather than seeking to categorise characteristics according to their compatibility or incompatibility with the image of the reasonable person, he adopted a transparently normative approach. He explicitly rejected the notion of the reasonable man, with or without attribution of characteristics. Instead, he said, judges might find it more useful to explain the principles of the doctrine of provocation to the jury:

[46] *Supra* n. 1, 308.
[47] *Ibid.*, 316.
[48] *Ibid.*, 308.

"First, it requires that the accused should have killed while he had lost self-control and that something should have caused him to lose self-control . . . Secondly, the fact that something caused him to lose self-control is not enough. The law expects people to exercise control over their emotions . . . The jury must think that the circumstances were such as to make the loss of self-control sufficiently *excusable* to reduce the gravity of the offence from murder to manslaughter. This is entirely a question for the jury. In deciding what should count as sufficient excuse they have to apply what they consider to be appropriate standards of behaviour; on the one hand making allowance for human nature and the power of the emotions but, on the other hand, not allowing someone to rely upon his own violent disposition. In applying these standards of behaviour, the jury represent the community and decide, as Lord Diplock said in *Camplin's* case . . . , what degree of self-control 'everyone is entitled to expect that his fellow citizens will exercise in society as it is today' ".[49]

Lord Millett differed from the majority on some points of law, and in particular on whether characteristics affecting self-control could be relevant. But his (*obiter*) observations on the issue of domestic violence, like those of Lords Hoffmann and Clyde, appear to show a greater openness to entertaining a plea of provocation in such cases.

Accepting that abuse might erode the "natural inhibitions" against resorting to violence in the same way that other forms of provocation might, he noted that the requirement of a "sudden and immediate loss of self control" nevertheless posed an obstacle to a provocation plea. He went on:

"In many situations this is a useful test for the jury to have in mind . . . But in the case of the battered wife the test is unhelpful. There is no legal requirement that the defendant's reaction must be triggered by an event immediately preceding his loss of self-control . . .

The question for the jury is whether a woman with normal powers of self-control, subjected to the treatment which the accused received, would or might finally react as she did. This calls for an exercise of imagination rather than medical evidence, but it does not dispense with the objective element. It does not involve an inquiry whether the accused was capable of displaying the powers of self-control of an ordinary person, but whether a person with the power of self-control of an ordinary person would or might have reacted in the same way to the cumulative effect of the treatment which she endured. The more difficult question in such a case is likely to be whether she lost her self-control at all, or acted out of a pre-meditated desire for revenge. On this issue the jury may be assisted by expert evidence to the effect that ill-treatment can act as a disinhibitor, and that the defendant's outward calm and submissiveness may be deceptive; they may have masked inner turmoil and suppressed rage".[50]

For abused women, then, the possibility of successfully raising the defence of provocation depends first, on whether the jury accept that there has been a loss of self-control in fact and, secondly, on whether they accept that the sustained violence endured by the defendant renders the killing partially excusable. In relation

[49] *Ibid.*, 312.
[50] *Ibid.*, 350.

to both these issues, juries will continue to impose murder convictions unless they are made aware of the dynamics, the severity and the effects of domestic violence.

(c) Diminished responsibility

It is apparent from the case law that there are difficulties in establishing either self-defence or provocation, particularly where a killing is preceded by any deliberation or planning. A killing becomes more easily comprehensible to law and, in some sense, reasonable or excusable if the abuse has engendered in the woman a state of, at least partial, unreason. And indeed, it is diminished responsibility that has thus far proved to be most successful as a defence for battered women who kill.

Diminished responsibility is defined in terms of section 2(1) of the Homicide Act 1957 as "such abnormality of mind (whether arising from a condition of arrested or retarded development of mind or any inherent causes or induced by disease or injury) as substantially impaired his [the defendant's] mental responsibility".

Despite the court's *obiter dicta* relaxing the requirements for provocation, it was the defence of diminished responsibility that ultimately succeeded in *Ahluwalia*. A medical report showing that the defendant had been suffering from endogenous depression had been overlooked at the trial. At her retrial in 1992, she was found guilty of manslaughter on the grounds of diminished responsibility (ROW (1993)). The court in *Hobson*, quashing a murder conviction and ordering a re-trial, appeared to accept that BWS could also support a finding of diminished responsibility.[51]

As Wilson (1999) points out, cases like *Ahluwalia*'s do not fit comfortably within the framework of diminished responsibility. Her "abnormality was symptomatic rather than systemic. It disappeared when her husband disappeared". McColgan (1993) observes that the Homicide Act requires that the diminished responsibility must stem from some abnormality of mind rather than emotional upset. This does not, she says, on the face of it apply to battered women who kill because they can see no escape except through violence. The prosecution, she cautions, might not always accept such a flawed version of a plea of diminished responsibility. Nevertheless, it remains the case that thus far, the defences that have succeeded in the reported cases dealing directly with domestic homicide have relied on the abnormality of the accused, and this is usually couched in terms of BWS.

4. BATTERED WOMAN SYNDROME

While it was initially thought that evidence of BWS would operate to normalise the defendant's behaviour (Raitt and Zeedyk (2000)), the syndrome has since been

---

[51] *Supra* n. 11. BWS was also relevant to provocation (at 33).

classified as a sub-category of post-traumatic stress disorder (PTSD) (Raitt and Zeedyk (2000)) and has had the effect in court of pathologising it. In addition to its stigmatising effect, the use of evidence of BWS has been criticised as being inappropriate. It is questionable whether BWS affects many women who are abused. Dobash and Dobash (1992) suggest that rather than exhibiting learned helplessness, women in their study tried actively to negotiate safety and frequently attempted to leave. And as one Canadian judge observed, it is possible that women who do not match the stereotype of passive, helpless victimhood may find themselves unable to rely on the defence.[52] In addition, Nicolson and Sanghvi (1993) point out, reliance on learned helplessness involves a logical inconsistency: if battered women are helpless, how do they come to kill?

This raises the question of the relative success of BWS in establishing a defence. For Wilson (1999), diminished responsibility is a way of circumventing the "moral holes" left uncovered by other defences. Norrie (1993), too, argues that psychiatric discourse can be seen as an aid to rescue the law from the "embarrassing consequences of its harsh narrowness". At the same time, he says, the individualising power of psychology combines with that of law to avoid focusing on the social conditions that led to the crime in question. In this way, psychology helps to maintain law's legitimacy.

Norrie's argument stems from his analysis of the way in which law constructs the legal subject. "Legal individualism", he maintains, "affixes a badge to our clothing or a mask to our face which has nothing to do with what we really are or resemble" (1993) p. 13. He goes on: "Legal justice is limited and partial because it deals with individuals in a particular abstract fashion. It picks out certain aspects of individuality, but excludes others" (p. 16). In particular, he says, with the possible exceptions of duress and necessity, the law precludes consideration of context or motive.

Yet it is not only duress and necessity that introduce context and motive into the law. It is surely the case that, albeit to a limited degree, the defences of provocation and self-defence do likewise. The defendant's motive is, for instance, read off from context in the shape of the method used and the timing of the act. The problem for women is that, to the extent that context and motive are taken into account, they are generally examined from a point of view that best reflects typical male experiences. The obstacles to reliance on provocation and self-defence for abused women lie in the "inherent masculinity" of the law's understanding of context and the male model of conduct from which motive is read off. Women who kill instead of leaving their abusers and women who attack a sleeping victim are taken to be acting out of vengeance or other similar motives, unless they can show some mental abnormality. In short, women's actions and responses frequently do not conform to those of the reasonable man.

---

[52] *Malott* v. *The Queen* [1998] 121 CCC (3d) 456, 471.

5. THE REASONABLE MAN

The concept of reasonableness, say Lacey and Wells (1998), is one "which is apparently gender-neutral but in reality discriminates against women". Indeed, O'Donovan (1993) says, the reasonable person of law is "in his physical ability, in action and response . . . embodied as a male". For instance, as the Canadian court in *Lavallee*[53] observed, the paradigm of the law of self-defence is a "one-time barroom brawl between two men of equal size and strength". It appears to fit more easily into a scenario involving public violence than into one involving sustained private violence deployed by men in order to keep women, who are generally physically weaker, and often trapped, isolated and terrified, under control.[54] Battered women tend not to react with instant force to taunts of violence in the way that men do (Dobash and Dobash (1984)) but delay may make the use of force unreasonable.

While it might be said that *Smith* has abandoned the reasonable man, it is nevertheless the case that neither the concept of reasonableness nor its male character have disappeared altogether. Self-defence relies on the concept of the reasonable person. Even Lord Hoffmann's formulation of provocation in terms of social norms or Lord Millett's reference to an exercise of the imagination can be interpreted as importing notions of reasonableness; it is still open to the jury to assess the excusability of a response to provocative conduct in terms of its reasonableness, taking into account the defendant's circumstances. The question, then, is how the court and the jury can be made aware of the context of a defendant's act in terms that better reflect her experiences, provide clearer insight into her state of mind or reasons for acting as she did and so lead to a less masculine conception of reasonableness.

6. LAW AND EXPERTISE

Domestic violence has come to be constructed as a serious social problem and the law has increasingly been expected to be seen to be doing something about it.[55] Moreover, revelations that some women who kill do so in response to violence have presented a potential challenge to law's legitimacy; a legal system that ignores the victimisation of the perpetrator in allocating blame for the killing may be seen as unjust. Indeed the campaigns that took place in relation to cases such as those of *Ahluwalia* and *Humphreys* indicate that the convictions did evoke a sense of outrage. In order to soothe the anxiety manifested by at least some sectors of the

[53] *Supra* n. 17, 876.
[54] This is not to postulate an essentialist view. Rather it refers to the likely effects of serious domestic violence as well as the view that norms and practice coalesce to entrench sexual difference (Butler (1993)).
[55] See Dobash and Dobash (1992); Diduck and Kaganas (1999).

public and to maintain its legitimacy, law has had to take cognisance of the issue of domestic violence and to explore the relationship between the experiences of women who kill and legal responsibility for their actions.

This need to respond to anxiety produces problems for law. Law's established categories of excusable and inexcusable behaviour are disrupted if domestic violence is taken into account. And the way the new boundaries are drawn depends on the way in which domestic violence is perceived and understood. The law is faced with a large and complex body of knowledge about domestic violence. In order to simplify complexity and so to process knowledge and apply it, the law has to turn to experts. In addition, passing difficult decisions to experts also invests law's decisions with the legitimacy offered by science (Nelken (1998)). However, law also has to keep "science and expertise within proper bounds" (*ibid.*). So, while "[e]xpertise is called for where legal competence or lay common sense is not deemed sufficient", (*ibid.*) certain aspects of human behaviour are assumed to be within the judge's or jury's competence.

In *R* v. *Turner*[56] the Court of Appeal stated:

> "An expert's opinion is admissible to furnish the court with scientific information which is likely to be outside the experience or knowledge of a judge or jury. If on the proven facts a judge or jury can form their own conclusions without help, then the opinion of the expert is unnecessary".

"Jurors" said Lawton LJ, "do not need psychiatrists to tell them how ordinary folk who are not suffering from mental illness are likely to react to the stresses and strains of life".[57]

In contrast to the position of the English courts at the time, the Canadian court in *Lavallee*[58] adopted a more receptive attitude; it allowed expert evidence to highlight the falsity of the "myths" on which the jury might rely:

> "The need for expert evidence in these areas can . . . be obfuscated by the belief that judges and juries are thoroughly knowledgeable about "human nature" and that no more is needed . . . Expert evidence on the psychological effect of battering on wives and common law partners must, it seems to me, be both relevant and necessary in the context of the present case. How can the mental state of the appellant be appreciated without it? The average member of the public (or of the jury) can be forgiven for asking: Why would a woman put up with this type of treatment? Why should she continue to live with such a man? . . . Such is the reaction of the average person confronted with the so-called 'battered wife syndrome'. We need help to understand it and help is available from trained professionals".

This attempt, albeit within the context of BWS, to make visible what research suggests are the typical dynamics of domestic violence stands in stark contrast to the, presumably "common sense" assumption in *Thornton* that she had the simple option of walking out. Yet, according to Nelken (1998), there is little scope for the

---

[56] [1975] 1 QB 834, 841.
[57] *Idem.*
[58] *Supra* n. 17, 871–2.

deployment of expertise to dispel myths; the use of expert evidence to correct the misconceptions held by lay people would, he said, make the task of science "unending, given that its mandate is precisely to show that 'lay' understanding and reasoning rests on corrigible misconception and error".

Nelken (1998), and other scholars, saw the role of the expert in English law as being confined to "interpreting the abnormal". Raitt (1998) observed that the "average juror is assumed to be at ease with all aspects of normal human behaviour". And McColgan (1993), reviewing the case law in 1993, predicted that, "Short of claiming that the experience of battering has produced psychiatric abnormality sufficient to amount to diminished responsibility . . . , it is unlikely that defence counsel could persuade the courts that expert evidence of the effect of such abuse has anything to add to jurors' understanding of a woman's perceptions of danger and the reasonableness of her response to it".

Given the prevailing view that expert testimony could be deemed helpful only when it attested to abnormality, it is not surprising that criminal law's knowledge of abused women's experiences has, in the past, been largely confined to psychiatric accounts of BWS. Apart from this "syndrome", the body of research revealing the experiences and responses of abused women has remained outside criminal law's remit. Instead, common-sense conceptions of "normal" human behaviour have prevailed in the reported cases. It has, apparently, been easier for law to accommodate a new, discrete category of abnormal people than for it to re-think its construct of the ordinary, reasonable person.

Law has addressed the problem of domestic violence in the context of murder trials by selectively invoking science, while excluding any evidence that might disrupt its own hegemony over the normal world. Such an approach simplifies the complexity of the knowledge law has to confront and enables it to maintain the use of "conduct rules" which ensure that decisions do not need to become too individualised and concerned with subjective experiences (Nelken (1998)). It also curtails the proliferation of expert witnesses, with the attendant costs in terms of time and money (*idem*).

However, if an expert is someone who knows more than the jury, and is there to fill in gaps in knowledge, it can surely be argued, particularly in the light of the long-term invisibility of the nature of domestic violence, that juries are not cognisant with the experiences of normal battered women. Law's internal rationale for the use of experts supports their use in this situation, despite the unfortunate consequence of increased costs. And it seems that the courts have already come to adopt an approach to expertise that goes beyond the evidence of mental illness referred to in *Turner*.

Courts are now admitting evidence in the form of expert evidence or in the form of testimony by an intervenor to attest, not simply to the abnormality of a particular person, but to the typical responses of people or classes of people to certain situations. For example, in family proceedings the Court of Appeal[59] has allowed

---

[59] *Re L (Contact: Domestic Violence); Re V (Contact: Domestic Violence); Re M (Contact: Domestic Violence); Re H (Contact: Domestic Violence)* [2000] 2 FLR 334.

an expert psychiatric report[60] detailing, in general terms rather than in terms specific to the children in question, the advantages and the risks of contact between children and absent parents. This report, which included discussion of the possible effects on children of domestic violence, was described by the judge as setting out "the psychiatric principles of contact between the child and the non-resident parent".[61] Those "principles" were founded in large part on the experts' knowledge of "normal" or typical experiences and behaviours.

Even more significant was the willingness of the House of Lords in *Smith* to permit intervention by Justice for Women, Southall Black Sisters and Liberty in order to explain the typical effects of domestic violence on victims. The joint petition of these three organisations sought to de-pathologise BWS and to bring the responses of battered women who kill within the range of reasonableness demanded by the defence of provocation: "by definition, battered woman syndrome is a condition which many women, in the same situation, would develop. It is a reasonable woman's reaction to an abusive relationship".[62] The petitioners argued that BWS should not be seen as a special characteristic setting the defendant aside from the ordinary person. Rather, it should be seen as "a complex of responses to be expected from a reasonable woman who has been subjected to cumulative provocation" and should be treated by the jury as one of the circumstances to be considered in judging the conduct of the defendant.[63] In support of their contention, the petitioners presented the House, inter alia, with a psychiatric report showing "a consistent pattern of psychological and emotional effects arising out of the abuse" (para. 1.11(a)) and a literature review of "research on the impact on and coping strategies of victims of domestic violence" (para. 1.11(c)). While the petition in *Smith* did employ the term BWS, it sought to remove it from the realms of medicalised and abnormal conditions and to identify it as a term referring to a set of typical and normal responses. That the House took heed of the petitioners' evidence is apparent from the *obiter dicta* accepting the possibility that the ordinary or reasonable[64] woman might lose control and kill her abuser and that this act might be excusable.

It appears, then, that expert evidence may be adduced to attest to the normality of the extreme act of killing in the context of extreme circumstances. Moreover, the dicta in *Smith* offer the hope of a move away from relying on syndrome evidence and towards a consideration of typical as well as individual responses to violence. That this is a real possibility seems to be supported by the fact that the evidence that can be adduced is not limited to psychiatric or psychological testimony; the courts now admit social science research findings under the rubric of

---

[60] See Sturge and Glaser (2000).
[61] *Supra* n. 59, 336.
[62] Petition for leave to intervene, *R* v. *Morgan James Smith*, 3 January 2000, para. 1.4.
[63] *Ibid.*, para. 1.8.
[64] This approach seems to suggest that, contrary to the view of Raitt and Zeedyk (2000), BWS is compatible with reasonable conduct.

expert evidence.[65] The signs are that such evidence may assist women in raising a defence of provocation. Moreover, there seems no reason that expert evidence should not be deployed in support of a plea of self-defence.

7. EXPERT EVIDENCE AND REASONABLENESS

It is surely possible, for the purposes of establishing self-defence, to adduce expert evidence to the effect that the normal woman's perceptions of danger are affected by abuse and her levels of fear heightened when faced with violence or the threat of violence emanating from an abusive partner. However, just as the excusability of the defendant's conduct in response to provocation is not a matter for the experts, nor is the reasonableness of the defendant's response for the purposes of self-defence; the normative judgement is one for the jury alone. Nevertheless, since that judgement has to be made in the light of all the circumstances, in the case of provocation, experiences of violence and typical responses to violence will be relevant; evidence such as that offered in *Smith* highlighting the severity of the abuse and its impact would inevitably colour the way in which the moral judgement is made. Similarly, in relation to self-defence, the reasonableness of the defendant's actions must surely be judged in the context of her experiences and history. Expert evidence as to the relationship between abuse and woman killing, as to separation violence and as to typical as well as individual levels of fear will go to establishing the defendant's perception of danger and so influence the assessment of reasonableness.

This is not to argue for a "reasonable woman" standard, a possibility that has been mooted in relation to tort law. It is to argue for an expanded, context-sensitive version of the reasonable person. It is true that not all agree on the wisdom of going down this route. Conaghan (1996b), for example, rejects the possibility of a "context-based standard" as too vague and as potentially making it impossible to articulate any normative standard at all. However, it is not being suggested here that all normative standards be abandoned in favour of a subjective test. It is already the case, in relation to provocation and self-defence, that the law contextualises the act of killing. What is being suggested is that, unless the context brought to the law's attention reflects the material conditions of the lives of many abused women, there can be no understanding of the defendant's predicament. Accordingly the assessment of the moral significance of her act cannot be an informed one.

Of course there are different degrees of abuse and different reactions to it. Nevertheless, if the law could be made to acknowledge that the reasonable woman

---

[65] The literature review compiled by Dr Liz Kelly and submitted to the court in *Smith* was a review of social science research. Dr Kelly has also written a number of expert reports based on social science knowledge of domestic violence in cases involving asylum seekers as well as women who kill. Her reports have not been challenged in any of those cases (personal communication from Dr Liz Kelly, 25 October 2000).

subject to abuse does not necessarily strike back immediately when threatened, that delay before she acts does not necessarily imply that she is behaving vengefully rather than in self-defence, and that the option of leaving is often not a realistic one, the prejudicial nature of the established self-defence rules might be countered. If there is evidence of severe abuse and of high levels of fear, for example, the law could take account of what a reasonable woman who sees her demise as inevitable and who perceives no escape might do under those conditions. This contextualisation is necessary to counterbalance the context that is already implicit in the law of self-defence: mutual combat, usually outside of intimate, continuing relations, between opponents who are broadly speaking of comparable strength. And for the present, it seems that the expert is essential in providing this counterweight. Expert evidence is necessary to embody women victims of violence as, say, smaller than their assailants, dominated, afraid and trapped.

8. SIMPLIFYING COMPLEXITY

This process of embodying the defendant has its inherent problems, however. The image of the battered woman produced by the experts and taken on board by the courts can operate to the disadvantage of some abused women who kill. According to McColgan (1993), the experience in the USA calls into question the benefits of admitting expert evidence; it has been used to construct stereotypical images of battered women and women who do not fit the stereotype are prejudiced.

In addition, there are even more fundamental difficulties in getting the law to understand the circumstances of the defendant. Even if complex and inclusive versions of battered women were presented to the courts by experts versed in the knowledge produced by the "psy" professions and by social science, such versions will be unlikely to survive the transition into the courtroom. The law will inevitably deal with knowledge of this kind selectively in order to simplify complexity. Typical or likely responses tend to be transformed into rigid "principles".[66] In its quest for "clear normative principles"[67] the law will reinterpret this knowledge to create new and simplified rules. These rules will undoubtedly ill-serve some abused women; the new norms will marginalise those individuals and groups of women who fail to conform. Yet expert evidence has the potential at least to broaden the already selective and even narrower perspective of women's experiences that currently inhabit the world of judicial and popular common sense.

9. CONCLUSIONS

Domestic violence has come to be constructed as a public rather than merely a private problem and it is a problem that law, in order to maintain legitimacy, must

---

[66] See Kaganas (2000).
[67] King and Piper (1995).

confront in the context of domestic homicide as elsewhere. In order to appear just, the law has to take into account the abuse suffered by the defendant in apportioning blame. However, the rules that have developed around the defences of provocation and self-defence mirror common-sense understandings of violence that exclude the experiences of abused women and it seems that the only way to counter these is through the deployment of expert evidence. Through expert evidence, the defendant who has suffered abuse is embodied for law and invested with the perceptions and understandings of her world. It is only once these become visible to law that any cogent inferences can be drawn from her actions. Through expertise aimed at revealing these women's states of mind and their reasons for acting as they did, law's interpretation of their physical acts through its focus on timing and method can become less blinkered. Moreover, it is through expert evidence that the court has shown signs of accepting the normality and, potentially, the reasonableness of abused women's responses to violence. It is through expert evidence that the defence of provocation has come within the reach of battered women who kill. And it is through expert evidence that the defence of self-defence might also be brought within their grasp.

Of course, expert evidence is no guarantee of success. For one thing, juries might take the view that, despite what they have been told about domestic violence, it is insufficient to provide a moral excuse or justification for killing an abuser. It has been said, in the sphere of tort law, that the law, while quick to protect the interests traditionally valued by men, is slow in its response to women's concerns (Conaghan (1996a)). Yet there are signs, in family law for example, that the law's resistance to women's perceptions is softening a little.[68] And these shifts, although they may ultimately be incorporated into the law's common-sense understandings of the world, all stem from social science and "psy" knowledge.

There is little doubt that there are difficulties inherent in the use of expert evidence. In particular, the law has a tendency to reinterpret and simplify expert knowledge. But unless and until common sense comes to embrace the perceptions of abused women, it is the experts who offer the prospect, at least to some defendants who kill, of being judged as something other than mad or bad.

REFERENCES

ASHWORTH, A., "Self-defence and the Right to Life" (1975) *CLJ* 282.
ASHWORTH, A., "The Doctrine of Provocation" (1976) *CLJ* 292.
BARRON, J., *Not Worth the Paper . . . ? The Effectiveness of Legal Protection for Women and Children Experiencing Domestic Violence* (Bristol, WAFE Ltd, 1990).

[68] In relation to contact with children by abusive men, courts have begun to advert to the potential danger to mothers posed by such contact. There is some understanding of separation violence and the LCD (2000) has now issued a document recommending guidelines to be used in cases of violence. Admittedly, it may be that concern about violence in this field took hold more easily because of research linking woman abuse with child abuse; the state and the law appear to respond more readily to the plight of children in danger than to that of women.

Blackstone's Criminal Practice 2000 (London, Blackstone Press Limited, 2000).

BORKOWSKI, M., MURCH, M., and WALKER, V., *Marital Violence. The Community Response* (London, Tavistock Publications, 1983).

BUTLER, J., *Bodies that Matter: On the Discursive Limits of "Sex"* (London, Routledge, 1993).

CAMPBELL, J.C., "'If I Can't Have You, No One Can': Power and Control in Homicide of Female Partners" in J. Radford and D.E.H. Russell (eds.), *Femicide. The Politics of Woman Killing* (Buckingham, Open University Press, 1992).

CONAGHAN, J., "Gendered Harms and the Law of Tort: Remedying (Sexual) Harassment" (1996a) 16 *OJLS* 407.

—— , "Tort Law and the Feminist Critique of Reason" in A. Bottomley (ed.), *Feminist Perspectives on the Foundational Subjects of Law* (London, Cavendish Publishing, 1996b).

CRETNEY, A. and DAVIS, G., "Prosecuting Domestic Assault" (1996) *Crim L Rev* 162.

—— , "Prosecuting Domestic Assault: Victims Failing Courts, or Courts Failing Victims?" (1997a) 36 *The Howard Journal* 146.

—— , "The Significance of Compellability in the Prosecution of Domestic Assault" (1997b) 37 *Brit J Criminol* 75.

DIDUCK, A. and KAGANAS, F., *Family Law, Gender and the State* (Oxford, Hart Publishing, 1999).

DOBASH, R.E. and DOBASH, R.P., *Violence Against Wives* (New York, Free Press, 1979).

—— , "The Nature and Antecedents of Violent Events" (1984) 24 *Brit J Criminol* 269.

—— , *Women, Violence and Social Change* (London, Routledge, 1992).

EDWARDS, S., *Reducing Domestic Violence. . .What Works? Civil Law Remedies* (Policing and Reducing Crime Unit, 2000).

HOME OFFICE, *Information on the Criminal Justice System in England and Wales, Digest 2* (1993).

—— , *Home Office Agenda on Violence Against Women* http://www.homeoffice.gov.uk/ domesticviolence/hoagen.htm (2000).

HOYLE, C., *Negotiating Domestic Violence* (Oxford, Oxford University Press, 2000).

KAGANAS, F., "*Re L (Contact: Domestic Violence; Re V (Contact: Domestic Violence); Re M (Contact: Domestic Violence); Re H (Contact: Domestic Violence).* Contact and Domestic Violence" (2000) 12 *CFLQ* 311.

KERSHAW, C., BUDD, T., KINSHOTT, G., MATTINSON, J., MAYHEW, P. and MYHILL, A., *The 2000 British Crime Survey* (Home Office, 2000).

KING, M. and PIPER, C., *How the Law Thinks About Children* (Aldershot, Arena, 1995).

LACEY, N. and WELLS, C., *Reconstructing Criminal Law. Text and Materials* (London, Butterworths, 1998).

LAW COMMISSION, *Family Law, Domestic Violence and Occupation of the Family Home* (No. 207, London, HMSO, 1992).

LCD, *The Advisory Board on Family Law: Children Act Sub-Committee. A Report to the Lord Chancellor on the Question of Parental Contact in Cases Where There is Domestic Violence* (2000).

MAHONEY, M., "Victimization or Oppression? Women's Lives, Violence and Agency" in M.A. Fineman and R. Myktiuk (eds.), *The Public Nature of Private Violence. The Discovery of Domestic Abuse* (London, Routledge, 1994).

McCOLGAN, A., "In Defence of Battered Women who Kill" (1993) 13 *OJLS* 508.

—— , *Women Under the Law. The False Promise of Human Rights* (Essex, Pearson Education Limited, 2000).

McGee, C., *Childhood Experiences of Domestic Violence* (London, Jessica Kingsley Publishers, 2000).

Mirrlees-Black, C., *Domestic Violence: Findings from a New British Crime Survey Self-Completion Questionnaire. Home Office Research Study 191* (London, Home Office, 1999).

Mirrlees-Black, C., Mayhew, P. and Percy, A., *The 1996 British Crime Survey. England and Wales* (London, HMSO, 1996).

Morley, R. and Mullender, A., "Hype or Hope? The Importation of Pro-Arrest Policies and Batterer's Programmes from North America to Britain as Key Measures for Preventing Violence against Women in the Home" (1992) 6 *Int J of Law and the Family* 265.

Nelken, D., "A Just Measure of Science" in M. Freeman (eds.), *Science in Court* (Aldershot, Ashgate, 1998).

Nicolson, D. and Sanghvi, R., "Battered Women and Provocation: The Implications of R v. Ahluwalia" (1993) Crim LR 728.

Norrie, A., *Crime, Reason and History. A Critical Introduction to Criminal Law* (London, Butterworths, 1993).

O'Donovan, K., "Law's Knowledge: The Judge, The Expert, The Battered Woman, and Her Syndrome" (1993) 20 *JLS* 427.

Peacock, G., "Domestic Abuse Research" (1998) *Family Law* 628.

Polk, K., *When Men Kill. Scenarios of Masculine Violence* (Cambridge, Cambridge University Press, 1994).

Raitt, F., "A New Criterion for the Admissibility of Scientific Evidence. The Metamorphosis of Helpfulness" in H. Reece (ed.) *Law and Science, Current Legal Issues,* Vol. 1 (Oxford, Oxford University Press, 1998).

Raitt, F. and Zeedyk, S., *The Implicit Relation Between Psychology and the Law: Women and Syndrome Evidence* (London, Routledge, 2000).

ROW, *Bulletin* (Spring 1993).

Stanko, E. A., *The Day to Count . . .* , http://www.domesticviolencedata.org/5_research/count/count.htm (2000).

Stanko, E. A., Crisp, D., Hale, C. and Lucraft, H., *Counting the Costs: Estimating the Impact of Domestic Violence in the London Borough of Hackney* (Wiltshire, Crime Concern, 1998).

Sturge, C. and Glaser, D., "Contract and Domestic Violence – The Experts' Court Report" [2000] Fam. Law 615.

Straus, M., "Physical Assaults by Wives. A Major Social Problem" in R. Gelles and D. Loseke (eds.), *Current Controversies on Family Violence* (London, Sage, 1993).

Wilson, W., *Criminal Law* (London, Longman, 1999).

Wilson, M. and Daly, M., "Till Death do Us Part" in J. Radford and D.E.H. Russell (eds.), *Femicide. The Politics of Woman Killing* (Buckingham, Open University Press, 1992).

8

The Many Appearances of the Body in Feminist Scholarship

ANNE BOTTOMLEY

1. INTRODUCTION

"In nova fert animus mutatis dicere formas corpere".[1]

WORK ON "The Body" has become one of the most important themes of contemporary feminist scholarship; some would argue *the* most important. The basic argument is that a focus on TB[2] cannot but reveal gender specificity. Not only are there differences in the ways gender has been inscribed and used in a society that has favoured one gender at the expense of the other, but also attention is drawn to the extent to which knowledge, of ourselves and of our world, has been predicated upon binary constructs of mind/body, male/female, and so on. In other words, the very fabric of the way we think and theorise, a seemingly natural and neutral process, is revealed as gender specific. By beginning with the ways in which TB of women has been thought and constructed in our social order, we are led to fundamental epistemological questions that focus on the way in which TB itself has been constructed and thought.

Feminist work has used TB in a number of ways. Sometimes it connotes the corporeal body, sometimes it is used to insist on TB as more than corporeal, bringing into the account mind and also, for some, spirit or soul. Sometimes TB is used more figuratively, thinking, for instance, of the figure of the maternal body. I have tried to indicate these differences by using in my title the notion of the "many appearances" of TB, with the extra element that, for feminist work, the very notion of the need to make TB "appear" has been important. Underlying the different uses made of TB, differing concepts and constructions of TB, and the demand by feminists for new forms of embodiment, there is an important sense in which TB morphs. This means more than simply differing uses; it emphasises change, transition and the fluidity of body use and image.

---

[1] The first lines of Ovid's Metamorphoses. I like the Miller translation for Loeb (1916): "My mind is bent to tell of bodies changed into new forms".

[2] Initially writing "TB" was simply a time saving device, but I have now come to regard it as a useful sign: a sign that we are actually talking about many different aspects of the notion of "the body". TB then signals the empty/plenitude of the site.

I have constructed my chapter as, in part, a review of feminist work on TB. As a review it is, however, necessarily partial, both because of the space available to me and also because it is marked by my own authorship and therefore is structured around an argument informed by my own approach to this work. So much more could have been said, references to important debates and disagreements remain unexplored here, and many readers will wonder why certain writers in the field have been omitted. However, no chapter of this kind can be more than one feminist's exploration of a very rich area of work. My political and scholastic biography sets the frame for my own engagement and the argument I construct is one which I recognise many feminists, let alone others, will find contentious. A central theme of feminist work is the need for "embodiment", which, in this context, emphasises that we think and write from a position in which we are never simply "mind", the abstract academic who reviews the literature and, from a distance, formulates a rational argument; we are so much more and therefore so much less than that.

2. "BODIES HAVE A HISTORY . . . WE START IN THE MIDDLE"[3]

Taking "embodiment" seriously, I will begin my chapter not with academic literature, but rather from the context of a broader feminism, the feminism of "lived experience". Recognising that my own account is imbued with my own biography (a white, middle class woman who intended becoming a lawyer but became an academic, a student in the 1970s and a participant in the London women's movement throughout the late 1970s and early 1980s), I want to remind the reader that feminist work within the academy can never, finally, be separated from its political context.

(a) Recovering/reclaiming our bodies

For many of us, as women, the experience of being objectified led to a sense of dispossession of our bodies. Whether as objects of desire or as objects of medical science, what we experienced was a sense of intrusion, lack of control and being subjected to "the gaze". We moved, with difficulty, between wanting to claim our bodies as ours and yet being unsure as to how to be "authentic" to ourselves. Could/should we take pleasure in beauty? What did that mean? How were we to explore our sexuality? Themes of resistance became entwined with questions of "self": as woman—as something more than we were being allowed to be. We were working through a radical sense of displacement—the appearance of our bodies to others did not seem to "fit" our sense of what was possible for us. We were being required to conform to body images that fractured and violated our sense of what it could/should mean to be a woman.

[3] Richardson (1998) p. 114.

I want to try and recall and inscribe the very real sense of "body loss" that motivated so much feminist politics in the 1970s. The form of embodiment that we were offered seemed so over-determined: We were about body, but not about "our" body. We were objects of desire, of lust and passion, who could become so desirable that we became dangerous creatures to be feared. We were sexual but our own potential sexuality was so voracious that it had to be kept in check. We were expected to be maternal, emotional and caring, but we had to learn not to "cling" and "stifle". We were the agents of good behaviour, but when we were bad, we were worse than any man. We were brought up by mothers' warnings not to "scare off" men, we learnt by watching them how to hide our power(s), learn the value of sacrifice, and keep on the tightrope of being just attractive enough/just sexual enough/just caring enough—we learnt to manage our bodies. We hid the signs of menstrual bleeding, valiantly ignored PMT and spoke only in hushed tones about sex and childbirth.

To resist these pressures to conform became encoded in the idea of "reclaiming" our bodies, our corporeal bodies, along with the wish to reclaim our pleasures in our bodies—our sexuality. This led to an emphasis on TB as a site of struggle. We began to realise that by reclaiming TB, we could begin to use our own bodies as expressions of self and, in so doing, we also began to "listen to our bodies". We began to explore an interactive play between body/mind which allowed a sense of (to use contemporary therapeutic language) "being centred" and of "becoming whole".

Understanding the force of this experience, amplified by the feminist politics of the women's movement, might help, in part, to explain two factors which have dogged feminist work ever since: first, we could speak an experience of "loss", but how could we speak/imagine/explore our "real selves"? What did it mean to be "woman", other than those meanings we resisted because we felt/knew them to be a denial of "us"? The expression of "loss" and the demand of "reclamation" required (at least rhetorically), a positing of a figure of woman before/outside the dominant discourses, which led to the dangerous territory of essentialism/ naturalism and the related problems of asserting a category of "women" and pre-suming a subjectivity for women.

Secondly, at the very same time, in reclaiming our bodies, we were resisting a discourse that drew its authority from a claim to "naturalism". We argued that our present condition was a social construct and that different ways were possible, if only we could resist the force of the "claim to nature". To achieve this we challenged the seeming biologism of gender and argued that it was a social construction. We showed how gender (and sexuality) had been reinscribed as "natural" through the most "scientific" of discourses: how the attempt to present data rationally actually reproduced the dominant patriarchal discourse and was imbued with the prejudices, pleasures and privileges of the purveyors of these discourses— men. We would bring up our daughters not enslaved by the loss of their bodies and our sons with the benefits of the feminine; it was all merely a matter of "learnt behaviour" and resisting the power of the dominant discursive practices.

In fact, we have since had to learn hard lessons with our own children—watch (too many of) our boys make guns and (too many of) our daughters love Barbie; we are now having to deal with the depth of "difference" and re-engage with the idea of "gender". But, at the time, what was important was to see possibilities for change, to affirm these possibilities and to move from a politics dominated by resistance, to a politics based on future possibilities. From the beginning of my generation's encounter with struggles over TB, we experienced, at root, a fundamental paradox: the seeming need to claim the idea of a "real" woman as an assertion against the "natural" woman which was the figure presented to us.

(b) Becoming academic . . . the disappearing body

I was a student of law and criminology in the 1970s and, in common with an increasing number of female students, entered the academy inspired by a romantic notion that this would be a place in which we would explore ideas and become "ourselves". We wanted our talents recognised, a right to a career based on merit, and an end to the presumption that we were destined for marriage and motherhood. The university seemed the place where we would accomplish this leap into emancipation. What we actually found was that so much material we dealt with simply projected the masculine as the "norm" without any consideration of the partiality of this; that "women" hardly appeared at all, except on the margins and then as deviations from "the norm"; and that when these deviations did appear, they were very obviously, to women students, figures of masculine imagination, replete with "sexist" value judgements about "good" and "bad" women, the role of women and the necessary dependence of women as the "weaker sex".[4]

I took a course in crime and criminology at LSE: statistics on crime and then a resume of the reasons that had been given for why crime is committed. The absence of women from this agenda did not even merit a moment of questioning. Luckily for me, a doctoral student introduced me to Foucault, warning me, however, not to bring any of this material into an examination answer! And so I, with so many others of my generation, became more sophisticated in our analysis of the production of "knowledge", we began to unpack the power relations involved in projecting academic work as the disembodied voice of universal reason. We began, for instance, to think about the disciplining of men as "criminal" (with responsibility) and women as "mad" (without responsibility). We began to realise that we, as women, were placed as the emotional/problematic outsiders. We wanted to insist on bringing women into the picture, making them appear, bringing them into the body of knowledge. A strange dissociation arose for us—we demanded the right to be "seen" but we were resistant to becoming simply "objects of study", and we wanted to join the viewers, to be given entry into the "academy". But to become scholars, it became increasingly clear, we had to become "as men": learning to

---

[4] One account of the development of the figure of "woman" in modernity is found in Jervis (1999).

discard the messiness of unreason and enter the world of the objective, dispassionate observer. Leaving our bodies behind, we could become seemingly asexual, but actually masculinised, "scholars". The mind would triumph—a masculine mind that could order and thereby control. We were in a vortex of swirling in/out, appear/disappear, recover/lose, viewer/viewed.

For many women scholars this schizoid existence resulted in an experience of "disappearance", "fracture" and "violence". "Disappearance" in both the sense we had of the disappearance of "women" from the sight of the academic project and our own sense of disappearance as women becoming academics. We experienced a fracturing of ourselves, a violent act of refusal: we had to deny a great deal of our sense of "self", as the academic persona we sought insisted on this denial. The immediate struggle became a struggle over the margins: challenging the taken-for granted portrayals of women, whether in the fields of crime, madness or medicine;[5] looking at the power of definition, the power of marginalisation and the disruptive power of finding and giving voice to those voices that had not been heard.

3. "SEEKING TO EXERT CONTROL OVER THE REALITY OF BODILY EXPERIENCES"[6]

One way in which concerns over TB found expression was in the subsequent development of work on medical and health care issues. In *Feminist Perspectives on Health Care Law*, Sheldon and Thompson (1998) p. 2 recognise that both elements of their title are contentious to any traditionalist law academic, a specific site for healthcare law is as problematic as the idea of feminist perspectives:

"Both of his concerns, it seems to us, stem from the same problem. They both raise real issues of inclusion and exclusion, of what counts as 'real' law, 'real' knowledge and 'real' legal scholarship, of what is appropriate to be taught or researched in the law school and of what has no place there. In a volume which was a precursor to the series of which this book forms a part, Anne Bottomley speaks of 'the construction of these narratives, their partiality and their violence towards the excluded'. The choices made in structuring a law curriculum and in developing teaching practice are all fiercely political ones which the cloak of tradition helps to present as natural, objective and rational".

Making TB appear is here made possible by creating a site in which TB is the focus, not a series of incursions into, mostly on the margins of, other areas of "knowledge". By organising around the practices and disciplines of/on the medicalised body, what is rendered visible is the sexed/gendered nature of TB.

Making TB appear in this way tends to emphasise certain themes. Revealing the power of professionals and law is an account of TB as a contested site, a site of interference and colonisation. How are such potential threats and incursions to be

[5] See, e.g., Smart (1976)
[6] Farsides (1992) p. 37.

not merely revealed but resisted? Unsurprisingly recourse is made to such terms as "bodily autonomy" and "bodily integrity", a kind of rights discourse for the body. Despite the fact that many scholars recognise how problematic these terms are, either when facing such difficult questions as the maternal/foetal relation or in terms of a more abstract concern with the presumption of a unitary subject, they are difficult to avoid.[7]

It is all too easy to slip into an account of TB in which TB becomes a passive site of exploitation—a place onto which sex and gender are inscribed and somehow, within which, a "real woman" is fighting for survival. Further, "the law" becomes too easily characterised as another "body", of which evidence drawn from one situation/site can become evidence of "the whole". One active, monologic, agent acts upon a passive, monologic, subject thereby creating TB. Ironically, the call for the appearance of TB, can become rendered as the appearance of TB constructed and thereby, again, denied, a site upon which so much power is inscribed that it is difficult to conceive of anything more than moments of resistance:

> "This book has, we hope, demonstrated that women's engagement with law does not occur in a uniform fashion. Women come to law as mothers (potential and actual) as survivors of sexual and physical abuse, and as criminal offenders. They offer up to the scrutiny of the legal system their reproductive bodies, their sexual bodies and their offensive bodies. If this book has offered the possibility of glimpsing pockets of resistance at the juncture of this moment of scrutiny—this is, resistance to male power and agency, to legal discourse and to predominant constructions of women, their bodies and their behaviour—it will have gone some way towards achieving its aim".[8]

Woman has become victim through body, revealed through bringing together all those aspects of law which feature female corporeality and sexuality. I do not deny the very real importance of bringing together this material, of tracing the corpus through a number of legal sites, but the impact is such that a critique is created which reproduces woman reduced to body, passive body, and law as amplified to an all-controlling all-powerful external force.

The correlation between the image of TB as passive object and the image of law as active agent, is grounded in an unexamined presumption of a unitary subject and utilises a series of binaries, of oppositions: woman/law, internal/external. Such an approach is often sustained by utilising the internal/external further and positing a "real woman" with a "real body" as external to law. When Farsides writes:

> "women are trying to establish ownership over their own bodies, and control over their bodily functions; first by creating their own metaphors and then by seeking to assert control over the reality of their bodily experiences".[9]

one can slip, all too easily, into a dualism in which women are not merely trying to assert control over their bodies vis-à-vis men, but actually women's minds are

---

[7] See, e.g., Stychin (1998).

[8] Bridgeman and Millns (1998) p. 760.

[9] Quoted in Bridgeman and Millns (1998) 3.

trying to assert control over their own bodies. It is then all too easy, seemingly necessary, to presume a "real woman" inside a body she seeks to reclaim.

Avoiding this essentialism, a claim to universalism and naturalism has been a major concern of much internal critique within feminism. Smart, for instance, has spent a great deal of time addressing this issue.[10] Her move to assert law as "gendered" (rather than "sexist" or "male") is an attempt to avoid being caught in the essentialist trap:

> "the idea of 'law as gendered' does not require us to have a fixed category or empirical referent of Man or Woman. We can now allow for the more fluid notion of a gendered subject position which is not fixed by either biological psychological or social determinants to sex. Within this analysis we can turn our focus to those strategies which attempt to do the 'fixing' of gender to rigid systems of meaning rather than falling into this practice ourselves".[11]

However, having achieved "fluidity" in relation to gender, law remains a "rigid system":

> "law is now redefined away from being a system which can impose gender neutrality towards being one of the systems (discourses) that is productive not only of gender difference, but quite specific forms of polarised difference. Law is seen as bringing into being both gendered subject positions as well as (more controversially?) subjectivities or identities to which the individual becomes tied or associated".[12]

Therefore, our focus is on how "the woman of legal discourse" is constructed, and how that construction is based on male/female duality:

> "Woman represents a dualism, as well as being one side of a prior binary distinction. Thus in legal discourse the prostitute is constructed as the bad woman, but at the same time she epitomises Woman in contradistinction to Man because she is what any woman could be and because she represents a deviousness and a licentiousness arising from her (supposedly naturally given) bodily form, while the man remains innocuous".[13]

4. "THERE IS NO FEMALE SUBJECT IN THE TEXT OF THE CRIMINAL LAW"[14]

Duncan (1996) p. 189 carries forward the project of examining the way in which gender is constructed by focusing on the excluded-woman-subject, the necessary exclusion of woman as subject in order to sustain the seemingly neutral, but actually masculine, body of law:

> "The female body is disciplined as a sexual body, disciplined to mirror the sexual desire of the male subject, to expand the space of his legitimate desire. Where her body is constructed as sexual, the space for her consent is consistently contracted; where her body is

---

[10] See, in particular, Smart (1989, 1992).
[11] Smart (1992) p. 33.
[12] Smart (1992) p. 34.
[13] Smart (1992) p. 36.
[14] Duncan (1996) p. 177. See also Duncan (1994).

not construed as sexual, that space is expanded. The criminal law disciplines the female body; as it denies subjectivity to the woman/girl".

She argues, drawing from Irigaray, that the exclusion of female subjectivity is a necessary condition for the construction of male subjectivity. Law is a system of representation. Woman is beyond representation and therefore only appears as "body" before law, a sexual body which reproduces the binaries of men/women and emotion/reason:

"The woman appears only as a mirror to male subjectivity. She is constructed to mirror him and his desires and, to this end, her body is differentially disciplined within the law to allow space for his subjectivity".[15]

Thus:

"the law constructs the female as Other not as freely consenting subject but as Other for the male subject in the space of unreason, for the logic of desire.
   In these constructions, lie the paradox of the law of sexuality. It exists purportedly to defend and protect 'victims' of rape, incest and prostitution but even as far as it does so, it reasserts, through its constructions, the power of the speaking male subject through and the exclusion of woman as Other from, the dominant male discourse as it is expressed in and enshrined by that law'.[16]

This moves from "gendering", as construed by Smart, to a much more decisive argument that woman is not simply "other" but "Other": excluded from discourse to enable the development of a male subjectivity, based on reason but threatened by unruly desire, the figure of woman, and presented as neutral and universal but revealed as male, as sex specific. A revelation made apparent by, and through, an examination of TB.

Running through all the appearances of TB examined so far, questions about the construction of knowledge emerge: about scientific rationality, objectivity, and the power of knowledge claims based on the duality between body/mind and female/male. These challenges coalesce in the theme of "embodiment", in the requirement to context and situate the production of knowledge. However, at this point the very idea of subjectivity is contended: not only as produced by the violent disappearance of women, but within the male psyche itself.

5. "THE BODY IS A BETRAYAL OF AND A PRISON FOR THE SOUL"[17]

One of the primary objectives of contemporary work on TB has been to challenge the dualisms fundamental to Western knowledge and to patriarchal privilege—mind/body, men/women, reason/emotion and culture/nature. From Plato to Descartes, the scene was set in which body/women/emotion/nature coalesced into

[15] Duncan (1996).
[16] Duncan (1994). See also Brown (1986).
[17] Grosz (1994).

that which was rightfully governed by mind/men/reason/culture as the basis for the development of civilised society. These dualities not only privilege one side at the necessary expense of the other, but also carry the promise of an "overcoming" in which mind can triumph—in being able to see, and therefore control, "the other".

Subjectivity is grounded in acts of overcoming through sight and thought, a rational apprehension of "the other", and the ability to resist that which could hold back the fully developed "self". Rigid divisions are policed by carefully controlled boundaries and by extenuating difference. The subject comes into subjectivity within his mind—escaping the betrayal and prison of the body and entering into rational, universal knowledge, a self-reflecting and transparent consciousness:

> "This subject is a monological one . . . in contact with an 'outside' world, including other agents, the objects she or he and they deal with, her or his own and other bodies, but this contact is through the representations she or he has 'written'. The subject is first of all an 'inner' space, a mind to use the old terminology, or a mechanism capable of processing representations if we follow the more fashionable computer-inspired models of today. The body, other people, or objects may form the content of my representations . . . But what I am is definable independently of body or other. It is a centre of monological conscience".[18]

The attack on this most fundamental structural notion of the rational subject forms the core of much contemporary academic work. The psychoanalytical challenge to the Cartesian subject, for instance, implodes the rational unitary subject:

> "The subject of the unconscious demands that the subject of philosophy—in so far as the latter claims the prerogative of rationalism—faces his/her incompleteness, recognises the libidinal, bodily roots of intelligence and accepts the partiality of his/her modes of thinking".[19]

Further, Grosz (1994) argues that:

> "Freud problematised the ways in which both the psychical and the biological have been conceived, showing that each, in its very existence and operations, implies the other. It is therefore not surprising that he returns again and again in his psychological writings to the question of integration of psychology with biology".

Two processes are in action, one to reconnect TB to its many parts, the second, implicated in this, to overcome not only the binary of mind/body but also the reproduction of this binary in men/women, nature/culture etc. At this point we reach an interesting paradox between the "death" of the subject in post-modernist thinking, the reclamation of TB, and the specific project of feminism. I want to put it in two ways, which are actually saying the same thing: first, the reclaiming of TB in post-modernist thought presents a possibility for overcoming the binaries which reproduce sexual difference, but what is clear is that the work of Freud (and Neitzsche and Foucault), at best ignore sexual difference and at worst actively

[18] Taylor (1993), quoted in Pile and Thrift (1995) p. 14.
[19] Braidotti (1991) p. 34.

reproduce it. Secondly, at the very time as women seem to be on the threshold of female/feminist subjectivity (at least in the sense of entry in the polity and the beginning of the hard task of theoretical work), it seems that the thing we lack and desire (our own subjectivity) is not possible anyway.

I have talked in terms of "death", because that is the way in which men have talked about the loss of the subject: in fact I want to turn this around and think of it rather as the potential for conceiving new modes of thinking and representing "ourselves". The act of constructing the subject involved major acts of violence and separation, the division between mind/body, the division between male/ female:

> "I am struck by the violence of the gesture that binds a fractured self to the performative illusion of unity, mastery, self-transparence. I am struck by the terrifying stupidity of that illusion of unity, and by its incomprehensible force".[20]

So where do we begin to situate the potential for new beginnings? For feminists, the answer is in new conceptions of TB. Positive affirmations of TB: strategies for refiguring the body and therefore the notion of subjectivity:

> "a new form of 'corporeal materialism', the body is seen as an inter-face, a threshold, a field of intersection of material and symbolic forces; it is a surface where multiple codes of power and knowledge are inscribed; it is a construction that transforms and capitalises on energies of a heterogeneous and discontinuous nature. A body is not an essence, and therefore not an anatomical destiny: it is one's primary location in the world, one's primary situation in reality, the strategy of repossessing the body aims at elaborating alternative forms of knowledge and representations of the subject".[21]

6.   BODY MOVES, ONE: "TWO LIPS RETOUCHING"[22]

> "We want to do our work, we want to create and be critical too. But how can we create if we know that our theoretical tools, our handtools, our rewards and also in part our unconscious images of what it is like to be a creative person are produced by a culture which has excluded and devalued us? This is the question: how can we create, how can we create ourselves?"[23]

> "if the body is already engendered in this way, how can we claim our bodies without reproducing the inequities of the gender system? . . . so we become involved in explicating patriarchal relations without knowing where patriarchy begins and ends in the definition of a woman's or mother's body. What aspect of the body constitutes a women's potential capacities, and what part articulates her oppression?"[24]

---

[20] Braidotti (1994) p. 12.
[21] Braidotti (1994) p. 219.
[22] Irigaray (1985) quoted by Whitford (1991) p. 173.
[23] Minnikc (1978) p. 5.
[24] Eisenstien (1988) p. 93 and p. 97.

For Irigaray, the beginning of an answer to these questions lies in taking Lacan seriously, as exemplifying the system of representation which we refer to as phallocentric or phallologic. The construction of the male subject was/is dependent upon a regime of signification which allows the male subject to appear through not merely knowing what he is not (female) but by using the Other (female) to mirror back to him what he "is". The play of the mirror places Woman as the mirror itself, she is effaced into being no more than the surface of the mirror. This is the condition of representation, of knowledge of the world in which we live. We only encounter our bodies, as men do, through symbols of lack and projections of fear. The violence inflicted by this regime is not only on the bodies of women but also on the bodies of men. Woman becomes figured as "body" (corporeal) which men must escape and resist. The Platonic split asserts itself again. Further, Woman/Other are not merely relegated to "body" but constructed as "empty body": the maternal function being simply receptacle for male foetus, the sexual function being simply receptacle for male penis. Women are emptied and flattened: lacking subjectivity, agency or desire.

But even within this schemata, Irigaray finds openings, potential beginnings, for giving birth to (an)other. Two "seepages" exist within this otherwise seemingly tight structure. The first is that "I" know I am here: I don't know quite how I am here and I don't quite know how to articulate or envision my presence—but I, as woman, have not been finally silenced and effaced. I-as-woman, am an excess which cannot be finally contained and controlled. Irigaray posits this as a place of alteriority, in which my desire is still in play: my desire "to be". Secondly, my desire is an unboundaried, disruptive force which "I" can work with: my jouissance: my affirmative, celebratory sense of potential. The problem, for Irigaray, is how do "I" become representable within the current phallocentric regime, how do "I" enter into an economy of the sexes? For Irigaray's insistence is that the present economy of the sexes cannot accommodate "me". As Irigaray begins her analysis with an exposure of current representations of the body, so her strategy is then based on using the flesh of our bodies to disrupt and challenge these representations.

At this point the reader can take two quite distinctive approaches to Irigaray's work. Either she is trying to present a new ontology, and thereby an alternative epistemology, of/for Woman, grounded in an assertion of an essential, natural Woman which, following the traditions of the binary divide as well as the traditions of "the grand narrative", can triumph over the phallocentric regime. Or, and this is the position I take, one can read Irigaray as raising a series of strategic possibilities which mirror back the very fragilities of the phallocentric by mimicking them, moving in/out of dominant discursive techniques but never underestimating the power of phallologic representation. TB within the plays of Irigaray is both flesh and flesh to be represented, to provide an alternative economy of the symbolic, to provide the conditions that may make possible becoming-woman. She offers the following three particular strategies.

(a) The practice of ecriture feminine

This is more than writing as woman, it is an attempt to speak, in however an inarticulate fashion, from where we are now, exploring instinct and desire in the act of speaking/writing, as an attempt to construct potentials. Not a claim to truth but a play with potential: it is the struggle to articulate, the struggle to think, from an embodied sense of me/now, unwritten/unthought, for a potential me in a potential future. These are acts of performance, in which we are engaged in exploring (creating) multiple potentials. Specifically counterposed to the phallocentric act of "viewing", which emphasises distance, disembodiement and the attempt at a unitary vision, ecriture feminine is an extension of the tactile, the embodied, the connected and the multiple. It is about speaking and thereby hearing, inscribing and thereby finding a sense of authorship as well as a movement towards the performance of reading:

> "One (has) to listen with another ear, as if hearing an 'other meaning' always in the process of weaving itself, of embracing itself with words, but also of getting rid of words not in order to become fixed, congealed in them. For is 'she' says something, it is not, it is already no longer, what she means. What she says is never identical with anything, moreover; rather, it is contingent. It touches (upon). And when it strays too far from the proximity, she breaks off and starts over at 'zero', her body-sex".[25]

(b) The symbol of the lips

Entering into an economy of the sexes which recognises difference, requires an equivalent symbolic order. Irigaray finds this, as she must, situated in the female body, the lips of the female sexual organs are the alternative to the phallus. Lips mark an entry, a place of passage, which she envisions as both representational of the ignored and productive for imaging the becoming-woman. The position of the lips allows a play with surfaces that bring together an internal/external aspect to the body, allowing a recovery of an interiority. However, the emphasis is on bringing into relation, not simply a gateway between inside/outside, but a place that emphasises the surface in, as well as on, the envelope, the fold, of the skin. The lips are two which are also one. She emphasises this when she moves from the lips of the sexual organs to the lips of the mouth:

> "To seek to discover-rediscover a possible imaginary for women through the movement of two lips re-touching . . . does not mean a regressive recourse to autonomy or to a concept of 'nature', nor a recall to a genital order—women have more than one pair of lips!!! Rather it means to open up the autological and tautological circle of systems of representation and their discourses so women can speak (of) their sex [parler leur sexe]".[26]

[25] Irigary, quoted in Braidotti (1991) p. 249.
[26] Irigary, quoted in Whitford (1991) p. 173.

To be able to speak requires the two but the two function, in order to speak, by their coming together as well as their movement apart. This figurative device allows us to think differently about difference, and carries the advantage of encoding the female body in such a way as to allow us to celebrate potentials which are meaningful to "us".

(c) Recovering female genealogies

Recovering the suppressed figure of the female/feminine is central to Irigaray's work and has been a popular device in work in this country on histories of law. I do not have the time/space to explore this here, but I do want to signal one issue. There is a great deal of difference between the act of "recovery" if it is presumed to be an act of making a more complete history, and the act of recovery as a means of, again, challenging the symbolic order. The first tends to be presented, and understood, as an act of revelation, the second as an act of invocation: the first will tend towards the closure of completeness, the latter towards a celebration of the contingent and the multiple. It is only by working through, on, an understanding of TB that the latter is possible and the former avoided.[27]

7. BODY MOVES, TWO: "WE DO NOT KNOW WHAT THE BODY CAN DO"[28]

Spinoza offers the attraction of finding a counterbalance to Descartes, a chance to re-locate TB in which "connection" rather than "separation" is emphasised, and the focus is on possibilities rather than inevitabilities. For Gatens, Spinoza is a philosopher of the dynamic and of interconnectedness, refusing any separation between mind/body and moving to a refusal of a final separation between bodies:

> "Spinoza argues that there is only one substance, which is single and indivisible; body and mind enjoy only a modal existence and may be thought as 'expressions' or modifications of the attributes of substance, that is, extension and thought, respectively. Human being is conceived as part of a dynamic and interconnected whole".[29]

Gaten's project in reading Spinoza is clear:

> "Spinoza's largely neglected political and juridical theory offers a novel perspective from which to begin to think through the body of the law. This perspective should be of interest to those concerned to discriminate between different sorts of sociability without appeal to transcendent moral or crypto-theological categories. It offers an ethical stance without reducing ethics to a universal system of moral rules and so does not have pretensions to universalism. It provides a means by which one may value a sociability which has its basis in a community of rational beings, over one based on capture or utility, at

---

[27] This comes from a discussion with Nathan Moore and I am grateful to him for raising it with me.
[28] Spinoza (1988) p. 18.
[29] Gatens (1996a) p. 28.

the same time showing the difference in attitude of each type of sociability towards notions of ethical and legal responsibility".[30]

Gaten's use of Spinoza signals an interface between the feminist project of re-thinking TB and the Deleuzean exploration of the productive capacities of the body.

In the complex and radical work of Deleuze (often with Guttari), there is a challenge to think about the project of thinking which is grounded in a fundamental restructuring of body-image: a morphing of the body into a site of patterns, flows and intensities in which the emphasis is continually on movement. Figurations are used to enable us to think differently—the figuration of the rhizome (in opposition to the arboreal), of the nomad (in opposition to the territorialised, sedimented and stagnant) and the key figuration of "the body without organs" (BwO).

The BwO connotes two major themes—that we are playing on a series of surfaces, surfaces that refuse the binaries of in/out, interior/exterior, real/imagined. The BwO emphasises the energies in play that constitute our capacity to effect and be effected: it emphasises that we are (always) in the process of becoming. This process of becoming is "the line of flight" (the potential in the nomadic) which resists territorialisation: it is the opening up, the fluidity, which counters the hold of the Oedipal myth of separation and the consequent nostalgia/longing for rejoining/completing/ making whole. It is a celebration of desire as affirmative rather than as lack. It is a radical challenge to theory as usually thought and constructed, because it emphasises that the act of thinking/theorising has only one purpose: what it makes possible, what it enables. In this sense, the simple argument is that an epistemology constituted on the Oedipal fracture, the Platonic prison, is not only over but that we should welcome this. However, what Deleuze continually points out (and we are all too well aware of) is that it is very difficult to struggle out of this history, we continue to produce the echoes of it, we keep trying to return to, and invoke, it. This is not only because of its strength, but because of our fear of what lies ahead . . . is there anything? . . . is there too much?

Deleuze presents passageways for us, tracks for us, openings which signal a profound re-think but also provide routes/roots which we can recognise; hence his very careful and rigorous use of such thinkers as Spinoza. At the same time, he radically disrupts us by his figurations—nomads, war machines, BwO, and "becoming-woman". For many feminists, Deleuze has been a writer/thinker to deal with at a distance and with great suspicion. His concerns and his figurations, seem too often alien to feminists and reminiscent of the old story of neutral in appearance/masculine in practice. He is charged with not recognising/dealing with sexual difference, with appropriating the feminine in his "becoming-woman" and with reproducing and continuing the masculine economy, albeit in a new form.[31]

[30] Gatens (1996a) p. 40. See also Gatens (1996b).

[31] See, e.g., Grosz (1994) p. 187.

It is not my purpose, here, to go into a detailed account of these critiques and how they might be answered. I think that they should be accepted as a correct wariness, a series of concerns which keep open the position of a feminist reading of the text, not losing the specificity of "our" concerns, our issues, not to be overcome by/territorialised by a body of work which seems so all-engulfing. It is not whether Deleuze is or is not a feminist text, it is rather what Deleuze offers in terms of potentials to a feminist reader. I think, that these potentials are very rich indeed:

> "It is, of course, indispensable for women to conduct a molar[32] politics, with a view to winning back their own organisms, their own history, their own subjectivity . . . But it is dangerous to confine oneself to such a subject, which does not function without drying up a spring or stopping a flow".[33]

I do not find this patronising. I think it clearly represents the condition we are in now, the needs we have now and argues, correctly, that this is historically contingent. We want a new economy of the sexes and, unless one believes that this is not a possibility beyond continued and continuous essential difference, one has to welcome the potential of a replacing of binaries:

> "If we consider the great binary aggregates, such as the sexes or classes, it is evident they they also cross over into molecular assemblages of a different nature, and that there is a double reciprocal dependency between them. For the two sexes imply a multiplicity of molecular combinations bringing into play not only the many in woman but the woman in the man, but the relation of each . . . a thousand tiny sexes".[34]

Further, Deleuze and Guttari place both a responsibility on men, and a means by which men can begin to re-think their own position:

> "What we term a molar entity is, for example, the woman as defined by her form, endowed with organs and functions, and assigned as a subject. Becoming-woman is not imitating this entity or even transforming oneself into it . . . not imitating or assuming the female form, but emitting particles that enter into the relation of movement and rest, or the zone of proximity, of a microfemininity, in other words, that produce a molecular woman".[35]

I do not read this as a continued subjection for women, quite the opposite. It is, again, specifically oriented in time and place: it is the call, within our historically contingent situation, to let go of domination, of power, of the power of the subject, and enter the reality of the potential, which at this point can be figured as woman, becoming-woman. Not real women, not even the position of women, but women as representative of the affirmation of the multiple, the overcoming of the domination of "lack". It is actually posited as a transitional stage moving towards the process of becoming figured as the BwO:

---

[32] "Molar" is used by Deleuze to connote "large" scale, traditional attempts at unitary models—to which he counterposes "molecular", "small" scale assemblies.
[33] Deleuze and Guttari (1987) p. 276.
[34] *Ibid* p. 213.
[35] *Ibid* p. 275.

"You have to keep enough of the organism for it to reform each dawn; and you have to keep small supplies of significance and subjectification, if only to turn them against their own systems when the circumstances demand it, when things, persons, even situations, force you to; and you have to keep small rations of subjectivity in sufficient quantity to enable you to respond to the dominant reality. Mimic the strata. You don't reach the BwO, and its plane of consistency, by wildly destratifying. That is why we encountered the paradox of those emptied and dreary bodies at the very beginning: they had emptied themselves of their organs instead of looking for the point at which they could patiently and momentarily dismantle the organisation of the organs we call the organism".[36]

8. BODY MOVES, THREE: "THE BODY HAS REMAINED A CONCEPTUAL BLINDSPOT"[37]

Grosz's contention that the "body has remained a conceptual blind spot", is focused on both "mainstream Western philosophical thought and contemporary feminist theory".[38] This may seem rather dated, but I think that she is indicating something quite firmly here—that neither have really yet engaged with the full potential of TB, and also that neither has fully engaged with each other. Placing TB fully in focus requires a recognition of sexual difference, but equally, feminist work on TB cannot afford to ignore real engagement with "mainstream Western philosophical thought". Without such engagement we risk missing the depth of critique required, and hence there is the very real possibility of reproducing some of that which we need to avoid. In an important sense, the task that has been set is not merely to use a feminist critique of the former (a "lack" approach), but to see how far feminist concerns can be explored and grounded within careful conceptual analysis. There are very specific reasons for this: feminist thinking as it has "appeared" in the academy has been consistently subjected to a series of critiques, notably of essentialism and universalism, in other words those very same elements which feminism had set as its target. If feminism is to develop as more than critique, then what is required is an examination of foundations. This is particularly critical when, as the crisis in subjectivity has developed, feminists seemed to be situating their/our claims to their/our own knowledge based on a female subjectivity.

Butler (1993) and Grosz (1994) both insist on the need to think of TB as corporeal—the thing which they suggest has been particularly difficult for feminists to achieve, not merely because of the traditions of Western philosophy but because of our own fear of being regarded as essentialist, or as privileging the female body as an authentic site from which to challenge the male mind. Feminists have preferred to work with gender (see, for example, Smart) rather than face sex. Sex suggests determinism, either the biologism of being trapped in the female body or celebrated as the natural/maternal site of all that is good.

[36] Deleuze and Guttari (1987) at 160–1.
[37] Grosz (1994) p. 3.
[38] *Ibid.*

This fear of essentialism, a new naturalism, is often expressed as a critique of Irigaray who, in countering the duality of the phallocentric and the "lack" of woman (both in the sense of woman not appearing and woman herself lacking), emphasises a strategy that mimics phallocentric thinking by extenuating difference. The question for such feminists as Grosz is whether such a strategy is the only way forward, or the best way forward, at the present time. It is interesting that a major response, recently, has been to read across and through Irigaray/Deleuze: using one to read the other.[39] Thus Irigaray is used to keep open the specificity of the female body and the female condition in a reading of Deleuze, and Deleuze is used to keep open the emphasis on the multiple in any new form of subjectivity when reading Irigaray. However, one cannot, and should not, pretend that there are not major tensions in "reading the two" in relation to each other: it is important not to collapse, conflate or to confuse; the tensions between them are important to the movement between them:

> "I am reluctant to claim that sexual difference is purely a matter of the inscription and codification of somehow uncoded, absolutely raw material, as if these materials exert no resistance or recalcitrance to the processes of cultural inscription. This is to deny a materiality or a material specificity and determinateness to bodies. It is to deny the postulate of a pure, that is, material difference. It is to make them infinitely pliable, malleable. On the other hand, the opposite extreme also seems untenable. Bodies are not fixed, inert, purely genetically or biologically programmed entities that function in their particular ways and in their determinate forms independent of the cultural milieu and value. Differences between bodies, not only at the level of experience and subjectivity but also at the level of practical and physical capacities, enjoy considerable social and historical variation".[40]

For Grosz, we cannot either ignore sexual difference or, by stripping off the layers of cultural inscription, find a "true" body beneath; what is required is a much more careful examination of the sexed body, the way in which the sex of the body has been incoded and represented and an exploration of "difference" as a positive value:

> "This notion of sexual difference that is originary and constitutive, is not, strictly speaking, ontological; if anything it occupies a preontological—certainly a preepistemological—terrain insofar as it makes possible what things or entities, what beings, exist (the ontological question) and insofar as it must preexist and condition what we know (the epistemological question). The framework or terrain of sexual difference entails not the concept of a continuum, a wholeness, a predivisional world as plenum, but the simultaneous recognition and effacement of the spacings, of the intervals, the irreducible if unspecified positioning, the fissures and ruptures, that bind each 'thing' to every other and to the whole of existence without, however, linking them into an organic or metaphysical wholeness or unity".[41]

---

[39] See, e.g., Richardson (1998).
[40] Grosz (1994) p. 190.
[41] *Ibid* p. 209.

In terms of the present condition of T(female)B, Grosz, following Irigaray and Kristeva, emphasises the construction of T(female)B not merely as lack but as:

"a leaking, uncontrollable, seeping liquid; as formless flow; as viscosity, entrapping, secreting; as lacking not so much or simply the phallus but self-containment—not a cracked or porous vessel, like a leaking ship, but a formless that engulfs all form. A disorder that threatens all order . . . women, insofar as they are human, have the same degree of solidity, occupy the same genus, as men, yet insofar as they are women, they are represented and live themselves as seepage, liquidity. The metaphorics of uncontrollability, the ambivalence between desperate, fatal attraction and strong revulsion, the deep-seated fear of absorption, the association of femininity with contagion and disorder, the undecidability of the limits of the female body . . . its powers of cynical seduction and allure are all common themes in literary and cultural representations of women. These may well be a function of the projection outward of their corporealities, the liquidities that men seem to want to cast out of their own representation".[42]

TB of women had been subjected to a gaze that denied them bodily integrity and constructed their bodies as sites of lack and of excess. Male subjectivity had been made possible by the image of control over his body as well as the body of women, by the simple move of projecting onto women's bodies all those elements of all bodies (including his own) which were unboundaried, uncontrollable, uncomfortable. Thus to achieve an image of "wholeness" not only was the mind to be understood as the essence of male, civilised behaviour, but insofar as "he" had a body, it was under the control of the mind. TB came to represent the female, uncontrollable body. For women to claim back their body, we are faced not only with challenging the duality of mind/body, but also having to face the problematic equation which links their/our bodies with uncontrollable excess.

The task thus seems to be giving minds and bodies to women but also giving bodies (and therefore reconstructing minds) to men. These bodies/minds have to cease to be a projection of wholeness/completeness and we have to recognise the fine balance between "coming together" and "coming apart"; in other words, to recognise the plural, the multiple, the flows. The challenge to the modern subject, the disembodied unitary being, allows for this to come into play.

9. DIRECTIONS FOR FEMINIST WORK IN/ON LAW

This places feminist politics, and academic work, at an exciting but difficult juncture. Clearly, we have to be willing to engage more directly with the corporeal, sexed, and therefore differentiated, body rather than remain within the seemingly safer region of cultural representation, construction and encoding of gender. We have to confront biology, and in so confronting biology we have to lose our fears of essentialism and determinism, and engage with biology, biologism, as another

[42] Grosz (1994) p. 203.

aspect of the construction of knowledge.[43] The difficulties, and potential richness, of such a project are beginning to appear in print.[44]

Further, drawing from the work of Irigaray and Grosz,[45] there are a number of themes to be explored, one of which concerns "vision and voice".[46] The challenge to the dominance of the optical leads to a search for other forms of "relation", or apprehension of others, which do not feature the distance which vision requires. Irigaray emphasises the tactile, and, by reference to her image of the lips, relational apprehension. In moving to the lips of the mouth, she emphasises speech rather than vision.

Rose, considering Irigaray's approach in relation to her own discipline, geography, finds it a useful way to examine the orthodox rendition of the "geographic vision".[47] She calls for other ways of "visioning" as a way to move forward her discipline in a more plural form; vision which is low and small scale, vision which is involved in not merely seeing but understanding the construction of seeing. By playing with vision/voice in academic law, we can begin to challenge our own discipline by understanding how our work has been predicated on the use of disembodied voices and a lack of vision. One strategy, then, for us, is to begin by giving vision to voice, to expose the distancing which has been accomplished by lack of vision. I have found this useful when considering the academic land lawyers lack-of-vision of land, and there is still, I think, much to be gained from "giving vision" to law and "body" to land.[48] On a rather different trajectory, it is interesting that there are glimpses of an interest in giving body to property which are appearing in the literature.[49] "Giving body" insists on an "embodied" account, bringing into vision that which has been reified into an abstract formulation, as such it requires, and makes possible, a very different construction of "vision".

Meanwhile, an insistence on a consideration of the spoken has led to numerous examinations of the construction of narratives in legal discourse,[50] as well as the beginnings of an examination of conversations which might allow for the development of alternative narratives, alternative in style and therefore content.[51]

In terms of how we envision TB, the alternative figurations offered by Deleuze help us to explore, and when necessary overcome, the constraints of dualism. One most obvious example of this is in work on the maternal body, in which it has been very difficult to move beyond notions of autonomy and integrity when dealing with maternal/foetal "rights". Being able to find a construction in which we can figure the foetus as both of, and independent of, the maternal body (and therefore in which we figure the maternal body as an assemblage of parts), has become an

---

[43] See, e.g., Murphy (1997).
[44] See, e.g., Louizidou (1999).
[45] See especially, Grosz (1995).
[46] Other major themes (drawing also from Deleuze) are the dimensions of space and time.
[47] Rose (1993).
[48] Bottomley (1996).
[49] See e.g. Davies (1998) and on considering the body as property, see e.g. Stychin (1998).
[50] See e.g., Sheldon (1997).
[51] See e.g., Murphy (1997).

important way forward. Lim, using Harraway's figuration of the cyborg, is indicative of the potential.[52]

Treating TB as a site of instability, as well as potential, requires that we turn and give body back to law. This means that we have to be more clear-sighted about the instability and potential in law: we can no longer treat law as if it lives up to the positivist project of transparent rationality, or as a closed system of power. There is still much to expose and critique in law, but we also have to be much more aware of the aspects of instability and seepage. Feminist critique has to examine TB of law much more carefully; the potential of such an approach is well illustrated by the work of Noonan on criminal law.[53] A more embodied approach to law allows for a much more careful construction of "strategic" incursions into legal discourse which will not simply be moments of critique and defence, but represent a better understanding of both what is possible now and what potentials might be in play, envisioning "now" as a hinge, a threshold, a movement, between past and future. Deleuze continually emphasises the strategic, the ethical requirement to work now towards potential futures. In as far as this relates to aspects of legal discourse which have been continually subject to feminist critique, I would suggest that it means, for instance, having to recover very carefully such notions as responsibility and intention as ethical, strategic concerns rather than simply subjecting them to critique.

This brings us back to "the crisis" in subjectivity. What has to be understood is that this is a dynamic idea—not a "final place", but rather a site where two things are in play. First, a recognition that, in certain places and certain times, for strategic reasons, "the subject" will be represented as such, but will always in actual fact be contingent. Secondly, that this contingency is not due to lack, incompleteness or failure to foreclose, but rather is an affirmation of movement—of change, of possibilities of always "becoming". This is made possible both by recognising the actuality of the physical body and, at the very same time, thinking of the body as a figuration:

> "It is less a question of founding the subject than of elucidating the categories by which the feminist subject can be adequately represented".[54]

The feminist project has to incorporate not only a recognition of the actual condition of women now, but also be able to image and move towards a better future(s). This returns us to TB and again moves between what is possible now, without foreclosing what might be possible in the future. Thus, for example, the notion of "lived experience" has become highly problematic but it remains such an important focus for feminist work that it continues to have a resonance that cannot be easily dismissed. We have to take de Lauretis (1986) p. 9 seriously when she says: "Feminism differs from philosophical antihumanism in that it remains very much a politics of everyday life".

---

[52] Lim (1999).
[53] Noonan (1996).
[54] Braidotti (1991) p. 192.

There is, then, a very real sense in which the feminist project of beginning with what we have, situating ourselves and our desires, does resonate with the freeing of the monological subject by the pronouncement of "death" in post-modernism. But, if we are to avoid another betrayal and imprisonment (whether by nostalgia or by continuing with even more violent acts of fracture to attempt the impossibility of completeness), we must work with the figure of TB not as a place to become whole but as a site of multiplicity and potential.

REFERENCES

BOTTOMLEY, A., "Figures in a Landscape, Feminist Perspectives on Law, Land and Landscape" in A. Bottomley (ed.), *Feminist Perspectives on the Foundational Subjects of Law* (London, Cavendish, 1996).

BRAIDOTTI, R., *Patterns of Dissonance* (Cambridge, Polity, 1991).

——— , *Nomadic Subjects* (New York, Colombia University Press, 1994).

BRIDGEMAN, J. and MILLNS, S., *Feminist Perspectives on Law: Law's Engagement with the Female Body* (London, Sweet and Maxwell, 1998).

BROWN, B., "Women and Crime: The Dark Figures of Criminology" (1986) 15 *Economy and Society* 355.

BUTLER, J., *Bodies that Matter: On the Discursive Limits of "Sex"* (London, Routledge, 1993).

DAVIES, M., "The Proper: Discourses of Purity" (1998) XI.2. *Law and Critique* 147.

DE LAURETIS, T., *Feminist Studies/Critical Studies* (Bloomington, Indiana University Press, 1986).

DELEUZE, G. and GUTTARI, F., *Capitalism and Schizophrenia: A Thousand Plateaus* (Minneapolis, University of Minnesota Press, 1987).

DUNCAN, S., "The Mirror Tells its Tale: Constructions of Gender in Criminal Law", in A. Bottomley (ed.), *Feminist Perspectives on the Foundational Subjects of Law* (London, Cavendish, 1996) .

——— , "Disrupting the Surface of Order and Innocence: Towards a Theory of Sexuality and the Law" in (1994) 2 *Feminist Legal Studies* 3.

EISENSTIEN, Z., *The Female Body and the Law* (California, University of California Press, 1988).

FARSIDES, C., "Body Ownership", in S. McVeigh and S. Wheeler (eds.) *Law, Health and Medical Regulation* (Aldershot, Dartmouth, 1992).

GATENS, M., "Spinoza, Law and Responsibility" in P. Cheah *et al* (eds.), *Thinking Through the Body of the Law* (St Leonards, Allen and Unwin, 1996a).

——— , "Through a Spinozist Lens: Ethology, Difference, Power" in P. Patton (ed.), *Deleuze: A Critical Reader* (Oxford, Blackwell, 1996b).

GROSZ, E., *Volatile Bodies* (Bloomington, Indiana University Press, 1994a).

——— , "A Thousand Tiny Sexes: Feminism and Rhizomatics", in C. Boundas and D. Olkowski (eds.), *Gilles Deleuze and The Theater of Philosophy* (London, Routledge, 1994b).

——— , *Space, Time and Perversion* (London, Routledge, 1995).

IRIGARAY, L., *Parler n'est jamais neutre* (Paris, Minuit, 1985).

JERVIS, J., *Transgressing the Modern* (Oxford, Blackwell, 1999).

LIM, H., "Caesareans and Cyborgs"(1999) 7 *Feminist Legal Studies* 133.

LOUIZIDOU, E., "The Trouble with Rape: Gender Matters and Legal 'Transformations' (1999) 7 *Feminist Legal Studies* 275.

MINNIKC, R.K., *Creating Feminist Works* (New York, Barnard College Women's Centre, 1978).

MURPHY, T., "Feminism on Flesh" (1997) VII *Law and Critique* 37.

OVID, *Metamorphoses* (Cambridge, Harvard University Press, trans. Miller, F.J. 1916).

PILE, S. and THRIFT, N., *Mapping the Subject* (London, Routledge, 1995).

RICHARDSON, J., "Jamming the Machines: 'Woman' in the Work of Irigaray and Deleuze" (1998) XI *Law and Critique* 98.

ROSE, G., *Feminism and Geography* (Cambridge, Polity, 1993).

SHELDON, S. and THOMPSON, M., "Health Care Law and Feminism: A Developing Relationship", in S. Sheldon and M. Thompson (eds.), *Feminist Perspectives on Health Care Law* (London, Cavendish, 1998).

——, *Beyond Control: Medical Power and Abortion Law* (London: Pluto, 1997).

SMART, C., *Women, Crime and Criminology* (London, Routledge and Kegan Paul, 1976).

——, *Feminism and the Power of Law* (London, Routledge, 1989).

——, "The Woman of Legal Discourse" (1992) 1 *Social and Legal Studies* 29.

SPINOZA, *Practical Philosophy* (San Francisco, City Light Books, 1988).

STYCHIN, C., "Body Talk: Rethinking Autonomy, Commodification and the Embodied Legal Self", in S. Sheldon and M. Thompson (eds.), *Feminist Perspectives on Health Care Law* (London, Cavendish, 1998).

WHITFORD, M., *Luce Irigaray, Philosophy of the Feminine* (London, Routledge, 1991).

—— and TAYLOR, C., "To Follow a Rule", in C. Calhoun et al (eds.), *Bourdieu: Critical Perspectives* (Cambridge, Cambridge University Press, 1993).

9

Male Bodies, Family Practices

RICHARD COLLIER

"[T]he effects of oppression on the body—giving it its form, its gestures, its movement, its motricity, and even its muscles—have their origin in the abstract domain of concepts, through the words that formalize them" (Wittig (1992) p. xv, quoted by Hyde (1997) p. 3).

1. INTRODUCTION

THIS CHAPTER CRITICALLY assesses some of the conceptual themes and main developments taking place in recent scholarship on law and the body. It does so via a case study of some recent debates about how law might be used to "change" the behaviour of men in relation to the family (in particular, although not exclusively, in their position as fathers). Family law is a context in which questions of law and gender are well established within socio-legal scholarship. Specific engagements with the *bodies* of men (as men), however, remain rare. I argue that this is an area in which legal policy debates continue to be premised on an understanding of the relationship between the body, sex difference, and gender which is becoming increasingly problematic. Presenting an overview of a sociological literature termed the new "sexed bodies" scholarship, and questioning the continuing influence of social constructionist ideas of sex/gender within socio-legal work, I offer a re-thinking of the ways in which the male body has been understood in these debates. I place the male body at the centre of an analytic frame concerned with what it might mean to speak of embodiment, "family life" and changing gender relations between women and men at the beginning of the twenty-first century.

2. CONTEXTS: THE SOCIOLOGY OF THE BODY AND SOCIO-LEGAL STUDIES

Recent years have witnessed the emergence of a now considerable literature on the relationship between women's bodies and law (Bridgeman and Millns (1995); Naffine and Owens (1996)) as well as, more generally, law and "the body" (Cheah et al. (1996); Hyde (1997); Laciak (1996)). A number of texts have explored the ways in which law constitutes, "calls into being" and otherwise regulates male bodies within same-sex relationships (Estlund and Nussbaum (1997); Herman and Stychin (1995); Moran (1996); Stychin (1996)). The relationship between men's *heterosexual* bodies and law, however, is a topic that has tended to be somewhat less explored (Sheldon (1999)). Such an absence of engagement with the links between issues of embodiment, corporeality and male heterosexuality is striking given the voluminous socio-legal literature that exists on what might be termed the gender(ing) of family law in a more general sense.[1] This is work that has, after all, explicitly sought to address the relationship between law and the family using a range of interdisciplinary analyses, and has sought to contextualise law and legal practices within diverse and complex social relations.

Much of the scholarship on gender[2] originated from diverse feminist perspectives. But the idea that understandings of family life and "family values" have been historically enmeshed with the production of normative notions of gender or "sex roles"—of what it means, at particular moments, to be a "family" man, a "good" wife, and so on—is now a common theme in socio-legal scholarship.[3] Yet if this overarching framework of gender analysis is a well-established and accepted part of the socio-legal tradition,[4] an engagement with the relationship between family law and the sexed bodies of *men* remains rare. As many scholars have pointed out, discussions of gender and law continue, most usually, to be associated with either women and "the women question", with women's bodies and women's lives; or else, with regard to issues around homosexuality, the male body constituted as "perverted" (Moran (1996)), as Other (Herman and Stychin (1995); Stychin (1996)). The sexualised bodies of gays and lesbians are positioned in contrast to the (desexualised) heterosexual norm (Cooper and Herman (1991); Richardson (1996)). The "gender" of heterosexual men remains, notwithstanding the growth of writings about men and masculinities in recent years, a curious absence within this field of legal study.

Such a lack of engagement with the heterosexual male body in socio-legal studies might have seemed, at one time, to reflect the balance of broader sociological concern. This is, however, clearly no longer the case. Questions of embodiment, corporeality and the social meanings of sexual/sexed difference have become increasingly central to sociological scholarship, not least within a growing literature that has explored the changing nature of family life within the social conditions of late- or post-modernity (with the work of Giddens (1992), and Beck and

[1] The cases and materials text produced by Diduck and Kaganas (1999) provides a good overview of the scale and depth of this research.

[2] On the "socio-legal" approach more generally in the field of family law see further, e.g., Jolly (1996): *cf.* O'Donovan (1993).

[3] The influence of feminist scholarship here cannot be underestimated. See, e.g., work which continues to influence debates: Atkins and Hoggett (1984); Barrett and McIntosh (1982); Brophy and Smart (1985); Fineman (1995); Lacey (1998); O'Donovan (1993, 1985); Smart and Sevenhuijsen (1989); Smart (1984).

[4] By this I mean that "gender" is a now a clear presence within the socio-legal field, as evidenced by the number of papers on gender themes presented at the annual conference of the Socio-Legal Studies Association (SLSA). Note, more generally, the defined scope of the Law Unit of Assessment for RAE purposes as including "socio-legal studies and feminist/gender studies".

Beck-Gernsheim (1995) assuming a particular influence in this regard). Academic interest in the male body within the sociology of masculinities has, equally, been extensive.[5] More generally, over the past fifteen years or so, there has been an explosion of interest in embodiment in the academy, with much of the driving force for the work coming, not just from sociological, but also from philosophical, anthropological and historical scholarship.[6] A discussion of the core theoretical underpinnings and concerns of this diverse work is beyond the scope of this chapter. Nonetheless, it is possible to identify within this scholarship—whether it is concerned with "imaginary" (Gatens (1996)), "performative" (Butler (1993, 1990)) or "embodied" bodies (Davis (1997)), with "sexed", "sexy" (Grosz and Probyn (1995)), "communicative" or "discursively constructed" and "disciplined"[7] bodies—a number of recurring themes.

Core concerns have been, first, an attempt to challenge the idea that there exists a natural (naturally given) *pre-social* body (a body that exists, as it were, prior to discourse: see below); and, secondly, an attempt to question and transcend what are seen as a range of binary oppositions which, it is argued, have hitherto informed and constrained understandings of the body, sexuality and corporeality. Dualisms singled out for particular attention here include those of nature/nurture, the public/private divide, social/biological, hetero/homosexual (Edwards (1990)) and the distinction between sex/gender itself (Gatens (1983)). A project of disturbing or "bursting" (Murphy (1996)) these binaries has resulted in the posing of some very different questions about—and a very different conceptualisation *of*—the relationship between sex(ed) difference, gender and society. Taken together, these oppositions are seen as inextricably linked to what is depicted as the broader and far-reaching legacy of the rationalist primacy of mind over body within modernist thought more generally—a dualism that has historically been enmeshed with hierarchical notions of sex, gender and difference. Here the male/masculine has been systematically positioned as superior, and associated with qualities of rationality, activity, culture and the public sphere, whilst the female/feminine has been associated with emotionality, irrationality, passivity, and the private domain of the family.

---

[5] The work of R.W. Connell perhaps stands out, not only as one of the most influential writers in this area, but as one of the most systematic and sophisticated attempts to address the relation between men's bodies and masculinities. See, in particular, Connell (1995, 1987),

[6] It is not possible to do justice to the scope and depth of this work here. See further, and by way of illustration, the work of: Callard (1998); Davis (1997); Duncan (1996); Featherstone et al. (1991); Frank (1996); Shilling (1997, 1993); Turner (1996, 1992, 1984); Twigg (2000); Warren Perry and Sanchez (1998)).

[7] Following, most notably, Foucault's (1979, 1985, 1990) analysis of sexuality and power, the influence of which cannot be underestimated: also Foucault (1977).

Embodiment and the "sexed body"

If the above are prominent themes within the sociology of the body, what is meant by the term "sexed bodies" (Daly (1997)) or "new corporeal" scholarship?[8] What, in particular, might all this mean for law? In seeking to explore how a re-thinking of the idea of the *sexed* subject might facilitate an appreciation of how the "life of the body" can shed some light on understanding the family practices of men, it is possible to identify a number of key themes in current debates.

At the heart of recent work on the sexed body lies a critique of—and an attempt to transcend—the aforementioned sex/gender dualism. The idea that there exists a distinction between the biological "fact" of an individual's sex and their socially constituted gender identity continues to be seen as an analytic tool which, it is presumed, will "yield high explanatory returns" when seeking to account for the social, familial, discursive or legal constructions of subjectivities (Gatens (1996) p. 3). This enterprise embraces a politics of change and can be seen as politically progressive, whether conceived of in terms of changing men, changing society, changing women's aspirations and so on. However, it has been argued, this dualistic division between (biological) sex and (socially constructed) gender is itself a construction that has served to polarise accounts of the human subject in such a way that it becomes characterised as being either predominantly (or wholly) determined by the influence of, on the one hand, social relations (be they environment/society/gender) or, on the other, biological forces (be they heredity/the body/sex). But this involves presupposing the existence of a neutral, pre-social, *pre-discursive* body, which is then seen as the passive recipient of gender "roles" or "messages". Crucially, the sexed specificity of the bodies of women and men is here rendered completely irrelevant in determining subjective consciousness. In assuming that the body is, effectively, a passive *tabula rasa* upon which social lessons can be inscribed, the dominant philosophical model of sex/gender, arguably, is itself one that has negated what might be termed the sexed specificity of social subjectivity (Gatens (1983)).

The obvious charge that can be levelled against such an argument is, of course, that it amounts to an effective essentialism and/or reductionism in the way in which gender difference is conceptualised. Yet to accept that active processes are involved in becoming a (gendered) subject, a particular kind of "masculine" man or "feminine" woman, involves a recognition that some bodily experiences and life events (child birth, let us say), though they may lack any *fixed* significance in particular cultural contexts, are likely in all social structures to be privileged sites of significance. Thus, and as anthropological, ethnological and historical evidence shows, the body can, and clearly does, intervene to confirm or to deny certain social significances,[9] albeit that technological developments have transformed,

---

[8] A phrase adapted from Grosz (1994). Note also Diprose (1994); Gatens (1996); Grosz and Probyn (1995). See also Leng (1995).

[9] This argument follows Gatens (1996).

and are transforming, the contours of "what is possible" in this regard (as chapters elsewhere in this volume illustrate). From this perspective biology, understood as the complexity of products and capacities of the organism, is re-positioned. The *sexed* body, importantly, is seen as neither inherently (masculine) brute/active and so forth nor (feminine) passive/vulnerable, but as interwoven with *and constitutive of* a heterogeneity of systems of meaning, signification and representation.

In the light of the above, and perhaps unsurprisingly given the implicit focus on meaning and representation, what has followed in much academic work has been an engagement with the ways in which ideas of sexual difference have been made to signify hierarchically within specific discursive instances and contexts (such as law, legal discourse, literature, popular culture and so on).[10] There are a number of other themes which, in addition, relate to this more general attempt to re-think, transcend or otherwise disturb the sex/gender distinction. The sexed bodies literature has also sought to render contingent the idea of social identity, seeing identities as complex and heterogeneous, the social subject her/himself as composed of multiple and contradictory positionings or subjectivities.[11] For some writers, "gender" itself now appears, notably in a strand of work influenced by queer theory, as a "performative construction", something that is naturalised through repetition (most influentially in the work of Butler (1993, 1990); see also Bell and Valentine (1995); Gatens (1996); Grosz (1994); Grosz and Probyn (1995)).

Thus, far from suggesting that men and women have physically determined natures (a reductionist position) or embracing a wholly semiotic or cultural account (ultimately, no more tenable than a biological one),[12] social subjectivity is here understood as the lived experience of both a psychical and libidinally mapped body. The experience of the body is seen as giving meaning to subjects in ways that are socially and culturally inscribed. The intention is not to prioritise the body *over* "gender". It is, rather, to re-work the various dualisms between mind/body, nature/nurture and so on, in such a way that it becomes impossible to think *only* in terms of the "mind" or the "body" when approaching the idea of the sexed/gendered subject. At issue is an attempt to transcend what Gatens (1996) has referred to as the "tired and tiresome" charges of essentialism and biologism so often levelled at theories of sexual difference. To recognise sexual difference in such a manner is not to abrogate the field of the social and the political; to make reference to biology is not *necessarily*, as Brown (1990) p. 44 points out, to subscribe to

---

[10] Thus, Hyde (1997) presents readings of such subjects as the "body as machine", "the body as property" and the "fatigued body", "bodily narratives", "the legal vagina", "the legal penis", "tranquillising the prisoner", "body wastes", "the racial body" and "offensive bodies".

[11] See further, on male subjectivity Jefferson (1994).

[12] As Connell argues "social constructionist approaches to gender and sexuality underpinned by a semiotic approach to the body provide an almost complete antithesis to socio-biology. Rather than arrangements being the effects of the body-machine, the body is a field on which social determination runs riot" (1995) p. 50. Connell's concern is that "with so much emphasis on the signifier, the signified tends to vanish" (1995) pp. 50–1, resulting, he suggests, in a "disembodying" of sex. Gender, moreover, "is hardly in better case, when it becomes just a subject-position in discourse, the place from which one speaks, when gender is seen as, above all, a performance; or when the rendering contradictions within gendered lives become "an instatement of metaphor" (1995) p. 51.

any particular major biologistic premise and thus all the deduced implications of
that premise. What it *is* to do is to recognise a materiality of gender in/of bodies
(Hood-Williams (1996); Hood-Williams and Harrison (1998); see also Burkitt
(1998)); and, importantly, bodies that cannot be understood as simply categorised
into two, mutually exclusive groups, male and female, at once biologically fixed and
separate from the cultural context in which they exist. As Murphy notes (1996)
p. 41, in striving to acknowledge identity variables beyond the straightforward
sex/gender binary, many questions proceed to be asked about the status of sex,
gender and the body, questions which themselves re-figure understandings of the
relationship between the power of law and the social subject in a number of far-
reaching ways. The issue remains however: what questions? What, in particular for
the purposes of this chapter, might such a re-thinking of the "sexed body" mean for
developing an understanding of the relationship between law and the *male* body?

3. LAW, SEX DIFFERENCE AND THE BODIES OF MEN

It is now commonplace within both socio-legal and doctrinal legal scholarship to
state that law, in different ways, "influences" and "shapes our lives". Less explored,
however, at least until recent years, has been the way in which law relates to the
(presumed pre-legal) realm of nature and, in particular, to the idea of sexual difference as discussed above. Family law, perhaps more than any other area of legal
study, is concerned with this relationship between law and nature, with how "the
natural" connects, not just to the intimate, personal and "private parts" of life—
to sexual desires and activities, love and personal commitments—but also to ideas
of community, citizenship and sociality. It is perhaps ironic, therefore, that any
theoretical engagement with the sexed body has generally been avoided in family
law. When addressed at all, gender and sex difference have been marked by a seeming inability to go beyond the framework, concepts and reasoning of law's dominant (doctrinal, positivist) epistemology. Thus, whilst "the body" may have been
re-thought within sociological work, for a growing number of legal scholars there
is an immediate problem when seeking to re-think the bodies of women and men
in law. The epistemological and ontological frameworks of legal knowledge have
been largely structured around forms of philosophical understanding that conceptualise the body in terms of the dualistic distinction between (biological) sex
and (socially constructed) gender (Davies (1997)).

There are, however, signs that the sexed body is becoming an increasingly visible presence within legal studies. In recent years a number of texts have sought (in
the words of the title of one recent book) to *Think Through the Body of Law* via an
engagement with the new sociological and philosophical studies concerned with
embodiment and corporeality (Cheah et al. (1996)). A central question has been
the way in which law comes to have a "hold" over bodies; with how, in particular,
the "body of law"—legal codes, statutes and common law—is itself dependent on
ideas about the "lawfulness of bodies". The way in which legal studies has

addressed this question perhaps illustrates some of the central themes of the sexed bodies scholarship more generally, namely the ways in which ideas of sex difference are made to signify hierarchically within particular discursive contexts and a concern with the representation of bodies approached through the deconstruction of legal texts. This work has sought to explore the diverse ways in which the bodies of women and, to a lesser degree, men, have been constructed within legal discourse (whether cases, statutes or legal practices). And these legal bodies have been addressed via an exploration of a range of signifying practices which, importantly, have been understood to have functioned towards particular discursive and political ends (for example, and most notably, as being patriarchal, sexist, homophobic and/or racist in their effects).[13]

To illustrate. In seeking to "push the boundaries" of established critical theory, and in questioning the analytic and political utility of classic legal concepts such as consent, rights, privacy and equal treatment (e.g. Hyde (1997)), recent studies seeking to explore the (sexed) legal subject have produced analyses of how the bodies (and body "parts") of women and men have been constituted in legal discourse[14] within culturally specific contexts. For example, recent work has noted how, whilst the penis frequently appears in law as subject to a man's rational thought and control, the vagina tends to be presented as space, as an always-searchable absence deriving its identity from relations with other people (Hyde (1997) p. 172). Recurring assumptions have been made about the idea of there being a natural, sexual "fit" between the bodies of women and men, with particular notions of male (hetero) sexual activity, female passivity and a naturally given sex status informing legal determinations of what does, and does not, constitute a legal marriage (Collier (1995)).

In Naffine's (1994) discussion of rape law, similarly, the liberal rational individual central to criminal law is depicted not only as a sexed, autonomous and masculine subject, but as a peculiarly *dis*embodied being; as bounded, constituted as *male* as dependent on a separation from the bodies of other men and, crucially, on a hierarchical difference from female bodies. Naffine's approach, both here and elsewhere (Naffine (1997)), exemplifies the way in which a more general strand of feminist legal scholarship, particularly clear within the fields of medical and criminal law, has sought to chart the ways in which the bodies of women have been constituted in ways very different to those of men within legal texts. All too often, the bodies of women appear as incomprehensible, as fluid, *un*bounded, as defined by "openings and absences".[15] In the field of reproductive politics, Sheldon (1999) suggests that the bodies of men are marked more by absence and physical disengagement; here, men's safe, stable and bounded bodies signify what would seem to

---

[13] Some of this work, e.g. the Bridgeman and Millns (1995) collection, is positioned from the outset within the frame of (British) legal feminism and, specifically, the burgeoning literature on the female body. Recurring themes can be seen to be an attempt to question previous essentialist accounts in an exploration of "The Woman of Legal Discourse" (Smart (1992)) and an awareness of the challenges to feminism's "Woman" wrought by post-modernism.

[14] Again, the Bridgeman and Millns (1995) collection illustrates this diversity.

[15] For detailed discussion of this point, see Anne Bottomley (chap. 8).

be a somewhat tangential, contingent relation to gestation and reproduction. Feminism, Sheldon (1999) suggests, has thus produced a rich scholarship representing, in different ways, the female body as leaky, volatile, permeable and so forth. What it has not done, however, for understandable political reasons, is pay the same kind of attention to the (implicit) contrasted construction of the male body as bounded, stable and (it is assumed) non-permeable. Waldby (1995) concurs, delineating the contours of male heterosexuality more generally as being premised on assumptions about an impenetrable (in particular in relation to the anus), active, penetra*ting* and genitally-focused male body.

Such attempts to rethink the "bodies of law" cannot be confined to analyses of legal texts, be they cases or statutes. Recent work has also sought to explore how lawyers and other legal actors *talk* about the body. What metaphors, similes and other verbal constructions cumulatively form a discourse of the body within the legal field in this more general sense? Of particular concern here has been the ways in which the bodies of women have been routinely sexualised within the legal field in ways that the bodies of men have not. Here, the male body has been seen as systematically *de*sexed, evacuated from any sense of corporeality (with the sexuality of women and men in the legal profession itself serving as a case in point in this regard: Collier (1998); Thornton (1996)). What does it mean to say that the body is property that can be owned, or a machine that labours, or a privacy interest that needs to be somehow balanced? When, and how, are particular bodies figured as sites of difference, whether gendered, racial or other?

Throughout each of these analyses, importantly, questions of *difference* and *hierarchy* are seen as entwined. In some accounts, law's social power itself appears, at times, to be pervasive and seemingly inescapable.[16] What emerges from these readings of law and the body is not simply that there are multiple constructions of corporeality available to legal and other speakers in ways that are neither "natural" nor limited by biology. What we have here is a set of conversations about the bodies of women and men understood as discursive creations and approached from within a project of denaturalisation and deconstruction. And at issue has been a project of working towards what has been termed a *re*constructive politics of legal bodies, or what Hyde (1997) has usefully referred to as a "jurisprudence of human presence". What remains unclear within this work, however, is how such readings of the "male" body within legal discourse relate to the bodies of men in terms of social *practice* itself; how it relates, for example, to what men *do* in their "everyday" lives as, let us say, familial social subjects. It is this issue that I wish to explore in the next section.

4. RETHINKING THE MALE "FAMILIAL" BODY

The above readings of the body in legal texts can tell us something about how law produces notions of embodiment and corporeality; about how, for example,

---

[16] Smart (1995, 1989). See further Sandland (1996).

women's and men's practices are constituted as normal, deviant, legal or illegal, moral or immoral. What it does not do, however, is provide us with a way in to an account of the lived practices, the everyday experience as it were, of women and men. It is important to remember in this regard that precisely such a "lived" male body is, on one level, a ubiquitous presence within family law. It is, after all, the lived bodies of men which can be deemed by law at various moments to be sexually functional or dysfunctional, as capable or incapable of vaginal penetration (Collier (1995)); male bodies that may be fertile or infertile, capable or incapable of reproduction (Sheldon (1999)); bodies that may experience psychological and physical harms during marriage breakdown and the divorce process; bodies that are violent, can attack others, abuse, maim and kill (Burton et al. (1998); Dobash et al. (2000); Hearn (1998)); bodies that have been positioned by law in particular spatial relationships to children—bodies that do (or do not) touch and caress, feed and bathe, drop off and pick up (from school, from the house of the other parent); bodies that are experienced (by adults or children) as being physically distant or close; bodies that love, nurture, care and otherwise seek to protect; bodies that "work", whether at paid employment or at sustaining relationships (be it with partners and children, parents, grandparents and the wider family and community); bodies that experience sexual intimacy, desire and pleasure; bodies, in short, that are "there" in a most fundamental sense. As Morgan suggests, and as each of the above examples illustrates:

> "*Family practices are, to a very large extent, bodily practices.* Family themes and family concerns revolve around issues of birth, death and sexuality and the connections and relationships that are made and unmade through these . . . 'Our daily experiences of living . . . are intrinsically bound up with experiencing and managing our own and other people's bodies'" (Shilling (1993) p. 22, quoted in Morgan (1996) pp. 113–14, my emphasis).

There are limitations to what analyses of discursive constructions can tell us about the "family" or "family law"; those everyday family practices which are, as Morgan notes, "to a very large extent, bodily practices". In order to explore this question further, and to consider what it might mean for understanding the relationship between men, women and gender to integrate an appreciation of the lived body, I wish to consider how these issues have played out in the context of an ongoing debate about the possibility and limits of the use of law in seeking to change the practices of men in relation to the family: what has been termed the "men and change" debate.

(a) The example of the "men and change" debate

A concern with changing the behaviour of men in relation to what are seen as their familial commitments, responsibilities and duties—whether during subsisting marital or non-marital relationships, or else in the post-divorce/separation scenario—

has become a pressing issue in many Western societies. As part of a broader conversation about shifting gender relations, this is an issue that has come to pervade
newspaper and magazine articles, talk shows, television dramas, popular novels and
films. In these debates, the relationship between men and the *family* has come to
have a central significance and the question of how the law might be used in seeking
to promote, encourage or reinforce certain kinds of behaviour seen as socially desirable on the part of men, is often asked; for example, and to illustrate some of the
main concerns of this debate, around the issue of what are, and should be, the legal
responsibilities, rights and status of men, whether married or unmarried
(Lord Chancellor's Department (1998); Pickford (1999)), within the "new" or
"bi-nuclear" family (Silva and Smart (1999)); in relation to the ways in which family and employment policies conceptualise a need to change the behaviour of men
during marriage and cohabiting relationships (Collier (1999a); Lewis (2000)); with
regard to the promotion of equality between women and men in the workplace and
the family, or the more general promotion of more "positive" cultural images of
family men (and in particular of men as fathers: Inman (1999); Lloyd (1996);
Richardson (1998)); in relation to attempts to promote "good enough" responsible
post-divorce parenting on the part of men (Smart and Neale (1999a, 1999b)),
whether in the context of securing the provision of child support (Diduck (1995);
Wallbank (1997)) or in seeking to maintain post-divorce contact between fathers
and children (Smart and Neale (1997a, 1997b)); and, finally, in the context of
debates about families, crime and citizenship, where ideas of parental responsibility
have moved increasingly politically centre stage (Gelsthorpe (1999)). Thus, a concern with changing men's family practices—whether in promoting ideas of "good"
fatherhood, of men as good responsible employees who strike a balance between the
demands of work and family life, as good citizens—can be seen to be central to
ongoing political debates about the parameters of the family and understandings of
contemporary family life.

If we look a little more closely, it becomes clear that there are a number of
assumptions about men and gender being made in these debates. In relation, for
example, to the ideas of *gender neutrality* and the *individualising* of a well-
established feminist critique of men, what we have here is a more general assumption that "changing men" might best be understood in terms of a need to change
existing gender relations. Social change is thus conceptualised in terms of a need
to "address", "challenge", "transform" or "transcend" a range of existing gender
"norms" around what men do. What is more difficult to see is any consideration
of how material power and interest relates to how family practices are lived. This
itself connects, I suggest, to the ways in which a focus on gender has sometimes
served to efface any concern with questions of embodiment, power and the materiality of social practices.

(b) Embodiment, power and social practice: re-thinking family politics

Central to a range of legal interventions in relation to "the family" has been the core idea of gender neutrality.[17] By this is meant, not so much the idea that specific interventions are (and should) now routinely be couched in terms of formally gender neutral language, but the related assumption that women and men themselves come before the law, as it were, as gender-neutral, ungendered beings. Yet the concept of gender neutrality, as a number of scholars concerned with the idea of sex difference have now argued, is extremely problematic in relation to the family in several respects (see, for example, Boyd (1989); Fineman (1995, 1991, 1983)). We have seen above something of the way in which sociology's engagement with the complex ways in which structural and discursive practices both constitute and give meaning to sexual difference in specific instances has brought to the surface what might be described as the nature of the sexed *as different* experiences of women's and men's "gendered lives" in relation to contemporary family practices (Fineman (1995, 1994)); and, in so doing, whether it is in relation to the workplace or the family, the integration of a "politics of difference" (Young (1993, 1990a, 1990b)), not least around questions of corporeality and reproduction, leads to some fundamental and unsettling questions about recent attempts to promote social justice via the conceptualisation of the gender-neutral or ungendered citizen. Recent sociological work suggests that the family is not a pre-given site in or to which men and women "come" as fixed and finished gendered subjects. Family practices are, rather, active forces in the social construction of ideas about "family" men and women in the first place (Morgan (1999)). In seeking to engage with men's bodies at the level of these everyday practices in relation to the family—that is, what men "do" in their lives—David Morgan has suggested that family life itself might usefully be:

> "considered through a variety of different lenses and from different perspectives. Thus, family practices may also be gender practices, class practices, age practices and so on . . . family life is never simply family life and . . . is always continuous with other areas of existence. The points of overlap and connection are often more important than the separate entities, understood as work, family, politics and so on" (Morgan (1999) p. 13).

In approaching family as "a constructed quality of human interaction . . . an active process rather than a thing-like object of detached social investigation", this analysis shares with the sexed bodies approach discussed above a concern with performativity, fluidity and hybridity, and an attempt to transcend such binaries as the public/private distinction. It also, importantly, serves to question any pre-given, taken-for-granted notion of what "a family" (or family practice) might be. In contrast to those accounts which conceptualise family at the outset as "a relatively bounded unit exchanging with other, equally relatively bounded units" (Morgan (1999) p. 14), a focus on the "doing" of family life in this way embraces

---

[17] See, e.g., Andrew Bainham's discussion in chap. 10.

an attempt to appreciate difference and diversity in family forms, resisting the all too common slippage into a normative model of heterosexual "family life" (something which in any case is becoming increasingly untenable in the face of demographic changes: Reinhold (1994)). From this perspective, there are multifarious ways in which diverse social practices play a key role in the constitution of gendered "familial" subjects; via processes, for example, such as the encoding of cultural, social and economic capital, the construction of family work as a form of emotional labour and via normative notions of parental responsibility. It brings men into the picture, not least because men are clearly active participants in the doing of family life in this broader sense as much as women (on the diversity and complexity of contemporary fathering practices, for example, see Lewis (2000)). However, it also brings into question what we know about the reality, as opposed to any rhetoric, of equality within contemporary family life.

There exists a vast body of empirical research on family life which suggests that family practices, not least those in relation to parenting and domestic labour, continue to be sexed (as different) in some far-reaching ways.[18] In terms of what we might term the "day-to-day" realities of family life, numerous research studies indicate there to be a continuing disjunction between the *rhetoric* and the *realities* of contemporary family practices. Far from moves towards gender convergence and sex equality constituting the norm of the "new family", research continues to highlight the pervasive nature of the distinct and differential experiences of women and men in relation to the negotiation of responsibilities and commitments around the "inevitable dependencies" of family life (most notably, although not exclusively, in relation to childcare and, increasingly, elder care: Fineman (1995); see, for example, Arendell (1986, 1995); Brandth and Kvande (1998); Eichler (1990); Gray and Merrick (1996); Grbich (1995); Smart and Neale (1999a); Warin et al. (1999)). This is not simply to argue that men have been dissociated from the familial because of the way in which certain gendered discourses around the meaning of heterosexual masculinities have been historically institutionalised within dominant understandings of family and working life (Collier (1995)). Looking towards social action, everyday practice and to what the sexed bodies of women and men *do*—approaching parenthood, for example, as a material, embodied practice—involves recognising the importance of the ways in which ideas of sexual difference are given meaning. It involves, importantly, questioning *how* diverse gendered experiences of family life (again, let us say, the experience of parenting a child) come to be produced and reproduced; and it involves an analysis of how women's and men's gendered lives are themselves *lived*. "Gender" does

---

[18] Far from revealing any pattern of gender convergence based on a coming together of women's and men's "gendered roles", empirical research points to the continuing existence of a pervasive sexual division of domestic labour, neatly defined by McMahon as covering "all the necessary elements of care and maintenance of people which occur in households. Domestic labour ranges from cleaning the family toilets to sensitively nurturing the family psyches. It is labour because it requires effort and it must be done, continually, and it remains sexually divided—for whatever reason, the majority of domestic labour, whether toilet cleaning or soul soothing, is carried out by women" (1999) p. 2.

not "float free" from what women and men do. And it is in this regard that the dominant frame of gender neutrality has served to divert attention from what *men* do by problematising, not social practice, but the abstract notion of men's "gender", conceived, most usually, in terms of the seemingly ubiquitous "social problem" of their "masculinity" or "masculinities".

Let us be clear about what is happening in this process. When the issue of men's gendered bodies is addressed within so much socio-legal family scholarship—a literature which, we have seen, has been concerned largely with the representation of bodies in legal texts—it so often would appear to "float free" from what these bodies actually do.[19] Whilst men's practices may be criticised, it is the gender category "masculinity" that is most often seen to be the problem, with resulting calls for masculinity to be "redefined", "reconstructed", "dismantled", or "transformed" now becoming common in contemporary gender debates around the family. Instead of questioning whether men should change their *behaviour*, a debate has been constructed around ideas of men "wrestl[ing] with the meaning of masculinity". *Domination is an aspect of masculinity, rather than something men simply do.* Even practice-based analyses of masculinity find it hard to avoid constructing masculinity as some kind of thing-in-itself (McMahon (1993) p. 691, my emphasis). Yet the host of research on men, their masculinities and the day-to-day reality of family practices suggests that the context in which this core masculine identity is produced is itself one marked by a constellation of family and employment practices which continue to be sexed (as different) in far-reaching material and, importantly, psychologically complex ways (Day Sclater (1999, 1998); also Yates (2000)). Within this debate about men and change "good" fatherhood, for example, continues to be depicted as something that is to be learnt, something requiring practice and hard work. It is a status and a state of mind to be achieved in a "struggle" against other demands. As such, what we have here is a model of men's parenting which can itself be seen to involve a distinctly "masculine" notion of unconnectedness and endeavour, with "successful" fatherhood being routinely portrayed as "the product of acquired knowledge and mastery of action. Motherhood, in contrast, still tends to be represented as having an instinctive core" (Lupton and Barclay (1997) p. 147). Or, as Smart and Neale (1999b) put it, what we have here is a model of men's parenting which continues to be understood largely within psychologistic, personal and individualised terms, devoid of any appreciation of the complex social and economic developments which are constituting broader changes in family practices.

It is this notion of the *individualising* of a politics of gender that is central to my argument at this stage. If we begin, as McMahon seeks to do, to integrate perspectives from the oft neglected Other of French feminist thought, feminist materialist scholarship (that is, a literature concerned with a materialist analysis of labour: e.g. Leonard and Atkins (1996); Leonard et al. (1996)), what comes into view in

---

[19] This argument follows, and adapts, the analysis of McMahon (1999).

a consideration of contemporary family practices is men's direct *interest* in maintaining these existing (and well-documented) sexual divisions of domestic labour. And in marked contrast to the making of any assumptions about there being a positive "push for change" on the part of men—an idea inherent within so much of the contemporary rhetoric around gender and families—there exists a considerable body of research which attests to the existence of what might more accurately be termed a widespread resistance, stalling and reluctance to change on the part of men, as well as the continuing material, cultural and symbolic empowerment of men generally across a number of social fields—not least the supposedly increasingly egalitarian and equal workplace.

This argument supports the claims of those who have suggested that gender neutrality has itself, in many respects, led in practice to a devaluing and systematic negation of the social importance of mothers and mothering, a position which Fineman (1995) has described as "motherhood descending" (see also Dowd (2000)). In such a context, what is so revealing about present debates in this area is, McMahon (1999) suggests, how much of the rhetoric in conversations about families, men and change in fact constitutes an attempt to bolster and reaffirm heterosexual marriage *in the face of* the threat posed by the economic and cultural changes in women's lives and, importantly, the resulting dissatisfaction on the part of many women with existing sexual divisions of labour. What is consistently passed over, in short, is the way in which men, as a sex group, stall and resist change whilst, at the same time, and paradoxically, an entire debate about family life is being constructed in terms of a demand for men *to* change. A range of discourses about men, masculinities and social change would themselves be appearing to depict male personality "as a reification, or hypostatization, of men's practices (and, of course, the practices of women that support them). [This] reification is then employed to explain these same practices" (McMahon, 1993, p.689). It is in this regard that the sexual political effects of this debate can themselves be seen to be conservative because of the ways in which ". . . attention is directed away from *interested* male practices and toward [this] reified *personality*" (McMahon (1993) p. 689, my emphasis). At the very moment when a consideration of the materiality of family practices is effaced (the kind of analysis that, I have suggested, a consideration of the sexed body would lead to), a broader discourse around gender (neutrality) and (sex) equality itself has emerged as dominant.

Where does this argument leave the relationship between law and the bodies of men? Taking the sexed body seriously is, I suggest, both potentially productive and unsettling for understanding the relationship between law and the family. It is unsettling because of the way in which such a focus on fluidity, hybridity and disorder serves to side-step the disciplinary borders which have so often been policed by legal scholars. To state that the boundaries and conceptual unity of family law may be uncertain in this way is by itself, of course, far from original. Yet looking beyond the family towards an appreciation of how social and economic changes (not least those around employment) are transforming social experiences of family life,[20] serves itself to reposition male practices in a number of ways. It is productive, therefore, precisely because it calls for analyses which cross boundaries, not least in relation to the idea of the "private" family (Bennett Woodhouse (1999); Fineman (1999)). To address an issue such as the social structuring and experience of childcare, domestic labour, or the everyday (re)negotiations of men and women around the commitments (and pleasures) of work and home calls, for example, for an understanding of diverse areas of law (employment law, for example, is as much, from this perspective, a part of "family law" in as much as it regulates family life, as the traditional subjects of marriage and divorce). Such an approach does, however, serve to undermine some of the optimism that appears to run through the way in which notions of gender convergence and sex equality have played out in present debates. What we have here is, ultimately, an approach in which social practice is seen as being enmeshed with relations of power.

At the present moment a debate about family, gender and change has been constructed around ideas of the "new burdens" of men, the "obstacles" to changing men embodied in the structuring of the labour market, to the intractability of the work structure and the demands of employers and so forth.[21] What is not addressed is the way in which the present structuring of the labour market itself, overall, can be seen to "serve male interests, and be maintained by their practices. Instead, the [very] structure is used to explain why men cannot change" (McMahon (1993) p. 689). Any project of "changing men", as the sociologist Bob Connell has long argued (1987, 1995), cannot be reduced to either individual or collective projects of self-actualisation on the part of men. It is, rather, about the way in which a currently dominant social group continues to, or ceases to, exercise (or have taken away from them?) social power.

5. CONCLUDING REMARKS

The heterosexual male body, I have argued, remains a curious absence within much socio-legal scholarship concerned with the meaning of family values and family life. This is so notwithstanding the ways in which broader developments within sociology have themselves, in recent years, resulted in a profound questioning of the analytic utility and coherence of concepts premised on the epistemic frame of sex/gender (not least, for example, those of heterosexuality/heterosexualities and masculinity/masculinities). Drawing on recent work within this literature, this chapter has addressed a number of emerging themes within contemporary critical thought that have implications for our understanding of the

---

[20] The view that "the family" is constructed, moulded by or as otherwise reflecting broader social, economic and cultural shifts has been increasingly challenged within sociological scholarship. Far from being a passive recipient or object of social power, family practices themselves are now seen to impact on these broader changes: see further Smart and Neale (1999a).

[21] As McMahon (1993) notes, the empirical validity of this argument can itself be questioned. Many women do manage to occupy primary labour market positions whilst also taking major responsibility for family work.

relationship between law and the body, the family and the social. In seeking to read the biological in the light of the social, and in order to avoid the collapsing of "sex" with "gender", I have sought to contribute to a broader debate about the relationship between law and the family within Anglo-American legal scholarship. This is a debate in which the institution of heterosexual marriage is itself being reconceptualised as the foundation of stability and social cohesion.

In bringing to the fore the ways in which the very idea of the heterosexual family is a contested political terrain, a site of competing interests, I have suggested that the debate about men and change taking place at present can be seen as an aspect of a broader social conversation about the very meaning of the "private" heterosexual family (Fineman (1999)). Shifting the focus of analysis away from a concern with gendered (masculine) "roles", "identities", "personalities" and so forth, and towards an engagement with the nature of the epistemic frame within which ideas of the body and corporeality are conceptualised in the first place, a critical engagement with the heterosexual male body leads towards an analysis of the interwoven and complex networks of structured heterosexual social practices which derive legitimation from existing social arrangements (Collier (2000)). In relation to men, for example, the nature of men's *dis*embodiment from the family, the dominant cultural production of men's bodies as simultaneously *empow*ered, bounded, non-permeable and stable artefacts, itself speaks volumes about the ways in which Women's Otherness has been constructed in such a way as to side-step the issue of how the (heterosexual) "Man" of legal discourse has bound men to ideas of pre-given, sexually specific masculine/male bodies.

My analysis suggests that a range of cultural discourses are presently problematising what men do in relation to "family life" in far-reaching ways. This is happening, however, in such a manner that—behind the ostensibly progressive rhetoric of equality, gender convergence and gender neutrality—issues of power and material interest are systematically depoliticised within discussions of contemporary family practices. A consideration of the embodied nature of the social relations, of material practice, leads to a questioning of how ideas of familial commitment, dependency and responsibility continue to be sexed in some very different ways. For all the seeming heterogeneity of new ways of "being" a heterosexual man in a context in which the male body has itself been increasingly culturally commodified (Mort (1996); Nixon (1996)), what continues too rarely to be questioned is the autonomy of men to opt out of caring relations and, importantly, what this then tells us about the way society values intimacy. Crucially, the vocabulary of gender neutrality, like the epistemic frame of sex/gender from which it derives, paradoxically appears disconnected from any appreciation of the sexed nature and material realities of care and caring—a recognition, for example, that the choice and commitment to care *about* is not necessarily the same thing as caring *for*. Ultimately, I have suggested, an engagement with the bodies of men which transcends the level of textual, deconstructive analysis offers a way of questioning the epistemological frameworks through which the relationship between law, sex and the body has been understood. It opens up, importantly, an engagement with the politics of the family which might itself address what men and women do in such a way that theory remains grounded in material practice.

REFERENCES

ARENDELL, T., *Fathers and Divorce* (London, Sage, 1995).
—— , *Mothers and Divorce* (Berkeley, University of California Press, 1986).
ATKINS, S. and HOGGETT, B., *Women and the Law* (Oxford, Blackwell, 1984).
BARRETT, M. and McINTOSH, M., *The Anti-Social Family* (London, Verso, 1982).
BECK, U. and BECK GERNSHEIM, E., *The Normal Chaos of Love* (Cambridge, Polity, 1995).
BELL, D., and VALENTINE, G., "The Sexed Self: Strategies of Performance, Sites of Resistance", in S. Pile and N. Thrift (eds.), *Mapping the Subject: Geographies of Cultural Transformation* (Routledge, London, 1995).
BENNETT WOODHOUSE, B., "The Dark Side of Family Privacy" (1999) *George Washington Law Review* 67 (5/6) 1247.
BOYD, S., "From Gender Specificity to Gender Neutrality? Ideologies in Canadian Child Custody Law" in J. Brophy and C. Smart (eds.), *Feminism and the Politics of Child Custody* (London, Routledge, 1989).
BRANDTH, B. and KVANDE, E., "Masculinity, Child Care and the Reconstruction of Fathering" (1998) 46 *The Sociological Review* 293.
BRIDGEMAN, J. and MILLNS, S. (eds.), *Law and Body Politics: Regulating the Female Body* (Aldershot, Dartmouth, 1995).
BROPHY, J. and SMART, C. (eds.), *Women in Law: Explorations in Family, Law and Sexuality* (London, Routledge, 1985).
BROWN, B., "Reassessing the Critique of Biologism in Feminist Perspectives in Criminology", in L. Gelsthorpe and A. Morris (eds.), *Feminist Perspectives in Criminology* (Buckingham and Bristol, PA, Open University Press, 1990).
BURKITT, I., "Sexuality and Gender Identity: from a Discursive to a Relational Analysis" (1998) *The Sociological Review* 483.
BURTON, S., REGAN, L. and KELLY, L., *Domestic Violence: Supporting Women and Challenging Men* (The Policy Press, Bristol, 1998).
BUTLER, J., *Gender Trouble: Feminism and the Subversion of Identity* (New York and London, Routeldge, 1990).
—— , *Bodies that Matter: on the Discursive Limits of Sex* (New York and London, Routledge, 1993).
CALLARD, F., "The Body in Theory" (1998) 16 *Environment and Planning D: Society and Space* 387–400.
CHEAH, P., FRASER, D. and GRBICH, J., (eds.), *Thinking Through the Body of Law* (St. Leonards, Australia, Allen and Unwin, 1996).
COLLIER, R., *Masculinity, Law and the Family* (London, Routledge, 1995).
—— , "'Nutty Professors', 'Men in Suits' and 'New Entrepreneurs': Corporeality, Subjectivity and Change in the Law School and Legal Practice" (1998) 7(1) *Social and Legal Studies* 27.
—— , "'Feminising the Workplace'? (Re)constructing the 'Good Parent' in employment law and family policy" in A. Morris and T. O'Donnell (eds.), *Feminist Perspectives on Employment Law* (London, Cavendish, 1999).

COLLIER, R., "Straight Families, Queer Lives" in D. Herman and C. Stychin (eds.),*Sexuality in the Legal Arena* (London, Athlone Press, 2000).

CONNELL, R. W., *Gender and Power* (Sydney, Allen and Unwin, 1987).

——, *Masculinities*, Cambridge (Cambridge, Polity Press, 1995).

COOPER, D. and HERMAN, D., "Getting 'The Family Right': Legislating Heterosexuality in Britain, 1986–1991" (1991) 10 *Canadian Journal of Family Law* 41.

DALY, K., "Different Ways of Conceptualising Sex/Gender in Feminist Theory and their Implications for Criminology" (1997) 1 *Theoretical Criminology* 25.

DAVIES, M., "Taking the Inside Out: Sex and Gender in the Legal Subject", in N. Naffine and R. J. Owens (eds.), *Sexing the Subject of Law* (London, Sweet and Maxwell, 1997).

DAVIS, K. (ed.), *Embodied Practices. Feminist Perspectives on the Body* (London,Sage, 1997).

DAY SCLATER, S., "Divorce—Coping Strategies, Conflict and Dispute Resolution" (1998) *Family Law*, March, 150.

——, *Divorce: A Psychosocial Study* (Aldershot, Ashgate, 1999).

DIDUCK, A., "The Unmodified Family: The Child Support Act and the Construction of Legal Subjects" (1995) 22 *Journal of Law and Society* 527.

—— and KAGANAS, F., *Family Law, Gender and the State: Text, Cases and Materials* (Oxford, Hart, 1999).

DIPROSE, R., *The Bodies of Women: Ethics, Embodiment and Sexual Difference* (London, Routledge, 1994).

DOBASH, R.E., DOBASH, R.P., CAVANAGH, K. and LEWIS, R., *Changing Violent Men* (London, Sage Series on Violence Against Women, 2000).

DOWD, N., *Redefining Fatherhood* (New York, New York University Press, 2000).

DUNCAN, N. (ed.), *Body Space: Destablising Geographies of Gender and Sexuality* (London, Routledge, 1996).

EDWARDS, T., "Beyond Sex and Gender: Masculinity, Homosexuality and Social Theory" in J. Hearn. and D. Morgan (eds.), *Men, Masculinities and Social Theory* (London, Unwin Hyman, 1990).

EICHLER, M., "The Limits of Family Law Reform, or The Privatization of Female and Child Poverty" (1990) 7 *Canadian Family Law Quarterly* 59.

ESTLUND, D. M. and NUSSBAUM (eds.), *Sex Preference and Family: Essays on Law and Nature* (Oxford, Oxford University Press, 1997).

FEATHERSTONE, M., HEPWORTH, M. and TURNER, B. S. (eds.), *The Body: Social Process and Cultural Theory* (London, Sage, 1991).

FINEMAN, M.L., "Implementing Equality: the Rhetoric and Reality of Divorce Reform" (1983) *University of Wisconsin Law Review* 789.

FINEMAN, M.A., *The Illusion of Equality: The Rhetoric and Reality of Divorce Reform* (Chicago, University of Chicago Press, 1991).

FINEMAN, M., "Feminist Legal Scholarship and Women's Gendered Lives" in M. Cain and C. Harrington (eds.), *Lawyers in a Postmodern World* (Buckingham,Open University Press, 1994).

——, *The Neutered Mother, The Sexual Family and Other Twentieth Century Tragedies* (New York, Routledge, 1995).

——, "What Place for Family Privacy?" (1999) 67 *The George Washington Law Review* 1207.

FOUCAULT, M., *Discipline and Punish: The Birth of the Prison* (Harmondsworth, Penguin, 1977).

FOUCAULT, M., *The History of Sexuality Vol 1: An Introduction* (Harmondsworth, Penguin, 1979).

—— , *The Use of Pleasure: The History of Sexuality Vol 2* (Harmondsworth, Penguin, 1985).

—— , *The Care of the Self: The History of Sexuality Vol 3* (Harmondsworth, Penguin, 1990).

FRANK, A. W., "For a Sociology of the Body: an Analytic Review" in M. Featherstone, M. Hepworth and B. S. Turner (eds.), *The Body: Social Process and Cultural Theory* (London, Sage, 1996).

GATENS, M., "A Critique of the Sex/Gender Distinction" in J. Allen and P. Patton (eds.), *Beyond Marxism? Interventions After Marx* (Sydney, Intervention Publications, 1983).

—— , *Imaginary Bodies: Ethics, Power and Corporeality* (London and New York, Routledge, 1996).

GELSTHORPE, L., "Youth Crime and Parental Responsibility" in A. Bainham, S. Day Sclater and M. Richards (eds.), *What is a Parent? A Socio-Legal Analysis* (London, Hart, 1999).

GIDDENS, A., *The Tranformation of Intimacy* (Cambridge, Polity, 1992).

GRAY, C. and MERRICK, S., "Voice Alterations: Why Women Have More Difficulty Than Men With the Legal Process of Divorce" (1996) 34 *Family and Conciliation Courts Review* 240.

GRBICH, C., "Male Primary Caregivers and Domestic Labour: Involvement or Avoidance?" (1995) 1(2) *Journal of Family Studies* 114.

GROSZ, E., *Volatile Bodies: Towards a Corporeal Feminism* (St Leonards, New South Wales, Allen and Unwin, 1994).

GROSZ, E. and PROBYN, E. (eds.), *Sexy Bodies: Strange Carnalities of Feminism* (Routledge, London, 1995).

HEARN, J., *The Violences of Men* (London, Sage, 1998).

HERMAN, D. and STYCHIN, C. (eds.), *Legal Inversions: Lesbians, Gay Men and the Politics of Law* (Philadelphia, Temple University Press, 1995).

HOOD-WILLIAMS, J., "Goodbye to Sex and Gender" (1996) 44(1) *The Sociological Review* 1.

HOOD-WILLIAMS, J. and CEAREY HARRISON, W., "Trouble with Gender" (1998) 46(1) *The Sociological Review* 73.

HYDE, A., *Bodies of Law* (Princeton, New Jersey, Princeton University Press, 1997).

INMAN, K., "Invisible Men", *The Guardian*, 17 November 1999.

JEFFERSON, T., "Theorizing Masculine Subjectivity" in T. Newburn and E.A. Stanko (eds.), *Just Boys Doing Business? Men, Masculinities and Crime* (London, Routledge, 1994).

JOLLY, S., "Family Law" in P. Thomas (ed.), *Socio-Legal Studies* (Ashgate, Aldershot, 1996).

LACEY, N., *Unspeakable Subjects* (Oxford, Hart Publishing, 1998).

LACIAK, B., "Sex, Gender and Body in Polish Democracy in the Making" (1996) 10(1) *International Journal of Law, Policy and the Family* 37.

LENG, K.W., "New Australian Feminism: Towards a Discursive Politics of Australian Feminist Thought" (1995) 7(1) *Antithesis* 47.

LEONARD, D. and ATKINS, L. (eds.), *Sex in Question: French Materialist Feminism* (London, Taylor and Francis, 1996).

LEONARD, D., BARKER and S. ALLEN (eds.), *Dependence and Exploitation in Work and Marriage* (Longman, London, 1996).

LEWIS, C., *A Man's Place in the Home: Fathers and Families in the UK* (York, Joseph Rowntree Foundation, 2000).

LLOYD, T., *Fathers Group Evaluation* (London, Working With Men, 1996).

LORD CHANCELLOR'S DEPARTMENT, *Court Procedures for the Determination of Paternity: The Law on Parental Responsibility for Unmarried Fathers—Consultation Paper* (London, Lord Chancellor's Department, 1998).

Lupton, D. and Barclay, L., *Constructing Fatherhood: Discourses and Experiences* (London, Sage, 1997).

McMahon, A., "Male Readings of Feminist Theory: the Psychologization of Sexual Politics in the Masculinity Literature"(1993) 22 *Theory and Society* 675.

——, *Taking Care of Men: Sexual Politics in the Public Mind* (Cambridge, Cambridge University Press, 1999).

Moran, L., *The Homosexual(ity) of Law* (London, Routledge, 1996).

Morgan, D., *Family Connections: An Introduction to Family Studies* (Cambridge, Polity, 1996).

——, "Risk and Family Practices: Accounting for Change and Fluidity in Family Life" in E. Silva and C. Smart (eds.), *The "New" Family?* (London, Sage, 1999).

Mort, F., *Cultures of Consumption: Masculinties and Social Space in late Twentieth Century Britain* (London, Routledge, 1996).

Murphy, T., "Bursting Binary Bubbles: Law, Literature and the Sexed Body" in J. Morison and C. Bell (eds.), *Tall Stories? Reading Law and Literature* (Aldershot, Dartmouth, 1996).

Naffine, N., "Possession: Erotic Love in the Law of Rape" (1994) 57 *Modern Law Review* 10.

——, "The Body Bag" in N. Naffine and R.J. Owens (eds.), *Sexing the Subject of Law* (London, Sweet and Maxwell, 1997).

Naffine, N. and Owens, R.J. (eds.), *Sexing the Subject of Law* (London, Sweet and Maxwell, 1996).

Nixon, S., *Hard Looks: Masculinities, Spectatorshsip and Contemporary Consumption* (London, UCL Press, 1996).

O'Donovan, K., *Sexual Divisions in Law* (London, Weidenfeld and Nicolson, 1985).

——, *Family Law Matters* (London, Pluto, 1993).

Pickford, R., *Fathers, Marriage and the Law* (London/York, Family Policy Studies Centre/Joseph Rowntree Foundation, 1999).

Reinhold, S., "Through the Parliamentary Looking Glass: 'Real' and 'Pretend' Families in Contemporary British Politics" (1994) 48 *Feminist Review* 61.

Richardson, A., *Fathers Plus: An Audit of Work with Fathers Throughout the North East of England* (Newcastle, Children North East, 1998).

Richardson, D. (ed.), *Theorising Heterosexuality: Telling it Straight* (Buckingham, Open University Press, 1996).

Sandland, R., "Between 'Truth' and 'Difference': Poststructuralism, Law and the Power of Feminism" (1996) 3 *Feminist Legal Studies* 3.

Sheldon, S., "Reconceiving Masculinity: Imagining Men's Reproductive Bodies in Law" (1999) 26 *Journal of Law and Society* 129.

Shilling, C., *The Body and Social Theory* (London, Sage, 1993/1997).

Silva, E. and Smart, C. (eds.), *The "New" Family?* (London, Sage, 1999).

Smart, C., *The Ties That Bind* (London, Routledge and Kegan Paul, 1984).

——, *Feminism and the Power of Law* (London, Routledge, 1989).

——, "The Woman of Legal Discourse" (1992) 1 *Social and Legal Studies* 29.

——, *Law, Crime and Sexuality: Essays in Feminism* (London, Sage, 1995).

—— and Neale, B., "Good Enough Morality? Divorce and Postmodernity" (1997a) 17 *Critical Social Policy* 3.

—— and Neale, B., "Arguments Against Virtue: Must Contact Be Enforced?"(1997b) 28 *Family Law* 332.

——, *Family Fragments* (Cambridge, Polity, 1999a).

——, "'I Hadn't Really Thought About It': New Identities/New Fatherhoods" in

J. Seymour and P. Bagguley (eds.), *Relating Intimacies: Power and Resistance* (Basingstoke, Macmillan Press, 1999b).

SMART, C. and SEVENHUIJSEN, S. (eds.), *Child Custody and the Politics of Gender* (London, Routledge, 1989) .

STYCHIN, C., *Law's Desire* (London, Routledge, 1996).

THORNTON, M., *Dissonance and Distrust: Women in the Legal Profession* (Oxford, Oxford University Press, 1996).

TURNER, B. S., *The Body and Society* (1st edn., London, Sage, 1984).

—— , *Regulating Bodies: Essays in Medical Sociology* (London, Routledge, 1992).

—— , "Recent Developments in the Theory of the Body" in M. Featherstone, M. Hepworth and B. S. Turner (eds.), *The Body: Social Process and Cultural Theory* (London, Sage, 1996).

TWIGG, J., "Social Policy and the Body" in G. Lewis, S. Gewirtz, and J. Clarke (eds.), *Rethinking Social Policy* (London, Open University Press, 2000).

WALDBY, C., "Destruction: Boundary Erotics and Refigurations of the Heterosexual Male Body", in E. Grosz and E. Probyn (eds.), *Sexy Bodies: The Strange Carnalities of Feminism* (London, Routledge, 1995).

WALLBANK, J., "The Campaign for Change of the Child Support Act 1991: Reconstituting the 'Absent' Father" (1997) 6 *Social and Legal Studies* 191.

WARIN, J., SOLOMON, Y., LEWIS, C. and LANGFORD, W., *Fathers, Work and Family Life* (London, Joseph Rowntree Foundation/Family Policy Studies Centre, 1999).

WARREN PERRY, R. and ERIN SANCHEZ, L., "Transactions in the Flesh: Toward an Ethnography of Embodied Sexual Reason" (1998) 18 *Studies in Law, Politics and Society* 29.

WITTIG, M., *The Straight Mind and Other Essays* (Brighton, Harvester Wheatsheaf, 1992).

YATES, C., "Masculinity and Good Enough Jealousy" (2000) 2 *Psychoanalytic Studies* 77.

YOUNG, I. M., *Justice and the Politics of Difference* (Princeton, NJ, Princeton University Press, 1990a).

—— , "The Ideal of Community and the Politics of Difference" in L. Nicholson (ed.), *Feminism/Postmodernism* (London, Routledge, 1990b).

—— , "Together in Difference: Transforming the Logic of Group Political Conflict" in J. Squires (ed.), *Principled Positions: Postmodernism and the Rediscovery of Value* (London, Lawrence and Wishart, 1993).

10

Sexualities, Sexual Relations and the Law

1. INTRODUCTION

T HIS CHAPTER IS concerned with one of the most intimate aspects of the human
body—sexuality—and with the interactions of bodies in the context of sexual
relations. The law's fascination with different sexualities and sexual relations
apparently knows no bounds. In criminal law, there are numerous sexual offences
on the statute book and the law is currently the subject of a wide-ranging review
by the Home Office (Home Office (2000a); Lacey (2001)). In the civil arena, family law in particular has long attached significance to sexual relations, whether this
has been to insist on the physical consummation of marriage, to prohibit adulter-
ous associations or to impute to two people that dubious distinction of being
regarded as living together "as husband and wife".

Historically, the law's concern has been rooted in the need to uphold the connection between marriage, sexual relations and procreation, particularly to ensure the
orderly devolution of family property (Cornish and Clark (1989)). Yet, in a modern liberal democracy such as the United Kingdom, we might be surprised by the
continuing preoccupation of the law with sexual matters. We might expect, as a general proposition, that an individual's sexuality and all *consensual* and *private* acts[1]
would be regarded as important aspects of personal autonomy and not the business
of the law. Sexual relations, according to this view, ought to be governed by individual choice—the right to have control over one's body and to determine the
degree of intimacy that one is prepared to allow with others. Conversely, we might
expect the unambiguous and consistent condemnation of *non-consensual* sexual
relations as an equally clear violation of the principle of individual autonomy.

---

* I am very grateful to Belinda Brooks-Gordon for drawing my attention to, and obtaining copies
for me, of relevant materials in connection with the sexual offences aspect of this chapter and for her
helpful comments on an earlier draft. Any errors that remain are my sole responsibility.

[1] There may be a public nuisance justification for prohibiting those sex-related activities which take
place in the public domain. The fact that the homosexual activities in *ADT* v. *United Kingdom* [2000]
2 FLR 697 were never destined for public exposure clearly influenced the European Court of Human
Rights in finding that there had been a violation of the applicant's right to respect for private life. The
case is discussed in greater depth below.

It will be my central contention that having a particular sexuality (or indeed *no* sexual orientation in so far as this is possible) and engaging in consensual sexual acts ought not to attract legal consequences. Any qualifications to this principle need to be justified and to have a clear rationale such as, to take the best example, the restrictions on sexual activity involving children. These restrictions may be justified on paternalisitic principles though, even here, there is rightly an ongoing debate about the proper limits that should be imposed on the sexual autonomy of adolescents. We might also be entitled to expect that, in so far as the law does attach consequences to sexual relations, it does so without discrimination, on the basis of gender-equality and in a way that is consistent with the fundamental human rights guaranteed by the international community. In the case of the United Kingdom this latter consideration is immediately pressing given the imple-mentation of the Human Rights Act 1998 on 2 October 2000 (Wadham and Mountfield (1999)).

Whether a commitment to gender-equality also involves a commitment to *gender-neutrality* in the law is a matter upon which there is considerable debate but I have argued elsewhere that, at least in the context of family rights, it does (Bainham (2000)). Here it must be conceded that *absolute* gender-neutrality, even if in principle desirable, would be difficult to achieve in the context of the criminal law. Thus, for example, although the law governing rape has shifted perceptibly in recent years towards gender-neutrality in relation to the victim, it is bound to remain gender-specific as to the perpetrator in so far as it continues to be defined as an offence requiring penile penetration—whether of the vagina or anus. Whether the law's concentration on penetrative sexual acts is wholly justified is of course another issue to which I allude below.

My concern in this chapter is to question how far it can be said that English law is currently consistent with the above principles. I do this by examining the prin-ciples applicable to sexualities and sexual relations in family law and criminal law. It should be noted at the outset that there is no necessary congruence between the principles of family law and criminal law since the essential purposes of these two branches of law differ. Thus, for example, the prohibitions on marriage between those closely related by consanguinity, affinity or adoption extend significantly beyond those sexual relationships which are prohibited by the crime of incest (Lowe and Douglas (1998); Smith (1999)). This perhaps reflects the fact that a society may not consider that particular sexual relationships should be a matter for punishment and the ultimate censure of the criminal law but may, nonetheless, wish to attempt to regulate them by withholding from them the recognition and approval that marriage would clearly imply. In recent years the categories of those within the prohibited degrees have been narrowed by removing many of the restrictions that previously applied to affines.[2] It remains the case, however, that a

---

[2] The Marriage (Prohibited Degrees of Relationship) Act 1986 establishes the general principle that marriages between affines are now permitted, although conditions apply to marriages between a step-parent and step-child or between a parent-in-law and a son-in-law or daughter-in-law. Such marriages are still restricted but no longer prohibited altogether.

man may not marry his aunt or niece but may lawfully have sexual intercourse with either and, likewise, a woman vis-à-vis her uncle or nephew. Making due allowance for the different roles of family law and criminal law, the position argued here is that there should, as far as possible, be consistency in the fundamental approach taken throughout the law to the questions of consensual and non-consensual sexual relations.

I will be concerned with the principles of family law in the first section and with the reach of the criminal law in the second. The criminal law (subject to the important qualification that almost all attempts are also criminal) is concerned only when sexual acts have taken place or, for example, in the case of the kerb-crawling legislation (see Belinda Brooks-Gordon and Loraine Gelsthorpe (chapter 11)), where they may be imminent and there is a public nuisance justification. Family law, in contrast, attaches legal consequences to the *mere manifestation* of a particular sexuality—at least where this is in the context of living in the same household as another person—and it has also traditionally accorded a great deal of significance to consensual sexual activities, such as a single act of sexual intercourse following marriage (the requirement of consummation) or a single act of sexual intercourse outside it (adultery). Indeed, one of the most interesting issues in family law at the present time, discussed below, is the extent to which sexual relations (or at least the potential for sexual relations) is a *sine qua non* of family membership where that may not be established through the traditional links of blood, affinity or adoption, or of the legal characterisation of two people as "cohabitants".[3]

I argue that there has been a perceptible shift in English law towards compliance with the general principles articulated above. Family law has begun to attach less importance to sexual relations and is beginning to take heed of the necessity to avoid discrimination based on sexuality.[4] Likewise, the criminal law is beginning to assert more obviously the principle that non-consensual sexual acts should receive condemnation (as evidenced by the abolition of the marital rape exemption) and that consensual acts should not (as will be required in relation to the offence of gross indecency following the recent ruling of the European Court of Human Rights in *ADT* v. *United Kingdom*).[5] Nonetheless, I argue that there is still much to be done and make some suggestions as to the reforms that may be required.

---

[3] The term "cohabitant" or (now less frequently) "cohabitee" has a technical heterosexual meaning in English law. Only a man and a woman may be cohabiting in the legal sense, although of course many people of the same sex, whether or not they are in a relationship, might be said in ordinary language to be cohabiting in the sense of sharing a home together. But merely sharing a household will not normally trigger legal effects except now in relation to applications under Part IV of the Family Law Act 1996 (which governs remedies relating to domestic violence and occupation of the family home).

[4] See particularly the House of Lords decision in *FitzPatrick* v. *Sterling Housing Association* [2000] 1 FLR 271, discussed below.

[5] *Supra* n. 1.

2. FAMILY LAW: SEXUALITY AND SEXUAL RELATIONS

How far then can it be said that a person's sexuality and consensual sexual activity occupy a private zone beyond the reach of the law, attracting no particular legal consequences? I begin this review by looking at the legal significance of sex within marriage. Then I examine the same issue in relation to informal "familial" relationships. There is of course a wealth of literature on what might be described as "marriage versus cohabitation" but it is not my purpose to rehearse yet again the various arguments for and against treating married and unmarried relationships similarly in law. My concern is with something more specific. What is, and should be, the relevance of sexuality and sexual relations in each context? I will argue that there is evidence that the law is retreating from its interest in these matters but that this is a process which needs to be carried much further.

(a) Marriage

Historically, as is well-known, canon law and now the ordinary civil law has insisted that in order to constitute a valid marriage there must not simply be a proper marriage ceremony but also an act of physical consummation. Thus it was that the legal arguments surrounding Henry VIII's so-called "divorce" from Katherine of Aragon (in fact an annulment) turned ultimately on the question of whether or not her earlier marriage to Henry's elder brother, Prince Arthur, had been consummated. The fundamental requirement of consummation continues today. What is required is *one* act of sexual intercourse after the marriage ceremony.[6] This must be "ordinary and complete, and not partial and imperfect".[7] The law reports are replete with cases that have sought to clarify precisely what is involved in this. As Katherine O'Donovan memorably put it: "Reported cases reveal bizarre knowledge against which questions were asked about how long, and how wide, and how far, and whether, and what" (O'Donovan (1993)). The baseline requirement, however, seems clear enough. It is full penetration of the vagina by the penis. Ejaculation is not required and, in what in my view was a landmark decision which has massive implications for us today, the House of Lords held in 1947 that a marriage was consummated despite the husband's insistence on using a condom.[8] Thus, throughout the post-war period, it has been accepted that there is no necessary link between consummation of marriage and the potential for procreation. This, I submit, is hugely important when, at the start of the twenty-first century, the debate is about whether transsexuals and same-sex couples should be permitted to marry. This is because one of the principal arguments against allow-

---

[6] Under Matrimonial Causes Act 1973, s. 12(a), (b), a marriage will be voidable if it has not been consummated owing to the incapacity of either party or to the wilful refusal of one party.

[7] Dr. Lushington in *D-E* v. *A-G* (1845) 1 Rob Eccl 279.

[8] *Baxter* v. *Baxter* [1948] AC 27.

ing such marriages is that there is no possibility of producing children—at least not together and by conventional methods. But if the required act of heterosexual intercourse does *not* necessitate at least the possibility of conception, this argument rather falls apart.

There are, moreover, substantial grounds for believing that, in a modern society committed to equality and human rights in personal relationships, the essential requirement of consummation is outdated and ought to be removed from the law. Other jurisdictions (notably The Netherlands and some states in North America) are moving sharply in the direction of allowing same-sex marriage.[9] It is true that this may take time and there remains the alternative of following the Scandinavian model of the "registered partnership". The latter is not marriage as such and does not require an act of consummation. But suppose it was thought desirable on policy grounds to extend to same-sex couples the full option of marriage (as I would argue it will be in the foreseeable future), is it not the case that the requirement of consummation will get in the way? Certainly, if it were to be retained, it would have to be redefined since a same-sex couple would be incapable of satisfying the current requirement of one act of *heterosexual* intercourse. Yet it is surely hard to believe that the law would enshrine a requirement of one act of *anal* intercourse for gay men and any requirement of penetration would probably be thought inappropriate in the context of lesbian marriage. In any event, the law has long made concessions to the elderly who may reach an agreement prior to the marriage that sex is to play no part in it.[10] We might then view marriage as a companionate arrangement in which sex has no necessary role to play and as an institution that ought to be made available to those of heterosexual, homosexual and asexual dispositions together with transsexuals who, because of a change of sex, are unable to consummate in the terms currently required by English law[11] (Home Office (2000b)).

There are other reasons too why, it is suggested, we ought to do away with the requirement of consummation. One is that as a matter of practice the entire law of nullity has been largely eclipsed by the progressive liberalisation of divorce. In today's society, a marriage which fails for sexual incompatibility is much more likely to end in divorce than it is to be annulled.[12] And divorce law has long been more receptive than the law of nullity to this problem. There will have been many who were by no means incapable of one act of sexual intercourse, but for whom the sexual compatibility thought to be so important to successful relationships

---

[9] The Upper Chamber of the Dutch Parliament passed a Bill to allow same-sex marriage on 24 December 2000. It came into force on 1 April 2001.

[10] The effect of the case law is that although such agreements are thought to be contrary to public policy and hence unenforceable they may nonetheless operate to prevent one of the parties from successfully seeking a decree of annulment based on non-consummation. See *Brodie* v. *Brodie* [1917] P 271 and *Morgan* v. *Morgan* [1959] P 92.

[11] The leading cases, several of which have reached the European Court of Human Rights, are *Corbett* v. *Corbett (otherwise Ashley)* [1971] P 38; *Cossey* v. *United Kingdom* (1991) 13 EHRR 622; *Rees* v. *United Kingdom* [1987] 2 FLR 111 and *Sheffield and Horsham* v. *United Kingdom* [1998] 2 FLR 928.

[12] In 1998, e.g., there were 144, 231 divorces as compared with just 281 decrees of nullity.

perhaps dwindled for some time before disappearing altogether. The law of nullity, with its obsessive reliance on one act of penile penetration, was never going to help people in this situation.

The other side of the marital sexual obligation has of course been that of fidelity. But here too, it is suggested, we are witnessing a substantial retreat by the law. Just as the requirement of consummation insists that spouses have sex with each other, the law of adultery insists that they refrain from sexual relations with anyone else. Here again we can see clearly the law's fixation with heterosexual penetrative sex—though in this context a partial, as opposed to full, penetration of the vagina with the penis is sufficient.[13] We should note perhaps that, whereas the law of rape has been redefined to include anal intercourse, only vaginal penetration will constitute adultery. Anal intercourse and other sexual acts, sometimes quaintly referred to as "indecent familiarities", would however almost certainly constitute "unreasonable behaviour" for the purposes of the facts that prove the ground for divorce.[14]

When we consider what has happened to the law of adultery over the last few decades we can see that its significance has greatly diminished. When, for example, the Richmonds went on a caravan holiday in 1950 with the Burfitts and decided to indulge in a bit of "wife-swapping", Mrs Richmond found that she could not rely on her husband's adultery with Mrs Burfitt in which she had connived.[15] Thus, the old matrimonial offence doctrine that applied before the Divorce Reform Act 1969, involved an investigation into the sexual behaviour of *both* parties. Technical defences such as connivance, collusion and condonation have long since ceased to be part of the law and this is one illustration of family law's declining interest in sexual relations. It is by no means the only illustration. The advent of large-scale undefended divorce and the introduction of the "special procedure" (an administrative process which does not allow any realistic judicial investigation) in the 1970s meant that, henceforth, any investigation into the truth of allegations of adultery would be perfunctory at best. It seems entirely likely that many allegations of adultery over many years have been manufactured by at least some of those wanting a quick exit from an unhappy marriage (Booth (1985)). Even more strikingly than this, if the Family Law Act 1996 had ever been implemented, adultery would have disappeared from the law altogether in a new no-fault system of divorce.[16] We might well have questioned, if that had happened, whether the law would in any sense have continued to uphold the obligation of marital fidelity and, while such a change would have been most unwelcome to those with conservative views about family life, many others would have rejoiced

[13] *Dennis* v. *Dennis* [1955] P 153.

[14] Under s. 1(2)(b) one of the so-called "facts" which may evidence irretrievable breakdown is that "the respondent has behaved in such a way that the petitioner cannot reasonably be expected to live with the respondent".

[15] *Richmond* v. *Richmond* [1952] 1 All ER 838. In fact it did not in the end matter to the wife that she could not rely on her husband's adultery since she was able to argue successfully that he had deserted her and failed to maintain her.

[16] Divorce would then essentially have been based on a statement of marital breakdown and the passage of a period of time. "Grounds" for divorce, as such, would no longer have existed.

at the law's eventual recognition of the reality that, for a very large number of people, the obligation of *lifelong* fidelity to one partner was at best an impossible dream. The argument, then, in relation to the requirements of consummation and fidelity (underscored by the law of adultery) is that both have already been substantially eroded and that neither has any place in modern family law—an argument consistent with the general proposition that consensual sexual behaviour is a private, not public matter, and none of the law's business.

(b) Informal relationships

When we turn to informal relationships outside marriage we can again observe the law's concern to privilege heterosexual relations but the question of whether the law is requiring at least *some* sexual activity, or the potential for it, is an interesting one. This is made all the more interesting by the recent House of Lords decision in *FitzPatrick* v. *Sterling Housing Association.*[17] Here similar questions were raised in the context of a same-sex relationship. What of course is crystal clear is that there is no requirement of consummation outside the context of marriage.

The starting point must be the law's attitude to the position of a man and woman living in the same household. On a range of legal issues including means-tested social security benefits, occupation orders in relation to a family home, fatal accident claims and claims for family provision on death, it is important to determine whether a man and woman, undoubtedly sharing the same household, can be said to be doing so in the capacity of "husband and wife"—an ironic question given that in many cases such people will quite deliberately have avoided the institution of marriage. In the context of transmission of tenancies on death this same question may also have to be answered but, in that context, it may also be sufficient for a survivor to establish that he or she was a member of the deceased's "family" at the time of death and for a specified period before it.[18] Looking at these two possible characterisations, "living together as husband and wife" and " member of the family", it is the former which is much the more significant under English law since it applies in a wider range of situations than the latter. The question, for our purposes, is how far sexuality and sexual relations are relevant to these respective determinations and how far they should be.

It is clear that the state of "living together as husband and wife" has been given an exclusively heterosexual interpretation so that persons of the same sex may not, as the law stands, be regarded as "spouses". This was recently confirmed by the House of Lords in the *FitzPatrick* case but it ought to be said that in both the USA and Canada there have been landmark decisions at the constitutional level which are beginning to require states to adopt an interpretation of the term "spouse"

---

[17] *Supra* n. 4.
[18] The period under the Rent Act 1977, as amended, which applied to the tenancy in the *FitzPatrick* case is the period of two years immediately preceding the death of the tenant.

which would include same sex partners.[19] The position there is evolving and the wider interpretation has thus far applied only to certain statutes, such as those conferring benefits on death, though a decision in Vermont is potentially very wide-ranging. Given that in England we are, for the moment, only concerned with a man and a woman, will *any* man and woman do or does their relationship have to be a sexual one?

This is a matter that has had to be investigated for a large number of years by the Department of Social Security. For the purposes of means-tested benefits, of which income support (formerly supplementary benefit) is the most significant, those "living together as husband and wife" are aggregated—the effect being to deny to them two independent claims for benefit.[20] The part which a sexual relationship plays in this has never been certain, and it is fair to say that there has been some vacillation in the practice of the social security authorities and in the attitude of the Social Security Commissioners. What has always been reasonably clear is that the presence or absence of a sexual relationship is not necessarily decisive. The case law has confirmed that there are six "admirable signposts", only one of which relates to the sexual relationship, or its absence, between the parties.[21] The department's officers have been instructed not to question claimants on the physical aspects of their relationship, but it has been acknowledged that claimants might wish to make a statement about it. The other signposts are membership of the same household, stability, mutual financial support and economic interdependence, the presence of a child and whether the persons concerned have publicly represented themselves to be husband and wife.

The decision in 1994 of the Commissioner, Mr M. Rowland (effectively equivalent to a High Court ruling) in *Re J (Income Support)*[22] is certainly susceptible to the interpretation that the sexual side of relationships ought to receive greater prominence in these determinations. The Commissioner held, *inter alia*, that whether there was a sexual relationship between the parties was an important signpost and, perhaps more importantly, that where there had *never* been a sexual relationship, there would need to be strong alternative grounds for finding that there was a relationship akin to husband and wife. He went on to say that, notwithstanding the official advice to adjudication officers, it would in some cases be necessary to question claimants about their sexual relationship with those living with them. This was, however, in the context of his wider decision which was to the effect that the paramount factor was the "general relationship" between the persons concerned and that this could not be resolved solely by reference to specific criteria.

The state of the law on this question is thus rather vague and unsatisfactory. We cannot say that a sexual relationship at some point is crucial to being regarded as

---

[19] In the USA see the landmark decision of the Supreme Court of Vermont in *Baker* v. *State of Vermont* 1999 WL 1211709. In Canada see the decision of the Canadian Supreme Court in *M* v. *H* (1999) SCR 3.

[20] Social Security Administration Act 1992, s. 74A(5).

[21] R (SB) 17/81.

[22] [1995] 1 FLR 660.

husband and wife (as opposed to *being* a husband and wife where it is) but we cannot say either that it is not going to be decisive in a particular case. It is not surprising in the light of this that the Commissioner in *Re J* remitted the case to a differently constituted tribunal for reconsideration. The evidence was that the two people concerned regarded themselves as living together in the capacity of patient and carer. As to the sleeping arrangements it appears that, although they slept in the same bed, the woman would go to bed early, wait until the man came up at about 3 a.m., then get up and sleep in the living room.

The issue of the relevance of a sexual relationship to the test of living as husband or wife has also arisen in the context of applications for family provision under the Inheritance (Provision for Family and Dependants) Act 1975.[23] Here also there is doubt as to the weight which should be attached to the presence or absence of sexual activity, but in *Re Watson (Deceased)*[24] Neuberger J appeared to signal a flexible approach which "should not ignore the multifarious nature of marital relationships". In this case the applicant and the deceased had had an attachment stretching back for over 30 years and had undoubtedly lived in the same household for the requisite period. There had initially been some sexual intimacy but this had long since ceased before they started to share a household. In holding that their relationship could be characterised by "a reasonable person with normal perceptions" as that of husband and wife, Neuberger J dealt explicitly with the sexual question stating that "It cannot be doubted but that it is not unusual for a happily married husband and wife in their mid-fifties . . . not merely to have separate bedrooms, but to abstain from sexual relations". This, then, might be seen as a decision indicating a lessening significance for sexual relations in this context but it ought to be noted (especially in the light of what the House of Lords have had to say in the context of same-sex relationships) that this was not a case in which there was *never* sexual intimacy.

This same uncertainty about the precise relevance of sex surfaces again when we consider what the courts have made of the test of "family membership" under the Rent Acts. At one time it was clear that the obvious presence of an active heterosexual relationship was enough to sink a claim based on family membership.[25] But by the mid-1970s this had all changed and it was equally clear that a stable heterosexual relationship *would* qualify.[26] What remains much less clear is whether a

---

[23] Inheritance (Provision for Family and Dependants) Act 1975, s. 1A (the result of an amendment in 1995) brings within the list of qualified applicants a person who "during the whole period of two years ending immediately before the date when the deceased died . . . was living—

(a) in the same household as the deceased, and

(b) as the husband or wife of the deceased".

[24] [1999] 1 FLR 878.

[25] See *Gammans* v. *Ekins* [1950] 2 KB 328. The traditional attitude of the courts was grounded in the view that cohabitation outside marriage was immoral and, as such, any purported contract between a man and a woman in this position would be unenforceable. In *Upfill* v. *Wright* [1911] 1 KB 506, Darling J famously said of a woman who rented a flat where she received visits from her lover: "I do not think it makes any difference whether the defendant is a common prostitute or whether she is merely the mistress of one man".

[26] *Dyson Holdings Ltd* v. *Fox* [1976] QB 503.

non-sexual relationship between a man and a woman could give rise to family membership where it is a relationship falling outside the traditional range of family relationships constituted by blood, affinity or adoption. The House of Lords had appeared to answer this in the negative in the late 1970s when they held that a platonic "aunt/nephew"-like relationship between a 75-year-old widow and a man of 24 fell outside the range of relationships which could be regarded as familial.[27] So far so good—sex counts. But this must now be re-evaluated in the light of the *FitzPatrick* decision which is only directly concerned with *homosexual* relations but which clearly calls into question the previous decision in *Carega*. The majority in *FitzPatrick* held that the surviving member of a stable same-sex relationship could qualify as a member of the deceased's family, but the speeches leave uncertain the question whether an actual or potential sexual relationship is required. There is much in the speeches about such things as "caring, sharing lives, support, love and affection" and so on. But what about sex? On this the speeches are far less clear. There is an acknowledgment that, at some point, the *Carega* decision may need to be reconsidered, but it was found unnecessary to undertake this at this time. Only Lord Clyde, of the three in the majority, alludes directly to the need for a sexual relationship and he implies that at least a *potential* sexual relationship might be required. What he said was:

> " It seems to me that essentially the bond must be one of love and affection, not of a casual or transitory nature, but in a relationship which is permanent or at least intended to be so . . . It would be difficult to establish such a bond unless the couple were living together in the same house. It *would also be difficult to establish it without an active sexual relationship between them or at least the potentiality of such a relationship*".[28] (my emphasis).

This was a case in which there had undoubtedly been a long-standing, faithful, monogamous, homosexual relationship between the deceased, John Thompson, and Martin FitzPatrick. This included the final eight years of Thompson's life in which FitzPatrick undertook to care for his terminally ill partner twenty-four hours a day. The question which needs to be asked, however, is whether the same conclusion would have been reached if Thompson and FitzPatrick had merely been friends and the latter had provided the nursing care out of love and friendship while making no pretence of a sexual relationship or the potential for one. We do not know the answer to this question any more than we know whether the parties in *Carega* would today be regarded by the courts as members of the same "family". The relevance of sex to family membership or to heterosexual cohabitation thus remains tantalisingly unclear.

There is of course a good reason for this and it explains why the courts are keen to evade the issue. Admission to either the category of cohabitation or family membership will give rise to automatic legal effects which privilege certain kinds of relationships over others and which trigger the special principles and procedures of

[27] *Carega Properties SA v. Sharratt* [1979] 1 WLR 928.
[28] [2000] 1 FLR 271 at 293.

family law. Thus, to exclude certain relationships from the privileged class of relationships is effectively to utilise a rationing device. It is not perhaps fanciful to suggest that the presence or absence of a sexual relationship, or the potential for one, has been used in this way.

There is recent evidence which illustrates that when Parliament wishes to create a much larger category of persons who qualify to invoke "familial" remedies it will not be slow in doing so. The definition of "associated persons" under Part IV of the Family Law Act 1996[29] (which governs access to the remedies that protect from domestic violence) is extremely wide and the key criterion, among the many included categories, is that of membership of the same household—other than in a commercial capacity such as landlord and tenant. What is very plain is that a sexual relationship is *not* the dominant criterion and, ironically, the most passionate of lovers are excluded from the statutory definition if they have never shared a household together.[30]

Before leaving the question of the legal consequences of consensual sexual relations we ought to return briefly to the relationship between this and procreation. The fact that, in the context of marriage and the requirement of consummation, the law has made the break between sexual relations and procreation is of course far from saying that there is no link between the two. Indeed, I have argued elsewhere (Bainham (2001)) that the extensive liability for child support which can arise from one act of unprotected sexual intercourse is perhaps the most striking example of the continued relevance of fault in modern family law. Thus, the civil consequences that can arise from sexual relations will be extensive where they result in the conception and birth of a child. Yet, even here, it is possible to have a legitimate argument about the extent of the state's responsibility versus individual reponsibility for the children resulting from casual sexual encounters (Krause (1990)). It should perhaps be said that the significance of sexual relations in the process of becoming a parent has also diminished given the advent of assisted reproduction (which does away with the need for a sexual liaison) and the increasing debate about whether parenthood really is about the genetic connection or the child's social relationships. In short it is arguable that there has been a palpable decline in the legal significance of *parentage* and correspondingly greater emphasis on *parenting* or *parental responsibility* which may be exercised by those who are not genetically related to the child concerned (Bainham, Day Sclater and Richards (1999)).

To summarise, it can be argued that whether we are considering marriage, informal relationships or parenthood, the legal significance of a particular sexuality and of consensual sexual relations is declining though in some contexts there is doubt as to what significance, if any, is being given to the presence or absence of a past or potential sexual relationship. But we are still a very long way from being able to say that the area of consensual sexual intimacy is of no interest to the law.

[29] Family Law Act 1996, s. 62.
[30] Though there might be criminal prosecution or civil remedies under the Protection from Harassment Act 1997.

Indeed, we must now turn to an area of the law, criminal law, in which certain forms of consensual sex not only attract civil consequences but are prohibited altogether.

3. CRIMINAL LAW: PROHIBITED SEXUAL RELATIONS

How far can it be said that the criminal law is consistent with the principles set out in the introduction to this chapter? In the recent review of sex offences by the Home Office (Home Office (2000a)) similar principles are articulated as being the foundation of a coherent and fair code for governing sexual behaviour. The key guiding principles accepted in the Review are that "the criminal law should not intrude unnecessarily into the private life of adults . . . that most consensual activity between adults in private should be their own affair" but that " the criminal law has a vital role to play where sexual activity is not consensual or where society decides that children and other very vulnerable people require protection and should not be able to consent" (para. 0.7). Restrictions on consensual sexual activity would therefore require a strong justification based on the Millian "harm" principle. The criminal law, it was said, expresses society's view of what is right and wrong in sexual relationships and the guiding principle here should be that "what is right and wrong should be based on an assessment of the harm done to the individual (and through the individual to society as a whole)" (para. 0.6).

Other guiding principles accepted by the Review were that a reformed law would need to reflect "the looser structure of modern families" and that offences should be gender-neutral in their application, both as to victims and perpetrators, unless there was a good reason for departing from this principle (para. 0.6). For our purposes, it is worth noting another feature that emerges from the recommendations in the Review. This is that, if the proposals become law, there will be a significant shift away from the criminal law's traditional concentration on heterosexual relations whether consensual or non-consensual. Penile penetration of the vagina would lose its overwhelming significance and this, it may be argued, is consistent with some of the changes taking place in family law which we noted in the previous section.

Before looking at some of what is envisaged in the Review for the application of these principles to particular sexual offences, it should perhaps be said that the criminal law has already been evolving in a way that has brought it closer to the achievement of some of these principles. There is no better illustration of this than the changes made in recent years to the definition of rape—the most serious sexual offence on the statute book. Thus, since 1991, it has been accepted that a man might rape his wife and the so-called "marital rape exemption" has been removed from the law.[31] It is important to note the rationale for this change. The criminal

---

[31] *R* v. *R* [1992] 1 AC 599. The decision of the House of Lords was found not to be in violation of the European Convention on Human Rights by the European Court in *SW and CR* v. *United Kingdom* (1995) 21 EHRR 363.

law now concerns itself not with the *implied* consent to intercourse thought to be given on marriage (and we have seen that sexual relations are required for a valid marriage to be consummated) but with the *reality* of consent, doubtless reflecting a change in societal attitudes that, at least in relation to this matter, marital relations should not be viewed as an entirely *private* matter but as a legitimate sphere of *public* concern. This important principle will receive further impetus under the Review recommendations and underlines the vitally important point that non-consensual sexual activity should be recognised for what it is—although the determination of what is, and what is not, truly consensual is bound to remain problematical (Law Commission (2000)).

In 1994, important changes to the law of rape were made by Parliament that went quite some way in enshrining the principle of gender-neutrality and non-discrimination. Under the amended legislation men may also be the victims of rape, which now includes anal penetration, and further illustrates the law's gradual move away from an exclusive concentration on heterosexual penetrative sex.[32] In the following sections I briefly examine the law and the reform proposals as they bear on the key themes of this chapter: the principle of consent, the principle of gender-neutrality and the drift away from the law's concentration on penile/vaginal intercourse.

(a) The principle of consent

The issue of consent is crucial in sexual relations. As Andrew Ashworth has put it "consent may constitute the difference between the sexual expression of shared love between two people and the serious offence of rape" (Ashworth (1999)). At the same time the presence or absence of consent has been notoriously difficult to establish and the Review makes a number of welcome proposals which are again designed to affirm the general principle that only a *real* consent will do. The Law Commission has been engaged for some time in an ongoing review of Consent in the Criminal Law (Law Commission (1995)). At the request of the Home Office in 1999, the Commission refocussed its work to concentrate on consent specifically in relation to sexual offences and produced a Report in February 2000 (Law Commission (2000)). This Report engages with the many difficulties encountered in attempting to define and apply the requirement of consent in the context of sexual offences, including the capacity to consent of minors; mental incapacity; the effect of various deceptions, mistakes or threats; and the mental element of the

---

[32] Under Sexual Offences Act 1956, s. 1 (as amended by Criminal Justice and Public Order Act 1994, s. 142) rape is defined as follows:
"(1) It is an offence for a man to rape a woman or another man.
(2) A man commits rape if—
    (a) he has sexual intercourse with a person (whether vaginal or anal) who at the time of the intercourse does not consent to it; and
    (b) at the time he knows that the person does not consent to the intercourse or is reckless as to whether that person consents to it".

accused's belief in consent. Its central recommendation is that consent, for the purposes of any non-consensual sexual offence, should be defined as: "a subsisting, free and genuine agreement to the act in question". It goes on to recommend that this definition: "should make it clear that such agreement may be— (a) express or implied, and (b) evidenced by words or conduct, whether present or past" (para. 2.8). It also recommends that " a valid consent may be given only by a person who has capacity to give it" (para. 2.15).

Nowhere is the question of consent more important than in the law of rape where, under existing legislation, the defendant has a defence of honest belief that the victim was consenting even though (s)he was not in fact.[33] There has for some time been academic debate about whether the law should impose on men the express duty to inquire as to consent and this has now been accepted by the Review as a desirable change to the law. The defence of honest belief in free agreement would remain but would not be available where the accused did not take all reasonable steps in the circumstances to ascertain free agreement at the time. Consistent with what may be seen as insistence on the reality of consent, the Review also proposes that the law should define an age (13 is recommended) below which children should be regarded as wholly incapable of providing a valid consent to sexual relations (paras 3.5.8–3.5.11). But equally it recognises the other reality—that teenagers over that age may *in fact* consent to sexual activity which is unlawful as regards the other party. In an important concession to autonomy-based arguments about children's rights, the Review takes the position that it is "important, especially in the context of a national sexual health strategy and concerns about teenage pregnancy, not to deter those giving help, advice, treatment and support to children and young people in matters of sexual health or the young people from seeking such help". (para. 0.13). Proposals are also made which are designed to offer further protection to vulnerable people, who although possibly able to provide a consent may be the victims of exploitation and abuse, by the creation of a new offence of breach of a relationship of trust[34] (para. 0.17). This same concern to protect from breaches of trust would be reflected in a modern offence to replace the old law of incest. The key change would be that the new offence would not be limited to relationships with blood relatives (the rationale for which was thought to be at least partly eugenic) but would extend beyond this to include adoptive parents and siblings, step-parents, foster-carers and those in a position of responsibility in the family (chapter 5). The rationale of the law would then clearly

---

[33] The leading case is still the House of Lords decision in *DPP* v. *Morgan* [1976] AC 182.

[34] Such an offence has now been created by the Sexual Offences (Amendment) Act 2000 which received the Royal Assent on 30 November 2000. Under s. 3 it is an offence for a person aged 18 or over (a) to have sexual intercourse (whether vaginal or anal) with a person under that age; or (b) to engage in any other sexual activity with or directed towards such a person, if, in either case, he is in a position of trust in relation to that person. "Position of trust" is defined in s. 4 to include the situation of young people under 18 who are detained in institutions; residing in local authority accommodation; accommodated and cared for in hospital, various residential, nursing and children's homes; and receiving full time education at educational institutions. A person "looks after" the young person concerned if "he is regularly involved in caring for, training, supervising or being in sole charge of [him or her]".

be based on coercion and abuse of trust, consistent with the view that consent to sexual relations should be real and not induced by pressure. The new offence would also reflect the looser structure of modern families in which children and adults move in and out of households in a network of formal and informal relationships (Maclean and Eekelaar (1997)).

All of the above proposals may be seen as attempts to get at the reality of consent to sexual relations where there is good reason to believe that what occurred may not have been truly consensual. But what about those situations in which it is crystal clear that the parties were consenting? Can the criminal law ever intrude legitimately into such private consensual behaviour? As noted above, the intervention of the law may be justified on paternalistic principles in the case of young and vulnerable people who are considered unable to reach the considered judgement necessary to give a valid consent to sexual relations. In the case of minors, the Law Commission (Law Commission (2000)) has provisionally recommended the adoption in this context of a test not unlike the test of "*Gillick* competence" operating in the civil law.[35] It recommends that:

> "for the purposes of any non-consensual sexual offence, a person under the age of 16 should be regarded as having the capacity to consent to an act only if he or she is capable of understanding
>> (a) the nature and reasonably foreseeable consequences of the act, and
>> (b) the implications of the act and of its reasonably foreseeable consequences" (para. 3.16).

But what about *adults*? Most of those instances in which the criminal law has caught consensual sexual activities between adults have related to homosexual activities and sado-masochism. The criminalisation of these sexual encounters offends most of the general principles set out in the Review and urged in this chapter. As the law stands, the principal offences that apply to consensual adult activities are buggery and gross indecency. In the case of sado-masochistic acts, these are liable to fall foul of the Offences Against the Person Act 1861 which governs non-fatal offences of violence and provides a little understood "ladder" of assault offences of various gradations. Presumably because there are no specific sexual offences which cover sado-masochistic practices, the whole issue of sado-masochism appears to have fallen outside the terms of reference of the Review. The subject did, however, receive extensive examination in the Law Commission's 1995 Consultation Paper on Consent in the Criminal Law (Law Commission (1995)).

The scope of the offence of buggery was considerably narrowed in 1994 when non-consensual anal sex was brought within the definition of rape.[36] But this left within the definition cases of consensual anal intercourse, whether of the heterosexual or homosexual variety (together with acts of bestiality) except in so far as

---

[35] So-called because it was established in the House of Lords decision in *Gillick* v. *West Norfolk and Wisbech Area Health Authority* [1986] 1 AC 112.
[36] *Supra* n. 31.

those acts fall within the specified statutory exception. Thus, buggery since 1994 has not been committed where anal intercourse takes place in private and both parties are over the age of 18. The age limit has now been further lowered to 16 (see below). This 1994 amendment to the Sexual Offences Act 1956 had the effect, *inter alia*, of decriminalising anal sex between husband and wife. However, acts will not be regarded as taking place in private where more than two persons are present, or if they take place in a public lavatory.[37]

These same requirements are also features of the offence of gross indecency which is also open to the objection that it is gender-specific, applying only to male homosexual acts and not to heterosexual or lesbian activities. The law on gross indecency will now have to be changed following the recent ruling of the European Court of Human Rights in *ADT* v. *United Kingdom*.[38] In this case the police seized photographs and videotapes that contained footage of the applicant and up to four other adult men engaged in sexual acts, which included oral sex and mutual masturbation in the applicant's home. The applicant was convicted of the offence of gross indecency on the sole evidence of non-violent, purely private, homosexual acts involving more than two persons. The European Court of Human Rights upheld his complaint that the legislation and his conviction under it constituted a violation of his right to respect for private life under Article 8 of the European Convention. Such interference by the state in the particular circumstances could not be justified as necessary for the protection of health and morals given the narrow margin of appreciation that is available to states in relation to interferences with the intimate aspects of private life.

The Review takes the position that the law ought not to treat people differently on the basis of their sexual orientation and that consensual sexual activity between adults in private that causes no harm to themselves or others should not be criminal. Accordingly, it recommends that both offences of buggery and gross indecency should be repealed. This begs the question, in the case of sado-masochistic practices, of what amounts to unacceptable harm. The issue is an important one since the Law Commission took evidence that suggested that such practices, far from being a minority interest, were extremely widespread. Is there, for example, a reasoned justification for criminalising the spanking or caning of someone, with their consent, for the purposes of sexual gratification?[39] In *Brown*[40] the House of Lords upheld the position that it was not in law possible to provide a valid consent to those assaults or batteries which resulted in *actual bodily harm* or worse.[41] In other words, consent

---

[37] Sexual Offences Act 1956, s. 13, provides: "It is an offence for a man to commit an act of gross indecency with another man, whether in public or private, or to be a party to the commission by a man of an act of gross indecency with another man, or to procure the commission by a man of an act of gross indecency with another man".

[38] [2000] 2 FLR 697.

[39] On spanking see *R* v. *Court* (1988) 87 Cr App R 144. On caning see *R* v. *Donovan* [1934] 2 KB 498.

[40] [1994] 1 AC 212.

[41] It is possible to consent in law to what would otherwise be a common assault or battery which does not involve harm beyond a trifling level, but not to one which results in actual bodily harm or, *a fortiori*, grievous (meaning really serious) bodily harm.

would only be a defence to common assault and battery. By contrast, consent is a good defence in the case of certain activities, notably physical sports, which are thought to have social utility. The House rejected the argument that this magical ingredient of social utility could be found in the case of sado-masochistic encounters. The Law Commission, however, reached the provisional view that the threshold of harm should be raised and that the law should be changed to enable the "victim" to provide a valid consent to all but "serious disabling injury".[42] The real question in the case of sado-masochism is not whether these practices have social utility—so that they might be brought within the list of exceptions which the law recognises—but rather whether there is any real legal justification for criminalising consensual activity that does not result in significant harm to the victim or others. If not, then such activities should be lawful in accordance with the general principle that private consensual acts should be beyond the reach of the law.

(b) The principle of gender-neutrality

It is a feature of many of the sexual offences on the statute book that they are gender-specific (Review, chapter 6). We have seen that this is the case with gross indecency which applies only to male homosexual acts. But there is a range of other sexual offences which are gender-specific either as to the victim or the perpetrator, or both. The offences involving unlawful sexual intercourse, for example, apply only to girls and may be committed only by men or boys.[43] Moreover, as is widely known, the age of consent to sexual relations has been full of inconsistencies as it applies to girls and boys. Thus, 16 is the age at which girls may consent to heterosexual intercourse and to lesbian activity (because under 16 they would be unable to consent in law to an indecent assault).[44] But for boys their sexual orientation has been significant. For the heterosexual boy there is no age of consent as such except that he may not consent to anything which would constitute an indecent assault under 16. The age for consent to homosexual activity was until recently set at 18 but was equalised at 16 by the Sexual Offences (Amendment) Act 2000.[45] (Burnside, (2001)).

---

[42] "Serious disabling injury" was defined for these purposes as:
"an injury or injuries which—
(1) cause serious distress, and
(2) involve the loss of a bodily member or organ or permanent bodily injury or permanent functional impairment, or serious or permanent disfigurement, or severe or prolongued pain, or serious impairment of mental health, or prolonged unconsciousness;
and in determining whether an effect is permanent , no account should be taken of the fact that it may be remediable by surgery" (Law Commission (1995) , para. 4.51).

[43] Sexual Offences Act 1956, ss. 5, 6. The girl herself commits no offence by participating in sexual intercourse. See *R v. Tyrell* [1894] 1 QB 710.

[44] Neither girls nor boys under the age of 16 years may consent to an indecent assault. See Sexual Offences Act 1956, ss. 14, 15.

[45] The Bill was rejected by the House of Lords on 13 November 2000. The government invoked the Parliament Act 1911 to ensure that the Bill made it onto the statute book. The Act received the Royal Assent on 30 November 2000 and came into force on 8 January 2001.

The general position taken in the Review is that the criminal law should, as far as possible, offer protection in a gender-neutral way to men, women, boys and girls and ought not to treat people differently on the basis of their sexual orientation. Under these proposals, therefore, there would be a movement away from gender-specific towards gender-neutral offences which could be committed by and against both males and females. This does raise the question of what to do with the offence of rape. Could rape be committed by a woman who coerced certain sexual relations? This was an option seriously considered by the Review but ultimately rejected on the basis that the essence of rape, as widely understood by the public, was penile penetration. It did however make recommendations to cover other serious sexual violations including other forms of penetration (paras. 2.8–2.9).

(c) The significance of penetrative sexual relations

As noted above, the exclusivity of vaginal penetration in the context of rape was replaced in 1994 with the alternatives of vaginal or anal penetration. The central position of heterosexual vaginal intercourse in the law of sexual offences has now been further questioned by the Review. First, the Review favours a further extension of the definition of rape to include forced fellatio. Thus rape, although still a penetrative offence, would extend to penetration of the mouth, anus or female genitalia (para. 2.8). At the same time, it was thought that penile penetration was not the only form of serious penetrative violation and the Review proposes the creation of a new offence of sexual assault by penetration. This would catch violations involving penetration of the anus and genitalia by other parts of the body and with implements. The offence would be regarded as equally serious to rape and would, like rape, be punishable with a maximum of life imprisonment. Alongside this, it is proposed that the current offence of indecent assault be replaced by a new gender-neutral offence of sexual assault which would extend to other non-penetrative sexual touchings.

So here in the criminal law we can also see clear signs of the diminishing centrality of heterosexual, penetrative sexual relations which, I have argued, is also a feature of recent developments in family law.

4. CONCLUSION: THE IMPACT OF HUMAN RIGHTS

The Human Rights Act 1998 was implemented on 2 October 2000 and, as from that date, it has been necessary for the United Kingdom to ensure that its laws are compatible with the European Convention (Wadham and Mountfield (1999)). The key features of the Act are that public authorities, including the courts, must, so far as is possible, interpret and apply legislation in a way that is compatible with

"Convention rights", these are the rights enshrined in the Convention as interpreted by the jurisprudence of the European Court.[46]

For our present purposes, the key Convention rights are those enshrined in Article 8 which protects "private life" and "family life"[47] and Article 14 which protects against various forms of discrimination in the delivery of the substantive rights guaranteed by the Convention.[48] It should be noted that Article 14 is *not* a freestanding provision but may only be taken in conjunction with other articles. Thus, for present purposes, someone might wish to assert that he or she has been discriminated against in relation to actions or laws that interfere disproportionately with his or her private or family life. It is also important to note that these "Convention rights", like rights in general, are never absolute but are qualified. Indeed it is entirely possible that the Convention rights of two or more people may clash, in which case one is almost bound to give way to the other. What is of particular relevance in the present context is that laws which regulate sexual behaviour, and which appear prima facie to infringe the right to private life, may be justifiable interferences falling within the state's so-called " margin of appreciation" in complying with its Convention obligations.

The European Court has held that the concept of "private life" is not restricted to rights of privacy but extends to "the right to establish and develop relationships with other human beings".[49] Sexual life has been regarded as the most intimate aspect of private life.[50] In the context of sexual offences, the Review noted that there is "a particularly delicate and important interplay between the rights of the individual to the enjoyment of a private life, and the need of the state to provide protection and redress for citizens" (para. 1.2.3). The Review goes on to note that discrimination based on sexual orientation is likely to become increasingly difficult to justify, taking Articles 8 and 14 together: "Taken together with Article 8, the right for all citizens to enjoy a private life, the inexorable logic of the Convention is that there would have to be very powerful justification for the criminal law to continue to discriminate on the ground of sexual orientation" (para. 1.2.5). The same, it should be said, must go for the civil law and the principles of family law examined earlier.

It is not, however, entirely obvious that there is a requirement as such to refrain from discrimination based on sexual orientation under the European Convention.

---

[46] Human Rights Act 1998, ss. 3 and 6.

[47] Article 8 provides: "1 Everyone has the right to respect for his private and family life, his home and his correspondence. 2 There shall be no interference by a public authority with the exercise of this right except such as is in accordance with the law and is necessary in a democratic society in the interests of national security, public safety or the economic well-being of the country, for the prevention of disorder or crime, for the protection of health or morals, or for the protection of the rights and freedoms of others".

[48] Article 14 provides: " The enjoyment of the rights and freedoms set forth in this Convention shall be secured without discrimination on any ground such as sex, race, colour, language, religion, political or other opinion, national or social origin, association with a national minority, property, birth or other status".

[49] *Niemietz* v. *Germany* (1993) 16 EHRR 97.

[50] *Dudgeon* v. *United Kingdom* (1981) 4 EHRR 149.

It is not expressly included in the Convention among the heads of discrimination set out in Article 14. This may be contrasted with the position in North America where today many state constitutions do directly include sexual orientation in the list of prohibited forms of discrimination (Bailey and Bala (2000)). Under the European Convention, therefore, change is likely to be the result of the evolving jurisprudence of the European Court as it interprets the Convention as a "living instrument". Even more likely is the possibility that national courts and legislatures will simply take it upon themselves to make progressive changes. This is already a feature of legal developments in several European countries which have introduced laws going way beyond what might be strictly required by the Convention or the European Court .

One of the reasons for this is that the European Court has shown itself to be, on the whole, a conservative institution and this is compounded by its enthusiasm for evading issues of discrimination under Article 14 on the basis that, where it finds violations under other articles, it is unnecessary to consider head-on the arguments surrounding discrimination.[51] The enlightened majority decision in *FitzPatrick* was not required by the European Convention nor by the case law of the European Court which has, thus far, refused to recognise homosexual relationships as falling within "family life" as opposed to "private life". It should also be recalled that a European challenge to the moralistic decision of the House of Lords in the *Brown* sado-masochism case, failed in *Laskey* v. *United Kingdom*.[52] Although the application of the criminal law to consensual sado-masochistic activities did violate the applicants' rights under Article 8 to respect for private life, it was held that the presence of violence provided the state with a justification. The criminalisation of the activities in question was found to be "necessary in a democratic society for the protection of health or morals". Thus, as I have argued at length elsewhere, we ought not to be complacent in assuming that *mere compliance* with the minimum requirements of the European Convention is an adequate response to the challenge of upholding human rights in this or in other areas of the law (Bainham (2000)).

Looking to the future, one of the changes which needs to be followed through if the law is to cease from discrimination based on gender or sexual orientation is to remove, or at least dilute, the law's concentration on heterosexual relations and the legal significance of penile/vaginal penetration. As we have seen, there have been changes in both criminal law and family law which do constitute something of a gradual drift in this direction. As to the criminal law, the changes proposed in

---

[51] A recent example, directly relevant to this ch., is *ADT* v. *United Kingdom, supra* n. 1. Here the European Court, having found a violation of the applicant's rights under Article 8 did "not deem it necessary to examine his case" based on Article 14 taken in conjunction with Article 8. The applicant had argued that it was discriminatory for the offence of gross indecency to apply only to male homosexual acts and not also to sexual acts between heterosexual adults and lesbians. But surely there is a case to answer here and it is regrettable that the European Court failed to address the issue.

[52] *Laskey, Jaggard and Brown* v. *United Kingdom* (1997) 24 EHRR 39.

the Review of sex offences would, if made law, take this process much further while, at the same time, reflect a commitment to gender-neutrality. Whether legislation should be gender-neutral or gender-specific is, however, a matter that has generated considerable debate, particularly among feminist writers. Gender-neutral legislation achieves rule-equality but this is distinguishable from equality of results. The former has been condemned by some feminists as perpetuating, rather than removing, inequality between men and women (Fineman (1991, 1995)). Specifically in the context of sexual offences, rule-equality might be thought to obscure the reality that the vast majority of sexual offences are committed by men. Contrariwise, it might be argued that the basic commitment to human rights requires the adoption of gender-neutral rules at least as a starting point and that, as the Review acknowledges, a sound justification should be required for departing from this presumption. One such case, as noted above, is perhaps that of rape. The Review was primarily influenced by the societal perception of rape as an offence necessarily involving penile penetration. However, it might also be argued that an entirely gender-neutral offence of rape, such as exists in Australia, (in which men and women may be both perpetrators and victims and which would not necessarily involve penile penetration) would obscure the truth that it is *men* who commit rape. As Naffine has put it:

> "Perhaps we should recognise from the outset, as Hale did, that the crime of rape is basically a crime by a man against a woman: that the crime of rape occurs in a society in which it is men who rape women, not women who rape men. The retention of the sex-specific form of the crime in England therefore serves a positive purpose" (Naffine (1994)).

On the whole, what is proposed in the Review would take us a long way in the direction of upholding the privacy of consensual sexual relations and the consistent condemnation of non-consensual activity. The issue of sado-masochistic activities remains unresolved by the Review and it is at least doctrinally questionable that this type of behaviour should be classified along with crimes of violence rather than sexual offences. There is a strong case for adopting the Law Commission's provisional view that, in effect, it ought to be possible to consent to a moderate level of harm that does not also harm others.

In family law there is still a strong tendency to privilege apparent heterosexual relations, though how far this characterisation is dependent on sexual relations actually taking place is uncertain. Even in the context of marriage the requirement is for just one act of penile penetration of the vagina and the fact that sex may have become largely or wholly redundant in a particular marriage will not have any automatic legal effect. Outside marriage, decisions of courts and tribunals have clouded the issue of what function a sexual relationship may perform in the acquisition of the legal characterisation of cohabitation and the consequences that flow from it. But with the recognition that a single sex couple may constitute a family there are signs here too of a welcome departure from the heterosexual paradigm that has historically so dominated the law.

REFERENCES

ASHWORTH, A., *Principles of Criminal Law* (3rd edn., Oxford, Oxford University Press, 1999).

BAILEY, M. and BALA, N., "Canada: Reforming the Definition of Spouse and Child Related Laws" in A. Bainham (ed.), *The International Survey of Family Law, 2000 Edition* (Bristol, Family Law , 2000).

BAINHAM, A., "Family Rights in the Next Millennium" in M. Freeman (ed.) (2000) 53 *Current Legal Problems* 471.

—— , "Men and Women Behaving Badly: Is Fault Dead in English Family Law?" (2001) 21 *Oxford Journal of Legal Studies* 219.

—— , DAY SCLATER, S. and RICHARDS, M., *What is a Parent?: A Socio-Legal Analysis* (Oxford, Hart Publishing, 1999).

BOOTH, MRS. JUSTICE (Chair), *Report of the Matrimonial Causes Procedure Committee* (HMSO, 1985).

BURNSIDE, J. P., "The Sexual Offences (Amendment) Act 2000: The head of a 'kiddy-libber' and the torso of a 'child-saver'" [2001] *Criminal Law Review* 425.

CORNISH, W., and CLARK, G., *Law and Society in England 1759–1950* (London, Sweet and Maxwell, 1989).

FINEMAN, M., *The Illusion of Equality* (Chicago and London, University of Chicago Press, 1991).

—— , *The Neutered Mother, The Sexual Family* (New York and London, Routledge, 1995).

HOME OFFICE, *Setting the Boundaries: Reforming the Law on Sex Offences*, Vols 1 and 2 (Supporting Evidence) (London, Home Office Communication Directorate, 2000a).

—— , *Report of the Interdepartmental Working Group on Transsexual People* (London, Home Office, 2000b).

KRAUSE, H., "Child Support Reassessed: Limits of Private Responsibility and the "Public interest"" in H.H. Kay and S.D. Sugarman (eds.), *Divorce Reform at the Crossroads* (New Haven, Yale University Press, 1990).

LACEY, N., "Beset by Boundaries: The Home Office Review of Sex Offences [2001] *Criminal Law Review* 3.

LAW COMMISSION, Consultation Paper No.139 on *Consent in the Criminal Law* (London, HMSO, 1995).

—— , *Consent in Sex Offences: A Report to the Home Office Sex Offences Review* (2000).

LOWE, N. and DOUGLAS, G., *Bromley's Family Law* (9th edn., London, Butterworths, 1998).

MACLEAN, M. and EEKELAAR, J., *The Parental Obligation: A Study of Parenthood Across Households* (Oxford, Hart Publishing, 1997).

NAFFINE, N., "Possession: Erotic Love in the Law of Rape" (1994) 57 *Modern Law Review* 10.

O'DONOVAN, K., *Family Law Matters* (London, Pluto Press, 1993).

SMITH, J., *Smith and Hogan: Criminal Law* (9th edn., London, Butterworths, 1999).

WADHAM, J. and MOUNTFIELD, H., *Blackstone's Guide to the Human Rights Act 1998* (London, Blackstone Press Ltd, 1999).

11

Hiring Bodies:
Male Clients and Prostitution

BELINDA BROOKS-GORDON AND LORAINE GELSTHORPE

"The body and sexual practices are socially constructed and variable, involving changing assumptions about what is or is not 'natural' or 'normal'. They have, in other words a history and a geography" (McDowell (1998) p. 36)

T HE EXCHANGE OF money for sex has attracted wide interest amongst academics and policy-makers, but closer examination of the field highlights the fact that most of the attention has been given to the *selling* of sex. Indeed, "prostitution"[1] is widely known as one of the oldest professions and is still the subject of intense controversy because of the extremely polarised views that it represents either freely chosen work or a form of male domination. Also, prostitution continues to be seen as being at the heart of controversies about family and sexual mores. We want to take a rather different route in this chapter by focusing exclusively on the men who hire bodies in order to have sex. The chapter is somewhat historical, but this requires no apology since our purpose is to examine shifting conceptions of social and legal "deviance" in relation to men's use of sex workers and to highlight the changing gendered direction of the law. This direction has changed from protecting male "clients" and punishing female sex workers to recognition of the vulnerability of some sex workers whilst in more critical pursuit of the client.

1. AN HISTORICAL OUTLINE OF SOCIAL AND LEGAL ACCEPTANCE OF "PROSTITUTE" CLIENTS

Whilst our key interest is in the Victorian period and beyond, to set the scene we note that accounts of classical and Roman society suggest that it was commonplace

---

[1] The term "prostitute" has obviously attracted criticism over the years, and in some contexts has become laden with pejorative meaning. For example, in legal usage, the term "common prostitute" is viewed with opprobrium. The modern replacement "sex worker" is not unproblematic, however, because of its perceived patronising overtones, and because it rather assumes that there are no distinctions between sex working and any other contracted working relationship (see Pateman (1988)). Given these interpretative difficulties, we have tended to use each term in its historical context and we have aimed to use both terms in a non-pejorative way.

for a man to purchase sex from prostitutes, and evidence suggests that there was legal and social acceptance of this practice (Foucault (1986); Bullough and Bullough (1987)). Indeed, whilst it would appear that the women who provided sex were, along with their families, considered "disgraced" (Bullough and Bullough (1987)), their male clients were accepted and encouraged. These perspectives remained in place for some considerable time with a privileging of male sexual desire; throughout the medieval period there were claims that it was not the man's fault if he strayed sexually but the woman's, if he or she did (see Harras (1996) and Bullough and Bullough (1987)). Whilst the sexual licence and freedom of women was regulated whether or not it was commercial,[2] men were almost encouraged to engage in commercial sexual activities.

It was not until the Middle Ages that towns variously regulated or outlawed commercial prostitution. Prostitution was either banished to brothels outside the town or the whores punished, but there is no evidence to suggest that male clients were punished[3] (Harras (1996)). In towns like Southwark, where legal brothels or *stews* existed, they were regulated for the customers' protection.[4] Interestingly, this was so that the men could not be compelled to purchase food or transport at inflated prices (Harras (1996)). Prostitution continued to be considered an appropriate outlet for men who did not have access to women through marriage (Otis (1985))—an indication that this practice was normalised across the community. Paying for sex *only* became an offence if the client was married when this would involve committing adultery (fornication) and thus breaking the sacrament that marriage had become by the fifteenth century. Even clients who hit prostitutes were only obliged to pay their medical expenses or pay damages to a brothel manager for work time lost because of injury (Otis (1985)). Clients were only regulated when they committed an act of adultery or violence, and even here control was often limited to financial payment or humiliation for the harm done.

Concerns about brothels as centres of evil and corruption led to a transitory change in sexual morality in the late Middle Ages and consequently limited the indulgence towards youthful fornicators as purchasers of sex (Briggs et al. (1996)). But even under conditions of prohibition, the commercial client was seen as a weak soul to be saved from the depravity of women in brothels, rather than as an active agent seeking their services. Moreover, this enforced morality concerning male clients proved to be short-lived, and as Roberts (1993) p. 123 suggests, clients in late Elizabethan times outnumbered prostitutes especially in places like

---

[2] At this time a whore was someone who engaged in sex in a reprehensible way, for example with a large number of men, with a priest, or with a man other than her husband. This wider use of the term is reflected in court records which show women prosecuted as whores who were not commercial prostitutes, and there is no difference in medieval English between the words that mean "common women" for women common to all, and those who charge money (see Harras (1996) p. 131).

[3] The towns of Oxford and Cambridge categorised such women (including commercial prostitutes) as "immoral". In 1317 and 1327 the King required the local authorities of Cambridge to banish whores, and in 1459 the Chancellor of the University received the power to banish them himself.

[4] The portrayal of "Janet of the Stews" in *Piers Plowman* is an example of a practitioner plying a dishonest trade.

Southwark where they were said to have "constantly roved the area in pursuit of pleasure". By the 1700s, large numbers of unmarried men were increased by the tradition of the landed families to transmit their wealth through the male heir, leaving less money for younger sons, many of whom had to forego marriage (Stone (1977)). The purchase of commercial sexual services by such men was consequently looked upon benignly. They were not, however, the only client group, and married men also appeared to be frequent purchasers of sexual services according to noted diarists of the time, such as Pepys and Boswell (Stone (1977)). One suggestion that emerges from such diaries, and an important factor in understanding wider social attitudes to the men who purchased sex in the eighteenth century, is that it was often condoned within a marital relationship as a form of contraception. Women who did not want more pregnancies were more likely to condone their husbands' extra-marital sexual activities with prostitutes (Stone (1977)). Given the dangers of childbirth, this tradition continued until the following century, with Victorian husbands justifying their activities with prostitutes on this basis.

2. VICTORIAN ATTITUDES TOWARDS "PROSTITUTE" CLIENTS

It is well documented that it was a tradition throughout Victorian England for upper-class men to have their initial sexual experiences with prostitutes (Humphries (1988)), the first of which typically took place while away at university. These men received little more than a reprimand, however, if caught by the authorities.[5] In their broad history of prostitution, Bullough and Bullough (1987) suggest that Victorian clients mainly came from the middle and upper classes. A conflicting view is put forward by Briggs et al. (1996) p. 199, who argue that most clients were "poor men paying very small sums to even poorer women". Although attempts to reconstruct the Victorian client are difficult because of the inadequacies of records, Hall (1991) contends that it is nonetheless apparent that vast numbers of men of all classes paid for sex, and that the attitudes of legislators and judges provide important insight into how such men were regarded by society and the law. Examples of these attitudes can be seen in debates concerning the Criminal Law Amendment Bill of 1920, where it was proclaimed by Lord Dawson that men up to the age of 25 years were powerless against the "allurements" of girls under 17 (Hall (1991) p. 48). No doubt partly fuelled by concerns to protect men in the armed services from sexually transmitted diseases (Weeks (1981)) the image of the innocent male seduced by the self-seeking immoral female permeated the discourse on prostitution in Victorian England (and Ireland) to become enshrined in the Contagious Diseases Acts of 1864, 1866, and 1869 (Walkowitz (1992)). These Acts defined venereal diseases as transmitted by women, and

---

[5] Students at Oxford or Cambridge received only a verbal warning if caught with prostitutes, whereas the women were tried and sentenced by vice-chancellors' courts and later imprisoned in either the "Spinning House" in Cambridge or the "Clarendon rooms" in Oxford (Humphries (1988)).

forced the women to undergo medical checks to protect their male clients' health (Faugier and Sargeant (1997)). Indeed, the perception of the prostitute as potentially harmful, "abnormal" and "corrupting" remained pervasive (Lombroso and Ferrero (1986)). Their clients, by contrast, were ignored by legislative practice and were portrayed as behaving naturally in the eyes of the medical establishment and the law.

The first hint of the beginning of a change in attitude towards this situation was perhaps noted by Charles Frérè who observed the paradox whereby the prostitute was criminalised but her client was not (cited in Bullough and Bullough (1987)). Despite Frérè's observation, however, the client's legal position remained relatively stable because it was not against the law for a man to solicit a woman for sex. Only if he caused any nuisance by soliciting could he be "bound over" to keep the peace (according to the Justices of the Peace Act 1361). This has since been considered an uncertain and inadequate statute for dealing with the matter, and in 1993 Susan Edwards observed that it was rarely invoked and men remained free from censure.[6] Such freedom from censure occurred also because medical opinion continued to stress the need not only for men to be able to satisfy their sexual urges, but to do so in specific ways. Indeed, as the Victorian bourgeoisie began to medicalise sexuality and move it into the home, modern sexology began to penalise and stigmatise certain behaviours.[7] Havelock Ellis promoted the scientific study of sexuality from the 1890s (see for example, Havelock Ellis (1899)). Walkowitz (1992) suggests that as positivist science emerged as the authoritative discourse, it provided an account of gender that pathologised female sexuality (stressing sexual purity in women) whilst naturalising male sexuality. The general feeling amongst Victorian doctors and organisations, who saw male masturbation as self abusive and destructive,[8] provided the ground for accepting men's continued use of prostitutes throughout the Victorian period. This was because the purchase of sex was considered preferable to the perversion of self-abasement or its main alternative, the debasement of pure women. Following this period, however, a significant social movement was to alter general social expectations, which in turn changed the way in which male clients were perceived.

3. MODERNITY AND CHANGING IDEALS

The period 1890–1930 is generally taken to cover the major transformations of social and philosophical thought, aesthetic codes and practices that have shaped modern consciousness (Wolff (1994)). It is within this period that we can see

---

[6] Nottingham Anti-Vice Squad and Bournemouth Vice Squad revived the statute in 1995, for example (Benson and Matthews (1995)).

[7] Krafft-Ebing's various editions of *Psychopathia Sexualis* (from 1886 to 1903) stressed the destructive potential of sexuality and pathologised many sexual practices as perversions.

[8] The sexual purity movements such as the Association for Social and Moral Hygiene, which grew in England, Germany and the USA saw masturbation as the cause of physical, mental and moral decline (Hall (1991)).

significant social changes with regard to the payment for sex as the concept of conjugal love was progressively promoted, not least by Havelock Ellis in his pamphlet *Sex in Relation to Society* (cited in Segal (1994)). It gradually became less acceptable for a man to purchase sex from prostitutes and Hall (1991) p. 51 argues that many more men chose not to indulge in such a "crude financial transaction". This change in attitude is also convincingly illustrated in the correspondence Marie Stopes received from men following the publication of her book *Married Love* in 1918. These men wrote to express their sexual anxieties and to request advice and information. Men also began to see it as a slight on their attractiveness if they had to pay for company rather than attract it. The subsequent lower demand for services reduced prostitute numbers, and by 1930 convictions of prostitutes had gone down to 1,110 in England and Wales from a previous high of 2,350 the decade before (Briggs et al. (1996)).

Despite this conceptual shift in attitude towards men who purchased sex, involving an apparent valorisation of conjugal sex, some feminists (most notably Millet (1970)) identify conservative trends in sexuality between 1930–1960 due to the widespread influence of Freud.[9] Whilst interpretations of the writings of Freud may have influenced explanations as to why men paid women for sex, however, this is not without some difference of opinion as to the value of Freud's explanations. Millet (1970) p. 203 condemns Freudian ideas in which she contends "women are inherently subservient, and males dominant, more strongly sexed and therefore entitled to sexually subjugate the female, who enjoys her oppression and deserves it".[10] In contrast, feminists such as Segal (1994) credit Freud with the liberation of sexuality from essentialist biological discourses. Indeed, it is argued that Freud contributed towards a theory of sexuality that is socially constructed in that no part of a person's sexuality—paid or otherwise—can be separated from the influences on early psychic life. Chodorow's (1994) interpretation of Freud was that the stronger sex drive of the man, when faced with the sexual repression of his bourgeois wife (which developed during childhood), would also account for his turn elsewhere for sexual satisfaction (that is, towards prostitutes). Chodorow (1994) further supports other Freudian concepts concerning the Oedipus complex and ways in which they might fuel contempt for women (as penis-less creatures). In this way Freudian theory arguably explains the role of the client, who, because of his fear of and contempt for women, can only fully express himself sexually with an inferior (that is, a prostitute). Psychoanalysis therefore has arguably had a profound influence on the way in which male clients' use of sex workers' bodies has been interpreted.

In the decades before and after the Second World War prostitutes continued to be seen as "deviant pathological individuals", but the resort to prostitution for the male client, whilst still seen as inevitable given the dominance of male sexuality,

[9] Two papers in particular that are cited are *Some Psychical Consequences of the Anatomical Distinction between the Sexes* (1925) and *Female Sexuality* (1931).
[10] These ideas were subsequently developed in the work of Helen Deutsch (1945) and Marie Bonaparte (1965).

became less socially acceptable (Sullivan (1997)). In 1948, Kinsey, Pomeroy and Martin (somewhat controversially) implied that the trend of visiting prostitutes was diminishing in younger generations, especially within higher social classes who might have access to higher education (Kinsey et al. (1948)). In 1955, a study called *Women of the Streets* was published which portrayed the 150 sex workers studied as understandably alienated, but otherwise honest and hardworking. Their clients however, were described as cheating on their wives, and being dishonest in other ways (Rolph (1955)). Both these studies contributed to the increasing social disapproval of men who paid for sex, and the first statute in England specifically to outlaw the public purchasing of sex by men came in a section (section 32) of the Sexual Offences Act 1956.[11] It became an offence for "a man persistently to solicit or importune in a public place for immoral purposes". The aim of this statute was to penalise the soliciting of females either by the punter or by a pimp who touted for clients, but the Divisional Court later held that "it does not apply to the man who accosts women for sexual intercourse" and so, with few exceptions, it was applied to homosexual soliciting.[12] Whilst this first legal constraint missed its intended target, the clients of prostitutes came under scrutiny in the post-war era more and more, and from the late 1950s, the male client of the female sex worker increasingly became represented as a legal and sexual deviant for two reasons: the Wolfenden Report (1957) and the so-called sexual revolution of the 1960s.

The impact of the Wolfenden Report[13] was that some private consensual behaviours (including homosexuality and prostitution) became regarded as matters for private morality, and were removed from the law's jurisdiction, except when a "public nuisance" was created. Shortly afterwards, the Street Offences Act 1959 increased control over any such public behaviour, and Phoenix (1999) argues that prostitution became conceptualised as "publicly offensive". The Act also prompted a change in the conceptualisation of the client, making him more visible and problematic as the main offences included loitering and soliciting by a "common prostitute" in a street or public place for the purposes of prostitution (section 1(1)); solicitation of men for immoral purposes (section 32); kerb crawling (section 1 (1)); and persistent solicitation of women for the purposes of prostitution (section 2(1)). The Act therefore controlled the manner by which prostitutes and clients contact each other, and heralded the "negative regulationist approach" that arguably has framed English law on prostitution today (Phoenix (1999)). Discursive changes have also taken place in law-makers' understanding of those males who purchase female bodies for sex. These views have been underpinned by shifts in the sexual culture and subsequent understanding of what constitutes "normal" sexuality (Sullivan (1997)).

---

[11] This was drawn from The Vagrancy Act 1898, S. 1(1)(B).

[12] In case law, it was decided in *Crook* v. *Edmondson* [1966] 2 QB 81 that it did not apply to a man who accosted a woman for commercial sex, yet eleven years later in *Dodd* [1977] 66 Cr App R187 it was held to apply where the accused had accosted 14 year old girls.

[13] The Wolfenden Report on prostitution and homosexuality, published in 1957, offered a new encoding of sexual tolerance.

The "so-called" sexual revolution, with better contraception and greater acceptance of women's sexual freedom outside marriage, meant that the average "normal" male should have no need to visit prostitutes.[14] More companionate forms
of relationship, with an emphasis on love and mutual sexual desire, became dominant social themes, and Sullivan (1997) argues that paying for sex increasingly
became seen as a deviant sexual practice. Accordingly, by the 1960s, social scientists began to attempt to question what *kind* of men would consider paying for sex,
not least Mancini (1963), who could only explain the commercial sex client in
terms of deviance. It was argued that the men who go to prostitutes were those
who could not find sexual satisfaction elsewhere:

> "They are so physically unattractive, that only a prostitute would consent to having any-
> thing to do with them . . . others have too little time or money to obtain favours from a
> non-professional; others demand some unusual technique that they cannot get from an
> normal woman and are moreover attracted by the atmosphere of prostitution which
> excites them" (Mancini (1963) p. 70).

Thus men who paid for sex were now considered to be those with aberrant sexual desires that could not be accommodated within a "normal" relationship, or as
social misfits who could not forge relationships with "normal" women—perhaps
even because of a lack of a command of the English language in the case of immigrant men (Sullivan (1997)). By the late 1960s, not only were the actions of male
street clients beginning to be seen as a danger to non-prostitute women—thus
paving the way for increased legal surveillance and criminal penalties attached to
these aspects of prostitution—but also social expectations of relationships compounded the deviant status of men who went against such contemporary expectations of relationships by paying for sex.

4. THE TRANSFORMATION OF INTIMACY IN POST-MODERN SOCIETY

It is suggested that the sexual "libertarianism" proclaimed by movements of the
1960s and the emergence of "plastic sexuality"[15] sustained a rise in the ideals of
romantic love as a socially desirable *normative* state (Giddens (1992) p. 34).
Ostensibly, a change took place in the expectation of relationships, in what
Giddens (1992) p. 34 terms "the transformation of intimacy", and Beck (1992)
refers to as the "idealisation of modern love".[16] Within such concepts, reciprocal
sexual pleasure is a key element within a relationship, and sexual exclusivity the

---

[14] Whilst not the radical alteration of patriarchy it is sometimes claimed to be, Millet (1970) argues
that cultural change took place regarding a reformation of the abject legal status of women.
[15] This term encompasses both the separating of sexual practice from procreation and the plasticity
of sexual relationships (Giddens (1992)).
[16] Although the rise of romance arguably began in the late nineteenth century, the recent apotheosis only occurred with the "revalorisation of monogamy, loving commitment and heterosexual stability" (Lemoncheck (1997)).

ideal (Giddens (1992)). Monogamy came to refer not to the relationship itself, but sexual exclusivity as a criterion of trust: " 'fidelity' has no meaning except as an aspect of that integrity which trust in the other presumes" (Giddens (1992) p. 146). Such sexual exclusivity has arguably become an important way for commitment to another to be protected and integrity achieved in a relationship. Whilst this recently developed Western model of romantic heterosexual love claims dominance, there can be no *one* story of this social transformation and no neutral reading, because as Jamieson (1998) indicates, exceptions do exist and realities may differ. This model, however, circulated globally and as Connell (1998) points out, although it has not displaced indigenous models, it has interacted with, and heavily influenced them. It therefore remains a hegemonic influence on social attitudes and the law. To go outside a "relationship" and purchase intimacy or sexual practices violates these contemporary ideals and cultural customs.

Throughout the following decades, media treatment and portrayals have palpably strengthened attitudes and subsequent legislation against the male client. This is evident in the media anxiety surrounding the case of a single client whose dangerousness to vulnerable women was documented throughout the 1980s (Jouve (1986); Smith (1989); Segal (1990)). Between 1975 and 1981, thirteen women (of whom seven were sex workers) were killed by Peter Sutcliffe in the North of England. The case of the "Yorkshire Ripper" led to women's fear and anger, which Walkowitz (1992) argues fuelled a feminist anti-violence campaign. The Criminal Law Revision Committee of 1975 had already begun to address the issue of kerb crawling as the continued newspaper notoriety accorded to Peter Sutcliffe contributed to the public condemnation of men who purchase street sex.[17] Whilst the Sutcliffe case highlighted the vulnerability of sex working women, legislation continued to reverse the practice of blaming them, with the Criminal Justice Act 1982 amending the 1959 legislation and abolishing the use of imprisonment for women convicted of soliciting.

In Cambridge, a small conference explored the issue of sex offenders and one of the speakers, Lloyd Trott (1979) p. 134, concluded that an accurate typology of prostitutes' clients was necessary and that "much of the other research will be pointless if the role and needs of clients continue to be ignored". Trott's advice to consider clients continued to be ignored. The law thus proceeded to criminalise the client despite scant knowledge about him. In 1984, the Criminal Law Revision Committee published its Sixteenth Report and the Sex Offences Bill was first brought to Parliament by MP Janet Fookes (Criminal Law Revision Committee (1984)). The Report proposed three main offences. These were to prohibit the nuisance of kerb crawling; persistent soliciting by men; and the soliciting of a woman for sexual purposes (irrespective of whether or not she is a sex worker) "in

---

[17] At the same time, the Criminal Justice Act 1982 made the law more lenient towards sex working women by abolishing imprisonment for soliciting *by* women. Imprisonment was continued, however, for the non-payment of fines for soliciting.

a manner likely to cause her fear" (para. 46).[18] The repercussions of the Sutcliffe case resounded throughout the legal system, and many authors who subsequently explored the issue of soliciting or kerb crawling (either the Act or of the deliberations of the Committee) made mention of him (see, for example, Edwards (1984); Calvert (1986)).

The legal position of the street client in England and Wales changed in September 1985 with the Sexual Offences Act 1985. This Act criminalised a man for soliciting a woman (or women) in the street for sex. The Act specifically created an offence for any man who:

> "solicits a woman for the purposes of prostitution from or near a motor vehicle, persistently . . . or in such a manner likely to cause annoyance to the woman solicited, or nuisance to other persons in the neighbourhood" (section 1); or, in a street or public place "persistently solicits a woman for the purpose of prostitution" (section 2).

These offences were triable summarily only and subject to the maximum fines[19] and in the following year, 1986, 220 men were charged, of which 189 pleaded or were found guilty (Home Office (1986)). The statute thus created a new category of offence, that of kerb crawling, and constructed the kerb crawler as a different type of man from the ordinary, decent man in the street. Evidence of solicitation, however, was difficult to acquire and the legislation proved difficult to enforce (Edwards (1993)). Not surprisingly therefore, there were moves to make it easier to prosecute by removing the need for the police to prove the man's "persistence". In 1990 Sir William Shelton introduced a Sexual Offences Bill to Parliament that sought to remove the requirement that kerb crawling be "persistent or likely to cause annoyance or nuisance" (Hansard Parliamentary Debates, 6 July 1990, col. 1291). The Bill was ostensibly brought about in response to "constituency feeling and fear", but was talked out by Ken Livingstone who rightly pointed out that toughening approaches against kerb crawlers might increase the victimisation of both men and women. Reasons for this claim included the fear that the Bill would provide a Trojan horse with which to bring in a new "sus" law to use against black, Irish, immigrant and other working-class men police might want to charge for

---

[18] This third offence, more serious than the previous two, was recommended by the Criminal Law Revision Committee which wrote in 1984: "whereby such conduct, he puts a woman in fear, he should, we think, be guilty of a criminal offence" (Criminal Law Revision Committee (1984) working paper s. 3.44). This was similar to an existing offence of indecent assault, and it was assumed that the woman would almost always have to be called as a witness. This offence was to be triable summarily only, being punishable by a maximum fine on level 5 (£2,000 in 1984), or "a custodial penalty to be available on a second or subsequent conviction" (CLRC (1984) s. 50). When the Act received Royal Assent on 16 July 1985 there was no mention of the third offence. It transpired that the offence of soliciting in a way "likely to cause her fear" had not been drafted despite also being recommended by the Policy Advisory Committee (CLRC (1984) para 3.42). By the time the Home Office Circular 52/1985 explaining the provisions of the Act came out, all mention of it had ceased. Percipiently, Edwards (1984) had earlier surmised that "there exists a great lacuna in the law as far as the protection of prostitutes is concerned and the categories as presented may well in practice reinforce this" (p. 646). This vision was to be unerringly near the truth, and the following fifteen years saw the violation, mutilation and death of at least thirty-one sex working women at the hands of clients.

[19] That is, on level 3 on the standard scale, which was set at £400 at that time.

quite unconnected purposes. Using the persuasive arguments of the Campaign against Kerb Crawling Legislation (a coalition of anti-rape, black and civil rights organisations, AIDS prevention groups, lawyers, probation officers and Labour Party activists), it was thought that the Bill would add to prostitutes' and other women's vulnerability to violence by: "forcing working women further underground: curtailing the time available for prostitute women to 'sus out' clients nervous about arrest before going with them; committing more police time and resources to prostitution rather than rape and other violent crimes" (Hansard Parliamentary Debates, 6 July 1990, col. 1291).

There were two important elements concerning this Bill which illustrate wider social attitudes to kerb crawling: first, the strong support the Bill received from the House, indicating a political interpretation of public feeling and, secondly, subsequent media attacks on Ken Livingstone which illustrate a turn in the tide of media opinion of the time against the kerb crawler. Media coverage ran to large columns in all the national broadsheets, up to half a page in some papers (see, for example, *The Times*, 12 May 1990, p. 4; *Daily Mirror*, 12 May 1990, p. 9). The front page of the *Daily Express* unhelpfully suggested that "MP is condemned for putting women at risk" (12 May 1990). Unsurprisingly, the dust slowly settled on the Shelton Bill and the issues were not taken up by others.

Throughout the final two decades of the last century there were three other major social issues which seemingly impacted on how the prostitute client is perceived: the HIV crisis; an increasing awareness of the feminisation of poverty, and increased awareness of the sexual abuse of children and the subsequent rhetoric of fear around their abusers. During the 1980s, the media linked HIV infection to sexual excess, "perversity" or abnormality (McDowell (1998)). Whilst the homosexual body was linked to HIV via sexual activity and the heroin addict through intravenous drug use, sex working women were linked through their involvement in prostitution in order to support drug use. HIV infection was associated with behaviours deemed to be deviant and illegal and transmission of the disease was considered for criminalisation (Young (1996)). The client became linked with not only deceiving others, but also travelling from one site of infection to another, his body linking the world of the "morally correct" with the underworld of the "sexually deviant" (Young (1996) p. 200). Metaphors on the "war" against disease and the "war" against crime intersected and by 1990, the number of men proceeded against for kerb crawling was 1,470 (Edwards (1993)).[20] Four years later, and in parallel with an apparent slowing down of the spread of HIV and its accompanying media panic, the figures of men charged with soliciting dropped to 1,185 (Home Office Criminal Statistics (1994)) with little fluctuation in this figure throughout the remainder of the decade.[21] Reasons for the decline in the use of sex

[20] This followed a case law decision in *Paul v. DPP* (1989) which permitted prosecutors to move onto the next level of seriousness, allowing evidence of a nuisance of kerb crawling activities in the area to be produced as evidence without having to prove "persistent soliciting" (cited in Edwards (1993)).

[21] However, it has remained disproportionate to the number of women (and some children) charged for solicitation, of which there were 7,029 convictions in the same year (Edwards (1993)).

workers generally include, *inter alia*, women's greater sexual freedom, greater occupational choice, the availability of contraception, the increasing availability of divorce so that non-compatible couples need not stay together, the rise in non-marital cohabitation, and the erosion of the "culturally supported" myth that men enjoy, need or want sex more than women (Bullough and Bullough (1987)).

At the same time, recognition of the "feminisation of poverty"—the social change and lack of welfare policies in the wake of the Thatcher-Major regimes that arguably created and extended social hardship to women (Glendinning and Miller (1992))—may have played a part in the diminishing of social censure in some quarters towards sex working women. By the late 1990s, nine out of ten lone parent families were headed by a woman, with many single parent women forced to rely on benefits or low pay in the part-time work sector with a lack of childcare facilities, and struggling daily to avoid hardship and debt (Franks (1999)). Figures issued by the English Collective of Prostitutes showed 75 per cent of women sex workers to be lone mothers (ECP (1997) p. 90). Thus the choice of sex work has begun to be seen as rational "resistance", if not courageous choice, in the face of poverty[22] (Scambler and Scambler (1997)). The client therefore has increasingly attracted vilification for being prepared to cash in on the economic disadvantage of these women for his own gratification.

Awareness of the exploitation of women in this way has been accompanied by a growing awareness of the victimisation of vulnerable children. The involvement of children in prostitution as a strategy for survival has been amply illustrated in a series of reports by the Children's Society.[23] These reports have revealed children let down by the state in care systems, excluded from school, and at risk at the hands of punters and pimps, and they provide grounds for considering clients' involvement in prostitution in a more abusive vein. One report in particular, by Lee and O'Brien (1995), recommended that the police treat children under the age of 17 years involved in sex work as victims of crime, and more actively pursue the punters and the pimps who abuse and coerce them. Following pilot work in Nottinghamshire and Wolverhampton and support from the Association of Chief Police Officers (ACPO), Government guidelines (Home Office (1998)) recommended that the police respond to juveniles in terms of the Children Act 1989 rather than the criminal law, emphasising that children should be given protection from harm and abuse and the "*primary law enforcement effort must be against abusers*" (our emphasis).

A wider social factor that has possibly impacted on this concerns the emergence of a "risk culture", a culture in which, Beck (1992) contends, wealth production and patterns of society have changed along with new forms of pluralised unemployment (with all the associated hazards and opportunities) and efforts to lessen risk have

[22] This is not the case in the right-wing press, however, which maintains a less open attitude to both lone parents and sex working women.

[23] These included *Young Runaways* (Newman (1989)), *Hidden Truths* (Rees (1993)), *Running the Risk* (Stein et al. (1994)), *The Game's Up* (Lee and O'Brien (1995)), and *One Way Street* (Melrose, Barrett and Brodie (1999)).

become paramount. This is linked with notions of a culture of anxiety and fear of crime (Hollway and Jefferson (1997)) as public fear has increased further in the wake of cases of predatory paedophiles.[24] Public protection has become an increasing feature of criminal justice policy and the political ticket on which Nash (1999) argues that more punitive policies have been brought in. The Home Office White Paper *Protecting the Public* declared:

> "in the past, those who have shown a propensity to commit serious or violent sexual offences have served their sentences and been released only to offend again . . . The government is determined that the public should receive proper protection from persistent violent and sexual offenders" (1996) p. 48.

Within this wider political and legislative climate of increasing punitiveness, tougher approaches have been implemented which target those committing acts including violence, sex or drug abuse (Nash (1999)). As the penalties for all areas covered by sex offences legislation were moved "up-tariff", so has kerb crawling, and on 1 April 1997 kerb crawling became a recordable offence which signifies something of its perceived seriousness.

Subsequent legislation which allowed the police to obtain non-intimate samples for DNA analysis from offenders who are charged, reported or cautioned for any recordable offence came in section 4 of the Criminal Evidence (Amendment) Act 1997.[25] This legislation is deliberately inclusive, and specifies that "sexual offences include all offences with any sexual connotation whatsoever" (National Police Records (Recordable Offences) (Amendment) Regulations 1997, SI 1997/566, reg. 4). Since September 1998, samples have been taken from all men charged with kerb crawling under sections 1 and 2 of the Sexual Offences Act 1985, and these samples are maintained on a national database.

Despite this routine taking of DNA samples from men found guilty of kerb crawling (contributing to the national database of more than one million samples by March 2001),[26] little is known about the subjective implications of this process. Instances of people being caught for offences they committed months or even years ago are increasing due to matches being made between recent samples and stains recovered at original scenes of crime. Indeed, the utility of DNA as a means of purchasing power regarding prosecution has been proved in cases spanning auto-crime to abduction (Packman (1998)). The use of this material not only has the potential to uncover previously unknown connections between kerb crawling and other offences in a way that, say previous criminal histories alone cannot, but

---

[24] These include the Dutroux case in Belgium in 1996, the case of Sidney Cooke in 1997, and Robert Oliver in 1998.

[25] This empowered any constable to require a person who has been charged with a recordable offence, or informed that he will be reported for such an offence, to attend a police station so that a non-intimate sample may be taken. The legislation was ostensibly to "correct an omission" from the Police and Criminal Evidence Act 1984. Whilst non-intimate samples include, amongst other things, saliva or hair, saliva is the recommended type of sample to take in these instances.

[26] University of Leicester Bulletin, *Pioneering Scientist Supports "DNA" Bank* (Leicester, University of Leicester, 2001), p. 6 (http://www.le.ac.uk/bulletin/).

its mere existence has the power to affect the lives of male sex clients in more far-reaching ways than police records.

The implications of these developments for future commercial sex transactions are clearly relevant to our understanding of the behaviour of sex clients. The human rights debates, stemming from the implementation of the Human Rights Act 1998, surrounding potentially dangerous offenders and DNA sample-taking continue at a rapid pace (especially in relation to Article 3 concerning degrading and inhumane treatment and Article 8 concerning the right to respect for private and family life), but it remains to be seen what will happen in practice. The formulation of policy remains theoretically and empirically on thin ground with regard to the taking of body particles from men who hire women's bodies without further consideration of client behaviour (see Brooks-Gordon (2000)).

A second contemporary issue concerns the utility of rehabilitation for men who purchase sex. In the early 1990s, "schools" for clients began to gather momentum, particularly in the USA; the first school developed in the United Kingdom was in 1998 (Bindel (1998, 1999)). The idea of schools is essentially that clients/offenders might be rehabilitated or "educated" out of their desire to hire bodies for sex. The schools largely involve one day workshops during which clients (some of whom are not convicted) are warned of the penalties of reoffending, lectured on the effects of prostitution and soliciting on neighbourhoods, and alerted to various health dangers concerning sexually transmittable diseases. There are also presentations from "prostitute survivors" who tell their stories of abuse by and repulsion for clients, and from families which have experienced the death of a child through prostitution (Monto (2000)).

The schools have attracted wide criticism, however. On a theoretical level it is argued that the curriculum is wide of the mark by ignoring gender and power issues, and the economic marginalisation of women sex workers. As one critic put it: "such procedures ... abstract prostitution from its systemic and structural roots and treat it merely as a question of individual morality" (O'Connell Davidson (1998) p. 199). On a practical level, the schools are often run in conjunction with intensive policing strategies and so create a fear of arrest amongst sex working women. Many of the women have reported that they have worked longer hours or in more isolated areas (with no obvious sources of support) as a consequence of this. Others have indicated that intensive policing makes the whole business of negotiating with clients on the street a hasty affair; as a result, their power to intuit safety in the first stages of the negotiation has been eroded. There have been further criticisms that the operation of the schools diverts resources from other developments revolving around women's safety needs, and that the course content—designed to humiliate and shame clients—has had the effect of increasing violence towards women sex offenders as a displacement activity. Moreover, the practice of sending unconvicted men to such "schools" once again raises human rights issues regarding the right to a fair trial (European Convention on Human Rights, Article 6). In the United Kingdom, health organisations, social justice organisations, and academics expressed concern about such schools shortly after their inception. Following a ground-swell of critical opinion led by the UK co-ordinator of the European Organisation for the Prevention of AIDS for Prostitutes (EUROPAP), the Executive Committee of the Josephine Butler Society and the ECP, and the systematic lobbying of politicians and policy-makers, the UK schools ceased to exist, although some schools remain in the USA (Kinnell (1999); Self (1999)).

5. CONCLUDING REFLECTIONS

Nash's (1999) turn of the century reflections include the point that the protection of the public and the fear of dangerous offenders has reached the top of the criminal justice agenda. The perceived importance of public protection heralded the Sex Offenders Act 1997 and the creation of a sex offenders register, placing the onus on the police to assess and manage risk.[27] The rhetoric of public protection was also enshrined in proposals of the Crime and Disorder Act 1998 (for example in sections 2 and 3 regarding sex offender orders, in which the police also have to assess risk).

The public mood on punitiveness thus shifted most dramatically in the last two decades of the twentieth century and aligned the punter alongside the pimp as a coercive and abusive character from whom the public should be protected. Further, it has culminated in the Home Office Review of Sex Offences (Home Office (2000)). Whilst this points towards the penalisation of specific categories of client (Recommendation 51), it holds back from full-scale condemnation of the client in the light of awareness of the complexities of intersections of gender, prostitution and the law, but nevertheless suggests that there should be a further review of the law on prostitution (Recommendation 53). Should such a review of the law on prostitution take place, it will necessarily involve consideration of the legal construction and signification of both the "prostitute" body and that of her client. At the time of writing the Report of the Sex Offences Review is out for consultation and it remains to be seen how far public and political opinion will support the general tenor and recommendations of the Review (Home Office (2000)).[28]

This chapter has outlined the social and legal construction of the status of men who have purchased sexual access to women's bodies throughout history.[29] The Victorian man who went to prostitutes was normalised in the discourses of medicine and the law. However, a transformation took place in the twentieth century, and as

---

[27] Offences that are "dangerous" include rape, unlawful sexual intercourse with a girl under 13 years, intercourse with a girl 13 to 16, incest by a man, buggery, indecency between men, indecent assault on a woman, indecent assault on a man (both if under 18), assault with intent to commit buggery, causing or encouraging prostitution of, or intercourse with, or indecent assault on a girl under 16.

[28] The consultation period ended on 1 March 2001, and a further report will be expected in due course.

[29] As Connell (1998) points out, not all men will behave in the same way and the hegemonic form of masculinity might not be the most common form of behaviour. Many men live in a state of some tension with or distance from hegemonic forms of masculinity. Perhaps we should make it clear that this chapter merely serves to place in context general historical patterns that emerge from the evidence.

Norbert Elias (1994) points out, practices that were once typical and acceptable, are now "deviant". In the past two decades the client has become criminalised to the degree that purchase of sexual access to a woman's body is not only perceived as criminally and sexually deviant, but he has also become a generally "dangerous" figure.

Despite some historical and cultural variation, this historical outline captures broad structures of change, and notions that the client's "deviance" was perhaps first viewed through a social, and then legal lens. An historical outline can thus reveal the "trends and shifts in moral, ideological and symbolic images and associations" relating to this aspect of prostitution (O'Neill (1997) p. 19), and can provide a glimpse of how the disciplines of philosophy, theology and law have variously approached the question of the person who hires bodies for sex. Given that social phenomena cannot be studied without an investigation of the underlying mechanisms that make such phenomena possible in the first place (May (1993)), it has been essential to explain the policies and practices that preceded and underpin present-day kerb crawling legislation. This legislation came into force, without consultation, on 1 September 2001 in the Criminal Justice and Police Act 2001. It provides the police with the power of summary arrest over kerb crawlers. This enables them to take men into custody and question them rather than having to summons kerb crawlers to appear in a magistrates court to answer a charge. The role of the contemporary "punter" is essential to an understanding of prostitution, for it is often argued that if men did not create a demand for it, prostitution would cease to exist (Kinnel (1989); Sharpe (1998)). Whilst the past decade has seen a decrease in the numbers of women working in red-light areas and a concomitant increase in advertising for off-street sexual services, both in local newspapers and telephone boxes (Holmes (1996)), the proportion of men looking for sex on the streets appears to have increased. A recent audit calculated the average number of kerb crawlers in London during any one week to be 7,600 (Matthews (1997)).[30] Despite up-tariffing in terms of the categorisation of kerb crawling and increasingly punitive interventionist policies and strategies, the person who hires bodies for sex has become increasingly problematic to criminal law and, looking to the future, human rights law.

REFERENCES

Beck, U., *Risk Society* (London, Sage, 1992).
Benson, C. and Matthews, R., *The National Vice Squad Survey* (Enfield, Middlesex University School of Sociology and Social Policy, 1995).
Bindel, J., "A New Way Forward in Tackling Prostitution: Kerb Crawler Rehabilitation Programme in West Yorkshire", paper presented at the National Vice Squad Conference, Northumbria Police Headquarters, Ponteland, Newcastle, 10–11 June 1998.

---

[30] This figure does not include men cruising around the area watching women, but only men actively involved in paying for street sex. It works out at 1 in every 170 males in the 20 to 40 year age group, according to Matthews (1997).

BINDEL, J., "Kerb Crawler Rehabilitation Scheme", paper presented at the National Vice Squad Conference, Avon and Somerset Constabulary Headquarters, Bristol, 29–30 June 1999.

BONAPARTE, M., *Female Sexuality* (New York, Grove Press, 1965).

BRIGGS, J., HARRISON, C., McINNES, A. and VINCENT, D., *Crime and Punishment in England* (London, UCL Press, 1996).

BROOKS-GORDON, B., *Prostitution in Public Space: Kerb Crawler Explanations and Malefactors* (Unpublished PhD Thesis, University of Cambridge, 2000).

BULLOUGH, V. and BULLOUGH, B., *Women and Prostitution* (New York, Prometheus, 1987).

CALVERT, J., "Protecting Men from Women" (1986) *Trouble and Strife* (8, Spring) 24.

CHODOROW, N., "Feminism and Psychoanalytic Theory" in *Polity Reader in Social Theory* (Cambridge, Polity, 1994).

CONNELL, R. W., "Masculinities and Globalisation" (1998) 1 *Men and Masculinities* 3.

CRIMINAL LAW REVISION COMMITTEE, *Prostitution in the Street* (16th Report, Cmnd. 9329, London, HMSO, 1984).

DEUTSCH, H., *Female Sexuality: The Psychology of Women* (New York, 1945).

EDWARDS, S. S. M., "Kerb Crawling and Allied Offences—The Criminal Law Revision Committee's Proposals" (1984) *Justice of the Peace* (October) 13.

——— , "England & Wales" in N. J. Davis (ed.), *Prostitution: An International Handbook on Trends, Problems and Policies* (Greenwood Press, West Port, 1993).

ELIAS, N., *The Civilizing Process* (Oxford, Blackwell, 1994).

ENGLISH COLLECTIVE OF PROSTITUTES (ECP), "Campaigning for Legal Change" in G. Scambler and A. Scambler (eds.), *Rethinking Prostitution* (London, Routledge, 1997).

FAUGIER, J. and SARGEANT, M., "Boyfriends, 'Pimps' and Clients" in G. Scambler and A. Scambler (eds.), *Rethinking Prostitution* (London, Routledge, 1997).

FOUCAULT, M., *The History of Sexuality. Vol 3: The Care of the Self* (trans. R. Hurley, London, Penguin, 1986).

FRANKS, L., *Having None of It: Women, Men and the Future of Work* (London, Granta, 1999).

FRÉRÈ, C., "Sexual Degeneration in Mankind and in Animals" (trans. Ulrich Van Der Horst, reprinted, New York, Anthropological Press, 1932) cited in V. Bullough and B. Bullough, *Women and Prostitution* (New York, Prometheus, 1987).

FREUD, S., "Some Psychical Consequences of the Anatomical Distinction between the Sexes" (1925) in S. Freud, *The Standard Edition of the Collected Works of Sigmund Freud* (Hogarth Press, London, 1953).

——— , "Female Sexuality" (1931) in S. Freud, *The Standard Edition of the Collected Works of Sigmund Freud* (Hogarth Press, London, 1953).

GIDDENS, A., *The Transformation of Intimacy* (Cambridge, Polity, 1992).

GLENDINNING, C. and MILLER, J., *Women and Poverty in Britain: The 1990s* (London, Harvester, 1992).

HALL, L. A., *Hidden Anxieties. Male Sexuality, 1900–1950* (Cambridge, Polity, 1991).

HARRAS, R. M., *Common Women. Prostitution and Sexuality in Medieval England* (Oxford, Oxford University Press, 1996).

HAVELOCK ELLIS, *Studies in the Psychology of Sex: Volume 1: The Evolution of Modesty; the Phenomena of Sexual Periodicity: Auto-Erotism* (Leipzip and Watford, 1899).

HOLLWAY, W. and JEFFERSON, T., "The Risk Society in an Age of Anxiety: Situating Fear of Crime" (1997), 48, *British Journal of Criminology* 255.

HOLMES, R., *The Laws Dealing With Street Prostitution* (Unpublished BSc. dissertation, University of Portsmouth, 1996).

HOME OFFICE, Circular No. 52/1985 (London, Home Office, 1985).

—— , *Criminal Statistics. England and Wales* (London, HMSO, 1986).

—— , *Criminal Statistics. England and Wales* (London, HMSO, 1994).

—— , White Paper, *Protecting the Public* (Cmd. 3190, London, HMSO, 1996).

—— , *Guidelines for Responding to Juveniles Under Children Act 1989* (London, HMSO, 1998).

—— , Review of Sex Offences, *Setting the Boundaries: Reforming the Law on Sex Offences* (London, HMSO, 2000).

HUMPHRIES, S., *A Secret World of Sex: The British Experience 1900–1950* (London, Sidgwick and Jackson, 1988).

JAMIESON, L., *Intimacy: Personal Relationships in Modern Societies* (Cambridge, Polity, 1998).

JOUVE, N., *The Streetcleaner* (London, Marion Boyers, 1986).

KINNELL, H., "Male Clients of Female Prostitutes in Birmingham, England: A Bridge for Transmission of HIV?" paper presented at the Fifth International Conference on AIDS in Montreal, 1989).

—— , *Europap Annual Report* (European Network for HIV/STD Prevention in Prostitution, 1999).

KINSEY, A. C., Pomeroy, W. B., and Martin, C. E., *Sexual Behaviour in the Human Male* (Philadelphia and London, W. B. Saunders, 1948).

KRAFFT-EBING, R. C., cited in L. Segal, *Slow Motion: Changing Masculinities, Changing Men* (1st edn., London, Virago, 1990).

LEE, M. and O'BRIEN, R., *The Game's Up: Redefining Child Prostitution* (The Children's Society, 1995).

LEMONCHECK, L., *Loose Women, Lecherous Men. A Feminist Philosophy of Sex* (Oxford, Oxford University Press, 1997).

LOMBROSO, C. and FERRERO, G. (1885 [1895]), *The Criminal Woman and the Prostitute* (trans. L. Melville, M. St. Auben, Milan, 1997).

MANCINI, J. G., *Prostitutes and their Parasites* (London, Elek Books, 1963).

MATTHEWS, R., *Prostitution in London: An Audit* (Middlesex, Middlesex University Press, 1997).

MAY, T., *Social Research. Issues, Methods and Process* (Buckingham, Open University Press, 1993).

McDOWELL, L., *Gender, Identity and Place* (Cambridge, Polity, 1998).

MELROSE, M., BARRETT, D. and BRODIE, I., *One Way Street* (London, The Children's Society, 1999).

MILLET, K., *Sexual Politics* (New York, Doubleday, 1970).

MONTO, M., "Why Men Seek Out Prostitutes" in R. Weitzer, *Sex for Sale* (New York, Routledge, 2000).

NASH, M., *Police, Probation and Protecting the Public* (London, Blackstone Press, 1999).

NEWMAN, C., *Young Runaways: Findings from Britain's First Safe Houses* (London, The Children's Society, 1989).

O'CONNELL DAVIDSON, J., *Prostitution, Power and Freedom* (Cambridge, Polity, 1998).

O'NEILL, M., "An Overview" in G. Scambler and A. Scambler (eds.), *Rethinking Prostitution* (London, Routledge, 1997).

OTIS, L. L., *Prostitution in Medieval Society* (Chicago, University of Chicago Press, 1985).

PACKMAN, D., "Success all the Way with DNA" *Metropolitan Police Inside the Job*, 8 November 1998, p. 16.

PATEMAN, C., *The Sexual Contract* (Oxford, Blackwell, 1988).

PHOENIX, J., *Making Sense of Prostitution* (Hampshire, Macmillan, 1999).

REES, G., *Hidden Truths: Young People's Experiences of Running Away* (London, The Children's Society, 1993).

ROBERTS, N., *Whores in History* (London, Harper Collins, 1993).

ROLPH, C.H. (ed.), *Women of the Streets* (London, Secker and Warburg, 1955).

SCAMBLER, G. and SCAMBLER, A. (eds.), *Rethinking Prostitution* (London, Routledge, 1997).

SEGAL, L., *Slow Motion: Changing Masculinities, Changing Men* (1st edn., London, Virago, 1990).

——— , *Straight Sex* (London, Virago, 1994).

SELF, H., "Fair Game", *Police Review*, 21 May 1999, p. 26.

SHARPE, K., *Red Light, Blue Light: Prostitutes, Punters and the Police* (Aldershot, Ashgate, 1998).

SMITH, J., *Misogynies* (London, Faber, 1989).

STEIN, M., FROST, N., and REES, G., *Running the Risk: Young People on the Streets of Britain Today* (London, The Children's Society, 1994).

STONE, L., *The Family, Sex and Marriage in England 1500–1800* (New York, Harper and Row, 1977).

STOPES, M., *Married Love: A New Contribution to the Solution of Sex Difficulties* (A. C. Fifield, 1918).

SULLIVAN, B., *The Politics of Sex: Prostitution and Pornography in Australia since 1945* (Cambridge, Cambridge University Press, 1997).

TROTT, L., "An Understanding of Prostitution, with Particular Reference to Mayfair, London" in D. J. West (ed.), *Sex Offenders in the Criminal Justice System* (Cropwood Conference No. 12, University of Cambridge, Institute of Criminology, 1979).

WALKOWITZ, J., *City of Dreadful Delight* (London, Virago, 1992).

WEEKS, J., *Coming Out: Homosexual Politics in Britain from the Nineteenth Century to the Present* (London, Quartet, 1977).

——— , *Sex, Politics and Society: The Regulation of Sexuality Since 1800* (Harlow, Longman, 1981).

WOLFENDEN REPORT, *Report of the Committee on Homosexuality and Prostitution* (Cmnd 247, London, Home Office, 1957).

WOLFF, J., "Feminism and Modernism" in *The Polity Reader in Social Theory* (Cambridge, Polity, 1994).

YOUNG, A., *Imagining Crime* (London, Sage, 1996).

12

Villain, Hero or Masked Stranger: Ambivalence in Transactions with Human Gametes

RACHEL COOK

GAMETE DONATION[1] DIFFERS from other kinds of medical donation (whether of body parts or products) in that donors give something that does not merely contribute to or extend life, but which provides the potential for new life. In the United Kingdom, additional factors distinguish gamete donation from other types of medical donation: the fact that donation takes place mainly in the context of private rather than public medical practice and that so-called donors are often vendors, or paid volunteers, receiving money for their "donation" (Daniels and Lewis (1996); see Martin Richards (chapter 16). A more accurate term might be "gamete providers" (as suggested by Evans (1995)), and this will be used here in an exploration of the nature of transactions with human gametes.

1. OWNERSHIP AND COMMODIFICATION OF GAMETES

There is nothing in law in the United Kingdom to suggest that people do not, to all intents and purposes, own their own gametes.[2] The view of gametes-as-property has not gone unchallenged, however, and questions have been raised about whether gametes belong to the individual (Dickenson (1997)). But if gametes do not belong to an individual, to whom do they belong? Do members of a couple have any claim on their respective partners' body and its products? In England, individuals can donate gametes without informing their partners. The Human Fertilisation and Embryology Authority (HFEA) Code of Practice states:

"5.19 The centre does not have to obtain the consent of a donor's partner to the donation of their gametes. However, if the donated gametes are to be used for treatment, and the donor is married or has a long-term partner, centres should encourage donors to ask

---

[1] For reasons of space, this discussion is restricted to the provision of gametes by living people for reproductive rather than research purposes, and in medical contexts, rather than private arrangements between individuals.

[2] See the discussion of the body and body products as property by Jonathan Herring (chap. 3) in this volume.

their partner to consent in writing to the use of the gametes for treatment" (HFEA (1998a)).

It has been suggested that wives may have proprietorial feelings about their husbands' sperm (Dickenson (1997)) but there is little doubt that, in law, marriage does not entail control over the body or bodily products of one's partner (McLean (1997)).

Dickenson (1997) argues that we should look at gametes differently from other aspects of the body, because they are concerned with future generations and current partners, as well as our selves. In this sense, we might be seen as guardians of the genetic information in our gametes, rather than as owners of those gametes. However, there is no requirement for gamete providers to inform relevant members of past or future generations of their donation. In addition, if we examine people's behaviour in relation to their gametes, whatever law or regulation might prescribe, or ethics might have us do, we can see that people behave as though gametes belong to them alone. Many choose to keep information about their donation from partners, parents and children (Cook and Golombok (1995); Price and Cook (1995)). For this reason alone, we might deem gametes to be a kind of property (as described by Resnik (1998)). In addition, Jonathan Herring (chapter 3) notes that we might infer that gametes *can* be sold from the fact that the HFEA specifically prohibits their sale—if gametes could not be sold, then their sale would not require prohibition.

Furthermore, gamete providers can use the products of their bodies to express personal values (Andrews and Nelkin (1998)). They might choose a known recipient or, if making an anonymous donation, specify conditions for the use of their gametes. The HFEA Code of Practice states:

> "5.16 In all cases, people giving consent may specify additional conditions subject to which their gametes or embryos produced from them may be used or stored, and may vary or withdraw their consent at any time provided that the genetic material has not already been used" (HFEA (1998a)).

This permits gamete providers some control over the kind of person that the recipient is, for example, choosing not to donate to single women.

If individuals can be said to own their gametes, we might regard gametes as commodities. Body products are clearly transferable, and in some circumstances—when there is free informed consent—commodifiable. In the case of gamete transactions however, it is not always clear exactly what is being transferred. For example, both the Human Fertilisation and Embryology (HFE) Act 1990 and the HFEA place strong emphasis on the genetic aspects of parenthood, referring to gametes as "genetic material" and gamete providers as "providers of genetic material" (e.g. HFEA (1998a)). This perspective on gametes may be, from a biological point of view, misleading at least. As Johnson (1999) points out, the provision of gametes is not just the provision of genetic material; gametes have other components which are essential to the process of conception. Furthermore, the HFEA does not clarify whether it regards gametes as a commodity or whether the focus of the transaction is merely the services provided. Thus, for example, it refers to payment of gamete providers as "payment to donors" and "payment . . . per donation" but does not state what the payment is for (HFEA (2000a)). Although it has been argued that this payment should be regarded as compensation (British Fertility Society (1996)) it does not appear to be intended to be compensation, given that donors can in addition receive expenses to cover costs such as accommodation, childminding fees and financial loss. Similarly, it does not appear to be compensation for accepting the physical risks of the procedure, as male and female gamete providers are not differentiated.[3] The implication is that gamete providers are being paid either for their services or for their gametes. Given that their reproductive services have no value without their reproductive materials (Resnik (1998)), we have to assume that the payment is for the gametes themselves. The purpose of gamete donation is clearly important: the value of gametes lies in their potential for new life, and without this potential, they have no value. Gametes may, however, be seen as incomplete commodities—on their own, they have little or no value and they need to be used in a very specific way for their value to become apparent. Provision of gametes therefore needs to occur in a context that permits this value to be exploited. Eggs might objectively be seen to have a greater value than sperm, because, although both are products of the body, sperm is renewable and eggs are not. Perhaps more importantly, the procedure for retrieval of eggs is more difficult and riskier for the provider, and therefore where a free market is allowed to operate, as in much of the USA, the price of eggs is much higher than the price of sperm (see also Martin Richards (chapter 16)).

As with many other body parts and products, the language of gamete provision is commercial. We refer to the "products" of conception; eggs can be "harvested", like a crop; sperm can be "banked", like money (Dickenson (1997); Andrews and Nelkin (1998); Soules (1999)).[4] Cohen (1999) argues that within US reproductive medicine, the demands of the marketplace have led to replacement of the "reproductive paradigm" with the "manufacturing paradigm", and that this is detrimental to our view of reproduction as a human activity. He concludes that commodification of the body of this kind is unethical. In contrast, Resnick (1998) argues that selling gametes is morally acceptable, although concerns about commodification and its negative social consequences should be addressed by regulation of gamete transactions.

Most people have gametes, and there is a real demand for them; whilst some regard gamete donation as unethical, it has also been suggested that it would be unethical not to obtain gametes from providers willing to part with them, for recipients who need them (Sauer (1997)). Demand always exceeds supply (Murray and Golombok (2000)). Many people therefore have the potential to be involved in transactions with human gametes but few from the pool of potential

---

[3] Although it has been argued that they should be, e.g. see Evans (1995).

[4] The use of the term "gamete providers" in this chapter may just be another example of this.

donors become actual donors. There are a number of reasons for this. First, unlike blood donation, there is no national recruitment agency; many people therefore are never aware of the need for donors (Cook and Golombok (1995)). Secondly, as a priority for licensed centres is maintaining the supply of gametes, and as donors are always scarce, populations which have produced a reasonable supply of donors in the past are targeted. In the case of semen donation, this has usually meant college or university students. People outside such targeted populations may therefore be unlikely to see advertisements. Thirdly, potential gamete providers often have concerns about the procedures and risk involved, such that a large proportion withdraw from donation programmes at an early stage (Horne et al. (1993)). Potential gamete providers may also have concerns about the possible outcomes of their donation, such as loss of anonymity, which lead them to withdraw (Cook and Golombok (1995)). Fourthly, there is stigma attached to gamete provision, especially sperm provision; and a particular constellation of personality characteristics may be required for donation under these circumstances (Nicholas and Tyler (1983); Schover et al. (1992b)). Fifthly, some gametes have more value than others. Only a very small proportion of semen providers have semen with the right characteristics and therefore there is only a market for the "best" sperm: that which has a high fertilising potential, and comes from donors without genetically or sexually transmittable disease (Barratt and Cooke (1993); British Andrology Society (1999)).

2. EFFECTING GAMETE TRANSACTIONS

There is considerable variation between countries in the nature of these transactions. In some countries, gamete provision is not permitted (Gunning (1998)). This legislation, however, will not prevent some citizens of these countries from obtaining gametes as a consequence of the increasing availability of gametes via the Internet and the potential for medical tourism (Sauer (1997)).

Gamete provision is normally represented as either a gift (so-called altruism) or a purchase (payment). Some countries prevent payment to donors, some limit payment and others do not. The HFE Act 1990 states that a condition of a licence to treat patients using donated gametes is:

"12.(e) that no money or other benefit shall be given or received in respect of any supply of gametes or embryos unless authorised by directions".

Leaving the HFEA the option of authorising payments was seen as a way of ensuring that donors were not paying to donate (Morgan and Lee (1991); Lee and Morgan (2001)) but the intention behind the Act seems to be that gamete providers should not be paid. Directions were issued to licensed centres allowing them to pay up to £15 per donation plus expenses when the HFEA assumed its powers in August 1991, in order to reflect practice at the time. Since then the HFEA has repeatedly stated that its intention was always to remove payment to donors, believing that gametes should be a gift. This principle would be consistent with other types of donation of body parts or products in the United Kingdom, where costs associated with the donation (taking time off work, travelling to the centre and so on) are borne by the donor. Practice, however, does not reflect this principle. In February 1998 a consultation document was issued by the HFEA as a preliminary to removing payment (HFEA (1998b)), but the Authority succumbed to the pressure of medical practitioners who were concerned about the consequences for the supply of gametes should payment be removed. Gamete providers therefore continue to be paid for their donations (HFEA (2000b)).

We can contrast this somewhat ambivalent situation with other countries where, generally, gametes are not paid for and are seen as a gift of some kind (for example, France and New Zealand) and other countries where gametes are clearly sold (for example, the USA). In the latter case, payment might be seen as compensation for the risks of the procedure, as egg providers are paid considerably larger sums than sperm providers, and this market-driven economy of gametes has resulted in ever-increasing payments, which clearly act as inducements (Sauer (1997)). Fairly recently there has been a pilot program in one US state to provide organ donors with money toward their funeral expenses (Kahn (1999)) (despite federal law which prohibits the sale or trade of organs). The purpose of this is to provide compensation and to avoid a situation where the payment or benefits offered act as an incentive. However, to state the obvious, a fixed sum of money does not have a fixed value for everyone. Thus even the smallest sum may act as an inappropriate incentive to donate.

There are some differences between the provision of sperm and eggs which might affect who is deemed suitable as a gamete provider. In contrast to the notion that gametes could be given or sold by any female adult whose eggs were suitable, recently some medical practitioners have argued instead that some categories of donor should be prevented from providing gametes. Specifically, the increasing evidence of potential risks associated with egg donation[5] might lead us to consider whether women unrelated to the recipient and who are not infertility patients themselves should be encouraged or permitted to undergo donation procedures at all (see e.g. Ahuja, Simons and Edwards (1999); Lockwood (1997)). Some countries, such as Israel and Denmark, actively discourage or do not permit non-patient volunteers to provide eggs (Ahuja and Simons (1998)).

Whilst it may be reasonable for patients undergoing medical procedures to accept some risk in view of the therapeutic effects of their treatment, in the case of volunteer donors there are no medical or therapeutic benefits. Rather the benefits are potentially psychological or social, and these are difficult to quantify. The General Medical Council's (GMC) guidance on good practice advises doctors that they should not:

---

[5] In the short term the possibility of ovarian hyperstimulation syndrome and in the longer term, malignant disease (Ahuja et al. (1999)).

"put pressure on (their) patients to give . . . benefits to . . . other people . . . recommend or give patients investigation or treatment which (they) know is not in their best interests" (GMC (1998) p. 6).[6]

It might therefore be argued that encouraging non-patients to donate eggs is an abuse of their trust.

There are other differences between the nature of transactions with sperm and eggs. The shortage of eggs is represented as being more severe than that of sperm (Murray and Golombok (2000)). If fewer women express an interest in gamete provision, or fewer become providers, this may be due to factors such as differences in recruitment strategies and perception of risks; for most women, the costs may just be too great and the benefits too few. Other areas of medical donation also show sex differences: women appear to be more likely than men to donate blood (Ferguson (1996)), and yet men appear to be more willing to volunteer for bone marrow donation than women (Briggs et al. (1986)). These different patterns of donation may reflect different gender role perceptions, as well as being related to differential opportunity to donate. It has been suggested that the motives of women who provide oocytes are different from those of semen providers: women appear to be less concerned about anonymity, and less concerned with financial reward. It is likely, however, that such factors are influenced by the context of donation. Because of the differences between the retrieval of sperm and eggs this means in practice that sperm providers are paid and egg providers (like other types of medical donors) are not. In fact it has been suggested that women in the United Kingdom essentially pay to provide their eggs and, because most treatment takes place in the private sector, others benefit financially from this transaction (Dickenson (1997)). Thus, women who wish to be rewarded financially will not be recruited. However, in the USA, where female donors are paid, women with a financial motivation come forward (see e.g. Schover et al. (1992b)).

Studies of altruistic behaviour demonstrate that men are not unwilling to help others, but that the male gender role appears to require agentic helping, such as acts of heroism or chivalry: if men are to help, they benefit from an audience (Eagly and Crowley (1986)). Semen donation as currently practised is not consistent with helping behaviour as prescribed by the male gender role: it is not heroic (for it is low risk), nor chivalrous (for men are paid). Men may be discouraged from donating for these reasons. This suggests that we should not accept the conventional view of all men as inevitably instrumental in their approach to the provision of gametes (as opposed to the men who provide sperm in our current set of circumstances).

---

[6] The first of these points is retained in the draft version of the third edition (see: http://www.gmc-uk.org.uk).

3. SOCIAL LEGITIMACY OF GAMETE TRANSACTIONS

It has been suggested that the social legitimacy of gamete provision is closely tied to recognition of the donor's role (Novaes (1989)). A number of features of transactions provide evidence of the extent to which they are perceived to be acceptable, including general social attitudes, payment and anonymity. Some of these appear to be deliberately maintained to excise the presence of the donor from the creation of a family.

The supply of gametes depends to some extent on public attitudes, in that they exert a general influence on both the number and type of prospective donors as well as the decisions of potential recipients. Whilst insemination using donated semen was an established treatment for infertility by the 1960s, the motivations of participants were still viewed with suspicion. Intensive media coverage of new reproductive technologies may have encouraged contemporary society to view the predicament of infertile couples more sympathetically, but there is little doubt that, even today, many people have misgivings about those who decide to transfer their gametes to others.

Attitudes towards and acceptance of donation and treatment using donated gametes have been assessed in both the general public and interested groups. Unsurprisingly, participants in gamete donation have more positive attitudes than the general public, and recipients are more positive than donors (Bolton et al. (1991)). A US study showed sperm donation to be more acceptable than egg donation, whereas a UK study showed similar levels of acceptance. Attitudes towards gamete provision amongst the general public have become increasingly more favourable, yet there remains a proportion of people who find its use abhorrent, whether for concern about the welfare of the resultant offspring or because of the whiff of adultery.[7]

The concern about "adultery" may be particularly apparent with sperm provision. Whilst other kinds of medical donation may be socially acceptable and valued, the motives of semen providers are viewed with suspicion and their behaviour stigmatised. The semen provider therefore faces social risks to which other donors, including egg providers, are not exposed. Egg donation may be viewed as a clinical and passive procedure, whereas the image of sperm provision may be sexual (Achilles (1993)). Whilst there are no penalties attached to not giving sperm, the public perception of sperm donors and the social stigma attached may mean that there are penalties attached to this particular transaction. Many men who are willing to donate blood are ambivalent about donating sperm (Novaes (1989)).

Whether donation is acceptable therefore also depends to some extent on the freedom with which gamete providers make their decision. The HFEA stresses its

---

[7] Note that in law, it is not adultery, which is a "voluntary act of sexual intercourse between a married person and a person (other than his or her spouse) of the opposite sex" (Cretney and Masson (1997) p. 363).

commitment to altruistic donation and its belief that gamete provision should be a consequence of consent free from inducement and pressure (HFEA (1999)). In practice when money is provided as compensation, it can also act as an inducement. There is little doubt that most egg providers in the United Kingdom do not receive sufficient payment or benefits for this to act as a motivation to donate. This is certainly not true for sperm providers, many of whom clearly state a financial motivation for their donation, even if they express other motives in addition to this (see e.g. Sauer et al. (1989); Pedersen, Nielsen and Lauritsen (1994) (Denmark); Cook and Golombok (1995) (United Kingdom)).

This raises serious, but often unacknowledged, issues of free consent to the procedures that they undergo. In addition, it may have later psychological consequences for individuals; psychological well-being can be threatened by the use of body tissue without consent (Andrews and Nelkin (1998)). We could hypothesise that gamete providers who are induced to donate for financial gain, or who are emotionally detached from their behaviour, and therefore not freely consenting, could later experience regret and a compromised sense of self. Research suggests that some sperm donors are uninvolved and detached from the process of donation (Lui et al. (1995)) and this kind of evidence supports the idea that consent may be compromised in current practice.

There is little information about recipients' views on the motivations of gamete providers. In the absence of such information, it has been suggested anecdotally that recipients may prefer sperm donors to be paid as a reward for their services, this being a healthier[8] motivation than altruism (Gazvani et al. (1997)). Another way to interpret this "healthiness" is that by paying the donor, and maintaining her/his anonymity, we terminate a relationship which barely existed, and are not faced with the social and psychological implications of the process and the kinship issues which are raised (see e.g. Novaes (1989)).

The provision of compensation or payment is dubious not only because it compromises informed consent. Although it has been argued that we can have commodities which are both sold/bought and given as gifts (such as food and clothes), it has been argued that when such commodities are donated, they are more highly valued and used with greater care (Titmus (1978)). Furthermore, payment may devalue the notion of altruistic donation and may make it less likely: at the level of society we come to accept that this is something that is paid for and therefore, at an individual level, people become unwilling to provide gametes without payment. Some activities and behaviours provide their own reward, intrinsic to the activity (Deci (1971)). There is evidence from some countries that it is feasible to recruit donors without payment, which suggests that this qualifies as an intrinsically motivated activity. The question which arises is: what happens to this intrinsic motivation when we offer extrinsic rewards for the behaviour? One possibility is that external rewards, which include money but also symbolic rewards, might actually undermine intrinsic motivation (Deci et al. (1999)). This is important,

---

[8] The authors do not clarify what is meant by "more healthy".

because people who would offer to act as gamete providers in the context of so-called altruistic donation, would not offer to do so in a climate of paid gamete provision.

From the perspective of cognitive evaluation theory (Deci (1971)) however, rewards can have conflicting effects on people's behaviour. Where they are seen as informational (providing satisfaction of the need for competence), they may enhance intrinsic motivation to perform an interesting activity. They can also be seen as controlling and reducing an individual's autonomy, which might have implications for the individual's sense of self and bodily identity.

Control over one's self (which includes one's body) is seen as vital for psychological well-being. We can use our bodies to express ourselves, our attitudes and our values (as donors may do when they place restrictions on the use of their gametes). An invasion of the body or a threat to bodily integrity is likely to cause distress and have implications for our sense of self. In an era of increasingly sophisticated medical technology, such invasions and threats need not be experienced physically, but may be the consequence of provision of information about invisible malfunctions of the body.[9]

Whilst body products can be seen as part of the body, and therefore as property, they are different from body parts in terms of our view of self, in that they can normally be separated from us without loss of sense of self. A woman breast-feeding her child, whether or not she feels that she transmits something of herself via her milk, does not lose part of herself by this act. Gametes could be seen rather differently from other body products. The man whose act of masturbation produces semen does not lose his sense of identity by this act, but that semen has the potential to transmit his genetic information, which may form the basis of his own sense of self, to new life. Furthermore, whilst egg provision is often referred to as the female counterpart of sperm provision, eggs may be different from other body products in another way. The donation of eggs requires invasive procedures. It is only recently that we have been able to think of human eggs as products of the body, they are not separated from the body by a simple or natural process, such as cutting one's hair or urinating, but have to be surgically retrieved. In this way we might see women's eggs as more a part of their bodies, and more fundamental to their sense of self, than men's sperm.

Societal lack of acceptance of this mode of family formation also appears to be reflected in both the lack of provision of any information about the donor to her or his offspring, and parents' decisions not to inform their children conceived by donor insemination of their origins. Under the HFE Act 1990, the donor gives up their legal parenthood and passes their rights and responsibilities as a parent to the recipient(s). Furthermore, the Act prevents the disclosure of identity of, or any other information about, donors to their offspring. This information is kept, however, on a register of information about licensed treatments and their outcomes.

---

[9] For example, receipt of a positive result on a screening test may impair our view of our self as healthy (e.g. see Marteau et al. (1992)).

In somewhat inconsistent fashion, one of the four main reasons for keeping this register is to "provide information to children born as a result of such treatments" (HFEA (2000a)).

Parents report that they decide not to tell their children conceived from donated gametes from a wish to protect the child or the father (see e.g. Snowden et al. (1983); Daniels and Taylor (1993); Cook et al. (1995)). Note that motivation of parents may be to protect, but may be perceived by children as deception (Landau (1998)). Only a minority of heterosexual couples who plan to use this method of family formation set out with expectations of telling children about their origins (Milsom and Bergman (1982); Berger et al. (1986); Humphrey and Humphrey (1986); Daniels (1988); Schover et al. (1992a)) and even fewer fulfil these expectations once a child is born (Snowden et al. (1983); Amuzu et al. (1990); Klock and Maier (1991); Brewaeys et al. (1993); Cook et al. (1995)). Studies of attitudes of the general public towards gamete provision indicate that such views are not limited to users of donated gametes (Rowland and Ruffin (1983; Bolton et al. (1991)). Some commentators have argued that the benefits of secrecy outweigh the potential costs.

However, lack of openness within the family is thought by many to be psychologically damaging (e.g. Sants (1964); Brandon and Warner (1977); Rowland and Ruffin (1983); Berger et al. (1986)). As well as creating boundaries between those who know and those who do not (Karpel (1980); Imber-Black (1993)) there is the additional strain of fearing that someone else will disclose information to the child (Karpel (1980); Bruce (1990)). Such disclosure is a real risk, given that between one and two-thirds of couples using donated gametes confide in others (Ledward et al. (1979); Humphrey and Humphrey (1986); Rowland (1983); Cook et al. (1995); Gottlieb et al. (2000)).

In contrast with the experiences of heterosexual couples who use donated gametes, lesbian couples and single women are almost unanimous in their decision to tell their child about her or his origins (Sparks and Hamilton (1991)). Consistent with this, an increasing number of sperm banks are being set up in the USA aimed primarily at lesbian or gay couples with gamete providers who are prepared to permit recipients or offspring varying amounts of information about them (for example, Pacific Reproductive Services: http://www.hellobaby.com) or release the donor's identity (Xytex: http://www.xytex.com) or encourage and facilitate ongoing relationships between donors and recipients (Rainbow Flag Health Services: http://www.gayspermbank.com).

The psychological and ethical advantages of openness may be apparent, and the comparison with adoption is easily made. It is important to note, however, that there continue to be several ways in which the experience of adoption is different from the experience of gamete donation and which may discourage openness in parents: the use of gamete donation invariably necessitates explanation of infertility, which adoption does not; parents with children of gamete donation lack the "scripts" as well as the support available to adoptive parents; and legislation operates against openness amongst parents with children of gamete donation, for no information is available about the genetic father (Cook et al. (1995)). Parents who are considering whether or not to tell their child may receive mixed messages about the importance of doing so; those who initially favour openness may be discouraged when institutions themselves are secretive (Haimes (1993)).

There has been no exploration of the effects of secrecy by comparison of families who plan to tell with those who do not, primarily because so few parents do plan to tell. Although there is evidence to suggest that young children do not suffer psychologically as a consequence of not being provided with information about their origins (see e.g. Golombok et al. (1995)), there is little if any systematic information about the consequences for older children, adolescents and adults. It remains to be seen whether difficulties become apparent as children mature. Children's understanding of their origins seems likely to be limited in the early years (Brodzinsky (1987)), and secrets are easier to keep from young children (Mahlstedt and Greenfeld (1989)). Greater challenges for parents and children lie in meeting the child's increased need for understanding and knowledge which characterises middle childhood and adolescence. There is some evidence of distress and other negative consequences of this secrecy, but it comes from studies which are small and unrepresentative (see e.g. Baran and Pannor (1989); Turner and Coyle (2000)). We therefore cannot generalise about the psychological consequences of lack of information about origins from this research.

Recipients of gametes and donors demonstrate a "need" for secrecy; some adults conceived using donated gametes report "a need" to know of their origins. It has been suggested that both of these needs are socially constructed (O'Donovan (1989); Evans (1995); Freeman (1997)). In particular, O'Donovan argues that rather than changing practice, we should consider changing society's emphasis on the importance of genetic relationships. This seems an unlikely option, given the cultural significance of gametes at a time increasingly dominated by the search for genetic explanations of behaviour. Further, that needs are socially constructed does not imply that such needs should be ignored. Maintaining secrecy in assisted conception using donor gametes may be tempting for many of the parties involved: for clinics, it means easier recruitment of donors; for donors it means relative detachment from the implications of their actions; for recipients it means sustaining the façade of a traditional family (Landau (1998)).[10] However, it raises issues concerning the welfare of the child.

When considering the rights and welfare of children (and potential adults), we need to bear in mind that there is debate about whether decisions made on behalf of children should be made in objective terms (what the decision-maker thinks would be best for the child) or more subjectively (what the child would want for her or himself) (see e.g. Bainham (1998); Cretney and Masson (1997)). Any belief that secrecy is detrimental to the well-being of a child is in conflict with the provision of the HFEA Code of Practice, which requires clinics to:

---

[10] Although note that this strategy may be counterproductive, since keeping secrets requires considerable effort and may lead to obsessive preoccupation with the secret subject, see e.g. Lane and Wegner (1995).

"take account of the welfare of any child who may be born or who may be affected as a result of the treatment" as well as "a child's potential need to know about their origins and whether or not the prospective parents are prepared for the questions which may arise while the child is growing up".

Furthermore, clinics are asked to consider whether there might be any risk of harm from neglect or abuse of a child conceived in this way. Whereas in other arenas when there is a dispute over children, for example, as a result of divorce, the child's welfare is paramount, in contrast to this the HFEA makes the adults' rights predominant over the potential child's.

Perhaps the most startling aspect of the nature of transactions with gametes is the extent to which traces of the most vital member of the transaction—the gamete provider—continue in many countries to be excised. This marginalisation of a key person in these transactions may be supported by the commodification of gametes, as argued by Daniels (2000). There may however be changes ahead. Article 8 of the Human Rights Act 1998 states that "Everyone has the right to respect for his private and family life, his home and his correspondence" (Wadham and Mountfield (1999)). It is expected that this will lead to challenges from those who feel that their sense of identity is compromised by an absence of information about their origins (Liberty (2001)). There has been considerable discussion in both academic and clinical circles concerning the relative benefits of openness and secrecy and in December 2000 the UK Department of Health announced that it was planning to reconsider the provision of information to those conceived using donated gametes, although this would not operate retrospectively. A consultation document is planned for mid-2001 (Carvel (2000)).

There is a difference, however, between constructing regulations or laws that do not permit anonymity, or which are aimed at enabling an understanding of our origins, and ensuring that these are complied with. Allowing people conceived by donor insemination, whether as adults or children, access to information about the gamete provider, currently depends upon those responsible for the child providing initial information about their conception. In Sweden, where donor offspring have, as adults, the right to learn their genetic father's identity, parents are nevertheless unlikely to tell their children about their conception. A recent study found that only 11 per cent of parents had told their child, although 59 per cent had told others (Gottlieb et al. (2000)).

It has been noted that "converting social goals into law cannot automatically improve children's lives" (Cretney and Masson (1997)). In order for this to happen, relevant parties must both have the will and be enabled to do so, by the development of appropriate mechanisms or procedures and the provision of appropriate support (Cook et al. (1995)). Legislation is not enough.

All these factors support the notion that gamete provision is not a use of the body that is socially legitimate. Whilst there are ongoing debates in the United Kingdom about the future provision of information to persons conceived by donor insemination, it seems unlikely that in the short term such information will include identifying information.

4. WHY IS THE DONOR NOT THE HERO?[11]

What can we say with certainty about this "use" of the body? It seems appropriate to define gametes as an incomplete commodity; given suitable legislation they can be sold for a high price to the highest bidder. Such a price is, however, not a necessary condition for gamete provision, for in some countries, it has been argued, gamete providers effectively pay to donate. Against a background of debate over the status of gametes, people and societies continue to treat them as commodities. Whilst use of reproductive technologies has been seen in the past as a threat to the family, transactions with gametes are sanctioned in a set of circumstances which is designed to support, rather than threaten, conventional family structure. Yet despite more than one hundred years of history of this kind of transaction, there is evidence for continued ambivalence and lack of social acceptance.

Our understanding of the psychology of gamete provision is incomplete. Research has tended to be driven by practical rather than theoretical considerations, and has been limited by focusing on discovering stated reasons for this uncommon behaviour, rather than developing an understanding of the more common alternative: why people do not donate. One consequence of this has been the maintenance of the payment/altruism dichotomy in the literature, which tends to encourage two opposing views of the donor, particularly the semen donor. He may be the villain: unengaged, emotionless and driven by financial reward. Alternatively he might be viewed as the hero: gallant, benevolent and compassionate. However, in viewing the actions of the gamete provider, we cannot realistically characterise him/her as the villain or the hero. First, it is clear from research evidence so far from countries that enable or permit gamete provision in different climates that gamete providers are not impelled by a single motivation. Donors see themselves, or can be seen, to be using their bodies in a variety of ways and to achieve a variety of ends: as a resource, to obtain other resources; to state values and opinions; to exploit a talent (for fertility); to express personality characteristics; or even to achieve an otherwise impossible genetic continuity. What is not clear is what constitutes an appropriate motivation; furthermore we are still a long way from understanding the psychological consequences of this most secret activity. Secondly, even if we accept a dichotomy of motivations for gamete provision, whilst the behaviour of the financially-motivated might be dubious and the behaviour of the "altruistic" gamete provider laudable, the social illegitimacy of their actions means that in neither case are they sufficiently visible to be characterised as either the villain or the hero. Irrespective of motivation, the gamete provider is more like the masked stranger: central to the plot, but of uncertain identity. As yet, the story is unfinished: we have to read on, to discover whether he is to be unmasked.

---

[11] A paraphrase from Achilles (1993) p. 171.

REFERENCES

ACHILLES, R., "Protection from What? The Secret Life of Donor Insemination" (1993) 12 *Politics and the Life Sciences* 171.

AHUJA, K. K. and SIMONS, E. G., "Cancer of the Colon in an Egg Donor: Policy Repercussions for Donor Recruitment" (1998) 13 *Human Reproduction* 227.

AHUJA, K. K., SIMONS, E. G. and EDWARDS, R. G., "Money, Morals and Medical Risks: Conflicting Notions Underlying the Recruitment of Egg Donors" (1999) 14 *Human Reproduction* 279.

AMUZU, B., LAXOVA, R. and SHAPIRO, S., "Pregnancy Outcome, Health of Children, and Family Adjustment after Donor Insemination" (1990) 75 *Obstetrics & Gynaecology* 899.

ANDREWS, L. and NELKIN, D., "Whose Body is it Anyway? Disputes over Body Tissue in a Biotechnology Age" (1998) 351 *The Lancet* 53.

BAINHAM, A., *Children: The Modern Law* (2nd edn., Bristol, Jordan Publishing Limited, 1998).

BARAN, A. and PANNOR, R., *Lethal Secrets: The Shocking Consequences and Unsolved Problems of Artificial Insemination* (New York, Warner Books, 1989).

BARRATT, C. L. R. and COOKE, I. D., *Donor Insemination* (Cambridge, Cambridge University Press, 1993).

BERGER, D. M., EISEN, A., SHUBER, J. and DOODY, K. F., "Psychological Patterns in Donor Insemination Couples" (1986) 31 *Canadian Journal of Psychiatry* 217.

BOLTON, V., GOLOMBOK, S., COOK R. et al., "A Comparative Study of Attitudes Towards Donor Insemination and Egg Donation in Recipients, Potential Donors and the Public" (1991) 12 *Journal of Psychosomatic Obstetrics and Gynaecology* 217.

BRANDON, J. and WARNER, J., "AID and Adoption: Some Comparisons" (1977) *British Journal of Social Work* 335.

BREWAEYS, A., Ponjaertkristoffersen, I., VanSteirteghem, A. C. and DeVroey, P., "Children from Anonymous Donors—an Inquiry into Homosexual and Heterosexual Parents' Attitudes" (1993) 14 *Journal of Psychosomatic Obstetrics and Gynaecology* 23.

BRIGGS, N. C., PILIAVIN, J. A., LORENTZEN, D. and BECKER, G. A., "On Willingness to be a Bone-Marrow Donor" (1986) 26 *Transfusion* 324.

BRITISH ANDROLOGY SOCIETY, "British Andrology Society Guidelines for the Screening of Semen Donors for Donor Insemination (1999)" (1999) 14 *Human Reproduction* 1823.

BRITISH FERTILITY SOCIETY, *Document on the Payment of Semen Donors* (1996) http://www.britishfertilitysociety.org.uk.

BRODZINSKY, D. M., "Adjustment to Adoption—a Psychosocial Perspective" (1987) 7 *Clinical Psychology Review* 25.

BRUCE, N., "On the Importance of Genetic Knowledge" (1990) 4 *Children's Society* 183.

CARVEL, J., "Sperm Donors Face Loss of Privacy", 27 December 2000 *The Guardian*: http://www.guardianunlimited.co.uk/uk_news/story/0,3604,415559,00.html

COHEN, C. B., "Selling Bits and Pieces of Humans to Make Babies: The Gift of the Magi Revisited" (1999) 24 *Journal of Medical Philosophy* 288.

COOK, R. and GOLOMBOK, S., "A Survey of Semen Donation: Phase II—the View of the Donors" (1995) 10 *Human Reproduction* 951.

COOK, R., GOLOMBOK, S., BISH, A. et al., "Disclosure of Donor Insemination: Parental Attitudes" (1995) 65 *American Journal of Orthopsychiatry* 549.

CRETNEY, S. M. and MASSON, J. M., *Principles of Family Law* (London, Sweet & Maxwell, 1997).

DANIELS, K. R., "Artificial Insemination Using Donor Semen and the Issue of Secrecy: the Views of Donors and Recipient Couples" (1988) 27 *Social Science and Medicine* 377.

——, "To Give or Sell Human Gametes—the Interplay Between Pragmatics, Policy and Ethics" (2000) 26 *Journal of Medical Ethics* 206.

DANIELS, K. R. and LEWIS, G., "Donor Insemination: the Gifting and Selling of Semen" (1996) 42 *Social Science and Medicine* 1521.

DANIELS, K. R. and TAYLOR, K., "Secrecy and Openness in Donor Insemination" (1993) 12 *Politics and the Life Sciences* 155.

DECI, E. L., "Effects of Contingent and Non-Contingent Rewards and Controls on Intrinsic Motivation" (1971) 18 *Journal of Personality & Social Psychology* 105.

DECI, E. L., KOESTNER, R. and RYAN, R. M., "A Meta-analytic Review of Experiments Examining the Effects of Extrinsic Rewards on Intrinsic Motivation" (1999) 125 *Psychological Bulletin* 627.

DICKENSON, D. L., "Procuring Gametes for Research and Therapy: the Argument for Unisex Altruism—a Response to Donald Evans" (1997) 23 *Journal of Medical Ethics* 93.

EAGLY, A. H. and CROWLEY, M., "Gender and Helping Behaviour: a Meta-analysis Review of the Social Psychology Literature" (1986) 100 *Psychological Bulletin* 283.

EVANS, D., "Procuring Gametes for Research and Therapy" (1995) 21 *Journal of Medical Ethics* 261.

FERGUSON, E., "Predictors of Future Behaviour: A Review of the Psychological Literature on Blood Donation" (1996) 1 *British Journal of Health Psychology* 287.

FREEMAN, M., "The New Birth Right: Identity and the Child of the Reproduction Revolution" (1997) 4 *International Journal of Children's Rights* 273.

GAZVANI, M. R., WOOD, S. J., THOMSON, A. J. M., et al., "Payment or Altruism? The Motivation Behind Gamete Donation" (1997) 12 *Human Reproduction* 1845.

GENERAL MEDICAL COUNCIL, *Good Medical Practice. Guidance from the General Medical Council* (2nd edn., London, GMC, 1998).

GOLOMBOK, S., COOK, R., BISH, A. and MURRAY, C., "Families Created by the New Reproductive Technologies: Quality of Parenting and Social and Emotional Development of the Children" (1995) 64 *Child Development* 285.

GOTTLIEB, C., LALOS, O. and LINDBLAD, F., "Disclosure of Donor Insemination to the Child: the Impact of Swedish Legislation on Couples' Attitudes" (2000) 15 *Human Reproduction* 2052.

GUNNING, J., "Oocyte Donation: the Legislative Framework in Western Europe" (1998) 13 *Human Reproduction* 98.

HAIMES, E., "Issues of Gender in Gamete Donation" (1993) 36 *Social Science and Medicine* 85.

HORNE, G., HUGHES, S. M., MATSON, P. L. et al., "The Recruitment of Oocyte Donors" (1993) 100 *British Journal of Obstetrics & Gynaecology* 877.

HUMAN FERTILISATION AND EMBRYOLOGY AUTHORITY, *Code of Practice* (London, HFEA, 1998a).

——, *Consultation on the Implementation of the Withdrawal of Payments to Donors* (London, HFEA, 1998b).

——, *Annual Report* (London, HFEA, 1999).

——, *Annual Report* (London, HFEA, 2000a).

——, "Payment of Expenses to Donors" (2000b) 4 *HFEA Update* 2 (http://www.hfea.gov.uk).

HUMPHREY, M. and HUMPHREY, H., "A Fresh Look at Genealogical Bewilderment" (1986) 59 *British Journal of Medical Psychology* 133.

IMBER-BLACK, E., *Secrets in Families and Family Therapy* (New York, W.W. Norton and Company, 1993).

JOHNSON, M., "A Biomedical Perspective on Parenthood" in A. Bainham, S. Day Sclater, and M. Richards (eds.), *What is a Parent? A Socio-Legal Analysis* (Oxford, Hart Publishing, 1999).

KAHN, J. P., "Organ Donation—We'll Make it Worth Your While", *Ethics Matters CNN Interactive*, 3 May 1999, http://www.cnn.com/health/bioethics

KARPEL, M., "Family Secrets: I. Conceptual and Ethical Issues in the Relational Context. II. Ethical and Practical Considerations in Therapeutic Management" (1980) 19 *Family Process* 295.

KLOCK, S. C. and MAIER, D., "Psychological Factors Related to Donor Insemination" (1991) 56 *Fertility and Sterility* 489.

LANDAU, R., "The Management of Genetic Origins: Secrecy and Openness in Donor Assisted Conception in Israel and Elsewhere" (1998) 13 *Human Reproduction* 3268.

LANE, J. D. and WEGNER, D. M., "The Cognitive Consequences of Secrecy" (1995) 69 *Journal of Personality and Social Psychology* 237.

LEDWARD, R. S., CRAWFORD, L. and SYMONDS, E. M., "Social Factors in Patients for Artificial Insemination by Donor (AID)" (1979) 11 *Journal of Biosocial Science* 473.

LEE, R. G. and MORGAN, D., *Human Fertilisation and Embryology* (London, Blackstone Press, 2001).

LIBERTY (2001), http://www.liberty-human-rights.org.uk/

LOCKWOOD, G. M., "Donating Life: Practical and Ethical Issues in Gamete Donation" in F. Shenfield and C. Sureau (eds.), *Ethical Dilemmas in Assisted Reproduction* (New York, Parthenon Publishing Group, 1997).

LUI, S. C., WEAVER, S. M., ROBINSON, J. et al., "A Survey of Donor Attitudes" (1995) 10 *Human Reproduction* 234.

MAHLSTEDT, P. P. and GREENFELD, D. A., "Assisted Reproductive Technology with Donor Gametes—the Need for Patient Preparation" (1989) 52 *Fertility and Sterility* 908.

MARTEAU, T. M., COOK, R., KIDD, J., et al., "The Psychological Effects of False-Positive Results in Prenatal Screening for Fetal Abnormality: a Prospective Study" (1992) 12 *Prenatal Diagnosis* 205.

McLEAN, S., *Consent and the Law. Review of the Current Provisions in the Human Fertilisation and Embryology Act 1990 for UK Health Ministers* (London, Department of Health, 1997).

MILSOM, J. and BERGMAN, P., "A Study of Parental Attitudes after Donor Insemination (AID)" (1982) 61 *Acta Obstetricia et Gynecologica Scandinavica* 125.

MORGAN, D. and LEE, R. G., *Blackstone's Guide to the Human Fertilisation and Embryology Act 1990. Abortion, Embryo Research, the New Law* (London, Blackstone Press, 1991).

MURRAY, C. and GOLOMBOK, S., "Oocyte and Semen Donation: a Survey of UK Licensed Centres" (2000) 15 *Human Reproduction* 2133.

NICHOLAS, M. K. and TYLER, J. P. P., "Characteristics, Attitudes and Personalities of AI Donors" (1983) 2 *Clinical Reproduction and Fertility* 47.

NOVAES, S. B., "Giving, Receiving, Repaying. Gamete Donors and Donor Policies in Reproductive Medicine" (1989) 5 *International Journal of Technological Assessment in Health Care* 639.

O'DONOVAN, K., " 'What Shall We Tell the Children?' Reflections on Children's Perspectives and the Reproduction Revolution", in R. Lee and D. Morgan (eds.), *Birthrights. Law and Ethics at the Beginnings of Life* (London, Routledge, 1989).

PACIFIC REPRODUCTIVE SERVICES, http://www.hellobaby.com

PEDERSEN, B., NIELSON, A. F., and LAURITSEN, J. G., "Psychological Aspects of Donor Insemination. Sperm Donors: their Motivations and Attitudes to Artificial Insemination" (1994) 73 *Acta Obstetrica Scandinavica* 701.

PRICE, F. V. and COOK, R., "The Donor, the Recipient and the Child–Human Egg Donation in UK Licensed Centres" (1995) 7 *Child and Family Law Quarterly* 145.

RAINBOW FLAG HEALTH SERVICES, http://www.gayspermbank.com

RESNIK, D. B., "The Commodification of Human Reproductive Materials" (1998) 24 *Journal of Medical Ethics* 388.

ROWLAND, R., "Attitudes and Opinions of Donors on an Artificial Insemination by Donor (AID) Programme" (1983) 2 *Clinical Reproduction and Fertility* 249.

ROWLAND, R. and RUFFIN, C., "Community Attitudes to Artificial Insemination by Husband or Donor, *In Vitro* Fertilization and Adoption" (1983) 2 *Clinical Reproduction and Fertility* 35.

SANTS, H. J., "Genealogical Bewilderment in Children with Substitute Parents" (1964) 37 *British Journal of Medical Psychology* 133.

SAUER, M. V., "Reproductive Prohibition: Restricting Donor Payment Will Lead to Medical Tourism" (1997) 12 *Human Reproduction* 1844.

SAUER, M.V., GORRILL, M.J., ZEFFER, K.B. and BUSTILLO, M., "Attitudinal Survey of Sperm Donors to an Artificial Insemination Clinic" (1989) 3415 *Journal of Reproductive Medicine, Obstetrics and Gynaecology* 362.

SCHOVER, L. R., COLLINS, R. L. and RICHARDS, S., "Psychological Aspects of Donor Insemination—Evaluation and Follow-up of Recipient Couples" (1992a) 57 *Fertility and Sterility* 583.

SCHOVER, L. R., ROTHMANN, S. A. and COLLINS, R. L., "The Personality and Motivation of Semen Donors: a Comparison with Oocyte Donors" (1992b) 7 *Human Reproduction* 575.

SNOWDEN, R., MITCHELL, G. D. and SNOWDEN, E. M., *Artificial Reproduction: A Social Investigation* (London, George Allen and Unwin, 1983).

SOULES, M. R., "Posthumous Harvesting of Gametes—a Physician's Perspective" (1999) 27 *Journal of Law, Medicine and Ethics* 362.

SPARKS, C. and HAMILTON, J. A., "Psychological Issues Related to Alternative Insemination" (1991) 22 *Professional Psychology: Research and Practice* 308.

TITMUS, R., *The Gift Relationship: From Human Blood to Social Policy* (London, Allen and Unwin, 1978).

TURNER, A.J. and COYLE, A., "What Does it Mean to be a Donor Offspring? The Identity Experiences of Adults Conceived by Donor Insemination and the Implications for Counselling and Therapy" (2000) 15 *Human Reproduction* 2041.

WADHAM, J. and MOUNTFIELD, H., *Blackstone's Guide to the Human Rights Act 1998* (London, Blackstone Press, 1999).

XYTEX CORPORATION, http://www.xytex.com

13

Court-ordered Caesarean Sections

JANE WEAVER*

T HIS CHAPTER ADDRESSES the phenomenon of court-ordered caesarean section: the application by doctors or hospital administrators to courts to obtain
the legal right to impose the operation upon pregnant women who refuse to follow obstetric advice. These cases raise several important issues. One set of issues
concerns the imposition of unwanted treatment on the childbearing woman in a
day and age when it is conceded that women should be able to have choice and
control over their care during pregnancy, labour and birth (Department of Health
(1993)). Related to this are arguments about the pregnant or labouring woman's
competence to consent and about the relationship between the medical and legal
profession. Another set of issues concerns the respective interests of mother and
foetus. Maternal-foetal conflict, an emotive term, has sometimes been employed
in this context. Many of these issues are not only of interest and importance to
members of the legal profession, but also to social scientists, feminists and health
professionals.

The majority of cases appear to have arisen in the USA and the United
Kingdom. Many applications were presented as emergencies requiring a rapid
decision and thus precluding the production of a written court order. Therefore
exact numbers are unknown (Rhoden (1986)). Some of the UK cases were decided
without legal representation for the woman (Hewson (1996)) and sometimes
without even her knowledge. No further cases of enforced caesarean section upon
mentally competent women have been reported in the United Kingdom since two
appeals in 1997[1] and 1998.[2] However, there have been recent press reports of a case
involving surgery, without obstetric indication, on a schizophrenic woman who
was deemed likely to be unco-operative in labour (Beech (2000a)).[3] Although
some of the cases are old, many of the underlying issues and assumptions made by
the courts resonate with current attitudes in maternity care. Before these are
addressed, however, it is necessary to examine the issue of caesarean section and

* I would like to thank Martin Richards, Kirsty Keywood and Shona Chaib for reading, and giving
detailed comments on, previous drafts of this chapter. The author's research on decision-making for
caesarean section is supported by a grant from the Nuffield Foundation.
[1] Re MB [1997] 8 Med LR 217.
[2] St George's Healthcare Trust v. S [1998] 3 All ER 673.
[3] A brief, unattributed report of the case was also published under the heading "Forced Caesarean
baby is safe and well", in a Welsh Newspaper, Western Mail, 22 June 2000.

obstetric technology more generally. It is in the light of changes in both that court-ordered caesareans arose.

1. CAESAREAN SECTION

Caesarean section is carried out either for medical and obstetric reasons or because of social factors, for example, maternal request (Mould et al. (1996); Jackson and Irvine (1998); Paterson-Brown (1998)). The latter set of issues will not be addressed in detail here. Medical and obstetric indications include situations where it is considered impossible for the baby to born vaginally. Examples would include cephalopelvic disproportion, where the pelvis is not wide enough to allow the passage of the presenting part of the fetus, and placenta praevia, where the afterbirth is covering the outlet from the uterus. Indications of this nature are sometimes termed *absolute*. However, there is another set of indications where the features of the individual case, and the mode of practice and level of experience of the obstetrician, will determine whether vaginal birth is attempted or not. These indications are sometimes described as *relative*. They include poor progress in labour, and foetal distress (Francome et al. (1993); Churchill (1997)). Although national statistics have yet to be published,[4] one study, at a large teaching hospital, identified poor progress in labour (36.7 per cent of cases) and foetal indications (18.9 per cent of cases) as the most frequently cited justifications for caesarean section (Leitch and Walker (1998)). Another commonly cited indication for the operation is a previous caesarean, because of fears of rupture of the old uterine scar during labour. However, in recent years, the likelihood of this occurrence has been challenged (Enkin et al. (1989)).

Caesarean sections are also categorised according to their predictability. Unexpected caesarean sections are usually classed as emergencies, whilst those that are planned prior to the date of birth are elective. Some emergency situations are clear-cut, for example, when the mother is haemorrhaging, when any delay could prove fatal. However, not all emergencies are acute. In some cases there is fore-warning, and the woman and her partner can be prepared for the growing likelihood. For example, if progress in labour is poor but there is no maternal or foetal distress, both woman and obstetrician might prefer to await events for a while before making a final decision.

The caesarean section rate in England has risen steadily over the past twenty years. In the early 1980s the rate across England was just above 10 per cent of all births (Macfarlane (1998)). Ten years later this rate had risen to 15.5 per cent. By 1998 a quarter of all hospitals had rates of 20 per cent to 29.9 per cent, whilst another 2 per cent had rates of over 30 per cent (Anderson (2000a)). Nevertheless the main obstetric indications are the same as twenty years ago. It is the threshold for taking operative action that appears to have been lowered (Leitch and Walker (1998)).

---

[4] A national audit is in progress at the time of writing and the findings will be disseminated in autumn 2001 (Callwood and Thomas (2000)).

The reasons for this increase are debatable. Some writers blame the growing number of obstetricians who promote the operation as simple and safe (Kitzinger (1998)), whilst others attribute the rise to consumer demand (MacKenzie (1999)). There is still only limited research on the attitudes of mothers towards the operation, and this issue requires further investigation. Although it is sometimes assumed that all women would prefer a normal delivery, and that a caesarean section can never be more than the "next best thing" (Francome et al. (1993)), some women do find caesarean section to be a very positive experience (Clement (1992)). However, many women are emotionally and physically traumatised after the operation, describing feelings of alienation from their baby, bereavement, or being cheated (Clement (1992)).

To some extent the rising rate is understandable. Because of improved surgical and anaesthetic techniques the operation is considerably safer than it was two decades ago (Savage and Francome (1993)). However, caesarean section still carries an increased risk of complications, over and above vaginal birth, for both mother and child. Maternal mortality is six times higher than for vaginal birth (Hall and Bewley (1999)). Major maternal morbidity arises in 9 per cent to 15 per cent of cases (Churchill (1997)), and more minor problems in over 50 per cent (Hillan (1992)). In the longer term there are more likely to be complications with subsequent pregnancies and births. In terms of foetal morbidity, respiratory distress of the newborn is higher after caesarean section. Less commonly, babies can suffer scalpel lacerations, fractures and brachial plexus paralysis. There is also some suggestion that maternal hypotension during spinal anaesthesia might cause foetal distress (Hillan (1991a)). At the same time there is a lack of any convincing evidence of a concomitant reduction in perinatal or maternal mortality as the caesarean rate has risen (Enkin et al. (1995); Anderson (2000a)). The optimal caesarean rate is hotly debated, but absolute indications only account for between 5.8 per cent and 8.5 per cent of all births (Francome et al. (1993)). This is not to argue that caesarean section, except in life and death cases, holds no advantages for the childbearing woman. It might avoid psychological morbidity associated with fear of vaginal birth. It can also prevent severe perineal damage leading to dyspareunia or anal sphincter involvement (Sultan and Stanton (1996)).

2. OBSTETRIC TECHNOLOGY

Something that has changed alongside the rising rate of caesarean section is the image of childbirth. Several authors have traced a historical progression from representations of birth as a normal bodily function to its depiction as a medical problem, and from thence to a pathological event (Oakley (1984); Martin (1987); Campbell (1990); Schwarz (1990)). This process began in the last century alongside the development of obstetrics as a profession. However, the medical to pathological transition—the redefinition of birth from an event with the potential to go wrong, to an event that should only be considered normal in retrospect—has taken place since the 1950s. Alongside this redefinition has run a development in obstetric technology of which the refinement of caesarean section is just a part. Much of this technology has been in the hands of obstetricians and has thus been achieved at the expense of women's autonomy; women as both childbearers and as midwives.[5]

This obstetric control has also resulted in other changes in the way that pregnancy and birth is perceived. The obstetrician is often represented as the saviour of both mother, and especially child. Of course there are situations where, indubitably, the fetus has been saved because technology has correctly diagnosed a problem and a timely extraction of the child by caesarean section has ensued. Nevertheless, what women do not always realise is that many of the technological aids routinely used to monitor and facilitate childbirth can help to create an obstetric emergency in the first place. These aids were frequently developed with small specialised groups of women, then employed wholesale without full evaluation of their usefulness to the obstetric population at large (Beech (2000b)). Their deployment often disturbs the normal physiological responses that make labour effective (Anderson (2000b)). Each intervention also has side-effects. These often require management in the form of further intervention. This can set in motion a "cascade of intervention", the endpoint of which is frequently an instrumental or operative delivery (Wagner (1994)). Despite this, clinical recommendation and implementation of intervention is usually represented as value-free, rational and scientific (McLean (1999)).

Another change has been in the management of the foetus. The maternal-foetal relationship was once regarded as something integral. This was largely because the foetus was not visible during pregnancy, neither was it able to survive outside of the mother until near term. There was a division of labour between obstetricians and paediatricians, but because of this foetal invisibility, the paediatrician had little involvement in the woman's care until the birth was nearly or wholly accomplished (Richards (1975)). Today the developing foetus is visualised by ultrasound, monitored electronically and even operated upon *in utero.* Consequently mother and foetus are, more often than not, contemplated and managed as two separate individuals (Hornstra (1998)) and, as a result, as the court cases described below demonstrate, obstetricians have become increasingly involved as defenders of foetal interests (McLean (1999)).

3. THE CASES

It is well recognised in English law that a competent adult has the right to withhold consent to medical treatment. However, the court-ordered caesarean cases were often based upon reservations about the extent of this right particularly when the

---

[5] Men have also been able to train as midwives since 1975, although they are still a small minority within the profession.

adult's choice might lead to the death of a viable foetus.[6] Despite this, in English law the foetus has no legal right of action until birth, and only then if the child is born alive (Fovargue and Miola (1998); Mason and McCall Smith (1999)). Moreover, English law precludes claims by a child against a negligent mother, except in the case of injuries sustained during a traffic accident. This is a different situation to the USA where there tends to be strong support for state interest in the well-being of a viable foetus (Kordus (1997); Mason and McCall Smith (1999)). Thus in both the American and the English cases the issue has been obstetric concern for the well-being of the foetus, and often for the mother too (despite her legal right to refuse treatment, whatever the outcome), set against the unwillingness of the mother to comply with obstetric recommendation. However, the different status of the foetus in law in the two countries perhaps helps to explain why court-ordered caesareans have been particularly prevalent in the USA, and why so many applications for orders were successful there (RCOG (1994)). The issue in the United Kingdom revolves more strongly around the efforts of judges to address the concerns of the medical profession, whilst not according the foetus a legal status to which it is not entitled. Nevertheless, the Ethics Committee of the American College of Obstetricians and Gynaecologists, like the Royal College of Obstetricians and Gynaecologists in the United Kingdom, has stated that obstetricians should not perform procedures that are declined by a pregnant woman (ACOG (1987); RCOG (1994)). Therefore, many of the moral questions around attitudes towards, and management of, the pregnant women in these cases remain the same.

As explained above, written evidence of cases is in short supply. However, it is claimed that court-enforced caesareans have been performed in the USA since 1973 (Rowan (1998)). Most of these early American cases involved women who were poor, or members of ethnic minorities. Many of them did not speak English and had beliefs and attitudes about childbirth which did not coincide with the medical model of their doctors (Kolder et al. (1987)). They included cases where the pregnant woman had her wrists and ankles forcibly secured with leather cuffs, and where judicial authority had been granted over the telephone (Thomson (1998)). In most of these cases the order was easily obtained. In both the USA and the United Kingdom, the medical case has usually claimed that the operation was a life-saving necessity for both mother and child. The judges have invariably accepted this medical argument without question, even on the rare occasions when they have then gone on to defend the woman's right to imperil her own life and that of her infant. Nevertheless, when the woman has managed to escape the obstetrician's knife, either by such a defence of her rights or by giving birth before the operation could be performed, events have sometimes belied the life preservation argument. In one such case[7] the certainty of foetal death was put at 99 per cent

---

[6] *Re T (adult: refusal of medical treatment)* [1992] 4 All ER 649.
[7] Interestingly, a case of complete placenta praevia, a condition obstetrically considered an absolute indication for caesarean section.

and the chance of maternal survival at not better than 50 per cent.[8] The mother gave birth spontaneously, and with no ill effect to either herself or her infant, before the court-ordered operation could be carried out. In another, the hospital argued that a woman's infant, which had the umbilical cord wrapped around its neck, would strangle itself at birth. In this case the court refused to order surgery, and the mother gave birth to a healthy child (Field (1989)).

In what was probably the most notorious case in the USA, in 1987, a hospital administration went to court to force a pregnant woman who was critically ill with cancer to undergo a caesarean section at 26 weeks' gestation. At this point in pregnancy the foetus is barely viable outside of the uterus. Nevertheless, the hospital told the judge that there was a 50 to 60 per cent chance that the baby would survive and a less than 20 per cent chance that it would be handicapped.[9] This move was not only opposed by the woman herself and her family, but also by her obstetricians. The baby died two hours after the surgery, and after being told that her infant had not survived, the woman died two days later. The caesarean section was noted to be a contributing cause of her death (Field (1989)). Her life had also been foreshortened by the hospital's decision to withhold chemotherapy because of the dangers it posed for the foetus (Thomson (1998)). Three years afterwards the decision went to appeal and was successfully overturned.[10] This was the first American case to go to a fully considered appeal.

The first known British case occurred in 1992. A Nigerian woman refused to consent to the operation for religious reasons when her baby was found to be lying in a transverse position,[11] a lie incompatible with vaginal birth. The hearing lasted only twenty minutes, and the woman was not represented (Montgomery (1997)). It was agreed that she was competent to make decisions, but it was argued that the proposed surgery was to save her life and that of her child, and that it could therefore be performed without her consent. In fact the foetus died before the order was finally made (Hewson (1996)).

The next case to be widely reported was different.[12] A woman who suffered from schizophrenia had experienced deterioration in her mental state during pregnancy, her medication having been stopped because of an adverse reaction and for fear it would harm the foetus. By 37 weeks gestation there were clear signs of poor placental function, and concerns that, although the mother was at no risk, the foetus might die *in utero*. Although the woman consented to an induction of labour it was feared that, should foetal distress occur and a caesarean be required, she might resist. The NHS Trust sought a declaration that the operation could be performed without the woman's consent and that physical restraint could be used if necessary. The treatment (and by implication the use of restraint and reasonable force) was authorised under the Mental Health Act 1983, section 63. The justification was that

---

[8] *Jefferson* v. *Griffin Spalding County Hospital Authority* [1981] 247 Ga. 86; 274 SE 2d 457.

[9] *Re AC* 533 A 2d 611 [DC, 1987].

[10] *Re AC* 573 A 2d 1235 [DC, 1990].

[11] *Re S (adult refusal of medical treatment)* [1992] 4 All ER 671.

[12] *Tameside and Glossop Acute Services Trust* v. *CH* [1996] FLR 762.

a successful outcome of the woman's pregnancy was a necessary part of her overall treatment for mental disorder. It was argued that her mental health would be jeopardised further if she gave birth to a dead baby, and that expediting the birth of the baby also allowed a resumption of her antipsychotic treatment. The verdict in this case was widely criticised by academic writers, both in terms of obstetric management (Bewley (1997)) and in the use (or misuse) of the Mental Health Act (Bastian and Conroy (1997); Dolan and Parker (1997)).

By this time court-ordered caesareans were becoming more common and it was reported in April 1997 that the High Court in London had sanctioned around six such operations in the past year (Dyer (1997)). The first English case to go to appeal was heard the same year.[13] The term foetus of a 23-year-old woman was lying in a footling breech position—one of the baby's legs was extended and presenting at the cervix. It was considered that, whilst posing little danger for the mother, vaginal birth for a foetus in this position would put the child at risk of serious consequences. This was explained to the woman, and she agreed to a caesarean section. However, she suffered from a phobia of hypodermic needles, and despite signing a consent form for the operation, not only did she refuse the pre-requisite blood tests prior to the surgery, but she also refused insertion of the intravenous cannula for administration of the anaesthetic. By this time she was also too frightened to consent to anaesthetic administration by a mask, and the hospital sought and obtained judicial approval to perform a caesarean section with, if necessary, the use of reasonable force against the woman. The woman instructed her solicitor over the telephone to appeal against this judgment, and the Court of Appeal met that same night. The appeal was refused, the woman subsequently consented to administration of the anaesthetic, and a healthy baby was born by caesarean. The appeal judges had agreed that the woman was incapable of making a decision because her mental function was impaired by her needle phobia. However, in reaching this conclusion they did make several important statements, which have helped to shape subsequent decisions. They held that it would be unlawful for a doctor to perform a caesarean section on a *competent* woman who refused the operation, even if the life of the woman and her child would be thus endangered. Therefore the President of the High Court's family division misdirected himself when he approved the first forced caesarean section in 1992. They also pointed out that because a woman was willing to endanger her own life or that of her child this was not, in itself, reason enough to pronounce her incompetent. They also specified that the woman should be represented in all cases where application for an order was made—something that had frequently failed to happen previously.

The second, successful appeal was in 1998, although the original case had arisen in 1996,[14] prior to the one discussed above. A 30-year-old woman, at eight months gestation, visited her GP to register as a patient. She was found to be pre-eclamptic: suffering from a disorder of pregnancy that had the potential to threaten the life of

---

[13] *Re MB* [1997] 8 Med LR 217.
[14] *St George's Healthcare Trust* v. *S* [1998] 3 All ER 673.

both herself and her unborn child. The woman, a veterinary nurse, refused to go into hospital as her GP recommended, arguing that she wanted to give birth at home. She believed that pregnancy was a natural process and that it should proceed without medical intervention, regardless of the outcome. Unhappy with her refusal, the GP summoned the help of a social worker and the woman, who had a history of moderate depression, was detained under section 2 of the Mental Health Act 1983. She was taken first to a psychiatric hospital, but soon transferred from there to an obstetric unit. The woman was able to explain her views and the reasons for them in an explicit and highly articulate written note. However, this did not stop the hospital's application to the High Court for permission to carry out investigations and treatment of the pre-eclampsia without the woman's consent. No attempt was made to inform the woman of this move, although she had already appointed solicitors to act on her behalf. The judge was misled into believing that the woman had already been in labour for twenty-four hours, when she was not in labour at all, and that her life and that of her child were in imminent danger. The issue of the woman's competence was not raised in court, although the psychiatrist who had dealt with her believed that her capacity to consent was intact. The woman's baby daughter was born by caesarean section after the court ordered the operation. At no time during her detention in hospital did the woman receive any treatment for a mental disorder. In fact, two days after the operation a consultant psychiatrist found no abnormalities in her mental state.

The case went to appeal and it was ruled that the use of the Mental Health Act to effect forced obstetric intervention had been unlawful. The Court of Appeal reiterated the competent adult's right to autonomy and the lack of independent existence or legal recognition of the foetus as a person. The woman was awarded damages, and the guidelines laid down at the appeal the year before were clarified and expanded. It was stressed that, in the future, the courts would only attend to cases in which the woman was deemed incompetent. In all other cases the woman's decision must stand. The manner in which capacity to consent should be assessed, when it was in doubt, was laid out, and it was stressed that the judge should be supplied with accurate and relevant information. Nevertheless a rider was added that, assuming the incompetence of a patient, certain cases might arise when the situation was so urgent that it was impracticable to adhere to the guidelines. Thus a loophole was left for the guidelines to be circumvented whenever an obstetrician believes it to be necessary, at least until such times that NHS Trusts or the various statutory bodies, such as NICE,[15] develop guidelines of their own.

[15] National Institute for Clinical Excellence: a special Health Authority for England, set up in 1999, to appraise systematically health interventions and to produce national guidelines.

4. THE ISSUES

(a) Common law rights and maternal-foetal conflict

As stated above, the right of a competent patient to refuse treatment is long-standing. However, in the cases described above this right has been set against what health professionals deem to be requisite for maternal and foetal well-being. The term "maternal-foetal conflict" has been used in some written commentaries on the court-ordered caesareans. However, this conflict was never very clearly articulated by the courts in the cases in question. Although it might be argued that the envisioned conflict is one of interests—those of the woman versus those of the foetus—McLean (1999) points out that the word implies hostility. Because the foetus has no capacity to be hostile, she contends, this must mean hostility of the mother towards the foetus.

The reports of the court-ordered caesarean cases only give limited space to the arguments of the woman herself—indeed, some give her no voice at all. But what can be gleaned is that, by and large, the women involved see no conflict of any kind between themselves and the foetus. Generally they are insisting upon what they see as best for both themselves and their unborn child, and indeed, in some of the early cases where court action failed, it can be seen that the mother was wholly right. In actuality, if there is a conflict, it must be between the woman and those who are trying to subject her to unwanted surgery. The fact that in some cases the use of force has been endorsed supports this.

In many of the court cases both the woman and the foetus were deemed to be at risk. However, if the woman had not been pregnant her right to refuse treatment would have been less contentious. Thus, it can be argued, it must have been the perceived needs of the foetus that underlay the impetus to seek court action, and the fact that the mother's decision was likely to impinge upon the child she carried. The separate right to life of mother and foetus has been an issue for a long time. In earlier centuries, when survival of either mother or foetus from caesarean section was highly doubtful, the question of if and when the operation should be attempted was an important one. From early Christian times until the sixteenth century it was generally accepted that any attempt to save the foetus by caesarean section should only be made when the mother had died. However when, in 1733, doctors consulted Sorbonne theologians as to what should be done when the life of only one party could be saved, the response was that it was better to preserve the baby and assure it of a Christian baptism, thus saving it from Hell. Even as late as the 1930s this view persisted in some quarters. By the end of the eighteenth century many medical men still approached the operation with great caution. However, it was advocated by some in order to preserve the life of one party when the other was clearly dead, and to attempt to save both mother and child when vaginal birth was impossible (Francome et al. (1993)).

As described above, the very fact that the foetus can be visualised and treated as a separate entity from the mother is a consequence of relatively recent obstetric technology. It appears to be this separation which has resulted in the notion of the woman whose own interests conflict with those of her unborn child. Prior to this it appears to have been inconceivable that a woman could be at variance with something that was a part of herself. Thus the concept of maternal-foetal conflict is closely related to the development of the obstetric technology which has separated the two. It is not the biological relationship between mother and foetus that has changed, but the medical model that has shifted its emphasis from unity to duality (Hornstra (1998)). Nevertheless, woman and child are not separate; the implicit dualism within the social construction of maternal-foetal conflict sits less than comfortably with the uniquely integrated physical relationship between mother and unborn child. This relationship is not easily described using the essentially male dominated language of obstetrics which positions the birth canal as the passage, the foetus as the passenger and the doctor, more often than not, as the supervisor of the process (Martin (1987)). Within these power-laden images there is no word for a relationship in which, although the foetus is not separate from the woman (and competing with her), neither is it one with her, no more than a body part (Bailey-Harris (1998)).

It is the very nature of this relationship between mother and foetus that makes it impossible to position the foetus as a separate patient with individual rights without violating the rights of the mother (Martin and Coleman (1995)). In other words, in the cases where there has been no risk to the mother, the courts' championing of the case for the unborn child has implicitly made the foetus more important than the woman. Even when the woman herself has been at risk she has still been accorded less respect than every other competent member of society, who can legally refuse treatment. It has been pointed out that post-viability terminations of pregnancy are legally allowed to protect the woman's health. In this context doctors never put the well-being of a foetus before that of the mother (Rhoden (1986)). This only serves to underline the lack of logic in pursuing legal backing to impose obstetric surgery, with all its attendant risks, on an unwilling woman.

(b) Competence and consent

Another issue is competence. There is a societal tendency to privilege medical opinion (Thomson (1998)). Therefore when a woman rejects this, the possibility that she might be right and her doctors wrong is unlikely to be raised. Thus, as a mother-to-be, she is seen to be jeopardising not only herself but also her unborn child. This leaves her open to questions about her sanity. Even in the most recent appeal case, Butler-Sloss LJ, whilst prohibiting the reasoning, pointed out that the argument is easily understood that no normal mother-to-be could possibly persist with a course of action that would result in harm to her child.[16] The implicit societal expectations

---

[16] *St George's Healthcare NHS Trust* v. *S; R* v. *Collins and others, ex parte S* [1998] 2 FLR 728.

that mothers must, if they are mentally normal, love their children, nurture and protect them (McLean (1999)), labels the woman who dares not to as either bad or mad (Ussher (1991)). To put herself before her child undermines the characterisation of the good mother as one willing to make sacrifices for her children (Lee (1998)).

That this notion should be verbalised in court, even whilst it was being condemned, exemplifies the danger that any pregnant woman could be considered incompetent if she disagrees with obstetric reasoning. Without a doubt there are women who have serious psychiatric disorders and such a distorted awareness of their situation that decisions have to be made for them. Nevertheless, that the last appeal case leaves the way open for doctors to override a woman in an emergency situation without the usual assessment of capacity to consent, raises serious concerns.

Perhaps part of the problem lies in the location of pregnancy within a discourse that forges a link between women's reproductive function and irrational behaviour (Ussher (1989); McLean (1999)). Women's "raging hormones" are responsible, it is argued, for over-emotionality and psychological morbidity. This is said to be particularly apparent during times of hormonal shift: in pregnancy, in the postnatal period, around the time of menstruation and during the menopause, in other words, for much of a woman's reproductive life. It is easy, therefore, to label the pregnant woman who does not follow the logic society expects of her as impaired in her judgement.

Fatigue, shock, pain and the effects of analgesic drugs can all be an integral part of labour and birth. In both the English appeals, the courts intimated that these could affect competence. Here then, are further grounds for deeming a labouring woman incompetent. Despite this many patients with other conditions experience pain and all the other effects listed above, and yet their ability to make decisions is seldom, if ever, questioned. An argument is made that the underlying issue in the court-ordered caesarean cases is the right of women to respect, that this respect would be shown if those concerned were not pregnant or were of a different gender (McLean (1999)).

(c) Medical hegemony and its challenger

As mentioned above, there is a general societal tendency to reify medicine as a value-free, rational science. However, this belies the unpredictability of birth and the frequently imprecise nature of medical prognosis. Within the courts, definitions of urgent or desperate situations have almost invariably gone unchallenged in the caesarean cases, despite the fact that the awful consequences that are threatened do not always come to pass. It is understandable that the courts tend to treat the medical "facts" with which they are presented as incontrovertible. Courts do not have the medical expertise to challenge them; even if they did, they would be likely to hold back, knowing that the individual characteristics of a case can dictate the nature of the management (Field (1989)). It is on this basis: that it is not their patient and that they were not there at the time, that one obstetrician can censure another who dares to criticise their practice (Bewley (1997); Goldthorp and McDade (1997)). Nevertheless obstetricians themselves do not always agree on the best management for certain conditions. Even the Royal College of Obstetricians and Gynaecologists agree that the medical evidence upon which doctors base their decisions is often fallible (RCOG (1994)).

Thus there are challenges to the notion of the infallibility of medical opinion. However, those from within the profession are minor compared with those from outside. The natural childbirth movement and organisations like AIMS[17] have continued to oppose the medical model of birth as something hazardous. They tell women that there is an alternative to this model and that the methods of birth management promulgated by obstetricians are seldom the only, or the best, approach (Bridgeman and Millns (1998)). In recent years there has also been an increased judicial willingness to contest medical opinion—to treat it as evidence to be weighed according to the circumstances (Brazier and Miola (2000)).

When the refusal of a pregnant woman to accept medical opinion is seen in this light, it appears less irrational. In fact S, the woman at the centre of the first English case had, in a previous pregnancy, been told that she would have to have a caesarean, and had then gone on to give birth naturally (Bridgeman and Millns (1998)). Thus there was an internal logic to her unwillingness to accept the operation.

The seeming reluctance of the courts to challenge medical opinion brings to light another problematic aspect of the cases. The legal and the medical professions, by and large, come from the same socio-economic space within society and share a mutual respect (Sheldon (1998)). It is easy for lawyers and judges to respect doctors; they understand each other and the pressures of their respective professions. This is not to argue that the legal profession is somehow colluding with doctors. It is rather that like minded people are less likely to be able to be objective about each other than they are towards someone from a different background. This perhaps helps to explain why a disproportionate number of women, particularly in the American cases, have been from backgrounds least like those of doctors and lawyers: poor women, black women, unmarried women, and women whose first language is not English (Kolder et al. (1987); Field (1989)). Similarly, these women are least like the archetypal media images of motherhood in Western society, images which are more likely to depict mothers as middle-class, white and married. It has been argued that this might also help to position these women as deviant (Bridgeman and Millns (1998)). These women who come from different social and economic groups, have different needs, customs and beliefs to the judges and might have reasons for rejecting caesareans that are wholly logical if their background is taken into account (Lindgren (1996)). Some might be returning at a later date to a country with poor surgical facilities, where a woman with a scar from a previous caesarean, might be at particular risk. For other women a caesarean might be culturally unacceptable or be censured within their religion.

---

[17] Association for Improvements in the Maternity Services.

(d) Best interests?

In most cases caesarean sections have been judicially sanctioned on the basis that the operation was in the best interests of the patient. This argument was used in an English case in which a woman was refusing a caesarean section on the basis that she had received one in her previous pregnancy and had suffered considerable pain and debility afterwards. Despite her obstetrician's insistence that without the operation she and her foetus would die, the woman continued to refuse. She maintained that she would rather die than be subjected to another caesarean.[18] Under such circumstances, it has been argued, "patient" could only mean the foetus (Fovargue and Miola (1998)). The woman was unlikely to benefit either physically or psychologically from the surgery.

The raised levels of maternal morbidity and mortality associated with caesarean section mean that it can seldom be to the woman's physical advantage to have the operation, unless her life is threatened by the pregnancy. On top of these risks are those associated with general anaesthetic (necessary when caesarean is being imposed upon an unwilling woman) (Holdcroft (1997)). Interestingly, even when the woman's well-being is not in question, the physical risks for her of operative delivery have not usually been raised by the judges involved with the court-ordered caesarean cases (Michaelowski (1999)).

In other words, in at least some of these cases the woman's physical best interests would be not to have a caesarean. In addition to this, the courts also appear to have taken a one-sided view of the possibilities of psychological damage to the woman as a result of a forced caesarean. There is ample evidence now that women can experience severe post-traumatic stress as a result of an adverse birthing experience (Menage (1996)). Even under normal circumstances women who experience emergency caesarean section are more prone to psychological morbidity than those who have a normal birth (Hillan (1991b; Ryding et al. (1998)). How much more likely are they to become traumatised if they have been subjected to the operation, perhaps under physical restraint, and without their consent? In sanctioning caesarean sections against the woman's will the courts are effectively deciding what risks she should take (Rhoden (1986)).

If a woman does have a physical or psychological condition that indicates the need for operative delivery, the stress associated with attempts to coerce and threaten her into the operation cannot do any good whatsoever to her existing condition. For example, it was argued that MB, the woman with the needle phobia, really wanted her child to be born alive and well and would therefore suffer long-term psychiatric damage if it was born handicapped or dead.[19] However, the psychological effects of enforced treatment upon someone suffering such a phobia were only superficially examined in court (Michaelowski (1999)). This woman's

---

[18] *Rochdale Healthcare (NHS) Trust* v. *C* [1997] 1 FCR 274.
[19] *Re MB (Medical Treatment)* [1997] 2 FLR 426.

GP was able to help her to agree to caesarean section with specific caveats, and after the court ruling she consented to anaesthesia without the use of authorised force. Thus her inflexibility was not absolute, indicating that, with more sympathetic handling she might have exhibited less antipathy towards the operation. Similarly, although much was made of the perilous risks S was taking in refusing hospital investigation and treatment of her pre-eclampsia,[20] there was no acknowledgement of the effects upon her blood pressure and consequently upon her condition, of confrontation and forced admission to a psychiatric hospital (Cronk (1998)). This woman was managed in such a way that her condition must have been exacerbated considerably. Cronk questions whether sympathetic support from a midwife (one is not mentioned anywhere in the reports of the case) might have resulted in quite a different outcome. The fate of the woman in future pregnancies must also be considered. The RCOG guidelines point out the damage this type of coercive treatment must have done to the doctor-patient relationship. They quite rightly make the point that women who have suffered thus will be much less likely to seek medical help in future pregnancies, despite being the very patients who need that help the most (RCOG (1994)).

Risks to the mother apart, the broad assumption in the cases discussed above is still that caesarean section is completely unproblematic for the foetus. However, even this must be challenged. There are some physical risks associated with caesarean section. These were mentioned earlier. However, there are also psychological ramifications for the infant in terms of the difficulties a caesarean section appears to place upon the mother-infant relationship (Hillan (1991b)). This is due to the lack of early infant contact that is the inevitable concomitant of caesarean section under general anaesthetic. Even when the operation is performed with the mother's full consent, it has been argued that separation after delivery can affect maternal-infant attachment adversely for several months (Klaus and Kennel (1982)). Once again it is not unreasonable to suggest that an enforced caesarean might have much more profound effects. It seems reasonable to assume that a woman who has been forced to undergo a procedure she did not want, might then turn against that child, the source of her trauma. It was reported, for example, that S[21] distanced herself from her baby in the early days after the birth. It cannot be assumed that any supposed maternal instinct will prove stronger than the effects of the birth. The assertion that a woman who has been forced to undergo caesarean later proves to be a "competent and independent mother" (Goldthorp and McDade (1997)), says nothing about the quality of the emotional relationship between mother and child. Neither does it indicate whether the child will suffer any psychological sequelae as a result.

---

[20] *St George's Healthcare Trust* v. *S* [1998] 3 All ER 673.
[21] *St George's Healthcare NHS Trust* v. *S; R* v. *Collins and others, ex parte S* [1998] 2 FLR 728.

(e) Moral responsibilities

As this chapter has shown, there are numerous practical problems in taking legal action to force a woman to submit to caesarean section. However, it must be remembered that the vast majority of women do submit to the care and advice offered by their doctors, and are ready to go to enormous lengths to have a healthy baby (Martin (1987)). The moral responsibility of a mother towards her unborn child is not in question, and most women accept this willingly and selflessly. The issue is whether it is ever tolerable to enforce this responsibility via the courts. Even the most fervent supporters of the moral responsibilities of mothers-to-be baulk at this prospect (Brazier (1999)).

5. CONCLUSION

The circumstances under which a caesarean section is essential are few. Beyond these there is a great deal of variation in practice between different doctors and one issue that needs to be explored is how and why such differences arise—how the decision to perform a caesarean operation is determined. Similarly, there is a need to understand the attitudes of childbearing women towards the operation, particularly in the light of women who are reported to be requesting caesareans when there are no obstetric indications. Although, on the face of it, this is a separate issue to that of court-ordered operations, they have in common that they involve childbearing women who dare to oppose the views and recommendations of their doctors. As has been shown in this chapter, in the light of developments in obstetric technology which have progressively worn away the childbearing woman's control over her own body, this represents an important challenge to medical hegemony. It is especially the case because both situations concern the caesarean section operation which, even more than other obstetric interventions, as a surgical procedure, tends to be considered the sole province of the medical profession.

These two issues are of particular interest at this point in time because in recent years childbearing women's requests concerning the management of their care have been legitimised (Department of Health (1993)), although the boundaries of such control, whether it was meant to include caesarean section, have not been clearly defined. A second pertinent issue, discussed above, is the rising caesarean section rate and the question of how many of these operations are really necessary. In the court cases discussed above the judges have almost always accepted doctors' definitions of essentiality and the need to act quickly. This willingness of the legal profession to accede to the medical point of view has been compounded by socio-economic similarities between the two professions, and differences to the women upon whom their judgements impinge. The gulf between the viewpoint of the courts (and doctors) and the women caught up in the cases is made wider by societal attitudes that represent obstetricians and their technology as scientific, objective and infallible. At the same time childbearing women are characterised as emotional and irrational. Nevertheless a closer scrutiny of the facts of the court cases demonstrates that doctors' dire predictions have not always been correct, whilst objective assessment of obstetric technology has shown it to be fraught with problems and side-effects. Moreover, the objections women have raised against the medical management proposed in these cases often have an internal logic that has been ignored.

It must be remembered that caesarean section has dangers for both mother and child that have seldom been taken into account when the operation has been imposed upon a woman. This means that the women in these cases have been forcibly exposed to unwanted risks. Because a competent person has a right to refuse treatment for herself, it seems that in the case of a woman *and* foetus at risk, the operation is being carried out for the sake of the foetus. However, although English law affords it recognition, the foetus has no legal right of action until birth, and then only if the child is born alive. Moreover, it is impossible to champion the rights of the foetus without violating those of the mother.

The concept of maternal-foetal conflict has been used to describe the situation when a woman refuses treatment that she has been told is to the advantage of her unborn child. However, the perceived conflict of interests has usually only been in the minds of the professionals, not the woman, who has often been able to give cogent reasons for her choice of action. From the woman's point of view, the conflict appears to be between herself and the professionals caring for her.

The unreasonableness of seeking an order to perform a caesarean section on a competent woman has now been recognised by the courts. Nevertheless the discourses which underpinned the earlier cases are still prevalent in society. One such discourse depicts the objectivity and accuracy of medical science against the emotionality and irrationality of women, particularly pregnant, working class women. Another revolves around a perceived need for the obstetrician to defend the cause of the foetus. Yet another set of themes represent obstetric intervention as safe, whilst normal birth is depicted as hazardous.

It is necessary to maintain the right of doctors to intervene on behalf of the foetus when a woman is clearly so mentally unwell that she cannot make a competent decision. However, as long as these discourses persist there will always be a danger that a woman will be deemed incompetent because she opposes the views of her doctor. Such a woman is still at risk of legal action, or more insidiously, of coercion via the threat of legal action.

REFERENCES

ACOG, *Patient Choice: Maternal-Fetal Conflict* (Committee on Ethics, American College of Obstetricians and Gynaecologists, 1987).
ANDERSON, T., "Editorial. Have We Lost the Plot?" (2000a) 3 *The Practising Midwife* 4.

ANDERSON, T., "Editorial. The Birth of Love" (2000b) 3 *The Practising Midwife* 4.

BAILEY-HARRIS, R., "Pregnancy, Autonomy and Refusal of Medical Treatment" (1998) 114 *Law Quarterly Review* 550.

BASTIAN, H. and CONROY, C., "Commentary: Is Caesarean Section a Treatment for Medical Paranoia?" (1997) 314 *British Medical Journal* 1187.

BEECH, B. A. L., "Another Enforced Caesarean" (2000a) 12 *AIMS Journal* 22.

——, "Over-medicated and Under-informed. What are the Consequences for Birthing Women?" (2000b) 11 *AIMS Journal* 4.

BEWLEY, S., "Commentary: Bad Medicine and Bad Law" (1997) 314 *British Medical Journal* 1184.

BRAZIER, M., "Liberty, Responsibility, Maternity" (1999) 52 *Current Legal Problems* 359.

BRAZIER, M. and MIOLA, J., "Bye-bye Bolam: a Medical Litigation Revolution?" (2000) 8 *Medical Law Review* 85.

BRIDGEMAN, J. and MILLNS, S., *Feminist Perspectives on Law: Law's Engagement with the Female Body* (London, Sweet and Maxwell, 1998).

CALLWOOD, A. and THOMAS, J., "The National Sentinel Caesarean Section Audit" (2000) 8 *British Journal of Midwifery* 379.

CAMPBELL, R., "The Place of Birth" in J. Alexander, V. Levy and S. Roch (eds.), *Intrapartum Care. A Research Based Approach* (London, Macmillan, 1990).

CHURCHILL, H., *Caesarean Birth. Experience, Practice and History* (Hale, Cheshire, Books for Midwives Press, 1997).

CLEMENT, S., *The Caesarean Experience* (London, Pandora Press, 1992).

CRONK, M., "Where was the Midwife?" (1998) 94 *Nursing Times* 18.

DEPARTMENT OF HEALTH, *Changing Childbirth. The Report of the Expert Maternity Group* (HMSO, 1993).

DOLAN, B. and PARKER, C., "Caesarean Section: a Treatment for Mental Disorder?" (1997) 314 *British Medical Journal* 1183.

DYER, C., "Appeal Court Rules Against Compulsory Casesarean Sections" (1997) 314 *British Medical Journal* 993.

ENKIN, M., KEIRSE, M. J. N. C. and CHALMERS, I., *A Guide to Effective Care in Pregnancy and Childbirth* (Oxford, Oxford University Press, 1989).

ENKIN, M., KEIRSE, M. J. N. C. , RENFREW, M. and NEILSON, J., *A Guide to Effective Care in Pregnancy and Childbirth* (Oxford, Oxford University Press, 1995).

FIELD, M. A., "Controlling the Woman to Protect the Fetus" (1989) 17 *Law, Medicine and Health Care* 114.

FOVARGUE, S. and MIOLA, J., "Policing Pregnancy: Implications of the Attorney-General's Reference (No. 3 of 1994)" (1998) 6 *Medical Law Review* 265.

FRANCOME, C., SAVAGE, W. and CHURCHILL, H., *Caesarean Birth in Britain* (Cambridge, Middlesex University, 1993).

GOLDTHORP, W. O. and MCDADE, G., "Debate over Mentally Ill Patient's Caesarean Section was Too Emotional" (1997) 315 *British Medical Journal* 1017.

HALL, M. H. and BEWLEY, S., "Maternal Mortality and Mode of Delivery" (1999) 354 *The Lancet* 776.

HEWSON, B., "Editorial. Court-ordered Caesareans: an Unnecessary Development" (1996) 4 *British Journal of Midwifery* 509.

HILLAN, E. M., "Caesarean Section: Perinatal Risks" (1991a) 5 *Nursing Standard* 37.

——, "Caesarean Section: Psychosocial Effects" (1991b) 5 *Nursing Standard* 30.

——, "Short-term Morbidity Associated with Caesarean Delivery" (1992) 19 *Birth* 190.

HOLDCROFT, A., "Women's Autonomy in Childbirth" (1997) 315 *British Medical Journal* 488.

HORNSTRA, D., *A Realistic Approach to Maternal-Fetal Conflict* (Hastings Center Report, 1998).

JACKSON, N. V. and IRVINE, L. M., "The Influence of Maternal Request on the Elective Caesarean Section Rate" (1998) 18 *Journal of Obstetrics and Gynaecology* 115.

KITZINGER, S., "Sheila Kitzinger's Letter from Europe: the Cesarean Epidemic in Great Britain" (1998) 25 *Birth* 56.

KLAUS, M. H. and KENNEL, J. H., *Parent Infant Bonding* (London, Mosby, 1982).

KOLDER, V. E., GALLAGHER, J. and PARSONS, M. T., "Court-ordered Obstetrical Interventions" (1987) 316 *New England Journal of Medicine* 1192.

KORDUS, T. A., "Did South Carolina Really Protect the Fetus by Imposing Criminal Sanctions on a Woman for Ingesting Cocaine during her Pregnancy in *Whitner v. State*, No. 24468, 1996 WL 393164 (S.C. July 15, 1996)?" (1997) 76 *Nebraska Law Review* 319.

LEE, C., *Women's Health. Psychological and Social Perspectives* (London, Sage, 1998).

LEITCH, C. R. and WALKER, J. J., "The Rise in Caesarean Section Rate: the Same Indications but a Lower Threshold" (1998) 105 *British Journal of Obstetrics and Gynaecology* 621.

LINDGREN, K., "Maternal-Fetal Conflict: Court-ordered Cesarean Section" (1996) 25 *Journal of Obstetrical, Gynecological and Neonatal Nursing* 653.

MACFARLANE, A., "At Last—Maternity Statistics for England" (1998) 316 *British Medical Journal* 566.

MACKENZIE, I. Z., "Should Women who Elect to Have Caesarean Sections Pay for Them?" (1999) 318 *British Medical Journal* 1070.

MARTIN, E., *The Woman in the Body* (Milton Keynes, Open University Press, 1987).

MARTIN, S. and COLEMAN, M., "Judicial Intervention in Pregnancy" (1995) 40 *McGill Law Journal* 947.

MASON, J. K. and MCCALL SMITH, R. A., *Law and Medical Ethics* (London, Butterworths, 1999).

MCLEAN, S., *Old Law, New Medicine: Medical Ethics and Human Rights* (London, Pandora, 1999).

MENAGE, J., "Post-Traumatic Stress Disorder Following Obstetric/Gynaecological Procedures" (1996) 4 *British Journal of Midwifery* 532.

MICHAELOWSKI, S., "Court-authorised Caesarean Sections—the End of a Trend?" (1999) 62 *The Modern Law Review* 115.

MONTGOMERY, J., *Health Care Law* (Oxford, Oxford University Press, 1997).

MOULD, T. A. J., CHONG, S., SPENCER, J. A. D. and GALLIVAN, S., "Women's Involvement with the Decision Preceding their Caesarean Section and their Degree of Satisfaction" (1996) 103 *British Journal of Obstetrics and Gynaecology* 1074.

OAKLEY, A., *The Captured Womb* (Oxford, Blackwell, 1984).

PATERSON-BROWN, S., "Should Doctors Perform an Elective Caesarean Section on Request? Yes, as Long as the Woman is Fully Informed" (1998) 317 *British Medical Journal* 462.

RCOG, *A Consideration of the Law and Ethics in Relation to Court-ordered Obstetric Intervention* (Royal College of Obstetricians and Gynaecologists, 1994).

RHODEN, N. K., "The Judge in the Delivery Room: the Emergence of Court-ordered Caesareans" (1986) 74 *California Law Review* 1951.

RICHARDS, M. P. M., "Innovation in Medical Practice: Obstetricians and the Induction of Labour in Britain" (1975) 9 *Social Science and Medicine* 595.

ROWAN, C., "Comment. Court-ordered Caesareans—Choice or Control?" (1998) 5 *Nursing Ethics* 542.

RYDING, E. L., WIJMA, K. and WIJMA, B., "Experiences of Emergency Cesarean Section: a Phenomenological Study of 53 Women" (1998) 25 *Birth* 246.

SAVAGE, W. and FRANCOME, C., "British Caesarean Rates: Have We Reached a Plateau?" (1993) 100 *British Journal of Obstetrics and Gynaecology* 493.

SCHWARZ, E., "The Engineering of Childbirth: a New Obstetric Programme as Reflected in British Obstetric Textbooks, 1960–1980" in J. Garcia, R. Kilpatrick and M. Richards (eds.), *The Politics of Maternity Care* (Oxford, Clarendon Press, 1990).

SHELDON, S., "'A Responsible Body of Medical Men Skilled in that Particular Art . . .': Rethinking the Bolam Test" in S. Sheldon and M. Thomson (eds.), *Feminist Perspectives on Health Care Law* (London, Cavendish, 1998).

SULTAN, A. H. and STANTON, S. L., "Preserving the Pelvic Floor and Perineum During Childbirth—Electric Caesarean Section?" (1996) 103 *British Journal of Obstetrics and Gynaecology* 731.

THOMSON, M., *Reproducing Narrative. Gender, Reproduction and Law* (Aldershot, Ashgate Dartmouth, 1998).

USSHER, J. M., *The Psychology of the Female Body* (London, Routledge, 1989).

——— , *Women' Madness. Misogyny or Mental Illness* (London, Harvester Wheatsheaf, 1991).

WAGNER, M., *Pursing the Birth Machine. The Search for Appropriate Birth Technology* (Camperdown, Australia, ACE Graphics, 1994).

14

Dehydrating Bodies: the Bland Case, the Winterton Bill and the Importance of Intention in Evaluating End-of-Life Decision-Making

JOHN KEOWN

1. INTRODUCTION

T HE QUESTION WHETHER voluntary euthanasia—the intentional termination of a patient's life at their request—should be permitted by law has ignited a global debate which shows little sign of abating. Legislators, judges, healthcare professionals and lay people, particularly in developed countries such as the USA and the United Kingdom, continue to grapple with the profound issues of principle and policy raised by this question. Euthanasia can reasonably claim to be the most important issue in contemporary medical law and ethics (see Keown (1995)).

Echoing campaigners for abortion law reform in the 1960s, advocates for voluntary euthanasia argue that the law should be relaxed out of respect for individual autonomy and in order to prevent useless suffering. By what right, they argue, does society deny adults of sound mind the choice to a medically-accelerated death when the alternative is unwanted suffering?

Opponents reply that intentionally to administer (or hand) lethal injections to patients, even at their request, is to deny the fundamental and inalienable "right to life" (or, more precisely, the right not to be intentionally killed), and to propel society on a "slippery slope" to uncontrolled killing, not least of its most vulnerable members.

Despite many initiatives, and a sympathetic media, campaigners for reform have hitherto met with limited success. In very few jurisdictions, the most notable of which is the Netherlands, are doctors permitted to perform voluntary euthanasia or physician-assisted suicide.

The worldwide euthanasia debate focuses on medical *acts* which are intended to kill. The other and no less important side of the coin, medical *omissions* which are intended to kill, is largely and strangely overlooked. This is regrettable, for what matters morally is not the *means* by which doctors carry out their intention to end life, but their intention to end life.

It is the intention to end life (*intention* bearing its ordinary meaning of aim or purpose) which is the badge of euthanasia and which distinguishes euthanasia from conduct in which the hastening of death is merely a foreseen side-effect. Consequently, it is not euthanasia to administer drugs to palliate symptoms, even if the doctor foresees that the drugs will, as a side-effect, hasten death. Nor is it euthanasia to withhold/withdraw treatment because it is adjudged futile or too burdensome, even if the doctor foresees that death will come sooner than would otherwise have been the case.

Unfortunately, many—including many lawyers—fail to grasp the central moral significance of intention and instead locate the moral watershed between acts and omissions. The result is an unwarranted moral and legal distinction between medical acts intended to kill and medical omissions with precisely the same intent.

This chapter highlights this vital yet largely overlooked aspect of the euthanasia debate. It does so by identifying a serious inconsistency in English criminal law (though examples could also be taken from other jurisdictions). It notes that while English law prohibits doctors from (say) injecting potassium chloride with intent to kill (even at the patient's request), it allows them, as a result of the reasoning of the Law Lords in the *Tony Bland* case[1] in 1993, intentionally to withhold/withdraw tube-delivered food and fluids from certain unconscious patients with intent to kill them by dehydration and starvation. In short, doctors may not intentionally kill by drugs, but they may do so by dehydration.

Having identified this inconsistency, the chapter proceeds to discuss a Bill introduced by Ann Winterton MP which attempted to restore consistency by reversing this aspect of the reasoning in the *Bland* case. It examines criticisms of the Bill by the British Medical Association (BMA) and the Government and rejects those criticisms as ill-founded. By analysing the Bill and the misguided criticisms of it, this chapter illustrates the moral and legal inconsistency which so easily follows from a failure to grasp the significance of intention in evaluating end-of-life decision-making.

Part 2 identifies the inconsistency introduced into the law by the *Bland* case. Part 3 outlines the provisions of the Winterton Bill. Part 4 considers the main criticisms levelled at the Bill.

2. INTENTIONAL MEDICAL KILLING BY ACTS AND BY OMISSIONS: THE INCONSISTENCY OF THE LAW AFTER *BLAND*

(a) Euthanasia by an act

A doctor who intentionally (purposefully) hastens a patient's death by an act, such as an injection of potassium chloride, commits murder. This is so even if the doctor

---

[1] *Airedale NHS Trust* v. *Bland* [1993] AC 789.

acts at the patient's request and is motivated by a compassionate desire to end the patient's suffering.

This prohibition is unlikely to be relaxed, at least in the near future. In 1994 a distinguished Select Committee of the House of Lords, having exhaustively considered the arguments for reform, unanimously recommended that the law should not be changed (House of Lords (1993–94)). The Government has on several occasions reiterated its opposition to any relaxation of this prohibition. For example, the report containing the Government's proposals for making decisions on behalf of mentally incapacitated adults stated: "The Government wishes to make absolutely clear its complete opposition to euthanasia, which is and will remain illegal" (*Making Decisions* (1999)).

By "euthanasia", however, both the Select Committee and the Government meant the intentional shortening of a patient's life *by an act* not by omission. The Select Committee, for instance, defined "euthanasia" as "a deliberate *intervention* undertaken with the express intention of ending a life to relieve intractable suffering" (House of Lords (1993–94); *Who Decides?* (1997)). Neither appeared to accept that "euthanasia" can be carried out *by omission.*

(b) Euthanasia by omission

The criminal law does not normally impose criminal liability for omissions, even omissions which will hasten another's death. Consequently, if A sees B starving in the street and walks by without offering B any food, with the result that B starves to death, A commits no crime. This is so even if B was pleading with A for food; even if A could easily have fed B at no significant cost, and even if A's intention in failing to feed B was that B should die. However callous A's omission, it would not be criminal.

The situation is different, however, if one person owes a legal duty to another. Parents are clearly under a duty to feed their children. Doctors are clearly under a duty to feed their patients. Or at least doctors *were* clearly under such a duty until a landmark decision of the House of Lords in 1993, a decision which substantially qualified that duty. In *Airedale NHS Trust* v. *Bland*[2] the Law Lords declared it lawful for a doctor to withdraw tube-feeding from his patient, Tony Bland, who was in a "persistent vegetative state". Although Tony was in a state of permanent unawareness he was neither "brain dead", nor dying, nor on a ventilator. Counsel representing Tony opposed the removal of his tube-feeding, arguing it would be murder: it would be analogous to severing the air-pipe of a deep-sea diver. Three of the five Law Lords accepted his submission that the doctor's intention was to kill Tony, a submission which the remaining two neither rejected nor accepted. As one of the three, Lord Browne-Wilkinson, said:[3]

---

[2] [1993] AC 789.
[3] [1993] AC 789 at 881.

"Murder consists of causing the death of another with intent to do so. What is proposed in the present case is to adopt a course with the intention of bringing about Anthony Bland's death. As to the element of intention . . . , in my judgment there can be no real doubt that it is present in this case: the whole purpose of stopping artificial feeding is to bring about the death of Anthony Bland".[4]

The case has its defenders, such as the BMA. But is also has its critics. One of the main criticisms levelled at the judgments has been their distinction between living human bodies and human "persons":

"The judgments all suggest a dualistic distinction between Bland himself and his body: e.g. 'his spirit has left him and all that remains is the shell of his body' (Sir Stephen Brown P); 'his body is alive, but he has no life . . . He is alive but has no life at all' (Hoffmann LJ). This sort of dualism, which thinks of the body as if it were some kind of habitation for and instrument of the real person, is defended by few philosophers indeed (religious or otherwise). It renders inexplicable the unity in complexity which one experiences in everything one consciously does. It speaks as if there were two things, other and other: a nonbodily person and a nonpersonal living body. But neither of these can one recognise as oneself. One's living body is intrinsic, not merely instrumental, to one's personal life. Each of us has a human life (not a vegetable life plus an animal life plus a personal life); when it is flourishing that life includes all one's vital functions including speech, deliberation and choice; when gravely impaired it lacks some of those functions without ceasing to be the life of the person so impaired" (Finnis (1993)).

By rejecting the law's long-standing view that *all* patients are persons, regardless of their level of consciousness, the judges endorsed the fundamentally arbitrary judgement that patients with a certain degree of mental disability are better off dead and it is lawful to kill them, albeit by dehydration. The case is no less vulnerable to criticism for leaving the law, as one of the Law Lords put it, in a "morally and intellectually misshapen" state[5]—prohibiting doctors from intentionally terminating life by an act but permitting them intentionally to terminate life by omission (Keown (1997)). Having identified this major inconsistency in the law, we may now turn to the Bill which sought to repair it.

3. THE WINTERTON BILL

In December 1999 Ann Winterton, MP for Congleton, introduced the Medical Treatment (Prevention of Euthanasia) Bill. The Bill was short, comprising three brief clauses. Clause 1 provided:

---

[4] Why the majority assumed it was the doctor's intention to kill is unclear: it does not follow that because the doctor foresaw the patient's death as certain he therefore intended it. A doctor who withdraws tube-feeding in such circumstances may do so because he regards it as a futile medical treatment. (Whether the doctor would be right in regarding pouring food down a tube as a "medical treatment" is another matter, which remains the subject of some dispute). See Keown (1997, 2000).

[5] [1993] AC 789 at 887 per Lord Mustill.

"It shall be unlawful for any person responsible for the care of a patient to withdraw or withhold from the patient medical treatment or sustenance if his purpose or one of his purposes in doing so is to hasten or otherwise cause the death of the patient".

Clause 2 stated:

"In this Act—
   'medical treatment' means any medical or surgical treatment, including the administration of drugs or the use of any mechanical or other apparatus for the provision or
   support of ventilation or of any other bodily function;
   'patient' means a person suffering from mental or physical illness or debility;
   'sustenance' means the provision of nutrition or hydration, howsoever delivered."

Clause 3 provided that the Act was to be cited as the Medical Treatment (Prevention of Euthanasia) Act 2000; that it should come into force at the end of one month beginning with the day on which the Act is passed; and should extend only to England, Wales and Northern Ireland.

The Bill was short, lucid and focused. It would, quite simply, have made it clearly unlawful for those responsible for the care of patients to withhold/ withdraw medical treatment, including tube-feeding *with the (or a) purpose of hastening death*. The Bill would, therefore, by prohibiting doctors from *purpose-fully* hastening death by a deliberate omission, have restored to the law the consistency it abandoned in *Bland*.

The Bill was narrowly drawn so as to prohibit only the *purposeful* hastening of death. It would *not* have rendered unlawful the withholding/withdrawal of treatment or tube-feeding because it was futile (that is, offered no reasonable hope of therapeutic benefit), or too burdensome to the patient, or refused by the patient. The purpose of a doctor who withholds/withdraws treatment or tube-feeding solely for one of these reasons is not to hasten the patient's death. This remains true even if the doctor foresees that as a result of withholding/withdrawing the treatment or tube-feeding the patient will die sooner than would otherwise have been the case. Foresight is not purpose. In short, the Bill would only have hit doctors whose purpose was to hasten death, doctors who *tried to kill* their patients. Despite the focused and important reform it proposed, the Bill encountered fierce opposition.

4. CRITICISMS OF THE BILL

Both the BMA and the Government have long reiterated their opposition to "euthanasia". Given that the Bill was designed to restore the integrity of the legal prohibition on doctors intentionally shortening patients' lives, it is odd that it was opposed by both.

(a) The BMA's criticisms

On 21 January 2000, shortly before the Bill's Second Reading in the House of Commons, the Chairman of the BMA Council, Dr Ian Bogle, wrote to all MPs.[6] The letter expressed the BMA's opposition to the Bill and made several criticisms.

(i) The competent patient's right to refuse treatment

First, Dr Bogle wrote:

> "The current legal position is that questions of treatment withdrawal are resolved either by agreeing to the wishes of a competent patient or, for a patient who is unable at the time to indicate his/her wishes, by considering their best interests. For any person, 'best interests' encompass a range of factors such as the individual's own moral values, religious or cultural beliefs, views of their own aim and purpose in life, as well as the degree and type of medical treatment they want. The Bill would diminish consideration of these values and make worthless any valid refusal by restricting the law to have regard only for the 'purpose or one of his purposes' of the doctor (Clause 1). Our interpretation of the Bill is that it has no regard for the autonomy of patients".

Dr Bogle was mistaken. The Bill would not "make worthless any valid refusal" of treatment (or tube-feeding) by a competent patient, whether the valid refusal was made while competent or prior to incompetence by way of advance directive or "living will". For one thing, most patients no doubt refuse treatment because they think it would either be futile or too burdensome for them, not with the purpose of hastening their deaths. For another, even if in a particular case the doctor had good reason to think that the patient's purpose was to hasten death, the Bill was concerned only with the *doctor's* purpose not the *patient's* purpose. The Bill would not have prevented doctors from withholding/withdrawing treatment with the purpose of respecting a patient's refusal. The Bill would only have prohibited doctors from withholding/withdrawing treatment (or tube-feeding) with the (or a) purpose of hastening death.

(ii) The incompetent patient's best interests

Dr Bogle was also wrong in claiming that, in the case of incompetent patients, the Bill would "diminish consideration" of the patient's values, beliefs and wishes. The law has always forbidden doctors from *giving* treatment with a purpose of hastening death. That prohibition in no way diminishes the doctor's duty and right to take into account the patient's wishes, values and best interests in deciding whether and what treatment *to give*. Equally, the Bill's prohibition on withholding/withdrawing treatment with a purpose to kill would in no way have diminished the doctor's duty and right to take those same factors into account in deciding whether and what

---

[6] Letter from Dr Ian Bogle, 21 January 2000 (ref IB/GR/wb).

treatment to withhold/withdraw. Moreover, the Bill would simply have restored the prohibition which was long part of the law until it was undermined by the *Bland* case in 1993. There was not the slightest evidence that that prohibition had hindered doctors from taking those factors into account in deciding whether to withhold/withdraw treatment.

(iii) Complexity

Dr Bogle also claimed:

> "This is a complex area where simplistic statements are unhelpful and increase confusion. By seeking to remove the emphasis in law from the wishes of the patient to the 'purpose or one of his purposes' of the doctor, the Bill further complicates an already complex decision making process".

However, the prohibition on *active* killing, which focuses on the doctor's purpose irrespective of the patient's wishes, is simple and creates clarity not confusion. Why would the restoration of the prohibition on intentional killing by omission not do likewise?

Dr Bogle noted that the BMA had issued guidance on withholding/withdrawing treatment in 1999. But that guidance openly embraced *Bland*. The guidance appeared to invite doctors to deprive certain mentally-impaired patients (not just those in permanent vegetative state) of life-saving treatment (and tube-feeding) on the basis of an opinion that their lives are no longer a "benefit" and that they would be better off dead, and even appeared to condone the purposeful ending of life by withholding/withdrawing treatment or tube-feeding (Keown (2000)). The guidance was part of the problem, not part of the solution. It strengthened, rather than weakened, the case for the Bill.

(iv) Two scenarios

To illustrate his arguments against the Bill, Dr Bogle presented two scenarios. The first was as follows:

> "Doctors caring for a patient with chronic kidney disease, controlled with dialysis, who develops a rapidly progressive and terminal cancer would not be permitted to agree to the withdrawal of dialysis at the request of the patient. The doctor in so doing would be acquiescing to the patient's purpose of hastening death although the patient is already dying; agreeing to the patient's wishes in this instance would open the doctor to the accusation that his purpose was to hasten the death of the patient".

The second scenario was:

> "A patient with a long standing but progressive cancer of the breast may wish to indicate in advance what treatment should be given, withheld or withdrawn should the cancer spread to other organs and the patient be unable to express a view. To follow the patient's informed and expressed view would clearly be open to the interpretation as having the purpose of bringing about the patient's death".

Dr Bogle was seriously confused. For one thing, why did he assume that in either case the patient's purpose in refusing treatment would be to hasten death rather than simply to refuse a treatment which would no longer—given the patient's terminal condition—offer a reasonable hope of benefit? For another, even if the *patient's* purpose were to hasten death, it by no means follows that this would be the *doctor's* purpose. So long as the doctor's purpose were to respect the patient's refusal and not to hasten the patient's death, the doctor would commit no offence. In the (most unlikely) event that the doctor were to be accused of having purposefully hastened death, the prosecution would inevitably fail. How could the Crown prove that the doctor had an unlawful purpose when the doctor in fact had a lawful purpose? Further, any argument that, because doctors may be falsely accused of seeking to hasten death by omission, the prohibition should not exist, is no stronger than the argument that, because doctors administering palliative drugs to alleviate pain in the terminally ill may be falsely accused of seeking to hasten death by an act, the prohibition on active killing should not exist.

(b) The Government's criticisms

The Government's reasons for opposing the Bill were similar to, and no more cogent than, those advanced by the BMA. During the Second Reading debate on the Bill, the Parliamentary Under-Secretary of State for Health, Yvette Cooper, started by reiterating the Government's opposition to "euthanasia":

"At the outset, I emphasise that the Government remain completely opposed to euthanasia, by which we mean the *intentional taking of life*, albeit at the patient's request or for a merciful motive".[7]

Addressing the doctor's duty, she pointed out:

"When a patient is in hospital there is no doubt that the doctor owes the patient a duty of care. *That certainly includes a requirement not to kill the patient intentionally by any means, action or omission*".[8]

She recognised that a doctor was under no duty to provide treatment which would not benefit the patient, but that a doctor's omission to provide beneficial treatment to a patient could be "just as culpable—just as unlawful—as a positive attempt to kill that patient using a toxic drug".[9]

However, having expressed the Government's opposition to intentional killing, by act or by omission, Ms Cooper went on, inconsistently, to express the Government's opposition to the Bill and its reasons for that opposition. Those reasons were a tangled skein of error.

[7] (2000) 343 Parl Deb HC 743 (emphasis added).
[8] *Ibid.* (emphasis added).
[9] At 742–4.

(i) The competent patient's right to refuse treatment

A central reason for opposing the Bill was:

"It would switch the focus from the rights and best interests of the patient to the purpose or one of the purposes of the doctors. If it were passed, the law would judge a situation in which treatment was withdrawn or withheld not according to the decisions, rights and interests of the patient, but according to what was in the mind of the doctor".[10]

The present law was, the Minister added, based firmly on the rights of patients to consent to or refuse treatment. Competent patients had the right to refuse treatment, including tube-feeding. That right could be exercised even if a refusal would lead to death, and even if it were exercised "to bring about" death.[11] The Bill, she said, introduced "a new test of 'purpose', as distinct from the existing tests based on the rights and interests of the patient or, alternatively, the criminal-law concept of intention" applied by the law of homicide.

The Minister's argument is a miasma of confusion. First, her claim that the Bill would "switch the focus" from the rights and best interests of the patient to the purpose or one of the purposes of the doctor betrays a profound misunderstanding of the criminal law.

The criminal law typically protects rights and interests by framing prohibitions against conduct performed with specified states of mind, not least intention. For example, the right to life is protected by the crime of murder which prohibits *intentionally* causing death. The Bill aimed merely to restore the criminal law to its long-standing condition before *Bland*; to restore the fullness and consistency of its protection of patients' rights and interests; *to switch the focus back* to the right of patients not to be intentionally killed by omission. The law would indeed "judge a situation in which treatment was withdrawn or withheld" according to "what was in the mind of the doctor" but this is nothing novel. The criminal law would equally judge the lawfulness or otherwise of a doctor *giving* a treatment which hastened death according to "what was in the mind of the doctor".

The Minister claimed that the patient's right to refuse treatment would be undermined if a purpose of the doctor was to hasten death. She argued:

"The doctor's main purpose may be to respect the competent patient's right to refuse treatment. The Bill means that any other purposes that the doctor may have in respecting that request should be relevant, too. That would make the lawfulness of respecting the patient's rights dependent on the mindset of the doctor, not the patient's right in the first place. The Hon. Lady [Mrs Winterton] has made it clear that she does not intend the

---

[10] At 744.

[11] *Ibid.* This apparent assertion of a right to commit suicide by refusal of treatment is unsubstantiated and contrary to principle. When Parliament enacted the Suicide Act 1961, which decriminalised suicide, it did not endorse suicide, let alone create a right to commit suicide. See (1960–61) 644 Parl Deb HC cols 1425–6; (1960–61) 645 Parl Deb HC cols 822–3 (Mr Charles Fletcher-Cooke MP). This is also evidenced by the fact that the Suicide Act retained the offence of assisting or encouraging suicide.

Bill to have any such impact, but making acts and omissions identical and focusing on the doctor's purpose would do exactly that".[12]

She illustrated this argument as follows:

"A patient with advanced motor neurone disease, for example, may develop disabilities that make it necessary for her to receive increasing help with the tasks of daily living, such as bathing and feeding. If the person subsequently develops pneumonia, which without treatment could be fatal, she may decide that she does not want to receive that treatment, in full knowledge of the likely consequences. If the doctor understands the patient's position and desire to hasten her own death, could it be held that the doctor's purpose, or one of the doctor's purposes, was also to hasten death? For fear of that, would the doctor feel compelled to provide treatment?"[13]

The objection is similar to that advanced by the BMA; it is no less spurious.

First, the fact that the patient has "full knowledge" of the likely consequence of refusing treatment does not mean she has the "desire to hasten her own death". Secondly, even if the patient's purpose in refusing treatment were to hasten her own death, a doctor who withheld/withdrew treatment with the purpose of respecting the patient's refusal, and not with the purpose of hastening the patient's death, would commit no offence.[14] And the Minister's speculation that the doctor might fear that a lawful purpose might be misconstrued as unlawful and therefore decide to impose treatment is unsubstantiated and, surely, fanciful. Forcing treatment on a patient against the patient's will would be much more likely to attract accusations of illegality, accusations which would be all the more to be feared by the doctor because they would be well-grounded rather than groundless. Further, by analogy, is there any evidence that doctors hesitate to prescribe palliative drugs for fear that their lawful purpose of alleviating pain might be misconstrued as an intent to kill?[15]

Thirdly, even if the doctor's purpose, or one of the doctor's purposes, were to hasten the patient's death, this would be relevant to the doctor's criminal liability, not the patient's right to refuse treatment. The Bill would in no way have permitted, much less required, a doctor with such an unlawful purpose to force treatment on a patient who had refused treatment. It simply proscribed one purpose for non-treatment: the doctor could lawfully be motivated by others, not least respect for the patient's refusal. Patients currently have a right to refuse treatment;[16] nothing in the Bill weakened that right.

---

[12] (2000) 343 Parl Deb HC 743 at 746.

[13] At 747.

[14] Whether and in what circumstances a doctor *may* lawfully override a suicidal refusal in order to keep the patient alive is an interesting question, but it is not the issue here, which is whether the Bill would have *required* a doctor to override a suicidal refusal and keep the patient alive for fear of falling foul of the Bill's prohibition on non-treatment with the purpose of hastening death. The criticism fails: nothing in the Bill prohibited the doctor from withholding/withdrawing treatment with the purpose of respecting the patient's refusal, nor allowed, let alone required, the doctor to override that refusal.

[15] Even if there were evidence of such hesitation, it would point to the need to elucidate confusions in practice, not create them in principle.

[16] See e.g. *Re T (adult: refusal of medical treatment)* [1992] 4 All ER 649; *St George's Healthcare NHS Trust v. S* [1998] 3 All ER 673.

Fourthly, the weakness of Ms Cooper's argument that the lawfulness of respecting the patient's right to refuse treatment would have been compromised by a doctor's purpose of hastening death can be illustrated by an analogy with the administration of palliative drugs in order to ease suffering where the drugs will also have the effect of shortening the patient's life. The present law allows doctors to administer drugs for the purpose of easing pain, even if they foresee that those drugs will shorten life,[17] but prohibits the administration of drugs with the purpose of shortening life. Yet this prohibition in no way compromises the lawfulness of giving patients life-shortening palliative care without that unlawful purpose, and it would be absurd to criticise this prohibition on the ground that the right of patients to have their pain relieved might be compromised by the fact that some doctors might form an unlawful purpose. Indeed, the analogy shows that the patient's right to refuse treatment is, and would have remained, more powerful than the right to be given palliative drugs which have a foreseen life-shortening effect. While a doctor may not give life-shortening palliative drugs with a purpose of shortening life, a doctor *must* withhold/withdraw treatment in the face of the patient's valid refusal, whether or not the doctor has a purpose of shortening life.

(ii) The incompetent patient's best interests

The Minister's central criticism that the Bill would "switch the focus" from the patient's rights and interests to the doctor's purposes was applied to both competent and incompetent patients. She criticised the Bill for not containing any reference to the "patient's interests", or the "welfare" of children, or for stating that treatment could be withdrawn if it was "burdensome".[18]

As we saw above, the Bill would not have diminished the doctor's duty and right to take into account all relevant factors in deciding whether treatment would or would not be in the best interests of an incompetent patient. Doctors would have remained free to take those considerations into account; the Bill did not seek to limit them.

Just as it was not the goal of the Bill to *limit* those considerations, nor was it the function of the Bill to *list* them. The Bill sought to amend and clarify the criminal law. It is not generally the role of the blunt instrument of the criminal law to permit but to prohibit. It tells people not what they may do so much as what they may not do. For example, the law relating to offences against the person specifies prohibited ways of harming others; its function is not to create model citizens. That is largely the role of parents, teachers and preachers. The criminal law's role is no less limited in relation to more complex and subtle areas of conduct such as medical practice. The criminal law properly lays down a basic framework of prohibitions which doctors must observe, but its role is not to teach doctors medical ethics.

---

[17] See e.g. *R* v. *Cox* (1992) 12 Butterworth's Medico-Legal Reports 38; *R* v. *Moor* (1999, Newcastle Crown Court, Hooper J) unreported but discussed by Anthony Arlidge QC, "The Trial of Dr David Moor" [2000] Crim LR 31.

[18] (2000) 343 Parl Deb HC 743 at 748.

That is largely the responsibility of medical schools and professional medical bodies. In keeping with the limited function of the criminal law, the Bill did not essay a treatise on medical ethics, but sought simply to repair a flaw in the basic framework of criminal law within which ethical medicine could be defined, refined and practised. To that end, the Bill confined itself to prohibiting one form of conduct as being seriously contrary to the patient's best interests—*trying to kill the patient by withholding/withdrawing treatment or tube-feeding.*

The Minister went on to claim:

> "The lack of reference in the Bill to consideration of the patient's interests means that there is a risk that doctors, to ensure that there could be no doubt about any of their purposes, may feel pressurised to provide treatment beyond the point at which it is in the patient's best interests".[19]

This fanciful speculation echoes her criticism that doctors might force treatment on competent patients for fear of their lawful purposes being misconstrued. It is equally vulnerable to the counter-arguments levelled against that earlier speculation.

Ms Cooper added that the Bill would change the present law under which artificial nutrition and hydration could not be continued if they were agreed not to be in the patient's best interests.[20] She was, again, mistaken. All the Bill provided was that sustenance could not be withheld/withdrawn with the (or a) purpose of hastening death. If a doctor judged that tube-feeding was not in the patient's best interests (because, for example, the patient could not tolerate the tube) it would have remained lawful to withdraw the tube. The doctor's purpose would be to withdraw a burdensome intervention not to hasten the patient's death, even if the doctor foresaw that death would come sooner than it otherwise would have. The mere fact that the doctor foresaw that death would come sooner would not make that the doctor's purpose. Which brings us to another unsound criticism advanced by the Minister.

(iii) Purpose and intention

In ordinary usage, the word "intention" connotes "purpose".[21] In legal usage, however, the word is (strangely) often used to include not only purpose but also foresight. The law of murder appears to define intention as including not only consequences which are aimed at but also those which are foreseen as virtually certain.[22] Had the Bill used the word "intention" rather than "purpose" it could well have been criticised as overbroad: of prohibiting doctors from withholding/withdrawing treatment and sustenance not only when hastening death was their purpose but also when they foresaw the hastening of death as certain. There are, of

---

[19] (2000) 343 Parl Deb HC 743 at 748.

[20] At 749.

[21] The OED defines "intent" as "the act or fact of intending; intention, purpose": *The New Shorter Oxford English Dictionary* (1993) I, 1389. See also *ibid.*, "intention".

[22] *Woollin* [1998] 4 All ER 103.

course, many cases, such as where treatment would be futile, in which it is universally agreed that doctors behave ethically in withholding/withdrawing treatment even though they foresee that death will come sooner. Any Bill which sought to criminalise such behaviour would indeed be objectionable. By using the word "purpose", which has the clear meaning in both ordinary and legal usage of "aim" not "foresight",[23] the Bill avoided the ambiguity created by the tension between the ordinary and the legal meanings of "intention" and was immune to any criticism that it prohibited conduct which had the foreseen consequence of hastening death. Had the Bill used the word "intention" it would have been open to the criticism of being ambiguous and overbroad. But it did not, and it was not.

Ms Cooper nevertheless criticised the Bill for its use of the word "purpose". She claimed:

> "It introduces a new test of 'purpose', as distinct from the existing tests based on the rights and interests of the patient or, alternatively, the criminal-law concept of intention, which is applicable to, for example, homicide laws".[24]

The test of "purpose" is, however, hardly new: it has long been the core meaning of the concept of intention in the criminal law.

She added that:

> "given that the criminal laws relating to murder and manslaughter use the concept of primary intention and gross negligence rather than the concept of purpose, it is not clear how the Bill would, in practice, fit in with those existing laws".[25]

It was, with respect, crystal clear. The Bill would have prohibited doctors from aiming to hasten death by omission. Apart from that single, modest, yet vital amendment the law would have remained unchanged. The liability of doctors hastening death by an act, purposefully or not, would be determined by the existing law. So too would the liability of doctors hastening death by omission when this was not one of their purposes.

The Minister claimed that it was not clear what "purpose" meant and that it appeared to mean "motive".[26] She was confused. There is a well-established presumption that in interpreting a statute words bear their ordinary meaning. The ordinary meaning of "purpose" is "aim". Moreover, a judge interpreting the word would be aware that the criminal law distinguishes between aims and motives and is generally concerned with the former, not the latter.

The Minister continued that attempts could well be made to interpret "purpose" in line with the legal meaning of "intention".[27] So, having criticised the Bill for being too narrow in using "purpose" rather than "intention" in its legal meaning, in the next breath she seems to criticise the Bill because even the word

---

[23] "A thing to be done; an object to be attained, an intention, an aim": *supra* n. 21, II, 2421.
[24] (2000) 343 Parl Deb HC 743 at 744.
[25] *Ibid.*
[26] At 745.
[27] *Ibid.*

"purpose" might not be sufficiently narrow to avoid misconstrual as "intention" in its legal meaning.

In addition to criticising the word "purpose" for being ambiguous, she argued that its use made the Bill overbroad. She went on to consider "some of the consequences of the change, whether it is to 'purpose' or to 'intent' (sic)":[28]

> "If a doctor knew, virtually for certain, that withholding or withdrawing treatment—even at the patient's request—would result in the patient's death, and if the current legal concept of intention were applied, the doctor could be held to have intended the patient's death. The Bill would make it unlawful for a doctor to respect a patient's rights".[29]

Her argument, with respect, courts the absurd. First, the Bill used the word "purpose" not "intent". Secondly, if the legal meaning of "intent" does include foresight of virtual certainty, and if she were right that the law already prohibits "intentional" life-shortening by omission, then the doctor would be liable *under the existing law*. Thirdly, under the Bill, the doctor would only be liable for purposefully, not foreseeably, hastening death. The Bill could only have *improved* the position of doctors in the circumstances she envisaged.

She continued that even if "purpose" were given "a more everyday meaning" the Bill "requires every one of the doctor's purposes to be considered before it is decided whether withholding treatment at the patient's request is lawful".[30] But this is as misleading as saying that the present law against active killing "requires every one of the doctor's purposes to be considered before it is decided whether" a doctor's administering of life-shortening doses of morphine to the dying is lawful. In either case, only if there were grounds to suspect a homicidal purpose would the doctor's state of mind warrant investigation.

Finally, the Minister's objections to the Bill seemed inconsistent with her statement of the Government's opposition to euthanasia. She began, it will be recalled, by reiterating the Government's opposition to "the intentional taking of life" and accepted that the doctor's duty of care to the patient "certainly includes a requirement not to kill the patient intentionally by any means, action or omission".[31]

By the Government's opposition to the "intentional" taking of life she presumably meant the "purposeful" taking of life. The Government is surely not opposed to doctors giving or withholding/withdrawing treatment which they merely foresee will hasten death. Why, then, did the Minister object to the Bill? If it was because she thought, as she appeared to, that it was already unlawful for doctors purposefully to shorten life by omission, then she misapprehended the ruling in *Bland* that it is lawful for doctors purposefully to shorten patients' lives in certain circumstances.

---

[28] (2000) 343 Parl Deb HC 743 at 744.
[29] *Ibid.*
[30] *Ibid.*
[31] At 743.

(iv) Ascertaining purposes

Another criticism voiced by the Minister was that the Bill would be unworkable. A doctor could state one purpose "But how can we know whether the doctor has another purpose as well?" She added: "the law has no mechanism for finding out every purpose of the doctor".[32] This is another distracting and irrelevant criticism. First, the criminal law does not need to ascertain "every purpose" of the doctor, only any criminal purpose. Secondly, the practical difficulty of ascertaining a defendant's state of mind is no argument against the criminal law requiring proof of that state of mind. The principle of *mens rea* (which requires proof of a blame-worthy state of mind) is foundational to the criminal law. Many criminal offences require proof of a state of mind, whether intention or recklessness. Thirdly, the same criticism, when made in relation to doctors *giving* treatment to the dying which would hasten death, was roundly rejected by the House of Lords Select Committee:

> "Some may suggest that intention is not readily ascertainable. But juries are asked every day to assess intention in all sorts of cases, and could do so . . . if in a particular instance there was any reason to suspect that the doctor's primary intention was to kill the patient rather than to relieve pain and suffering. They would no doubt consider the actions of the doctor, how they compared with usual medical practice directed towards the relief of pain and distress, and all the circumstances of the case" (House of Lords (1993–94)).

5. CONCLUSION

The key to a sound ethical analysis of end-of-life decision-making is the real distinction between intention and foresight, not a spurious distinction between acts and omissions. Historically, both law and medical ethics have adopted the distinction between intended and foreseen life-shortening, prohibiting the intentional termination of patients' lives but permitting the use of palliative drugs which have the foreseen side-effect of hastening death, and the withholding/withdrawal of treatment which is either futile or too burdensome, even if it is foreseen that death will come sooner than would otherwise have been the case. Regrettably, in *Bland*, the Law Lords subverted this historic distinction and, by inventing the arbitrary category of patients who are living bodies but not "persons", allowed doctors intentionally to end life by deliberate omission. The law cannot sensibly prohibit doctors from intentionally ending life by an act but permit them intentionally to do so by omission.

Bland introduced this grave inconsistency into the law; the Winterton Bill would have removed it. The criticisms made by the BMA and the Government disclose their serious misunderstanding of the Bill and the issues it raised. The BMA and the Government cannot consistently oppose medical killing by an act

---

[32] At 745.

yet condone medical killing by omission. In doing so, they, like the current law, are sawing off the intellectual branch on which they are sitting.

Of course, euthanasia supporters could argue that the inconsistency should be resolved by permitting intentional killing by an act, not just by omission. But if opposition to active killing, such as that exhibited by the Government, the House of Lords Select Committee, Law Lords and the BMA is right (and it is submitted that it is) then the only reasonable way to resolve the inconsistency is to restore the prohibition on intentional killing by omission. Regrettably, the Winterton Bill was "talked out" at Report stage on 14 April 2000. Until the reform proposed in the Bill is enacted, the law relating to euthanasia will remain morally and intellectually misshapen. Meanwhile, the category of living bodies who are "non-persons" whose lives may be terminated by dehydration shows every sign of being extended (Keown (2000)).

REFERENCES

FINNIS, J. M., "*Bland*: Crossing the Rubicon?" (1993) 109 *LQR* 329.

HOUSE OF LORDS, *Report of the House of Lords Select Committee on Medical Ethics* (Paper 21–1 of 1993–94).

KEOWN, J. (ed.), *Euthanasia Examined: Ethical, Clinical and Legal Perspectives* (Cambridge, Cambridge University Press, 1995).

—— , "Restoring Moral and Intellectual Shape to the Law after *Bland*" (1997) 113 *LQR* 481.

—— , "Beyond *Bland*: a Critique of the BMA Guidance on Withholding and Withdrawing Medical Treatment" (2000) 20(1) *Legal Studies* 66.

Making Decisions: The Government's Proposals for Making Decisions on Behalf of Mentally Incapacitated Adults (Cm 4465, 1999) para. 18.

Who Decides?: A Consultation Paper issued by the Lord Chancellor (Cm 3803, 1997).

15

Religion, Culture and the Body of the Child

CAROLINE BRIDGE

1. INTRODUCTION

ONE OF THE great challenges currently facing the law and law-makers is the task of recognising, understanding, and embracing religious and cultural diversity. With a population characterised as the most ethnically composite in Europe, a sense of common ethnicity, and thereby culture, is a major focus of identification by individuals in our society (Hutchinson and Smith (1996)).[1] How we define ourselves as a group is fundamental to our sense of self and our sense of the continuity of our existence. Our cultural and often our religious beliefs are characterised by outward markers such as language, customs, manners, and social and family organisation and rituals (Poulter (1986)) but they also incorporate the more reflective and attitudinal markers of life-style values, ethical understandings and faith. These in turn may be reflected in our attitudes towards healthcare generally, to certain non-therapeutic rituals and practices and to both minor and major medical procedures. As fully competent and autonomous adults we have the capacity to subscribe to whatever healthcare regime we choose. Our right to refuse is absolute (see Jane Weaver (chapter 13). Our choice almost so. Children without capacity have no such rights. Instead, parents are vested with the power to give a proxy consent and have the right and freedom to bring up their children according to their own values and beliefs. This may mean a wish to carry out particular procedures on the child's body which are out of step with generally accepted practice. The law has always had a role in protecting the weak and vulnerable—the child—but to what extent should it intervene when the proposed procedure, or the refusal or demand for treatment, is dictated by the demands of religious or cultural diversity?

The aim of this chapter is to explore the ways in which the law approaches such diversity in the context of the child's body. The emphasis will be on judicial attitudes towards the religious and cultural interests of parents when medical decisions are made. It will explore whether the law is bound by its own traditional

---

[1] Although the term "ethnicity" is recent it refers to age old notions of a common culture, a sense of kinship and group solidarity.

concepts and the norms of the dominant ideology in defining welfare for a specific child or whether it has begun to develop the notion of a religious or cultural welfare? What is its approach to cultural pluralism, the concept of "otherness" (see Day Sclater (chapter 1) or "difference", in relation to children and medical decisions?

2. RELIGION, CULTURE AND PARENTAL RIGHTS: THE BACKGROUND

(a) Religion

Defining religion and the nature of religious belief and practice is problematic, but for the purposes of this chapter a useful identification of the pertinent issues is discernible from Article 9 of the European Convention on Human Rights 1950, now incorporated into domestic law by the Human Rights Act 1998.[2] Article 9 has two aspects. First, in providing that "everyone has the right to freedom of thought, conscience and religion; this right includes freedom to . . . manifest his religion or belief, in worship, teaching, practice and observance", the Convention protects both freedom of religion and the manifestation of that religion and belief. Secondly, it provides that "Freedom to manifest one's religion or beliefs shall be subject only to such limitations as are prescribed by law". For our purposes the crucial distinction between these two aspects is that the right to hold a religious belief is unqualified while the right to manifest that belief is a restricted one, limited by "lawfulness" itself and the concept of "necessity in a democratic society" (Starmer (1999)).[3] Our concern with the law's approach to religious practices in relation to the body of the child is a search for the limits and boundaries of that restriction.

European Court jurisprudence plus recent considerations of the Convention under the Human Rights Act has already provided guidance on the protection of religious rights. In *Re J (Specific Issue Order: Muslim Upbringing and Circumcision)*[4] Wall J considered Article 9 and found that both parents had competing rights to manifest their religion, but this was limited by consideration of the child's best interests. In the absence of a religion having a particular adverse effect on the child, the courts are generally not in the business of discriminating between the comparative worth of different religions (Bainham (1998a)—the judicial function is not to comment on the "tenets, doctrines or rules of any particular section of society provided that these are legally and socially acceptable".[5] Article 9 protects the rights of "known" religions more generally. This has extended, without argument, to

---

[2] Section 13 of the Human Rights Act makes special provision for freedom of religion.
[3] In *Arrowsmith* v. *UK* (1978) 19 DR 5, it was emphasised that Article 9 does not protect "each and every act motivated or influenced by religion or belief".
[4] [1999] 2 FLR 678.
[5] *Re R (A Minor) (Residence: Religion)* [1993] 2 FLR 163 per Purchas LJ at 171E.

Jehovah's Witnesses[6] and the Church of Scientology,[7] for example. However, this does not mean that a parent's right to religious conviction will override a child's right to medical treatment. The implication from *Hoffman* v. *Austria*[8] for example, is that the approach currently taken by domestic courts where Jehovah's Witness parents refuse consent to a blood transfusion for their child, is unlikely to be affected (Swindells et al. (1999)). And certainly in the unprecedented case of the conjoined twins[9] where the Court of Appeal ordered an operation which would save the life of one twin at the expense of the other, their Lordships did not believe that the Strasbourg court would have reached any other conclusion.[10] That case, however, did not involve Article 9 but was concerned with the right to life as protected by Article 2(1).[11] Perhaps the most significant insight into the place of religious conviction in the court room was the Court of Appeal's response to the submission by the Roman Catholic Archbishop of Westminster: "the court has to decide this appeal by reference to legal principle . . . and not by reference to religious teaching or individual conscience".[12]

(b) Ethnic minorities and the family

Ethnic communities within the United Kingdom often carry a deep sense of the significance of the family and family matters. The notion of family honour, the perception of family as encompassing the extended family, the hierarchical and patriarchal structure of many ethnic family groups and the demands and duties of kinship, for example, may all be at variance with those of the majority. The concept of the family and the intimate relationships of those within it may contribute to an individual's sense of identity and belonging more overtly within ethnic communities than may be the norm. Bainham (1998b) refers to the "collective family interest" in his discussion of the child as a member of a family unit. The point is even more valid in relation to children in ethnic families, for the cultural traditions and religious practices of ethnic minorities carry particular significance when the family is intimately affected. This forms part of the background against which English law must fashion its approach to diversity.

It must also be remembered that some ethnic minority families subscribe to a system of personal law based on religious and cultural traditions. This is in broad

---

  [6] *Kokkinakis* v. *Greece* (1994) 17 EHRR 397.
  [7] *X* v. *Church of Scientology* v. *Sweden* (1979) 16 DR 68. It should be noted that the Court of Appeal condemned Scientology and its effect on children in the custody case of *Re B and G* (*Minors*) (*Custody*) [1985] FLR 493.
  [8] 17 EHRR 293. Here a Jehovah's Witness mother complained that she had been denied custody of her children on the ground of her religious convictions but the court treated this matter as one falling within Article 8 rather than Article 9.
  [9] *Re A* (*Conjoined Twins: Medical Treatment*) [2001] 1 FLR 1.
  [10] Per Ward LJ at 61G.
  [11] Even Article 8 provided a justification for what would otherwise have been a wrongful interference with the weaker twin's rights.
  [12] *Supra* n. 9, per Walker LJ at 117G.

contrast to the dominant and secular uniform legal system that is English civil law. Some Muslims living in the United Kingdom, for example, observe Muslim law or *shari'a* and, as Pearl observes, allegiance to the supremacy of *shari'a* continues whilst the modern state assumes and insists on the supremacy of its own rule of law model (Pearl and Menski (1998)). The same might be said of Jewish religious law in relation to divorce, for example. A couple might obtain a civil divorce according to English law but, because of their Orthodox Jewish faith, will not consider they are divorced until they have been through the procedure to obtain a *get*. A refusal to grant the *get* can result in injustice to Jewish spouses, particularly women who become known as "chained" and thereby forbidden by religious law to contract a second Jewish marriage or even feel comfortable entering another relationship (Schuz (1996), and also Katzenberg and Rosenblatt (1999), and Freeman (2000)).[13] A resolution of the problem has been addressed by legislation,[14] indicating that we are moving some way towards an official legal acceptance of cultural and religious practice.

(c) Parental rights

Adherence to cultural and religious norms is intimately related to a sense of ethnic or community *inclusion* rather than *exclusion*. As will be discussed later, the circumcision of male children is an intense part of the Muslim sense of cultural identity and *inclusion* and from this point of view is integral to the Muslim child's welfare. It symbolises his sense of belonging both to the family and to his wider ethnic community. It might also be perceived by his parents as an integral part of their cultural and religious freedom. Bringing up children according to one's own values and convictions—and consequently, religion and culture—is fundamental to parenthood. The interest of parents in moulding their children the way they wish underlies the legal rights they are accorded to determine religious upbringing (McCall Smith (1990), and also Barton and Douglas (1995), and Bainham (1993)). The notion of parental choice is integral to religious upbringing and, as Barton and Douglas (1995) suggest, there is "virtually no possibility for the state to assert that the parents may be damaging the child's emotional or psychological development". The right to choose extends to the rights of the local authority with respect to a child in care[15] and to those parents whose children are adopted. An agency placing a child must "have regard (so far as is practicable) to any wishes of a child's parents . . . as to the religious upbringing".[16] Nonetheless, it is clear that recognition of religious and cultural practices is circumscribed.

[13] It should be noted that the plight of Jewish "chained" wives has been the subject of several recent court cases: *N* v. *N* (*Jurisdiction: Pre-Nuptial Agreement*) [1999] 2 FLR 745 and *O* v. *O* (*Jurisdiction: Jewish Divorce*) [2000] 2 FLR 147.

[14] Family Law Act 1996, s. 9(3) and (4) (known as the "get clause"). However, in anticipation of Part II of the Family Law Act 1996 not being implemented the Divorce (Religious Marriages) Bill was introduced in the House of Lords in May 2000 to replicate the "get clause".

[15] Under the Children Act 1989, s. 33(6), it is precluded from changing the child's religion.

[16] Adoption Act 1976, s. 7.

Religious and cultural beliefs lead parents to take a particular view of what should happen to a child in a particular situation (Bridge (1999a). First, they may decline medical treatment for the child.[17] Here, the state has a duty towards the child and will not let her die for her parents' beliefs. Her welfare is paramount, and welfare invariably equates with the maintenance of meaningful life. Secondly, parents may act towards the child in a way that is not necessarily regarded by others as in her best interests. Here, the state will not intervene unless there is serious parental disagreement and the court is asked to determine the matter.[18] The religious and cultural background of the parents determines what happens to the child only to the extent that it does not overtly harm her. The determination of significant harm[19] resides with the state,[20] and here the court compares the child's health and development with that of a similar child. But does a similar child mean one of the same ethnic background or religion? Can the court explore the child's cultural background and take account of cultural considerations? During the parliamentary debates on the Children Act 1989, Lord McKay LC suggested that background should be left out of account.[21] The Department of Health, however, advises consideration of cultural characteristics.[22] Whether the court takes account of background in the determination of "significant harm" or weighs such factors later when determining what order welfare demands,[23] it seems that religious or cultural factors carry little weight if a child is suffering *significant* harm. There is a minimum standard of care which transcends diversity and it is plain that the state is prepared to override the parents' cultural or religious convictions.

3. THE BODY OF THE CHILD

Jonathan Herring (chapter 3) raises the question "is my body my own?" The answer is a complex one. It is even more so in relation to children. At its most basic, the infant belongs to his parents. All things being equal, they and not the state have a right to possession of him. As the child matures so the parents' rights of possession become limited and by the age of 16 a court is unlikely to insist on his residence with a parent, for example. The moral and legal, as well as practical

---

[17] *Re S (A Minor) (Medical Treatment)* [1993] 1 FLR 376; *Re R (A Minor) (Blood Transfusion)* [1993] 2 FLR 757; *Re O (A Minor) (Medical Treatment)* [1993] 2 FLR 149.

[18] *Re J (Specific Issue Orders: Muslim Upbringing and Circumcision)* [1999] 2 FLR 678 and *Re J (Specific Issue Orders: Child's Religious Upbringing and Circumcision)* [2000] 1 FLR 571, CA.

[19] Harm is defined in the Children Act 1989, s. 31(9).

[20] Children Act 1989, s. 31(2).

[21] (1990) 503 Parl Deb HL 354.

[22] The Children Act 1989 Guidance and Regulations Vol 1, para. 3.20.

[23] The Children Act 1989, s. 1(3)(d), requires the court to have regard to "age, sex, background and any characteristics of his which the court considers relevant" when determining matters of upbringing. Bainham (1990) regards this as the appropriate point at which cultural factors may come into play. Freeman (1990) takes an opposing point of view, arguing that cultural difference is significant in assessing reasonable care given that the requirement of the Act is to look at the particular child and her needs.

reality can be characterised as one of *temporary* possession. The parents' exercise of their rights of possession over young children is a matter of degree. They make decisions for him but the state will intervene if harm is caused and it is a right of the child not to suffer significant harm. Parents' rights are therefore interlinked with the rights of the child. So is it the right of the child to have all decisions about what is done to his body made in his best medical interests? Who has the right to decide that—and on what grounds?

The role of the court is significant in safeguarding the child's physical integrity but, of course, it can only determine matters when asked to do so.[24] In cases of conflict between parents and those treating their children the right course of action is to bring the matter to court.[25] A series of cases has considered the views of parents—centred on their personal convictions and natural desire to keep their child alive rather than from any religious or cultural beliefs—where these have been in conflict with the treatment prescribed by doctors (Bridge (1999a)). These concern both neonates and very ill young children and give some indication of where the court will strike the balance between parents' and children's rights where the child's body is concerned. Analysis of such cases serves to discern, first, the extent to which the views of parents play a part in the court's considerations, and secondly, the factors to be balanced in determining best interests. From there we may better see the law's developing approach to these issues when cultural and religious diversity is involved.

Since the early 1990s, the jurisprudence emerging from the higher courts has centred very much on "sanctity of life" and "quality of life" issues but has done so in a broad and general way. Clinical factors are overriding and the deference of the court to medical opinion has meant that the formulation of any legal standard for what is best for a child remains vague. Bainham (1998a) has questioned whether a more concerted attempt should be made to devise legal standards for decision-making but concludes that the moral questions raised by the issues depend so much on individual beliefs and values that there is never likely to be a societal consensus. We suggest that this is correct and for our purposes it is relevant simply to elucidate the broad principles that appear to have governed judicial determinations of welfare. Determination of the child's best interests is the court's paramount concern. The judicial approach has drawn heavily on the principles of an earlier Court of Appeal ruling in the well publicised case of *Re B (A Minor)* (*Wardship: Medical Treatment*).[26] In deciding that corrective surgery was in the best interests of this Down's Syndrome infant despite her parents' refusal of consent,[27] judicial reasoning centred on the child's future quality of life: would it be a

---

[24] However, the extent to which treatment may be withheld from a severely handicapped new born infant when parents and professionals are in agreement can only be the subject of conjecture.

[25] In *R* v. *Portsmouth Hospital NHS Trust, ex parte G* [1999] 2 FLR 905, Lord Woolf MR set out guidance that, in cases of grave conflict over the medical treatment of a child, the matter should be brought before the court.

[26] [1982] FLR 117.

[27] She was born with an intestinal blockage and the parents refused consent for a relatively straightforward operation.

life so awful that it ought to be extinguished? The court concluded that here was a life, albeit a handicapped one, with the potential for maturity. But had the damage been more severe and the child's future "full of pain and suffering, the court might be driven to a different conclusion". The decision demonstrates, first, the court's balancing procedure, weighing the risks and benefits of the treatment against the predicted quality of the future life whilst also being prepared to envisage a situation where the prognosis was so awful that prolongation of life would not be in the child's best interests. Secondly, it is clear that there is no absolute right to life for the child and, thirdly, no right at all for the parental wishes where these are contrary to medical and subsequently judicial views.

Two further Court of Appeal cases developed the jurisprudence. In *Re C (A Minor) (Wardship: Medical Treatment)*,[28] the court drew on the *Re B* principles in considering the nature of treatment to be administered to a severely handicapped baby who "[was] dying and . . . nothing known medical science can alter that fact".[29] The prognosis was hopeless and the current quality of life "demonstrably awful". In rejecting any sanctity of life argument, the court authorised the withdrawal of any treatment which might extend the child's life span, focusing instead on palliative care to provide a dignified and peaceful end to life. In *Re J (A Minor) (Wardship: Medical Treatment)*[30] a severely brain-damaged premature baby required artificial resuscitation. Was his life so "demonstrably awful" that treatment should be withheld? On the basis of *Re B* Lord Donaldson reasoned that "There is without doubt a very strong presumption in favour of a course of action which will prolong life, but . . . it is not irrebuttable . . . account has to be taken of the pain and suffering and quality of life which the child will experience if life is prolonged".[31] Ultimately, the Court of Appeal, purporting to assess the baby's best interests from his own assumed standpoint, sanctioned a decision not to pursue mechanical ventilation but left the doctors free to take measures to preserve the child's life if his condition improved. The principle was thus advanced that although there is a strong presumption in favour of preserving life it is not an absolute principle but part of a balancing exercise in assessing the child's future quality of life. In determining what is best for a child the courts undoubtedly place some weight on parental wishes, yet it has become common for their views to be overruled (Bridge (1997)). That was, until the Court of Appeal gave much more weight to the wishes of the mother in *Re T (Wardship: Medical Treatment)*[32] despite unanimous medical opinion that a liver transplant was in the child's best medical interests. The mother disagreed and the Court of Appeal considered that it would not be in the child's best interests to overrule the parent in such a situation: ongoing post-operative care of the child would be required of her and

---

[28] [1990] 1 FLR 252.
[29] [1990] 1 FLR 252, 254.
[30] [1991] 1 FLR 366.
[31] [1991] 1 FLR 366, 375.
[32] [1997] 1 FLR 502.

without her wholehearted support there could be grave difficulties.[33] Arguably, while the decision went against the child's medical welfare it supported an overall assessment of welfare. Academic commentators (Fox and McHale (1997), Bainham (1997), Bridge (1997)) were unanimous in condemning the decision and, in retrospect, it was indeed an aberration. But if the case risked a return to "nineteenth century notions of the natural rights of parents" its message was short-lived (Bainham (1997)).

Subsequently, several dramatic cases restored the assessment of best interests to a determination of quality of life with parental wishes playing a part but not a determinative part. First, and perhaps the most vivid example is *Re C (HIV Test)*[34] where, arguably, the child's medical status would remain unknown without an HIV test and doctors might thus overly prescribe on the off chance that she was HIV-positive or under-treat through ignorance of her condition. The baby was at risk without the test yet the intrusion demanded was slight. The parents' contention that the application was an affront to their parental autonomy was over-ruled and the court concluded that although there undoubtedly exists a space in which parental decisions are final, it exists subject to section 1(1) of the Children Act 1989. Thus, parental wishes may be significant but are only final when they advance the best interests of the child—as perceived by doctors and the court.[35] The child's welfare is thus a limitation on the exercise of parental powers. This case reveals a judicial stance robustly focused on welfare and the rights of the child with the strength of the welfare point illustrated by the claim that European Convention rights were not needed because "everything" was encapsulated in section 1(1) of the Children Act. The parents' belief in an alternative approach to medical matters was not in the best interests of their child and carried little weight with the court. Although not a hard case, in the sense that little or no distress or pain would be caused to the child yet the advantages would be great, *Re C* is as an example of judicial reasoning asserting the strength of conventional medicine and eschewing the unconventional. It could be likened to the espousal of the dominant in the face of a claim from the minority—the assertion of the traditional as against the alternative.

Secondly, in *A National Health Service Trust* v. *D*,[36] a declaration that doctors need not artificially ventilate a severely ill baby was granted after balancing the child's minimal quality of life against the pain and suffering that would be caused by giving him the intensive treatment his parents wished him to have.[37] The

[33] This was despite the mother being a paediatric nurse experienced in such care.

[34] [1999] 2 FLR 1004. Here an HIV-positive mother breast fed her baby despite medical advice and subsequently refused to have her tested for HIV. The local authority applied for a specific issue order to have a sample of blood taken from the baby without the parents' consent.

[35] This point was made in *Re Z (A Minor)* (*Identification: Restriction on Publication*) [1997] Fam 1, where Sir Thomas Bingham stated that if the court's judgment "is in accord with that of the devoted and responsible parent, well and good. If not, then it is the duty of the court . . . to give effect to its own judgment".

[36] [2000] 2 FLR 677.

[37] They wished him to be admitted to paediatric intensive care for mechanical ventilation despite unanimous medical opinion that ventilation and intensive care were not in his best interests.

declaration was based on the child's best interests as perceived from his assumed standpoint, the assumption being that he would have wanted full palliative treatment coupled with a clear way ahead for the medical team treating him.[38] He would not have wanted the pain and suffering of mechanical ventilation nor the prospect of future opposition from his parents, even if this meant a short extension to his doomed life.[39] In conceding to unanimous medical opinion the court confirmed the undisputed principles of law as set out by Lord Woolf MR in *R v. Portsmouth Hospitals NHS Trust, ex parte Glass*.[40] Although these take account of "the natural concerns and the responsibilities" of the parent they are unlikely to override the court's view of the child's best interests where there is conflict. The Court of Appeal here refused to grant an anticipatory declaration which would indicate to doctors what treatment should or should not be given in circumstances yet to arise. Lord Woolf's reasoning asserted that the best course was for doctors and parents to agree,[41] but where this was not possible the actual circumstances should be brought before the court so that a decision could be made on the facts at the time. It is clear that the court will overrule parents in life and death situations and that judges will not hamper doctors by restrictive anticipatory declarations. It is also clear that once a child requires medical intervention the prescribed relationship for doctors and parents is one of consultation.[42] The view that a process of negotiation, and ultimately compromise, is the best course was also apparent in *Re MM (Medical Treatment)*[43] where the Russian parents were adamant that their child continue with the treatment he had received in Russia albeit that medical opinion here unanimously favoured a different treatment regime. In approving the course proposed by the English doctors [44] Black J urged that health professionals should consult with parents and consider the alternative forms of disease management they might suggest.[45] But

---

[38] In *Re J (A Minor) (Wardship: Medical Treatment)* [1991] 1 FLR 366 Lord Donaldson MR stated at 376 that "Nothing could be more inimical to the interests of the child than that the judge should make an order which restricted the doctors' freedom to revise their present view in favour of more active means to preserve the life of the child, if the situation changed and this then seemed to them to be appropriate".

[39] This is closely paralleled by *Re C (A Minor) (Wardship: Medical Treatment)* [1990] 1 FLR 376 where the baby was dying and her current quality of life "demonstrably awful". There, the court authorised the withdrawal of any treatment which might extend the infant's life span and focused on allowing her to die with dignity.

[40] [1999] 2 FLR 905. Here, the mother of a 12-year-old severely disabled boy with a limited life span wished him to have whatever medical treatment was necessary to prolong his life and sought an anticipatory declaration as to what course would be followed if he were readmitted. The hospital argued that only treatment designed to relieve suffering was appropriate.

[41] [1999] 2 FLR 905 at 910.

[42] Lord Woolf requires the parent to be "fully consulted and to fully understand what is involved".

[43] [2000] 1 FLR 224.

[44] By the time the case came to court the parents had agreed with the doctors on the course to be followed.

[45] Although this latter point might appear to be conceding that parents' medical ideas carry weight where their child is concerned, her Ladyship was also of the view that had agreement not finally been reached she would have overridden the wishes of the parents.

in the end the views of parents count for little as against those of the doctors and certainly the court. [46]

Two general points emerge which help clarify the position of parents *vis-à-vis* the court. First, parental views may be overly but understandably optimistic. The need of parents to hold onto hope and the enormity of child death in a society with high medical expectations, accustomed to the most advanced life-saving techno-logy, often means a refusal to accept the inevitable. This may be exacerbated by poor communication between parents and doctors. In such situations the court often assumes the role of a compassionate authority, empathising with the parents but leading them to accept what doctors say is best for their child.[47] Emotion is the driving force and of course emotions can be handled by sensitive communication or counselling by skilful staff. In this sense the court becomes free to focus purely on the child's best interests as perceived from the clinical point of view. Religious and cultural beliefs, however, are of a different order, being fundamental to the parties to the conflict as well as to its very nature. Secondly, whilst the court, in these "emotion" cases, is ready to assert that parental views are of the greatest importance, judges inevitably claim—either outright or by implication[48]—that they are neither paramount nor decisive. In part such statements reflect the court's counselling/empathising process, endeavouring to assist the parents in reconciling themselves to the medical view. More significantly, they are a statement of the legal position, that the welfare of the child is the paramount consideration. In deter-mining welfare the parents' ability to assist the child is part of the equation[49] but nowhere is there any reference to the wishes or views of parents being of any real consequence.[50] This was also the position in the conjoined twins case.[51] There, Ward LJ stressed that parental rights and powers exist for the performance of their

---

[46] What can almost be called the "etiquette of the doctor/parent relationship" was raised again in *Royal Wolverhampton Hospitals NHS Trust* v. *B* [2000] 1 FLR 953 where a premature baby later devel-oped complex medical problems and was likely to die despite receiving full medical treatment. The High Court declared that the child be treated as clinicians saw fit despite the parents' disagreement. The paucity of communication and understanding between doctors and the parents here was such that only when the doctors heard the mother give evidence via a telephone conference call did they realise the extent of her misunderstanding of the situation.

[47] Although the Court of Appeal's approach in *Re T (Wardship: Medical Treatment)* [1997] 1 FLR 502 was not in line with this. Instead, it endorsed the mother's view as against that of unanimous med-ical opinion.

[48] In *Royal Wolverhampton Hospitals* Bodey J stated that the parents' views were neither paramount nor decisive; in *Re MM (Medical Treatment)* Black J urged that parents be consulted and their alterna-tive views acknowledged, although at the same time her Ladyship said she would not hesitate to over-ride their view; Lord Woolf took a similar position in *R* v. *Portsmouth NHS Trust, ex parte Glass* by stating that where consultation failed to achieve agreement the conflict should be brought to court; in *Re C (HIV Test)* the Court of Appeal held that the parents' views could not stand against the child's right.

[49] Children Act 1989, s. 1(3)(f).

[50] In *A National Health Service Trust* v. *D*, Cazalet J went further and stated that the first principle of the "settled law"—that the court's "prime and paramount consideration must be the best interests of the child"—involved "the most careful and anxious consideration" being given to the views of the parents and that while these views are given careful consideration they cannot override the court's view of the child's best interests.

[51] *Re A (Conjoined Twins: Medical Treatment)* [2001] 1 FLR 1.

duties and responsibilities[52] and they must be exercised in the best interests of the child: "parental right is subordinate to welfare".[53] Although the wishes of the Roman Catholic parents were not prompted by the "scruple or dogma" referred to in *Re T*[54] they did not coincide with the court's assessment of the children's best interests.[55]

In summary, the wishes of parents clearly have status during the child's treatment and hospitalisation in the sense that their consent renders medical intervention lawful. In this context parental wishes command very great respect.[56] Their views also have status in that their knowledge of the child may assist doctors in devising the best approach to treatment and their role in helping the child accept and cope with treatment is inestimable. But this all occurs in the absence of conflict and thus before legal intervention. Once in the courtroom the parents' wishes have no status at all. Their assessment of their child's best interests carries little weight when it conflicts with the clinical assessment of best interests.[57] In such grave matters overriding control is vested in the court.[58]

4. TOWARDS A RELIGIOUS WELFARE?

(a) Non-conventional medicine

There is an upsurge of interest in alternative medicine today to the extent that it has become almost part of the mainstream. Alternative approaches to health and sickness are part of the diversity of society itself rather than a facet of religious or cultural diversity. As Jane Weaver explains (chapter 13) it is a fundamental principle of law that fully competent adults have the right to make their own decisions on medical treatment. It is a right of the autonomous adult therefore to treat her cancer with a herbal remedy if she so chooses. But could she have her child treated in the same way?

Where non-life-threatening childhood illnesses are concerned parental discretion is at its greatest. Here parental freedom to treat the child according to a belief system, particular values or simply convenience, reigns (Lavery (1990) and Bridge (1997)). Parents are not obliged in law to agree only to those procedures which a court would find was in the best interests of the child. Rather, it is sufficient that

---

[52] At 33G.

[53] Per Ward LJ at 49E.

[54] *Supra* n. 47, per Waite LJ at 514.

[55] The best interest of the twins was to give the chance of life to the child whose bodily condition was capable of accepting the chance, even at the cost of the sacrifice of the life of the other twin.

[56] *Re A (Conjoined Twins: Medical Treatment)* [2001] 1 FLR 1, per Ward LJ at 49E.

[57] As parties to the proceedings parents will present an opposing point of view but one that is seldom based on clinical fact and usually based on understandable emotion. That is not to say that there is no value to the child in bringing proceedings.

[58] *Re A (Conjoined Twins: Medical Treatment)*, *supra* n. 51, per Ward LJ at 33C.

they agree to that which will *benefit* the child (Skegg (1973)). This has relevance in the context of routine treatments for children where parents wish to adhere to culturally acceptable methods or use those that come within the tenets of religious faith—medical non-intervention for the Christian Scientist child with a chronic ear infection, for example. The extent to which this broad discretion may be exercised by parents remains relatively unexplored in medical ethics. What we do know is that the state will step in if significant harm is either suffered or is likely. And if the condition becomes a life and death one, with parents either refusing treatment, demanding inordinate means to keep the child alive, or refusing to agree to a withdrawal of treatment, doctors are likely to ask the court to intervene. The court would invariably overrule parents if they tried to treat the child's cancer with a herbal remedy, for example. Failure of parents to provide adequate medical aid or failure to take steps to provide such aid constitutes the criminal offence of wilful neglect.[59] Parents are also subject to the ordinary criminal law where the death of a child is caused by their unwillingness to summon medical assistance. The use of non-conventional or alternative treatments for children is thus circumscribed.[60]

Our concern now is with those situations where the religious or cultural beliefs of parents have led to their refusal of conventional medicine when the child's life is in jeopardy.

(b) Refusing blood

Following a series of cases [61] in which Jehovah's Witness parents refused consent to life-saving blood transfusions for their children it is clear that the court will overrule their religious objections in the child's best interests. It is also clear that in these situations the court endorses medical attempts to treat the child in accordance with parental faith even though the unconventional treatment is inevitably abandoned. In *Re S (A Minor) (Medical Treatment)*[62] for example, doctors treated the Jehovah's Witness child with non-conventional, less effective therapy for some time in deference to the parents' wishes, albeit there was an exacerbation of the child's suffering,[63] and in *Re R (A Minor) (Blood Transfusion)* judicial sympathies with the parents' wishes resulted in an order granting them a measure of control over therapy in all but imminently life-threatening situations. The parental discretion that exists over routine treatment seems to extend to the seriously ill children of religious parents and, arguably, those treating such children do so as far as possible with therapy which honours the religious or cultural dictates of parents.

---

[59] Children and Young Persons Act 1933, s. 1(1).

[60] *Re C (HIV Test)* [1999] 2 FLR 1004, where the parents, both practitioners in holistic medicine, eschewed a blood test for their child, is an example.

[61] *Re R (A Minor) (Blood Transfusion)* [1993] 2 FLR 757; *Re S (A Minor) (Medical Treatment)* [1993] 1 FLR 376; *Re O (A Minor) (Medical Treatment)* [1993] 2 FLR 149.

[62] [1993] 1 FLR 376.

[63] This resulted in the child becoming "needle shy" due to the inability of doctors to insert a surgical long line because they were denied the necessary back-up of a blood transfusion.

Arguably, parental rights prevail until a life and death situation is reached, even if this means subjecting the child to inferior treatment and increased suffering. We suggest that this is a recognition of the parents' right to manifest their religion, as required by Article 9 of the European Convention, but qualified by the restriction that when the child's life is at stake the limits prescribed by law have been reached.

While the courts inevitably overrule parents when the child's life is at risk it is instructive to consider why there are so few reported cases, none relating to young Jehovah's Witness children since 1993, for example.[64] First, the importance of consent at all stages in the treatment of a young child must be reiterated. Without the consent of parents treatment is unlawful and therefore, in the absence of an emergency, doctors are obliged to limit their dealings with the child to that which the parents have agreed. This must account for the extent to which non-blood products are used in the treatment of childhood leukaemia, for example.[65] If a life and death situation arises doctors can use the common law powers granted by the doctrine of necessity and administer blood. Given the availability of court intervention and the opportunity it provides for parents to have their point of view heard, such an approach may be perceived as running roughshod over religious parents even though it may be in the best clinical interests of the child. Nonetheless, commentators have noted that this is "the choice hospital authorities will, in general, adopt" (Mason and McCall Smith (1999)). A second explanation may be that the persuasive powers of doctors armed with the knowledge that ultimately the courts, or the doctrine of necessity, will overrule the parents, prevent situations going as far as a court application. Anecdotal evidence indicates that this may well be the case.[66] The persuasive approach in cases of conflict generally is likely to have the full support of the courts.[67] For Jehovah's Witnesses the *authority* of the court becomes a major persuasive factor in conceding to clinical demands. When the spectre of legal intervention is raised parents must ready themselves to concede, given the inevitability of the likely outcome. When intervention actually occurs and

[64] Although this is not the case with older children. For example, *Re L* (*Medical Treatment: Gillick Competency*) [1998] 2 FLR 810 concerned a Jehovah's Witness girl of 14 who refused life-saving blood transfusions for burns. Her parents, however, were not asked for their consent and the issue for the court was the competence of the girl to refuse the treatment. She was found to lack competence and thus the court ordered the conventional treatment. For discussion of this case see Bridge (1999b). In the earlier case of *Re E* (*A Minor*) (*Wardship: Medical Treatment*) [1993] 1 FLR 386, where a 15-year-old boy and his parents all refused blood transfusions to treat his leukaemia, the issue for the court was the teenager's competence rather than his parents' refusal. Again the court overrode the child's and parents' refusal.

[65] In *Re S* (*A Minor*) (*Medical Treatment*) [1993] 1 FLR 376, doctors treated the child's leukaemia with non-blood products, avoiding conventional treatment, until it was clear that a cure could not be affected by such means.

[66] A children's hospital in Alberta, Canada, for example, has a Jehovah's Witness doctor on hand to assist parents confronted with these situations. His task is to inform parents about the legal processes and persuade them to allow doctors to treat the child conventionally. It is said that this has resulted in conflict being resolved without legal intervention.

[67] Lord Woolf made clear his endorsement of parental/medical agreement as the optimum approach in the child's interests in *R* v. *Portsmouth Hospitals NHS Trust, ex parte Glass* [1999] 2 FLR 905.

the rule of law prevails parents can do nothing more. As was said of the parents in *Re S (A Minor) (Medical Treatment)*, "[they] will recognise that the responsibility for consent was taken from them and, as a judicial act, absolves their conscience of responsibility".[68]

So how far should doctors go in meeting the religious demands of parents? The answer must be, only as far as is clinically possible without causing detriment to the child.[69] In our view doctors must seek judicial sanction without delay when a transfusion looks inevitable unless the parents can be persuaded otherwise. However, it must be recognised that receiving therapy in accordance with parental wishes, at least in the early stages, endows a benefit on the child by minimising any potential rejection by them.[70] This arguably accords with his overall welfare.

(c) Demanding resuscitation

Many of the cases discussed earlier resulted from parental unwillingness to agree to withdrawal of treatment. Invariably the parents' wishes to have the child re-ventilated were overruled on the basis that the child's quality of life was exceedingly poor with no hope of a cure and with further distressing procedures simply prolonging the inevitable. However, in *Re C (Medical Treatment)*[71] the wishes of Orthodox Jewish parents were accompanied by a belief that "[it was not] within their religious tenets to contemplate the possibility of indirectly shortening life",[72] and they demanded that the 16-month-old child be re-ventilated. The family lived by the values of Orthodox Judaism and believed that a person could not stand aside and watch another die where their intervention could prevent death—"in such a case the person who stands by will subsequently be punished by God. Failing to resuscitate is equivalent to a situation such as this".[73] Here the child's illness was so severe that continued ventilation would only delay death without alleviation of suffering.[74] Ultimately, the case was decided on a "right to healthcare" argument, that is, the parents were asking doctors to carry out a procedure which was contrary to clinical judgement. An earlier leading case had made clear that no doctor could be required by a court or anyone else to do this,[75] and thus the court in *Re C* was spared an assessment of religious and cultural welfare (Fortin (1998)).

---

[68] [1993] 1 FLR 376, per Thorpe J at 380.

[69] Although in *Re S, supra* n. 65, doctors waited until the child's health was deteriorating before seeking intervention.

[70] The risk that religious parents may come to see their child as "tainted" if blood is given is a tangible one but does not amount to an argument that will prevail when significant harm or even death is inevitable.

[71] [1998] 1 FLR 384.

[72] *Ibid.* at 386.

[73] *Ibid.* at 389.

[74] The medical evidence was unanimous and doctors were unwilling to carry out further resuscitation.

[75] The court relied on *Re J (A Minor) (Medical Treatment)* [1992] 2 FLR 165 where Lord Donaldson stated that a doctor cannot be required by a court or by parents to carry out a particular treatment.

Mason and McCall Smith (1999) have criticised *Re C*, considering that by ignoring parental values the court was "at best paternalistic and, at worst, culturally imperialistic". Perhaps this opinion could be re-phrased as a call for greater acknowledgement of religious views and thus greater weight placed on the residual rights of parents. However, an alternative interpretation of the court's handling of the religious issue can be proffered. The medical profession does not have to respond to a parent's demand for particular treatment, yet here, more prolonged ventilation than was clinically desirable was carried out, in deference to the parents' religious wishes. Only when paediatricians could no longer find any semblance of clinical grounds on which to re-intubate the child did they seek judicial approval to stop the treatment, in deference to the child. The prospect of a tiny child being kept alive by means which even her doctors could not bring themselves to use is at best unethical and at worst inhumane. Doctors must embrace cultural pluralism by recognising and acting upon religious wishes to the extent that the child benefits. But taking account of parents' beliefs to the detriment of the child, as Mason and McCall Smith would have us do, would be to grant parents more than merely residual rights. It would be to place their interests on a footing akin to that of the child. That is not to say that best medical interests must always be equated with a child's best overall interests. Adherence to the religious observances of the family may well be in the child's best interests, but only as long as this does not cause him harm.

5. INVASIVE PROCEDURES ON CULTURAL AND RELIGIOUS GROUNDS

The notion of religious welfare forming part of a child's overall welfare is replicated in the law on circumcision. Ritual circumcision of male infants as a religious and cultural practice is lawful in this country while the more drastic female circumcision, also part of the religious[76] and cultural beliefs of some ethnic communities, is banned. We allow parents to agree to a relatively minor, albeit irreversible procedure, in the interests of observing religious practices in the upbringing of their male child but that freedom stops short at the seriously invasive procedure on young girls. The tenor of this distinction is consistent with what we have already observed in relation to Jehovah's Witness parents, that is, we allow what is minor but disallow that which becomes seriously detrimental to the child. But whilst female circumcision is regarded with abhorrence by the majority, and rightly prohibited by legislation, male circumcision can be viewed as no less an attack on the physical integrity of a child unable to consent. Why does the law allow parents to consent to an arguably medically unnecessary and irreversible invasive procedure on male infants? Is this a recognition of cultural pluralism or simply part of a majority norm? Is the distinction between the male and female

---

[76] Freeman (1998) refers to the belief amongst some Muslims that female circumcision is scripturally mandated by the Koran, although this is disputed by others.

procedures drawn by the dominant ideology without recourse to true cultural understanding and tolerance?

(a) Male circumcision

Ritual circumcision of male children has been carried out by Jews, Muslims and some African peoples for centuries. [77] It has a deep religious significance and its practice is regarded as necessary to the fulfilment of faith. A parent's duty to have the child circumcised is thus fundamental. Jewish boys are circumcised on the eighth day after birth, in Israel invariably by a non-medical ritual circumcisor.[78] In Islam the practice varies, it being a father's duty to ensure it is done, either on the seventh day after birth or at least before puberty, while abandoning circumcision would amount to the abandonment of Judaism as a culture. Even secular Jews regard circumcision as a defining characteristic of their ethnic identity. The ritual, however, is one that has escaped from its cultural or religious context (Richards (1998)). In the USA a century ago circumcision was promoted as a hygiene measure indicated for such diverse conditions as eczema and tuberculosis (Gollaher (2000)). It soon took hold and by 1996 at least 60 per cent of male infants born in the USA were circumcised. In this country it became common outside the Jewish community in the early twentieth century but is now primarily carried out on Muslim and Jewish children.[79] It is, arguably, unnecessary mutilation for religious or cultural reasons.

Today medical as well as religious justifications are advanced for the removal of the foreskin of a child's penis. Besides the existence of medical conditions for which circumcision is indicated,[80] the potential benefits have been described in numerous studies (Szabo and Short (2000), Christakis et al. (2000), Halperin and Bailey (1999)). In summary these amount to some small protective effects [81] but may be outweighed "for some parents" by small risks of complication.[82] However, the major debate today about the medical benefits of circumcision centres on its relationship with HIV transmission. In 1989 a landmark study showed a greater than eight-fold increased risk of HIV infection for uncircumcised men (Cameron et al. (1989)). A decade later the links have become so compelling that lack of male circumcision is

[77] Evidence of circumcision appears in early Egyptian art and radiographs of 6000 year-old mummies show evidence of circumcision.

[78] In Tel Aviv a growing number of secular Jewish parents are having their babies circumcised in hospital thus avoiding the ritual.

[79] In *Re J (Specific Issue Orders: Muslim Upbringing and Circumcision)* [1999] 2 FLT 678, at 690 Wall J found that it has become an accepted practice amongst a significant number of parents in England.

[80] The consultant paediatrician called by the Official Solicitor in *Re J (Specific Issue Orders: Muslim Upbringing and Circumcision)* [1999] 2 FLR 678 at 692 gave evidence of three such conditions: true pathological phimosis, balanoposthitis and paraphimosis.

[81] Reduction in the risk of penile cancer, urinary tract infections and sexually transmitted diseases.

[82] For example, a US study showed that a complication is expected in one out of every 476 circumcisions (Christakis et al. (2000)).

one of the main causes of many regional discrepancies in rates of HIV infection and it is reported that increasing numbers of men in traditionally non-circumcising communities are seeking safe affordable circumcision to avoid AIDS and other sexually transmitted diseases (Halperin and Bailey (1999)). An even more recent study in Uganda revealed the dramatic protective effects of circumcision and it can now be said that there is conclusive epidemiological evidence that uncircumcised men are at a much greater risk of HIV infection than circumcised men (Szabo and Short (2000)). Returning to Skegg's argument that parents need agree only to those procedures which benefit their child it would seem that, religious motivation apart, circumcision is now within that realm, that it is not completely unnecessary surgery. Arguably the long term protective benefits of circumcision, coupled with its religious significance, contribute to the child's overall welfare and is in his best interests.

(b) Circumcision and the law

Where parents agree that their infant son be circumcised the procedure is lawful. This was held to be so in *Re J (Specific Issue Orders: Muslim Upbringing and Circumcision)*,[83] the first case to ask the court to authorise circumcision.[84] Both the BMA and the Law Commission accept that circumcision pursuant to parental consent is lawful.[85] In *Re J* a divorced Muslim father sought to have his 5-year-old son circumcised despite the objections of the nominally Christian mother with whom the child resided. The ethos of both parents' households was an essentially secular one. In his application for specific issue orders under the Children Act 1989,[86] the father argued that his son was a Muslim and that circumcision was an essential part of his personal and religious identity and thus of his upbringing. The mother argued that the procedure was not medically indicated, carried significant psychological and small physical risks, and that the child's association with Muslims did not justify circumcising him for social reasons. In determining whether to authorise the procedure despite the mother's veto, the court examined the issues under the relevant heads of section 1(3) of the Children Act and concluded that circumcision would not be in the child's best interests.[87] The medical

---

[83] [1999] 2 FLR 678.

[84] Lord Templeman had earlier referred to it, *obiter*, in *R v. Brown and others* [1994] 1 AC 212, 231D–F.

[85] At [1999] 2 FLR 678, 688, Wall J noted that the BMA's *Guidance for Doctors* stated that the assumption of lawfulness had never been challenged, and Law Commission, *Consent in the Criminal Law* (No. 139, 1995) stated that it was lawful under English common law. Wall J nonetheless pointed out at 690 that the GMC and the Medical Ethics Committee of the BMA highlighted the nature of the ethical debate with the latter commenting that "[the ethics of circumcision] are matters for society as a whole to decide".

[86] The father applied for two such orders, the first requiring the mother to raise the child as a Muslim and the second requiring her to have the boy circumcised.

[87] Even though circumcision would identify the child with his father and confirm him as a Muslim, it was a painful operation (with significant psychological risks for this child), opposed by the mother (a hostile contact battle between the parents was ongoing), and would make him an exception amongst his peers (the child's upbringing would be a secular one in England).

benefit in terms of its relationship with HIV transmission was not put to the judge in evidence. In confirming this decision the Court of Appeal clarified an important legal point: that section 2(7) of the Children Act 1989 does not enable a parent to arrange circumcision without the consent of the other parent with parental responsibility.[88] Circumcision belongs to a small group of important decisions which, in the absence of agreement, ought not to be arranged by one parent even though she may have parental responsibility.[89] In other words, where there is disagreement the issue of circumcision, like sterilisation or change of name, ought to go to the court for specific approval because it is an essentially religious concession.

This case turns very much on its own facts and is thus limited. That the issue had become such a major one between the parents could not help but raise the psychological stakes for this child and it is that aspect of the case that was decisive, not the father's religious views or the mother's lack of them. In other circumstances, if the particular religious or cultural context for the child were different, a court may well order circumcision. Wall J illustrated this with the example of a Jewish mother and an agnostic father with a number of sons circumcised as infants. If another son were born after the parents had separated and the mother wished him circumcised like his brothers but the father refused, the court would be likely to grant the mother a specific issue order.[90] That child's best interests would be served by being physically like his brothers and his Jewish peers. This example illustrates that religion and culture are simply part of overall welfare within the meaning of section 1(3) of the Children Act 1989 and even though the right to manifest religion under Article 9 of the European Convention includes circumcision, that right is restricted when it conflicts with the rights and freedoms of the other parent and is not in the best interests of the child.[91] However, this is not to say that recognition of cultural pluralism is lacking. That the law allows parents to agree to an irreversible and probably medically unnecessary procedure on a male child who cannot consent is, arguably, evidence of an acceptance of the religious and cultural wishes of the minority by majority norms (Bodi (2000)). In the absence of parental conflict English law concedes that it is a parent's right to interfere with the physical integrity of the child in the interests of religious belief. Why should this be so when, for example, Somali parents living in this country cannot have their daughters circumcised, or white Christian parents cannot have a discreet cross tattooed on their child's arm?

(c) Female circumcision

While circumcision generally involves the removal of healthy genital tissue the effects of female circumcision are much greater than those for males. Female cir-

---

88 [2000] 1 FLR 571, 576 per Thorpe LJ.
89 *Ibid.* at 577.
90 [1999] 2 FLR 678, 700.
91 *Ibid.* at 701.

cumcision is of an altogether different order, as graphically illustrated by Freeman (1998) in his account of the differing degrees of physical mutilation common in the Sudan, Somalia and Ethiopia. These range from ritualistic circumcision with minimal mutilation (this Type II excision is the most common) to the full horrors of infibulation (Type III excision of part or all of the external genitalia and stitching of the vaginal opening) carried out with "crude cutting instruments and with few or no precautions against infection, [which] is life-threatening, as well as resulting in a total loss of stimulation".[92] The detrimental effects are thus physical, sexual and psychological, with the impact on menstruation and particularly childbirth being hazardous. Most such women have to deliver their babies by caesarean section.[93]

The very existence of a report on female circumcision in a recent issue of the *British Medical Journal* indicates the concern that persists despite its being a criminal offence (Jones (2000)). The practice is banned by the Prohibition of Female Circumcision Act 1985 (although there have been no prosecutions) yet it is reported, anecdotally, that the law is flouted.[94] Why, when the mutilation and its consequences are so severe is the practice still continued? A gynaecologist carrying out circumcision reversals has commented that "parents who put their children through this procedure honestly believe that they are doing the right thing, with 600 years of tradition behind them" (Jones (2000)). Its cultural significance, in relation to control of female sexuality and preserving virginity until marriage, is still adhered to by parents who want the best, as they see it, for their children. Similarly the London mother who scarred the faces of her two young children with razor incisions in accordance with the rituals of her Nigerian tribe. She was convicted of assault occasioning actual bodily harm.[95] Cultural and, for some, religious tradition lies behind these practices, as it does with ritual male circumcision, but the fact that only the latter, the more minor procedure, is lawful, is evidence of the central place of health, quality of life and risk to individuals in our Western legal system. The Tattooing of Minors Act 1969, which imposes an absolute ban on the tattooing of anyone under the age of 18, is probably best described as aberrant legislation. It does not appear to have a cultural component but, rather, is part of a range of statutes enacted to prevent supposedly undesirable activities.[96] Consequently, a parent cannot tattoo a child's arm but is perfectly at liberty to have his or her ears or other body parts pierced.

---

[92] Per Wall J in *Re J, supra* n. 83, at 689.

[93] Many of the patients at an NHS clinic in London for African women seeking reversal of the procedure are either already pregnant or have just got married.

[94] *The Times* 20 December 2000, reports that a doctor was struck off the medical register for agreeing to circumcise three young Somali girls in the United Kingdom.

[95] *R v. Adesanya, The Times*, 16 and 17 July 1994.

[96] Other examples are the Crossbows Act 1987 and the Explosives (Age of Purchase etc.) Act 1976.

6. CONCLUSION

In his discussion of what the place of Muslim law might be in Britain, Pearl reflects that an "ambivalent approach to 'the other' persists today when English law remains willing to take account of 'cultural practices' in certain situations, but strictly imposes uniform rules in others" (Pearl and Menski (1998) p. 53). The point is equally pertinent to female and ritual male circumcision where English law prohibits the former and allows the latter. Clearly some cultural practices are recognised and others banned. The reason for this may lie in the way the specific practice is perceived and understood by the majority and the law-makers. It might well be said that the legal system allows or disallows the cultural practices of others on the basis of its own dominant ideology. It might also be argued that a form of "selective" acceptance of cultural practices is consistent with the approach of cultural pluralism (Freeman (1998), Poulter (1998)). That is, while attempting to incorporate the beliefs and morality of others into the mainstream, we select from that "otherness" those facets that accord more readily with the majority cultural and religious norms. Despite the support that various government ministers have given to the policy of respect for and tolerance of diversity [97]—the trademark of cultural pluralism—Pearl would go even further. In his view, the critical question posed for lawyers overall remains the extent to which recognition of ethnic diversity should extend to the legal sphere. Should the dominant law and Muslim personal law, for example, be harmonised? Should recognition be accorded generally to the legal institutions of ethnic minorities? Schuz (1996) p. 151 also makes this point but, interestingly, qualifies her call for harmonisation with a demand for an exception in those cases where "religious law causes hardship which can effectively be averted by the application of the civil law". This may be the key to an acceptance of *limited cultural pluralism* and, specifically in the context of medical procedures on children, a guide to acknowledging and respecting diversity whilst still averting undesirable consequences (Poulter (1998)).

English child law balances risk against benefit and comes down firmly in favour of the individual child rather than the family, community or culture. This is evident in the case of circumcision. Male circumcision is relatively harmless, albeit, like tattooing, irreversible. The risks are minimal, the cultural and religious significance very great to a large number of people, and it is now reported as having long term protective effects. This enhances its rational basis. Just as significantly, it is not a practice belonging to the fringes of society but is almost part of the mainstream. Female circumcision is the reverse. It is harmful, not widespread, and unlikely to be practised by influential people integral to the shape and nature of our society. It is very much a fringe practice. If a risk/benefit analysis were undertaken it would totally support the current prohibitive legislation.

---

[97] Poulter (1998) lists D. Hurd, J. Patten, J. Major and M. Howard.

Legal acceptance of one but not the other is thus not a matter of cultural understanding and tolerance. It is a matter of individual child welfare judged by the standards of the majority. Community or majority norms dictate the legal and ethical responses to child health and well-being. The dominant law seeks to protect the individual child from risk, pain and suffering, and enhance health and welfare. In the context of the child's body the focus is on quality of life as judged from an *individual, medical, welfare* perspective. Consequently, we sanction the withdrawal of treatment from a severely disabled neonate, for example, rather than prolong his or her life by distressing medical intervention. Parents' wishes *per se* do not prevail when they conflict with the medical welfare of the individual child.

However, this is not always the case where the interests of parents *vis-à-vis* their child's body are religious or cultural. Not only is male circumcision lawful despite the argument that it is an invasion of the child's physical integrity, but the use of non-blood products as the first choice of treatment for Jehovah's Witness children, despite its inferior effectiveness, is agreed to by doctors and approved by the courts. This is because the concept of welfare as enacted in the Children Act 1989 encompasses the religious beliefs and practices of parents.[98] The dominant law regards the embracing of the particular beliefs of parents as part of the child's welfare—but only up to a point. And that point is reached when the adverse impact is such that the child's medical welfare, whether it be the preservation of life or the cessation of intolerable life, is at risk. Diversity is acknowledged only to the extent that it complies with the majority norms of the *individual, medical, welfare* model. The approach of the law is to select and endorse those practices which fall within the accepted norms. We allow or disallow on the basis of the dominant ideology. Only within these traditional confines has the notion of religious and cultural welfare developed. "Otherness" that falls outside of this model remains on the outside.

REFERENCES

BAINHAM, A., *Children—The New Law* (Family Law, 1990).
——, *Children: The Modern Law* (Family Law, 1993).
——, "Do Babies Have Rights?" (1997) 48 *Cambridge Law Journal* 48.
——, "Honour thy Father and thy Mother: Children's Rights and Children's Duties" in G. Douglas and L. Sebba (eds.), *Children's Rights and Traditional Values* (Aldershot, Ashgate Publishing Ltd, 1998a).
——, *Children: The Modern Law* (2nd edn, Family Law, 1998b).
BARTON, C. and DOUGLAS, G., *Law and Parenthood* (London, Butterworths, 1995).
BODI, F., "The Law Says No to Circumcision" (2000) *Q-News* 12.

---

[98] [1999] 2 FLR 678, 686. Wall J stated that the attitude of the courts to religious upbringing was clear—the issues "are relevant factors to be taken into account when applying the paramountcy of welfare test".

BRIDGE, C., "Parental Powers and the Medical Treatment of Children" in C. Bridge (ed.), *Family Law Towards the Millenium: Essays for P.M.Bromley* (London, Edinburgh and Dublin, Butterworths, 1997).

——, "Religion, Culture and Conviction—the Medical Treatment of Young Children" (1999a) 1 *Child & Family Law Quarterly* 1.

——, "Religious Beliefs and Teenage Refusal of Medical Treatment" (1999b) *Modern Law Review* 585.

CAMERON, D. W., SIMONSEN, J. N. and D'COSTA, L. J., "Female to Male Transmission of HIV Type I" (1989) 2 *The Lancet* 403.

CHRISTAKIS, D. A., HARVEY, E., ZERR, D. M., FEUDTER, C., WRIGHT, J. A. and CONNELL, F. A., "A Trade-off Analysis of Routine Newborn Circumcision" (2000) 105 *Paediatrics* 246.

FORTIN, J., "Re C (Medical Treatment)—A Baby's Right to Die" (1998) 4 *Child and Family Law Quarterly* 411.

FOX, M. and McHALE, J., "In Whose Best Interests?" (1997) 60 *Modern Law Review* 700.

FREEMAN, M., "Care After 1991" in D. Freestone (ed.), *Children and the Law—Essays in Honour of Professor H.K. Bevan* (Hull University Press, 1990).

——, "Cultural Pluralism and the Rights of the Child" in J. Eekelaar and T. Nhlapo (eds.), *The Changing Family—Family Forms and Family Law* (Oxford, Hart Publishing, 1998).

——, "The Jewish Law of Divorce" (2000) *International Family Law* 58.

GOLLAHER, D., *Circumcision: A History of the World's Most Controversial Surgery* (New York, Basic Books, 2000).

HALPERIN, D. and BAILEY, R., "Male Circumcision and HIV Infection: 10 years and Counting" (1999) 354 *The Lancet* 1813.

HUTCHINSON, J. and SMITH, A., *Ethnicity* (Oxford and New York, Oxford University Press, 1996).

JONES, J., "Concern Mounts over Female Genital Mutilation" (2000) 321 *British Medical Journal* 262.

KATZENBERG, S. and ROSENBLATT, J., "Getting the Get" (1999) *Family Law* 165.

LAVERY, R., "Routine Medical Treatment of Children" *Journal of Social Welfare Law* 375.

MASON, J. and McCALL SMITH, A., *Law and Medical Ethics* (5th edn., London, Edinburgh and Dublin, Butterworths, 1999).

McCALL SMITH, R. A., "Is Anything Left of Parental Rights?" in E. Sutherland and A. McCall Smith (eds.), *Family Rights: Family Law and Medical Advance* (Edinburgh, Edinburgh University Press, 1990).

PEARL, D. and MENSKI, W., *Muslim Family Law* (3rd edn., London, Sweet & Maxwell, 1998).

POULTER, S., *English Law and Ethnic Minority Customs* (London, Edinburgh and Dublin, Butterworths, 1986).

——, *Ethnicity, Law and Human Rights* (London, Edinburgh and Dublin, Butterworths, 1998).

RICHARDS, M., "The Ill-treatment of Children—Some Developmental Considerations" in G. Van Bueren (ed.), *Childhood Abused* (Aldershot, Ashgate, 1998).

SCHUZ, R., "Divorce and Ethnic Minorities" in M. Freeman (ed.), *Divorce: Where Next?* (Aldershot, Dartmouth, 1996).

SKEGG, P., "Consent to Medical Procedures on Minors" (1973) 36 *Modern Law Review* 380.

STARMER, K., *European Human Rights Law* (London, Legal Action Group, 1999).

SWINDELLS, H., NEAVES, A., KUSHNER, M. and SKILBECK, R., *Family Law and the Human Rights Act 1998* (Bristol, Jordans, 1999).

SZABO, R., and SHORT, R., "How Does Male Circumcision Protect Against HIV Infection?" (2000) 320 *British Medical Journal* 1592.

16

Future Bodies: Some History and Future Prospects for Human Genetic Selection

MARTIN RICHARDS*

1. INTRODUCTION

As we enter the "biotech century" (Rifkin (1998)) there are many predictions about the ways in which society may change as new biomedical technologies are introduced. A theme that runs through several of these visions of the future, and indeed has been raised in relation to some of the technologies in current use, is that we will increasingly have societies divided into those who use technologies which can reduce the burden of inherited disadvantage and provide positive genetic enhancement and those who are excluded from this by their moral or religious principles or lack of resources to access services. Silver (1998) has written of the "GenRich" and the "naturals". While the latter will continue to rely on love, and perhaps marriage, to establish partnerships within which they will conceive children by the traditional means, or maybe simply get pregnant, the GenRich will shop in the markets provided by the germinal vendors. Silver believes that within the lifetime of those already born there will be technologies which will allow the production of children with added artificial chromosomes which will carry genes that will enhance capabilities and performance.[1] The natural chromosomes of these GenRich designer children will, of course, have been screened to ensure that all deleterious gene variants have been altered or replaced. As these techniques are applied over generations there will be increasing separation of the modified gene rich from the naturals.[2] An implication is, of course, that the GenRich will be rich in all senses and will run the world, a vision with some similarities to Aldous

* I would like to thank members of the Cambridge Socio-Legal Group for their helpful comments on earlier drafts of this chapter. I am also grateful to Helen Szoke of the Victorian Infertility Treatment Authority, Jenny Blood of the Royal Women's Hospital, Melbourne and some anonymous children of AID for helpful information. As always, Jill Brown and Sally Roberts provided invaluable technical support. Alison Krauss, Union Station and the Cox Family, in various combinations, sustained me while I was writing. And a special word of thanks to Railtrack for providing many unplanned hours for reading and contemplation.

[1] Needless to say there are others who do not believe that such technology will be feasible in the foreseeable future, if ever.

[2] Silver assumes that the two groups would remain reproductively isolated. History suggests that gene flow between elites and the remainder of a population will be extensive.

Huxley's *Brave New World* (1932), but created with somewhat different reproductive techniques.

My concern in this chapter is not to attempt to predict the future, but rather to raise questions about reproductive choices. What can current reproductive behaviour and recent history tell us about reproductive fears and aspirations for the future? How are we likely to employ developing technologies that allow genetic selection? I will look at both sides of reproductive planning; what in the past has been called positive and negative eugenics[3]—the encouragement of the production of children with the most desirable characteristics and the avoidance of those with inherited disadvantage and disability. What can the history of our attempts to modify characteristics of our children tell us about possible future use of reproductive technologies?

2. THE EUGENIC PAST

Animal and plant breeding is as old as agriculture. The domestication of wild species and their "improvement" depends on the simple understanding that like, more or less, begets like. By breeding from individuals with advantageous characteristics and avoiding perpetuation of those with undesirable traits, a slow process of change began which has populated our farms and gardens with domestic breeds and strains. At the dawn of industrialisation, the process of plant and animal breeding became more self conscious and systematic. The eighteenth and nineteenth century agricultural improvers were able to increase food production to levels that not only sustained the growth of industrial cities in Europe, but provided stock and crops which European emigrants carried to North and South America, Australia and New Zealand to found a neo-Europe that has dominated the world agricultural trade to the present (Crosby (1986)). Until the twentieth century, agricultural breeding owed nothing to genetics or the science of biology. The principles remained simple and relatively effective; breed from the best and cull the worst.

Not surprisingly, it became plain to many that the same principles would apply to our own species. Such thoughts led to a nineteenth century example of a human selective breeding programme. This was the practice of human "stirpiculture"[4] instituted by John Humphrey Noyes in his Perfectionist Community at Oneida, in Upper New York State in the 1860s (Carden (1998)). By this time the community,

---

[3] Traditionally at least, eugenics is the science related to the production of fine offspring. Today, the term is often taken to have overtones of coercion, so that a distinction is drawn between, for example, past programmes for the sterilisation of those regarded as genetically unfit and current programmes for pre-natal screening, diagnosis and abortion of fetuses carrying genetic conditions. However, not all past programmes which aimed to produce "fitter" children and which were described as eugenic were compulsory, and, some would question the supposed voluntary character of some contemporary pre-natal programmes (see Paul (1997); Caplan (2000)).

[4] According to the Oxford English Dictionary, "The production of pure races or stocks by careful breeding".

which had been founded in 1848, was highly successful economically with almost 300 members. Between 1869 and 1879 fifty-eight children were born at Oneida. Thirteen were accidental conceptions but the remainder were born as part of the stirpiculture programme (Karp (1982)).

After he received a licence from Yale University, Noyes became an itinerant preacher whose teaching was founded on the doctrine of perfectionism, believing that the Second Coming had taken place at the time of the destruction of Jerusalem. Noyes took the biblical injunction to "love thy neighbour" more literally than most.[5] He set up a community based on a system of "complex marriage" or, as described by a contemporary, "regulated promiscuity, beginning at earliest puberty. [Using] a method of his own invention . . . [he] separated the amative from the propagative functions. By this community of possession and of person he sought to root selfishness forever from the hearts of his disciples" (McGee (1891) p. 320).

In the early years of the community births were almost completely avoided, as was the usual pattern in nineteenth and twentieth century Utopian communities (Kanter (1972)). But, as the community became more economically secure through their manufacturing activities, Noyes set up his programme of "scientific propagation", based on the genealogy of Abraham and the ideas of Charles Darwin and Frances Galton. A committee headed by Noyes selected individuals for breeding on the basis of their genealogies, medical histories, intellect and physique. An essential condition was that "mutual attraction . . . must exist to at least a slight degree between persons mated" and, not surprisingly, a significant proportion of the children were fathered by Noyes himself.[6] Children were brought up co-operatively, much as in the children's houses of the early Kibbutzim. Their progress was carefully monitored and reports published by the community and in scientific journals. Mortality was lower than the national average and heights and weights of the children were superior to those of Boston school children. In young adulthood the boys were described as "tall—several over six feet—broad shouldered and finely proportioned; the girls . . . robust and well-built" (McGee (1891) p. 324) and despite the fact that most of their fathers had been farmers and mechanics, and their mothers employed in manual labour, most went into business working as clerks, foremen etc. and others into the

---

[5] Carden (1998) explains Noyes' theological argument for his position. Matthew's gospel (20:30) states that "in the resurrection they neither marry, nor are given in marriage". This was usually interpreted to mean that there was no sex beyond resurrection. However, Noyes took the view that sexual relationships exist in heaven as on earth. He interpreted Matthew's gospel to imply that there would be no monogamous marriage after death. He argued that monogamy makes men and women unable to practise two principles of Christianity, loving God and loving their neighbours. "Exclusive attachment to a spouse turns attention away from God and one's fellow men. It is preferable for a man (or woman) to love everyone equally and to give his (or her) greatest love to God. If there are sexual relations in heaven (or in the perfectionist Utopia on earth), then the ideal state is one in which all men are viewed as married to all women". Hence Oneida's system of "complex marriage" (Noyes (1847)).

[6] Noyes had a strong belief in the superiority of his family line. He fathered ten stirpicults (of which one was stillborn) and his eldest son (born before Oneida was founded) fathered a further three (Carden (1998)).

professions. McGee concludes his assessment of the experiment by saying that the results seem to indicate that "our race would doubtless be greatly benefited by more attention to the laws of breeding" (p. 329). The programme at Oneida ended when the community began to dissolve following a dispute over the succession of their leader. It became a joint stock company which continues to the present day as a major manufacturer of tableware.

As mentioned already, the Oneida selective breeding experiment was in part inspired by Charles Darwin and Frances Galton (1865). Darwin[7] was quite unequivocal in his concerns about unselective human breeding. He set out his argument in *The Descent of Man* (1871):

> "With savages, the weak in body or mind are soon eliminated, and those that survive commonly exhibit a vigorous state of health. We civilised men, on the other hand, do our utmost to check the process of elimination, we build asylums for the imbecile, the maimed and the sick; we institute poor-laws; and our medical men exert their utmost skill to save the life of everyone to the last moment. There is reason to believe that vaccination has preserved those who from a weak constitution would formerly have succumbed to smallpox. Thus the weak members of civilised societies propagate their kind. No-one who has attended to the breeding of domestic animals will doubt that this must be highly injurious to the race of man. It is surprising how soon a want of care, or care wrongly directed, leads to the degeneration of a domestic race; but excepting in the case of man himself, hardly anyone is so ignorant as to allow his worst animals to breed" (pp. 133–4).

But despite such arguments there was no widespread movement for planned selective breeding.[8] The Oneida experiment seems to have been unique until German Rossenhygiene which included the Lebensborn programme which encouraged racially "pure" women to bear the children of SS officers (Procter (1988)). Thus it would seem that only under rare and rather special social or political conditions have people willingly submitted to planned programmes of selective breeding. However, in a broader sense, concerns about unregulated and unselective breeding did lead to the establishment of eugenic programmes in most parts of the industrialised world in the first half of the twentieth century. These programmes did not set up selective breeding programmes as such (apart from in Germany) but they aimed to "improve the human stock" by encouraging childbearing by the fit (positive eugenics) and discouraging or preventing it by the unfit (negative eugenics). The latter included sterilisation of those deemed unfit in a number of countries including the USA, Canada, Sweden and Switzerland (Kevles (1985)), their detention in institutions in Britain (Mazumdar (1992); Thom and Jennings (1996)) and "euthanasia" in Germany (Burleigh (1994)). Positive eugenic programmes were very wide-ranging from the baby shows and "fitness" competitions for couples at the county shows of rural USA, through financial

---

[7] See Paul (forthcoming) for a discussion of Darwin and eugenics.

[8] Darwin himself cannot be regarded as an eugenicist. He supported charity and welfare for those in need and did not directly advocate controls on human breeding. However, his work was often influential for those who did advocate eugenic practices and policies.

incentives for those groups deemed to be superior to have larger families, to pre-marital couple counselling such as was offered as part of the Peckham experiment in South London.

In many countries, though not of course in Germany, eugenic policies and pro-grammes began to lose support in the 1930s. Reasons for this were complex but included a growing realisation that in many cases there was little or no evidence that the characteristics used to define the "fit" or "unfit" were strongly heritable. Like the agriculturists of earlier centuries, proponents of eugenics had simply assumed (or hoped or feared) that the characteristics of interest to them were inherited. Often they attempted to make their case by describing family clusters of desirable or undesirable traits. For example, in Britain, the Eugenics Society (1909) used the example of the interlinked "pedigrees" of the Wedgewood-Darwin-Galton families (Figure 1) which had been conveniently modified to omit children who had been institutionalised because of limited abilities (Resta (1995)).[9] By the 1930s, scientific evidence about inheritance had weakened the eugenicists' case. But contrary to popular belief, knowledge of the horrors of Nazi eugenics was not sufficient to end all eugenic programmes elsewhere and, for instance, sterilisation programmes persisted in Canada, Sweden and Switzerland at least until the 1960s.

3. CONTEMPORARY CLINICAL PRACTICE

A difference between present clinical practice and that of the heyday of eugenics is that we now have reliable diagnostic and predictive tests for many genetic single gene diseases which can be used for pre-natal screening and diagnosis. Throughout the industrialised world there are now screening and diagnostic pro-grammes based on ideologies of individual choice and public health which aim to diagnose serious fetal problems and offer parents the possibility of termination of pregnancy. There are other procedures available to those who wish to avoid births of children with genetic conditions but who find the possibility of termination unacceptable. A "high tech" solution involving *in vitro* fertilisation is now possi-ble for a few genetic diseases (pre-implantation genetic diagnosis). This involves removing cells for a genetic test from an early embryo which has been produced *in vitro* and then only implanting embryos found not to carry the relevant genetic disease. Costs are high and success rates for pregnancies following implantation are low and, not surprisingly, few such procedures are currently carried out in Britain (Lavery et al. (1999)). A "low tech" solution adopted by some commun-ities whose members carry a relatively high frequency of a recessively inherited dis-order is to use genetic carrier detection testing with young people and then for matchmakers to avoid arranging marriage between those shown to be carriers of

---

[9] Despite the fictionalised nature of this pedigree and the simplistic way in which abilities were clas-sified, this pedigree was used as evidence in a scientific paper in *The Lancet* in 1996 on the inheritance of mental abilities.

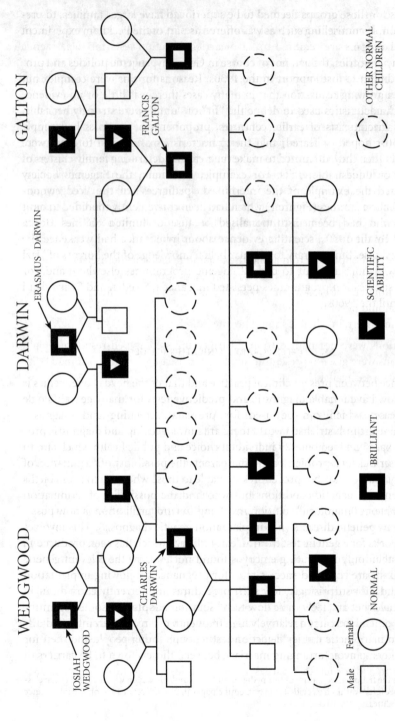

Figure 16.1 Inheritance of ability★

★ This chart showing the inheritance ability in the Wedgwood, Darwin and Galton families was originally published by the Eugenic Society in 1909. The names of some prominent individuals were added by Resta (1995) in which he provides evidence of how the pedigrees had been modified to avoid mention of members of the families with limited abilities. It will not escape the notice of readers that no women were regarded as having scientific ability or being brilliant the disease. Such programmes to avoid births of children with Tay Sachs disease are used by some Orthodox Jewish Communities in the USA. In Cyprus, Greek Orthodox couples are required to have carrier detection tests for thalassaemia before their weddings and, where both are carriers, pre-natal testing with the expectation of termination is encouraged. This programme has eliminated births of children with thalassaemia.

When used for serious medical problems, there is wide public support for pro-grammes for pre-natal screening, diagnosis and abortion. In a postal survey we carried out in 1995 with some 113 members of Women's Institute branches throughout the United Kingdom and seventy-three social science university stu-dents, we included a question about screening in pregnancy: "There are now many conditions in a baby that can be tested for in pregnancy. When a particular condi-tion is identified through testing, the mother is told and she is offered the possi-bility of an abortion. When do you think that testing should be offered for the following conditions?" Five response options were provided:

(a) Everyone should be told about the test and decide for themselves.
(b) It should be offered when doctors think it is appropriate.
(c) It should be offered when specifically requested by a mother.
(d) It should never be offered.
(e) I am uncertain when it should be offered.

Conditions were not named to avoid triggering stereotyped responses. Eight descriptions were given representing single gene diseases for which pre-natal dia-gnosis tests were available:

(i) For a foetal disorder of the nervous system which leads to death in the first two years of life [Tay Sachs disease].
(ii) For a disorder that needs treatment on a daily basis and reduces life expectancy to about 25 years [cystic fibrosis].
(iii) For a disorder which produces very small stature (a dwarf) [Achondro-plasia].
(iv) For a disorder that causes a loss of mind and control over the body in the 40s or 50s and death a few years later, but a normal and healthy life until this point [Huntington's disease].
(v) For a disorder which develops in middle age but with prompt treatment, including surgery, 60 per cent of those affected survive for at least 5 years [inherited breast cancer].
(vi) For a disorder which causes mental handicap so that education in a spe-cial school is likely to be necessary [Fragile X disease].
(vii) For a cancer that develops in middle age that can be treated successfully in many cases if it is diagnosed early enough [inherited breast and some other cancers].
(viii) For a disorder that causes progressive loss of control over muscular movement from early to mid-childhood and death by early adulthood [Duchenne muscular dystrophy].

In the square brackets I have added the name of the condition being described in each case but this information was not given in the survey questionnaire.[10] The results are presented in Table 16.1.

The first point to make about the results is the close similarity between the views of the women in the Women's Institute sample (average age 54 and slightly higher educational background than the general population) and the students (average age 19, of above average educational background) suggesting that there are rather stable views on these issues in the population. There was a much higher support for general availability of tests for diseases that develop in children and are fatal early in life (Tay Sach's disease, cystic fibrosis and Duchenne muscular dystrophy) and, interestingly, a non-fatal condition causing mental handicap (Fragile X disease) was viewed in a very similar way. Fewer respondents felt that tests for adult onset diseases (breast cancer, Huntington's disease) should be offered to everyone and a significant minority felt that such tests should never be offered. Perhaps rather surprisingly, more people thought that tests for achondroplasia should be offered to everyone than tests for potentially fatal adult onset diseases.

Rather simpler questions based on these were asked in the 1998 British Social Attitudes Survey (Stratford, Marteau and Bobrow (1999)). These concerned a "child . . . very likely to be born with a serious *mental* disability and never able to lead an independent life; a child with a serious *physical* disability not able to live independently; a child who was likely to be born with a condition that meant it would live in *good health* but die in its twenties or thirties, and a child who would be healthy but never grow taller than an eight year old". Respondents were asked whether or not they thought it right for women to have a legal abortion in each of these situations (Table 16.2).

Table 16.1: Percentage responses to questions on pre-natal screening*

	(a) Everyone told		(b) Doctors decide		(c) On request		(d) Never offered		(e) Uncertain	
Tay Sachs disease	73	82	22	11	3	6	0	0	2	1
Cystic fibrosis	66	67	21	21	6	7	4	0	4	1
Achondroplasia	59	44	21	27	10	8	14	14	6	7
Huntington's disease	35	34	29	23	8	16	16	15	12	11
Cancer	32	32	29	25	7	15	22	18	9	10
Fragile x disease	68	59	22	15	7	11	2	12	1	3
Breast cancer	39	37	29	25	3	11	22	19	7	8
Duchenne muscular dystrophy	71	62	21	18	5	11	0	4	4	4

* The first figure under each condition represents the percentage of women responding from the Women's Institute sample (N=113) and the second figure is from a survey of female and male first year social science students at an English University (N=73) using the same question (Richards and Ponder (1998)).

[10] In one of the questions related to breast cancer the word cancer was used. In fact results are very similar whether or not the word is used.

Table 16.2: British Social Attitudes Survey 1998*

	Serious mental disability	Serious physical disability	Healthy but dies in 20s or 30s	Healthy but height of an 8 year old
Never right	8	10	35	48
Sometimes right	39	45	42	32
Always right	49	41	18	16
Don't know	3	3	4	4

Data from Stratford, Marteau and Bobrow (1999).

* Percentages of respondents saying it would be right or not for a woman to have a legal abortion in each situation.

The results are broadly similar to our own survey, with a large majority saying it was at least sometimes right for women to have an abortion if a child was likely to have a serious mental or physical condition but less than a half believing this in the case of a child with short stature.

Pre-natal diagnosis programmes have become such a standard part of medical practice that in the USA courts have granted damages for "wrongful birth" when, for example, a child was born with Down's Syndrome after a doctor had failed to advise the mother to have an amniocentesis (Rifkin (1998)).

While public opinion supports the use of technology to avoid births of children with serious disorders, there are very different attitudes towards sex selection. Our own survey suggested that more than 90 per cent of respondents in each of the groups did not think pre-natal sex testing and abortion should be made available to couples. Even if a technique were to become available which allowed sex selection without the use of abortion, still more than 60 per cent of respondents were against this. So, there would seem to be strong public opposition to the use of reproductive technologies for the selection of children except when serious disease may be involved. However, we should note that there are cultural differences and that, for example, sex selection is widely practiced in India (Benagiano and Bianchi (1999)). A number of countries, including the United Kingdom, effectively ban sex selection. However, arguments have been put forward against this (see e.g. Savulescu and Dahl (2000)). It has been argued that, if abortion for maternal social reasons is permitted, it is inconsistent not to permit sex selection. Further, it is suggested that the objection that its availability might disturb the sex ratio would not hold in the United Kingdom or USA as demand will be largely from those wishing to balance their families (see Statham et al. (1993); Liu and Rose (1995)). Others have argued for a reproductive right or a procreative autonomy that couples should be able to decide what child to have, or even that there is a duty for parents to produce the "best" child they can, free from disease, and socially appropriate (which in some situations might include their sex) (Robertson (1996)).

The British Social Attitudes Survey 1998 (Stratford, Marteau and Bobrow (1999)) included a series of hypothetical questions about genetic engineering. A question asked, "Suppose it was discovered that a person's genes could be changed. Do you think this should be allowed or not allowed to reduce a person's chance of getting heart disease or breast cancer?" 68 per cent of respondents thought this definitely should or probably should be allowed for heart disease and 72 per cent for breast cancer. But support was very limited for what many think of as enhancement. Around 20 per cent thought that changing genes to make a person taller or shorter, more intelligent, straight rather than gay or lesbian should definitely or probably be allowed. This rose to around 50 per cent for making someone less aggressive or violent or average weight rather than very overweight, perhaps reflecting current cultural attitudes. But, as with any hypothetical questions about imagined technologies that do not exist, we should interpret these results cautiously. None of these things are possible, or likely to be possible, in the near future. Were any techniques of this kind ever to be developed, their use might reflect different values from those that may inform contemporary answers to hypothetical questions.

On the basis of the research I have discussed, I think we can make some generalisations about the current use of technologies which can prevent the birth of children with serious disorders. These technologies are acceptable and they are used widely by a majority. But where the issue is serious disease that develops in adulthood, rather than affecting a child, there is much less support, and almost none at all for a social selection such as the sex of a child. There is also little support for the hypothetical use of imagined possibilities to avoid the birth of children who might be overweight or undersized or for psychological attributes such as intelligence or aggressiveness. Of course, the only methods we have available at present to avoid births of affected children are pre-natal diagnosis and abortion, pre-implantation diagnosis or avoiding having children with particular partners known to be carriers of a genetic condition. People might feel differently about using technology to avoid less serious conditions or for enhancement if that technology was more benign than those available at present. Pre-natal diagnosis and abortion are not lightly undertaken and pre-implantation diagnosis is too complex (and expensive) and uncertain in its outcome to attract wide use. Less invasive technologies that avoid the necessity of abortion, perhaps involving the modification of gametes before fertilisation, might be more acceptable for less serious conditions (assuming of course that it proves possible to develop such technologies).

While most of the public do not like the hypothetical idea of genetic enhancement for non-serious conditions, it is taken for granted that we may change some characteristics of ourselves or our children once they are born (Parens (1998)). Children are subjected to all sorts of educational regimes to enhance their abilities and form their characters; their appearance is changed through cosmetic surgery or orthodontic work, or height increased through the use of growth hormones (Lantos, Siegler and Cuttler (1989)). But, as I want to argue, what many think appropriate to do after birth, may be rather different from what they are prepared to do before it—at least if that involves using genes from strangers.

4. A RETURN TO SELECTIVE BREEDING?

Are we heading for a world of the GenRich and the naturals? Certainly, there seems to be a belief amongst some biomedical scientists and technicians that the means will be available to create such a brave new world. For example, the men who brought us Dolly, in their modestly entitled book, *The Second Creation*,[11] (Wilmut, Campbell and Tudge (2000)) state that this will soon be possible: "In the wake of the research that has produced Megan, Morag, Dolly and Polly, we can look forward to an age in which the understanding of life's mechanism will be virtually total; at least, the principal systems will be understood molecule by molecule. From this total understanding will come—if we choose—control" (p. 288).[12] While these authors suggest that we have choices about how we may control our reproductive future, other biologists believe that this is constrained by our biology itself.

Arguing from the wilder shores of evolutionary psychology, Robin Baker (1999) states that "we are programmed to be attracted to features in a potential mate that indicate health, fertility and just generally good genes, . . . throughout the natural world, mate choice is and always has been a eugenic process" (p. 245). He asserts that eugenics is a biological imperative and that our "ancient urges" arising from our "genetic programming" will lead us to adopt reproductive technology which allows us to produce children with enhanced genetic potential. Others see this happening already in the markets for human eggs and sperm that exist in the USA (Silver (1998)). In Britain and many other countries the law prevents the buying and selling of eggs and sperm, or at least limits payments to nominal fees and/or the payment of expenses (Daniels (2000); see also Rachel Cook (chapter 12). But not so in the USA; there the free market reigns.[13] Are we already witnessing selective breeding through couples buying in eggs or sperm from carefully selected

---

[11] First time round the project involved all species, not just sheep, and included a world for them to inhabit. All that was achieved in six days without the assistance of government grants or venture capital. Dolly took much longer despite the fact that Roslyn technocrats had sheep somatic cells and ova as starting points and a ewe to gestate the resulting embryo.

[12] We should note that Wilmut, Campbell and Tudge argue against reproductive human cloning; "it would be more of a stunt, altogether too chancy". "As a medical procedure, superfluous and, in general repugnant". "A rather ugly diversion". But as others have commented, given these authors' interest in developing the potentially lucrative industry based on animal cloning and the evident public dislike of the idea of human cloning, they would say that, wouldn't they?

[13] There have been attempts in the USA to control the cost of eggs. The Ethics Committee of the American Society for Reproductive Medicine suggests that payments to egg producers "should reflect the time, inconvenience, and physical demands associated with the process" and should "minimise the possibility of undue inducement of donors and the suggestion that payment is for oocytes themselves". In practice, they recommend capping payments at US$5,000 which has been the market norm for the last couple of years. The ceiling for "expenses" payment to egg producers in the United Kingdom is £15 (Larkin (2000)).

individuals? Those who believe a future of the GenRich and naturals is already upon us make much of cases in the USA where tens of thousands of dollars are said to have been paid for eggs produced by beautiful young women who achieve out-standing grades at Ivy League universities (Mead (1999)). However, the realities of the trade in eggs and sperm that exists in the USA is rather different from this image. First, gametes are bought by infertile couples who typically have exhausted all possible ways of producing a child with their own gametes before they consider using eggs or sperm from others. And, as I will argue, selection of an egg or sperm provider has more to do with finding someone with whom the commissioning parents can feel a social and psychological affinity, and someone whose gametes may produce a child that in physical appearance could be their own, than any attempt to produce a "designer" baby.

Creating Families, Inc. is perhaps typical of American companies involved in what has been called germinal vending—the selling of human eggs and sperm. Creating Families, Inc. offers eggs for sale and the services of "surrogate" or birth mothers (www.eggdonorfertilitybank.com). Interestingly, like others in this trade, they describe women whose eggs are offered for sale as egg "donors" (see Price (1995)). Indeed, these companies present the women providing eggs as being altruistic and simply interested in helping infertile couples. This is how the company describes the profile of their typical "donor":

> "There is a large concentration of wonderful and accomplished young women in Southern California, who are willing and able to share their fertility with others. Almost all of the donors who have participated in the program have reported having an excel-lent experience which has been deeply moving and rewarding for them. Although the standards for the program are high, there are numerous donors on file. The number of candidates varies between 150–200 women at any given time, all of whom are ready and available to donate. Typically a couple may choose between 3–12 donors who would be suitably and closely matched. A typical donor would be between 21–32 years of age, have an excellent health history and a very personal, humanitarian reason for wanting to donate. She would have some years of schooling or master's degree, a career, and would range from attractive to strikingly beautiful" (www.eggdonorfertilitybank.com).

Creating Families, Inc. allows the potential buyer to define a profile of the kind of woman from whom they are interested in buying eggs. The characteristics that may be specified are age, race, ethnic ancestry, height, weight, physical build, hair colour, texture of hair, eye colour, complexion, tanning ability, hand co-ordination, vision, hearing, blood type, education (high school grade point average, college grade aver-age) and IQ score, and photographs are offered.

Information provided by sperm banks is generally similar to that for women but perhaps with a little more emphasis on medical tests and history. The Sperm Bank of California (www.thespermbankofca.org) offers a photo-matching service. The buyer provides photographs and the company will match these with those of a sperm producer. "Donor narratives" are also available which describe such things as their hobbies, languages spoken, athletic skill and goals and ambitions in life. Providers may state whether or not they want contact with children. Most seem to and give their reasons: "If it is important for the offspring to know me or contact me later in their lives, I would want them to have this possibility". "Because I don't have anything to hide I want the child to know who I am". They also answer the question "Why do you want to be a sperm donor?" Answers vary. "Because I think that this is one way to help those unfortunate couples that have problems with fertility". "Curiosity about the procedure, experience, fodder for cocktail party conversation, money. The latter is most important because my current non-profit work pays me nothing". The men can post messages to their customers, "You are getting very honest and ethical sperm. I lead a very principled life off the beaten track". "Love the child and be honest with him/her". (All these quotations are taken from information provided at www.thespermbankofca.org.)

As yet, we lack good studies of the buyers, so my arguments have to be indirect. Media stories repeat the theme that what couples are concerned with is finding a compatible and similar genetic parent for their children. The "bond" with the egg provider is seen as being important and some couples feel they want to meet donors and maintain some sort of relationship with them. Some companies offer "matchmakers" who are used to ensure a psychological fit between an egg producer and a couple. There is certainly an interest in excluding inherited disease but that, of course, these infertile couples have in common with couples reproducing in the old fashioned way. Strongly supportive of this view of the buying couples is the interesting fact that companies offering the services of a birth mother (women who will gestate a couple's embryo but do not sell their eggs) provide very similar profiles for couples to choose birth mothers and women offering eggs for sale. So, at least in the situation of choosing a birth mother, the issue cannot be a genetic one. However, while couples may not be seeking eggs with eugenic thoughts in mind, it has been suggested that some genetic "upgrading" may occur. An administrator of a Beverly Hills company is quoted as saying "It's like shopping. If you have the option between a Volkswagen and a Mercedes, you'll select the Mercedes" (Mead (1999) p. 62).

There is a point that should be made about inheritance. Some arguments seem to assume that couples chose the profile of their egg/sperm provider with the expectation that their children will closely resemble that person. Robin Baker (1999) in the book mentioned earlier describes a scene from a future "reproduction restaurant". A young man who is beginning to make his mark as a tennis champion is being encouraged by his mother to choose an egg provider for his child (whom his mother will gestate). He himself had been conceived by sperm bought from a tennis champion and in the story it is suggested that his main rivals on the tennis circuit have turned out to be his half-brothers. It is an implausible scenario; the real chances of a mother inseminated with sperm from a tennis champion producing a child who will succeed on the world circuit is very small indeed. Selective breeding is a long, slow process and, as all parents know, despite the shared genetic variation and all the shared environmental influences, children are often very unlike one another, or their parents. It is the old story of George Bernard Shaw and the actress. She was propositioning him and trying to persuade him to have a child with her. "With your brains and my looks, what a wonderful child we could have". Shaw made the obvious reply that the child might have his looks and her brains.

We have very strong evidence that most couples want to have their own children, and "own" means those they conceive with their own gametes. We know, for example, that couples who carry serious genetic disorders are much more interested in the reproductive options that allow them to have a child without the condition but using their own gametes than either adoption or gamete donation (Snowdon and Green (1997)). The same is true for infertile couples; only when all such options have been exhausted do they consider using gametes from others or adoption.

Haimes (1988) has commented on the way in which the institution of adoption has been viewed with unease, and has discussed the similarities it shares with assisted reproductive techniques that depend on the use of others' sperm or eggs in a society where the genetic relationship is often taken to be at the core of kinship structure. However, there is one major difference between adoption and conception using gametes from others. In Britain, it is usual practice for parents to tell adoptive children of their origins and they will generally provide at least some anonymised details of the birth parents. Increasingly adoption is becoming "open", where the child maintains some link with the birth mother, and sometimes the father. This contrasts sharply with the usual practice for children born of sperm or eggs from others. Here secrecy is the norm. Indeed parents are more likely to tell others in the family about their child's origin than inform the child directly (Snowden and Mitchell (1983); Feast and Brasse (2000)).[14]

It would seem that practices about telling children and the relationship with providers of eggs and sperm are governed by an ideology of a two-parent nuclear family. Parents either deny the involvement of others in the creation of their children or they incorporate the gamete providers in what Marilyn Strathern (1992) has called the "twentieth century extended family". In the first case parents (and indeed their physicians) may aim to get a good match for a gamete provider so, if possible, the child will look like a plausible genetic child of the parents. But, once the child is conceived, the gamete provider is written out of the family history.[15] Alternatively, the gamete provider becomes part of the family. The archetypal extended family here is Tony Barlow and Barrie Drewitt and their children Aspen

[14] There is growing debate about whether or not children should be told. At present, virtually all the follow up studies of *in vitro* fertilisation (e.g. Van Balen (1998); Golombok et al. (1996); Gibson et al. (2000)) are based on families where children are unaware of their origins. In 1993, the Donor Insemination Network was set up to support those who wanted to tell their children about their origins. It has about 300 members. There is a study of 83 DI Network parents who had told or intended to tell their children about their origins (Hunter, Salter-Ling and Glover (2000)).

[15] In the world of "no questions asked" DNA paternity testing available on the web (most commonly from companies in the USA and Australia) family histories may receive later additions. In the pre-regulation days of artificial insemination by donor in the United Kingdom, it was not unusual for a clinic repeatedly to use the same man for sperm donation. Some men are reported to have fathered several hundred children. In one such situation a group of adults wishing to trace their origins established that their conception took place in the same clinic around the same time. DNA testing established they shared the same genetic father and the genetic half-siblings are now in contact.

and Saffron (Hibbs (2000)). This gay couple then living in Essex bought eggs from Tracie McCune, a married woman in California. These eggs were fertilised *in vitro* with sperm from both the men. They then commissioned a birth mother and the twins were born in California. Under English law this woman, Rosalind Bellamy, would be the mother. However, the twins' birth certificate mentions neither of the women but (as decreed by a US Supreme Court judge) has the two men as "parent one" and "parent two". So in the USA the twins have two (male) legal parents. But in the United Kingdom this is not possible, nor can these men make a joint adoption application as that would require a marriage, but the Home Secretary granted the twins leave to remain indefinitely in the United Kingdom.[16] Once home the couple had their daughters christened and to cement the social relationship with the egg provider, Tracie McCune became a godmother and her husband a godfather. The birth mother was not involved in the proceedings—it is rumoured that she had fallen out with the couple over the matter of her fee (*The Times*, 19 July 2000).

5. CONCLUSIONS

Neither the evidence from public attitudes, nor that from the current practice of assisted reproductive techniques, suggests that there is likely to be any great rush for genetic enhancement of children.[17] It seems that our overwhelming desire is, if at all possible, to have children conceived with our own gametes.[18] If infertility prevents that and gametes from others are used, it seems that a concept rather like that of the child of the marriage prevails. Either the gamete provider becomes a member of the family or they are simply painted out of the picture leaving the child, and others, to presume that conception occurred by the usual route. Those offering reproductive services have assisted in building the fiction, as does English law. For instance, it used to be rather general practice in AID clinics to mix donor sperm and that from the (infertile) husband so that the improbable could always be imagined.

As we have seen, there is wide acceptance of the use of pre-natal screening and diagnosis but the evidence suggests that strong acceptance is restricted to serious early onset disease. Current attitudes to the use of sex selection do not suggest that

---

[16] They were also told by the Home Office that there would be no guarantee if they had any more children born abroad they would be allowed to join the family. Perhaps, not surprisingly, they have moved to the USA where a birth mother is expecting triplets conceived once again with their sperm and Tracie McCune's eggs.

[17] In this chapter I have not attempted to discuss the ethics of genetic enhancement. But some bioethicists have not been slow in springing to its defence. In the case of genetic enhancement and germline modification this has been attempted by the development of a concept of reproductive rights which claim that parents are morally obliged to produce the "best" children possible provided that this does not lead to harm to others (Robertson (1996)). However, this line of argument does not include possible future harm as such concerns are "too speculative" to justify denial of the use of germline interventions for treatment or for "quality control" of immediate offspring (Cohen (2000)).

[18] Indeed, if sociobiologists and evolutionary psychologists are to be believed, it is unclear why anybody would want to rear children conceived with gametes from others.

genetic enhancement for non-disease characteristics would, at least at present, receive wide support. Even with very serious medical conditions there seem to be limits. Our results quoted earlier suggest that almost a fifth of those asked did not think that pre-natal tests for adult onset diseases like breast cancer or Huntington's disease should be used. Pre-natal testing for Huntington's disease has been on offer for about a decade. What is very striking is that such tests are very seldom used by those at risk of having an affected child, who are well aware of the disease and its consequences (Haden (2000)). Perhaps this is another example of the importance some people may attach to genetic identity. Huntington's disease, which is a fatal degenerative condition usually developing in middle age, is caused by a gene mutation which almost inevitably leads to the development of the disease. It is passed on to, on average, half the children of someone who carries the mutation and who themselves will, in time, develop it. When a child inherits the gene mutation, he or she is in exactly the same genetic situation as the parent from whom the mutation was inherited. Thus, using pre-natal testing and aborting an affected fetus involves destroying a fetus that, as far as the gene associated with Huntington's disease is concerned, is identical with one of the parents. That would seem to be a step too far for most parents in affected families.

Of course, attitudes to genetic enhancement may change in the future. The temptation to produce a dynasty of the GenRich may prove to be too much, assuming of course that technologies to do this become available. Are we really going to be able to manipulate genes in the next few decades in the way that authors like Lee Silver suggest? Manipulating the genes associated with the rare Mendelian conditions such as cystic fibrosis, Huntington's disease or the inherited form of breast cancer is proving much more difficult than many scientists expected a few years ago. Enhancement of characteristics such as intelligence and personality present very different problems and may always be beyond our reach. These attributes are the product of highly complex developmental systems in which no single gene plays more than a minimal part in creating individual differences. There are no gene variants strongly associated with high intelligence or physical attractiveness. Very many weak gene variants interacting with each other and a host of environmental factors are involved. Such developmental systems are full of redundancy, there are different routes to the same ends (see Keller (2000)). Thus, it is likely to prove very difficult, if not impossible, even if the role of many specific genes are known, to intervene to produce specific developmental outcomes by genetic manipulation. Too often the world of genetic engineering has been characterised by over-confident and unrealistic statements about what may be achieved in altering human characteristics.[19] But I suggest that we can be

[19] Why has over-optimism about future capabilities been so prominent in this field? Some technological developments, such as the technique for sequencing DNA, have been unexpectedly fast. But the potential pay-offs of these technologies in terms of treating human diseases by genetic manipulation have almost entirely remained beyond our grasp, despite the confident predictions. Those predictions may be influenced by needs to justify research programmes and grants or to enhance share prices of biotech companies, while the failures to deliver may also reflect a tendency to underestimate the complexity and open-endedness of biological systems in a climate that favours genetic determinism.

confident that genetic enhancement of complex characteristics, such as intelligence or facial appearance, are beyond our capability for the foreseeable future. We should be grateful for this, because it gives us plenty of time to consider how we may use techniques when—or indeed if—they ever arrive. We could, given time, change human characteristics by selective breeding but as we have seen that has very seldom proved acceptable. Carefully selected and arranged matings would be required over many generations to bring about significant change. That seems an even more remote possibility than the employment of an, as yet, unimagined quick fix technique of genetic manipulation.

REFERENCES

BAKER, R., *Sex in the Future. Ancient Urges Meet Future Technology* (London, Macmillan, 1999).

BENAGIANO, G. and BIANCHI, P., "Sex Preselection: an Aid to Couples or a Threat to Humanity?" (1999) 14 *Human Reproduction* 868.

BURLEIGH, M., *Death and Deliverance: "Euthanasia" in Germany c.1900–1945* (Cambridge, Cambridge University Press, 1994).

CAPLAN, A. L., "What's Morally Wrong with Eugenics?" in P.R. Sloan (ed.), *Controlling our Destinies* (Notre Dame, University of Notre Dame Press, 2000).

CARDEN, M. L., *Oneida: Utopian Community to Modern Corporation* (Syracuse, Syracuse University Press, 1998).

COHEN, C. B., "Germline Interventions, the Right to Reproduce, and Harm to Future Generations", paper presented at the Fifth World Congress of Bioethics, London, 21–24 September 2000.

CROSBY, A. W., *Ecological Imperialism. The Biological Expansion of Europe, 900–1900* (Cambridge, Cambridge University Press, 1986).

DANIELS, K. R., "To Give or Sell Human Gametes—the Interplay Between Pragmatics, Policy and Ethics" (2000) 26 *Journal of Medical Ethics* 206.

DARWIN, C., *The Descent of Man* (London, John Murray, 1871).

FEAST, J. and BRASSE, G., "Embryological Secrecy Syndrome" (2000) *Family Law* 897.

GALTON, F., "Heredity Talent and Character" (1865) 12 *Macmiullan's Magazine* 157 and 318.

GIBSON, F., UNGEREN, J. A., McMAHON, C. A., LESLIE, G. I. and SAUNDERS, D. M., "The Mother-Child Relationship Following in vitro Fertilization (IVF)" (2000) 41 *Journal of Child Psychology and Psychiatry* 1015.

GOLOMBOK, S., BREWAYS, A., COOK, R., GIAVAZZI, M. T., GUERRA, D., MANTOVANI, A., VAN HALL, E., CROSIGNANI, P. G. and DEXEUS, S., "The European Study of Assisted Reproduction Families" (1996) 11 *Human Reproduction* 2324.

HADEN, M. R., "Predictive Testing for Huntington's Disease: the Calm After the Storm" (2000) 356 *The Lancet* 1944.

HAIMES, E., " 'Secrecy': What Can Artificial Reproduction learn from Adoption?" (1988) 2 *Int J Law and the Family* 46.

HIBBS, M., "Surrogacy—Who Will be Left Holding the Baby?" (2000) *Family Law* 736.

HUNTER, M., SALTER-LING, N. and GLOVER, L., "Donor Insemination: Telling Children about their Origins" (2000) 5 *Psychiatry Review* 157.

HUXLEY, A., *Brave New World* (London, Chatto and Windus, 1932).

KANTER, R. M., *Commitment and Community: Communes and Utopias in Sociological Perspective* (Cambridge, Mass., Harvard University Press, 1972).

KARP, L. E., "Past Perfect: John Humphrey Noyes, Stirpiculture and the Oneida Community. Part II" (1982) 12 *American Journal of Medical Genetics* 127.

KELLER, E. F., *The Century of the Gene* (Cambridge, Mass., Harvard University Press, 2000).

KEVLES, D. J., *In the Name of Eugenics* (New York, Knopf, 1985).

LANTOS, J., SIEGLER, M. and CUTTLER, L., "Ethical Issues in Growth Hormone Therapy" (1989) 261 *Journal of American Medication Associations* 1020.

LARKIN, M., "Curb Costs of Egg Donation Urges US Specialists" (2000) 356 *The Lancet* 569.

LAVERY, S. A., AURELL, R., TURNER, C., TAYLOR, D. M. and WINSTON, R. M., "An Analysis of the Demand and Cost of Preimplantation Genetic Diagnosis in the United Kingdom" (1999) 19 *Prenatal Diagnosis* 1205.

LIU, P. and ROSE A., "Social Aspects of >800 Couples Coming Forward for Gender Selection of their Children" (1995) 10 *Human Reproduction* 968.

MAZUMDAR, P., *Eugenics: Human Genetics and Human Failings: The Eugenics Society and its Critics* (London, Routledge, 1992).

MCGEE, A. N., "An Experiment in Human Stirpiculture" (1891) 4 *The American Anthropologist* 319.

MEAD, R., "Annals of Reproduction. Eggs for Sale", *New Yorker*, 5 August 1999, p. 56.

NOYES, J. H., *The Berean: A Manual for the Help of Those who Seek the Faith of the Primative* (Putney, Vermont, Office of the Spiritual Magazine, 1847).

PARENS, E. (ed.), *Enhancing Human Traits: Ethical and Social Implications* (Washington DC, Georgetown University Press, 1998).

PAUL, D. B., *Controlling Human Heredity: 1865 to the Present* (Amherst NY, Humanity Books, 1995).

——, "From Eugenics to Medical Genetics" (1997) 9 *J Policy History* 96.

——, "Darwin, Social Darwinism and Eugenics" in J. Hodge and G. Radick (eds.), *The Cambridge Companion to Darwin* (Cambridge, Cambridge University Press, forthcoming).

PRICE, F., "The Donor, the Recipient and the Child—Human Egg Donation in UK Licensed Centres" (1995) 7 *Child and Family Law Quarterly* 145.

PROCTER, R. N., *Racial Hygiene: Medicine Under the Nazis* (Cambridge, MA, Harvard University Press, 1988).

RESTA, R. G., "Whispered Hints" (1995) 59 *Amer J Med Genetics* 131.

RICHARDS, M. P. M. and PONDER, M., unpublished data, Centre for Family Research, University of Cambridge.

RIFKIN, J., *The Biotech Century. Harnessing the Gene and Remaking the World* (London, Gollancz, 1998).

ROBERTSON, J. A., "Genetic Selection of Offspring Characteristics" (1996) *Boston University Law Review* 421.

SAVULESCU, J. and DAHL, E., "Sex Selection and Preimplantation Diagnosis" (2000) 15 *Human Reproduction* 1879.

SILVER, L. M., *Remaking Eden. Cloning, Genetic Engineering and the Future of Human Kind* (London, Weidenfeld and Nicolson, 1998).

SNOWDEN, R. and MITCHELL, D., *The Artificial Family. A Consideration of Artificial Insemination by Donor* (London, Unwin Paperbacks, 1983).

SNOWDON, C. and GREEN, J. M., "Preimplantation Diagnosis and Other Reproductive Options: Attitudes of Male and Female Carriers of Recessive Disorders" (1997) 10 *Human Reproduction* 101.

STATHAM, H., GREEN, J., SNOWDON, C. and FRANCE-DAWSON, M., "Choice of Baby's Sex" (1993) 341 *The Lancet* 564.

STRATFORD, N., MARTEAU, T. and BOBROW, M., "Tailoring Genes" in R. Jowell et al. (eds.), *British Social Attitudes: The 16th Report* (Aldershot, Ashgate, 1999).

STRATHERN, M., *After Nature: English Kinship in the Late Twentieth Century* (Cambridge, Cambridge University Press, 1992).

THOM, D. and JENNINGS, M., "Human Pedigree and the 'Best Stock': from Eugenics to Genetics" in T. Marteau and M. P. M. Richards (eds.), *The Troubled Helix. Social and Psychological Implications of the New Human Genetics* (Cambridge, Cambridge University Press, 1996).

VAN BALEN, F., "Development of IVF Children" (1998) 18 *Developmental Review* 30.

WILMUT, I, CAMPBELL, K. and TUDGE, C., *The Second Creation. The Age of Biological Control by the Scientists who Cloned Dolly* (London, Headline Book Publishing, 2000).

17

Perceptions of the Body and Genetic Risk

ELIZABETH CHAPMAN*

1. INTRODUCTION

ADVANCES IN THE science of human genetics are beginning to change the way clinicians practise medicine by further expanding the ability to look at underlying biological mechanisms (Bell (1998)). It is currently possible to test DNA directly to determine predispositions for a small number of Mendelian single gene disorders and also to start investigating an increasing number of conditions where several genetic factors play a role in combination with environmental factors. It has been suggested that moves in this direction may lead to a society where individuals and their doctors are more likely to look for a genetic explanation over a societal one, where individuals consider themselves susceptible to genetic risks and the related responsibilities, and where the differences between individuals are reduced to their genetic codes. Lippman has called this "geneticization" (Lippman (1994)) and the extent to which genetic explanations are extended beyond their remit and through what means is further examined by Hedgecoe (2000). However, although it has been suggested that we could be moving towards a genetics paradigm (Conrad and Gabe (1999)), recent indicators suggest that the predictive ability of genetic analysis will generally be low (Wilkie (2001)). Furthermore, the predictive claims that can be made from examining the genetic basis of single gene disorders are very different from the claims made for complex disorders and this realisation has implications for the way genetic determinism is thought about and the way the information is used.

This chapter will focus on some of the issues that testing for a genetic condition raises for perceptions of the body, focusing on two Mendelian conditions, Huntington's disease and cystic fibrosis. The chapter starts by discussing the ways in which the body and identity might be altered by having a genetic test, also giving general background information about the process of genetic testing in at-risk

* I would like to thank Martin Richards specifically for his extremely helpful comments on earlier drafts of this chapter and the Cambridge Socio-Legal Group in general for their support in the writing of this chapter. I would also like to thank all the participants in the two empirical studies and the staff at the associated clinics and the Wellcome Trust for support of my current study.

families. The question of whether genetic testing gives rise to a unique perception of the body will be posed and assumptions challenged by consideration of how the body is perceived following infection with a virus such as HIV. The chapter then moves to some empirical research showing how perceptions of the body can be very different depending on the nature of the genetic condition involved. The final part of the chapter considers some of the implications of such tests, using as a basis for discussion some of the evidence from research on HIV and some data from the comparison of the two genetic conditions.

2. TESTING FOR GENETIC RISK

It has been accepted for some time that the way people feel about themselves is crucially dependent on how their body functions and appears to others (Helman (1994)), but also on the discourses prevalent in society (Bury (1997); Turner (1996)). Over and above the battle simply to maintain health, it is claimed that "risk" is now becoming an important way to think about our bodies, how we act, and our responsibility for our own health; the "risk society" (Beck (1992)). So can knowledge of genetic predisposition or a genetic test result alter the way we think about our bodies?

Following a genetic test, particularly for a condition that will arise in the future, research suggests that a person may begin to think very differently about their body and may consider their identity to be changed as a result (Ashcroft (1999); Cox and McKellin (1999); Juengst (1997). If a gene mutation is uncovered by testing, then this is, by extension, in almost every cell of a person's body,[1] has probably been there since conception, and can have implications for the individual's identity. Giddens (1991) suggests self-identity is reflexive and something that is continuously worked on. In forging our identity we think about who we are and from where we came. Genetic tests thus may have the power to make us think differently about what story we tell about ourselves and how we think about ourselves. The individual may come to feel that his or her identity is now bound up with the genetic condition in the sense that the illness, or risk of illness in the future, is incorporated throughout their body (Kavanagh and Broom (1998)). Those who have genetic tests, even where illness is not yet present or who will always be symptom-less gene carriers, are moved from the category of healthy to the category of "at risk" (Hallowell (1999)), and may experience discrimination (Wilkie (1993)), or altered self perceptions (Axworthy, et al. (1996)). This may be so despite the best efforts of genetic counsellors who continue to stress that, in late-onset conditions, having the faulty gene does not mean that one actually has the condition from testing point onwards.

Armstrong (1998) further reiterates that identity can be associated with one's genetic make-up and that if, through the testing and counselling process, a fault is

---

[1] In fact there is no DNA in red blood cells as these do not have a nucleus.

uncovered, something similar to a reversal of the stigmatising process may occur. Making use of early ideas of stigma and discrimination outlined by Goffman (1963), he maintains that instead of the spoiled identity being overlaid on someone's previously intact identity, the spoiled identity, which has always been there, is uncovered.

Genetic testing has often been considered to be special and to differ from other forms of diagnostic test because of these deterministic overtones; the promise to reveal who the individual has always been, and a future that cannot be altered. Experiences following a test may, however, depend upon whether the result is one in which the future outlook can be clearly defined or whether the result has to be given in terms of probabilities. One important misconception of genetic testing is that a positive test result implies that nothing can be done to change the future. This is not always the case and it may not make sense to think about the implications of genetic tests as being the same for all conditions; the implications for future treatments can vary considerably. An example of a late onset condition where it can often be advantageous to know about one's status is familial adenomatous polyposis (FAP). In this case if someone has the faulty gene, then small polyps form in the colon. Left untreated, one or more of the polyps in these patients will progress to cancer at a mean age of 44 years—approximately 20 years earlier than the appearance of colon cancers among patients with the non-hereditary forms. At-risk individuals can, however, undergo regular screening and have the polyps removed before they develop into cancers.

Furthermore genetic tests differ in the degree to which they can predict the severity of the illness. In cystic fibrosis (CF) (a recessively inherited genetic disorder affecting lungs and digestive organs), a pre-natal genetic test on the foetus can show a mutation in the CFTR gene, but there are many hundreds of different mutations with different effects on the developing individual and with different degrees of severity. If an individual inherits two faulty CF genes, this will result in a disruption in the flow of salt molecules in cells that line the walls of the lungs and pancreas. Thick and sticky mucus results but this can affect only the pancreas, only the lungs or, in the worst case, both organs. In the pancreas, this viscous fluid blocks the flow of enzymes to the stomach, enzymes that are essential for the breakdown of food. The patient fails to absorb nutrients, and bowel movements are often excessively fatty, foul smelling, and painful. In the lungs, the mucus restricts airflow and acts as a culture for bacteria. Over time, frequent infections inflame and then destroy lung tissue, decreasing the capacity for air progressively. In the past CF was considered a childhood disease and the survival rate into adulthood was low. Now, however, owing to improvements in early diagnosis and improved treatments, the median survival age is 30 years (Brown and Langfelder-Schwind (1999)) and environmental impact such as adherence to treatment can also make a significant difference to outcomes.

The examples in this discussion show that the results from genetic tests can vary considerably in their implications for treatment, the degree to which they predict the future course of illness and thus the impact on perceptions of the body.

Furthermore, several different kinds of tests are available ranging from a test on an infant *in utero*, or a pre-symptomatic test on an at-risk individual, to widespread screening. These are outlined in more detail in the following section.

(a) Pre-natal testing

First, there are pre-natal tests available to couples with a family history of a genetic condition where the parents may already have one child with a disorder and who wish to know whether their next child also carries the faulty gene. A couple may also know that they are symptom-less carriers for a recessive condition, having already been screened for the faulty gene, and wish to consider all options before having a child. For couples undergoing pre-natal testing there may be an unstated assumption that the pregnancy will not be continued if the result of the test is positive (Chadwick (1992)), but attitudes to termination of pregnancy in the case of foetal abnormality vary in different cultures and countries, as does legal regulation. In Cyprus and Italy, for example, termination is usually the expected outcome (Modell (1993); Schiliro et al. (1988). However, recent studies in the United Kingdom suggest that termination on the grounds of abnormality is deemed less acceptable, the views of affected groups are increasingly being sought (GIG (1999); RADAR (1999)), and women may now be under less pressure from professionals to have tests or to terminate (Statham and Solomou (1998)).

Making a decision about whether to terminate a pregnancy following a positive test result is more or less straightforward depending upon the condition under consideration and may vary in line with personal values (Evers-Kierbooms et al. (1993)). In a dominantly inherited condition only one parent has to have the faulty gene for the condition to be passed on to the next generation. The fact that the parent carries the same variant copy of the gene, and therefore suffers from the same condition, can have implications in decision-making surrounding termination. Terminating an affected pregnancy can then be perceived as saying "this baby carries the same variant gene as I do, does this mean I should not exist myself?" Empirical evidence that people do think in this way is also presented at the end of the chapter and only a tiny minority of parents who carry dominant disorders use pre-natal tests.

In other conditions, such as those that are recessively inherited, the issues are slightly different. The parents are not themselves affected by the condition and there may be less of a threat to genetic identity involved in terminating the pregnancy. Genetic identity here is used in the sense that one's genetic heritage is important in defining oneself. The parents themselves carry only one copy of the same flawed gene whereas two of these need to be combined in the offspring for the condition to manifest, as one faulty copy of the gene can be overridden by the functioning one. The chances of this happening are one in four for each pregnancy.

Furthermore if, following testing, the couple decides they will continue with the pregnancy, the resultant child's status will be known from birth (Braude et al. (1998)). This means that if the test was for a late onset condition, such as Huntington's disease (HD), the child will grow up knowing that he or she has a genetic condition that may not manifest until some time in the future (Adam (1993)). This may be very difficult for a young person and current professional guidelines are against testing of minors for HD (International Huntington Association (IHA) and the World Federation of Neurology (WFN) Research Group on Huntington's (1994)).[2] It also means that others have information about the health risk status of the child for which that child never gave permission and concerns remain about the influence of self-fulfilling prophecies on adolescents.

In disorders with more variable outcomes, affected pregnancies may not always be terminated as knowledge of the condition in the infant is used instead to ensure early treatment with quality of life benefits. A potential drawback to early knowledge of a condition in the child is that, where severity of the symptoms varies, there is a potential for a child with very mild symptoms (that would otherwise have gone unnoticed) perhaps being treated differently as a result of the genetic test outcome.

(b) Pre-symptomatic testing

This type of testing is available for a person who is not currently showing symptoms but wants to know whether they have inherited the faulty gene for the particular condition that has shown up in the family. This is more likely to be for a late-onset condition and uptake generally for late-onset conditions is highly variable (see e.g. Richards (2001)). In the case of HD (a late-onset neuro-degenerative disorder) the numbers of people having a predictive test were much lower than was estimated from data on expectations to take the test that were generated before tests were available (Harper et al. (2000); Hayden (2000)). Knowledge of the future can be difficult to handle, especially if no interventions are possible, but sometimes this knowledge can inform reproductive decisions and so have an impact on future generations. There are dozens of late-onset conditions and uptake of screening can vary considerably depending upon whether or not treatment is available (such as in FAP), and the degree of certainty of future illness that can be predicted. For example, in HD, the eventual outcome, but not the time of onset of symptoms, is highly predictable as the faulty gene has its effects in almost 100 per cent of cases. Conversely, for breast cancer the eventual outcome is much more probabilistic as the deleterious effects of the faulty BRCA 1/2 gene do not always manifest and there are also environmental factors involved.

---

[2] In the United Kingdom parents could in principle consent to a test for their child but most professionals would not offer it. However, a small number of "Gillick competent" young people have been tested at their own request (Binedell et al. (1997)).

(c) Screening

Thirdly, there are a few screening programmes that can identify carriers of recessive genetic conditions and affected individuals on a wide scale, not just couples with family histories. These are very often targeted at specific populations such as the Jewish population for Tay Sachs disease or those of Mediterranean origin for beta-thalassaemia.

Screening programmes involve both public health priorities and individual decision making and the extent to which these go hand in hand varies from country to country. In the United Kingdom, cystic fibrosis is the most common recessively inherited genetic condition for which screening might be appropriate. At the moment, the Government is still refusing to implement carrier screening on a national level because the economic benefits are not clear-cut (Super (1998)) and some problems remain concerning the psychological effects of carrier screening and understanding of results (Bekker et al. (1994); Axworthy et al. (1996)). In Cyprus, the situation for beta-thalassaemia is organised differently. Beta-thalassaemia is a recessively inherited condition causing extreme suffering in affected individuals from a young age. Both the individual members of society and the religious officials co-operate in a programme where individuals are required to be tested before they can marry. In most cases where the potential spouses are both found to be carriers the wedding goes ahead but there are strong social pressures to use pre-natal diagnosis and abortion of affected fetuses. In recent years there have been almost no births of affected children. Although the rationale is economic, as Cyprus is a poor country, the resources saved are used to provide service and care to those individuals who are living with the condition.

This first part of the chapter has outlined how genetic testing can have different implications for different individuals involved and depending on the conditions concerned. For a person who takes a pre-symptomatic test the impact on the body and identity may be considerable, changing the way that person conceives of him or herself. The extent to which interventions are available will further impact on this, in some cases limiting the fatalism that can sometimes go hand in hand with the outcome of a genetic test. Those individuals who are identified as carriers of a recessive condition, may, although never experiencing symptoms of the condition themselves, still feel differently about their bodies, perceiving themselves as less healthy than their counterparts who tested negatively (Axworthy et al. (1996)).

3. COMPARING THE IMPACT OF TESTS ON PERCEPTIONS OF THE BODY

In order to illustrate why issues of confidentiality and the right to know or not to know one's at risk status are especially important in genetic tests, more detail for one specific condition, Huntington's disease, will be outlined. However, HD lies at the most extreme end of the continuum of conditions caused by genetic mutations.

Unlike most other genetic conditions, in the case of HD those with a mutation will almost inevitably get the disease. The onset is usually late in a person's life, it is currently incurable and affects both the mind and the body. Like most Mendelian diseases it is very rare (about 1 in 5–9,000 births). For these reasons the implications for the body in HD may turn out to be unusual and there is a lot to be gained from comparative studies of other conditions. This section therefore looks first at HD and the special features arising, then moves to consider whether other, non-genetic conditions may also have similar effects for the body. The HIV test (although not a genetic test) is a theoretically strong comparison as there are significant implications for individuals who take the test and who are then designated as "risky", even in the absence of signs and symptoms of HIV. These two disorders, that could both be deemed late-onset, are then compared to cystic fibrosis. This recessively inherited genetic condition usually has an early onset with symptoms present from birth and may involve a different set of implications for the body that have little to do with risk.

(a) Huntington's disease (HD)

HD results from a dominantly inherited faulty gene. Each person whose parent has HD is born with a one in two chance of having inherited the gene mutation. Although the symptoms of the condition manifest in almost all individuals with the faulty gene, the onset of symptoms varies; generally it is from 30 to 50 years of age, but the range can be much wider. But of course a person may be killed in a traffic accident, or die from some other illness, before any symptoms of HD occur, so death from HD is not completely inevitable for those who inherit the faulty gene.

Symptoms result from degeneration of the nerve cells in the brain, which leads to gradual physical, mental and emotional changes. Early symptoms include slight, uncontrollable muscular movements; stumbling and clumsiness; lack of concentration and short-term memory loss; depression and changes of mood, sometimes including aggressive or anti-social behaviour. Difficulties in swallowing and choking are problems in later stages of the illness and weight loss is often a problem. The progress of the disease is slow, but gradual deterioration takes place over 15–20 years culminating in the need for full nursing care and, finally, death.

Huntington's disease is the best known of late-onset Mendelian conditions where predictive testing is possible, but treatment remains an elusive goal (Harper (1996)).[3] Predictive testing for the faulty HD gene is thus carried out following strict protocols. About 10 per cent of those at risk of HD have chosen to have predictive testing. The protocol involves genetic counselling before testing, and further

---

[3] Experimental work on stem cell transplantation for patients with HD is underway, but this raises considerable ethical problems (Hildt (1999)).

counselling upon receipt of the results, often with a companion present. The importance of counselling in the HD protocol is emphasised because either positive or negative results can have an impact on the individual. The realisation of future illness with little hope of cure is difficult to come to terms with and confirmation of HD in one person can also say something about the presence of the variant gene in other family members. Conversely, in some cases the individual may have been convinced that they *did* carry the faulty gene for HD and feel a sense of isolation from the family if they are confirmed as not having it (Juengst (1997)). Naturally, faced with this prospect, some individuals decide not to be tested (probably about one-third of those who enter counselling). The quotation below, from someone in the current study,[4] who is unsure about having the test, illustrates the difficult decision-making process:

> "And yes I was counselled in Manchester, I was at the time. And then when Mark started getting ill with it, then I got in touch with the HDA and I got lots of leaflets about it and read up about it, so I think I know a fair bit about it. And also I'd had, I'd been to the genetic clinic, they'd come down to Norfolk, I think they just sort of pursued me, like they do, they don't give up on you. I'd been to them two or three times and had blood taken in preparation for the test if I wanted it" (P15: 0148–154).

Furthermore, because of the implications for other family members involved in genetic testing, there may be subtle pressures applied to "do the right thing" (Hallowell (1999)):

> "Mum was tested in 1995 and I was tested in 1995 because although number two of my daughters had got her family, the younger one was still wanting to produce a family" (P39: 0023–0024).

The following quotation, from someone who decided to have the test and tested positive, clearly illustrates many of the points raised above such as the shock of finding out, how the diagnosis never leaves one, and the wider implications for other family members:

> "But no, it's very, very hard. My family tried to tell me you know, when I said, 'I haven't got it, I shall be all right' my son and my wife both said 'that could go wrong, this could go wrong'. So I think they had a feeling it was there, and they could see me perhaps more than I can see myself, doing things. You know and so it was quite a shock when they said 'yes you have'. I still think about that horrible day, but you know, you come to terms with that, but it's always in the back of your mind and especially now with the children thinking about having their children . . . and they're still not 100% sure whether to have families or

---

[4] Nine people with Huntington's disease (HD) in the family have been interviewed in this study that aims to investigate two contrasting genetic conditions to see if understanding of the body varies in late onset conditions compared to early onset conditions or depending upon whether inheritance is recessive or dominant. Thirty individuals with cystic fibrosis (CF) have also been interviewed, plus five carriers of one copy only of the faulty CF gene. All respondents answered questions relating to body image, visualisation of genes and genetic processes in the body, ethical dilemmas, and quality of life. The data were analysed using statistical tests or thematically as appropriate. At the time of writing, this study is ongoing.

not, they still really can't make their minds up . . . Yeah there's not a day goes past when I don't think of it, never, never. I just can't get it out of my head" (P3: 0036–0044).

The above section illustrates how one particular genetic condition, HD, epitomises many of the significant issues related to genetic testing, such as how one's perception of the body and future can be changed on the basis of the result, and how this changed perception may occur many years in advance of actual symptoms. The discussion has focused on the way that genetic information can lead to an altered risk status and identity, incorporating the knowledge of a deterministic outcome or "genetic prophecy" (Murray (1997)) and thus potential stigma and discrimination problems. However, the discussion will now be extended by thinking about how the body, identified by genetic testing as "at-risk for HD in the future", is either similar or dissimilar to a risky body identified by testing for HIV.[5] The question to be considered throughout is whether it is only genetic information that has such profound effects on consideration of the body or whether other tests can result in similar feelings.

(b) HIV

A test has been available to identify the HIV virus in the body since the early 1980s. The HIV test can detect the presence of the virus in the body many years before symptoms appear. This is in essence similar to the way that a predictive test for a late-onset genetic disorder can detect the gene fault that has been present in the body since birth, many years before symptoms materialise. The human immunodeficiency virus affects the body through a slow destruction of the immune system resulting, in time, in multiple effects on different body parts. Once the individual is confirmed as HIV-positive, there are implications for his or her identity (Waldby (1996)). The person may perceive the body as contaminated and feel a lack of touch contacts (Chapman (1998); Chapman (2000)). An HIV-positive individual may be treated as an element of society that needs to be contained and experience discrimination in many different contexts (Crawford et al. (1996); Sacks (1996); Schiller et al. (1994); Watney (1987)).

From the moment one is diagnosed HIV-positive it becomes necessary to think about, and adopt, anti-contagion measures in everyday activities; this means that the awareness of diagnosis never goes away. There are regular checks on a person's T cell count as a marker of the functioning of their immune system. This acts as a constant reminder of the virus' action within the body, struggling to overpower the body's natural defences. Regular monitoring of viral load within the body, especially for people who are taking triple combination therapies, means that even

---

[5] Eighteen HIV-positive individuals were interviewed and answered questions relating to body image, touch interactions, psychological health, and social support. The group consisted of five women and thirteen males. Six of these were gay or bisexual and the remaining twelve were heterosexual. The data were analysed either with statistical tests or thematically as appropriate. This work was carried out as a doctoral study between 1995 and 1998.

when fit and apparently well, one is not allowed to forget the HIV virus inside one's body. Although viral load may be reduced to "undetectable" levels, the virus may still be within the body, hidden deep in areas of the brain, lymph nodes or testicles and having potential to resurrect itself in optimum conditions (Zhang et al. (1999)). Linked to this is the idea of pollution and contamination within the body; every blood cell contains the potential to pass on the virus to someone else (Lawless et al. (1996); Weitz (1991)). Although individuals may try to conceal symptoms to avoid stigmatising interactions with others (Goffman (1959)), the body may betray its owner by suddenly breaking out with symptoms that one tries to conceal. For the person with HIV this sense of watchful waiting for symptoms to appear may give rise to a deterministic sense about the future body which is very similar to that identified by a genetic test for a late-onset condition.

In much the same way that genetic test results are confidential, legislation exists in the HIV arena to protect the medical privacy of the individual (Coles and Doughty (1999)). In the early years of the epidemic, approaches to HIV and AIDS were different from public health policies for other infectious threats or sexually transmitted illness; HIV exceptionalism (Bayer (1999)). It was hoped that these clear rules to guard strictly the confidentiality of HIV-related information would encourage people to come forward for testing voluntarily, and modify their behaviour without fear of exposure and resultant stigmatisation. Exceptions to this nondisclosure legislation are permitted in certain cases, such as in order to treat the individual effectively, or in cases of sexual assault if the victim requests it.

As the HIV epidemic has changed with the introduction of treatment therapies there are now calls to treat HIV in the same way as other public health threats and to remove its exceptionalist status. However, as with genetic conditions, an HIV test result can have implications for other members of the wider family or for people connected in social and sexual networks. For this reason there has always been an emphasis on counselling prior to and after an HIV test. Counselling prepares the individual for the knowledge of his or her altered risk status and highlights the dangers of passing on the virus to others. Questions may also be raised about partner tracing, bringing issues of confidentiality and rights to information once again to the fore.

The difficulty surrounding decisions about notification of sexual partners has been slightly eased in recent years. In the past, treatments for HIV were not particularly successful nor were there any apparent benefits for the individual of early, pre-symptomatic testing, only perceived negative effects and potential stigma. Many people thus refused to be tested (Simon et al. (1996)). Since the late 1990s more successful treatments have been introduced (only available in certain countries) and so the benefits of early diagnosis and treatment may now outweigh the drawbacks.

The situation in HIV, although not a genetic condition, is therefore similar in some respects to some serious late-onset conditions (such as HD) in terms of implications for the body, identity, relationships, and potential for stigma. There are also feelings of guilt and self-blame for people who have passed on HIV to a child or another sexual partner or for parents who have had children before knowing their own genetic risk status. The similarities lie mainly in the way that genetic and HIV tests have the power to indicate something about future illness in the body, the way that HIV and genes are widely distributed throughout, and the implications for others through infection or inheritance. Some aspects of body image and identity may be different between the two conditions although this is not well researched at the moment. Specifically, one might expect that feelings of contamination may not be a part of the identity of a person with a genetic condition to the same extent as it seems to be important in the identity of someone with HIV. These feelings of contamination may be a factor in how individuals with HIV react and interact with others through touch (Chapman (1999)). To what extent are consequences for the body and identity such as those outlined above always associated with genetic conditions? We shall turn now to another genetic condition to see; only this time one that has more complex environmental involvement, that is recessively inherited, and that may not give rise to the same feelings about risk and the body.

(c) Cystic fibrosis (CF)

In contrast to HD, there are other Mendelian genetic conditions that are inherited in a recessive fashion where it is necessary for a child to receive a faulty version of the gene from both parents in order to develop the disease. While the dominantly inherited conditions like HD generally manifest in adulthood, the recessively inherited conditions often show symptoms from birth. The carrier of recessive conditions will never experience any resultant health problems themselves but even so there may be implications for their sense of self (Axworthy et al. (1996)) or discrimination (Wilkie (1993)). About one in twenty-five of these are carriers of the faulty gene in European populations. If a child inherits two faulty CF genes, the varying symptoms of CF as described earlier will manifest.

Although CF is an inherited disorder, it may not result in the same sort of feelings about risk as either HD or HIV as each individual will probably have experienced some symptoms, and varying levels of treatment throughout their lives. Rather than waiting and watching for signs in an otherwise apparently healthy body, the majority of individuals with CF are identified at birth although there is considerable variation in symptoms and sometimes people are not identified as having CF until adulthood. For people with CF it is often the day-to-day experience of symptoms that is the most important factor as this person who has lived with CF for 32 years comments:

> "It's a big part, you have to think about before anything else. Like I say if you don't take your medicine, you don't eat as much as you can during the day or whatever, you just go downhill and get poorly. So yeah it's not the first thing on your mind, but it is a big part of you, a big part of your day" (P22: 0192–0195).

In terms of the impact of these disorders on the body, all three conditions (HD, HIV, and CF) are understood to be widespread throughout the body; the faulty gene is in every cell or the virus is in blood and body fluids. They do, however, differ greatly in terms of how each condition came into the body and according to their moral standing. The genetic disorders are present in the body from birth and as such the risk is embodied or corporeal rather than being externally introduced (Kavanagh and Broom (1998)) even if symptoms are not always present from birth. HIV breaches the body boundary though penetrative sex or enters the bloodstream through injecting drugs or blood products. Being HIV-positive carries a stigma and is often perceived as being acquired through morally reprehensible activities, whereas the genetic condition may not involve such clear moral overtones.

So it may well also be the case that people feel very differently about themselves depending upon how each specific condition enters their bodies, the physical manifestations that are occurring, the extent to which they have similarly affected others, and according to the moral status of the particular condition. From a comparison of these three conditions it becomes less obvious that genetic information always results in a unique sense of a risky body, an altered sense of embodiment that foretells the future, or indeed that a sense of a risky body cannot also come from different kinds of tests. Feelings of risk and embodiment also vary considerably, even within a class of Mendelian disorders that are perceived to be a homogenous group. Finally, many of the special features of genetic information, often seen as unique to genetics, can be seen in the HIV case also. Should we therefore still be considering genetic tests as having special implications or should each case where there might be a potential impact on the body be considered on its own merits? This point will be discussed in the next section.

4. FUTURE IMPLICATIONS

Having outlined some of the physical manifestations of these three conditions, it should be obvious that none of them would be acceptable in a world where the emphasis is so often on the creation of a perfect fit, healthy, beautiful body (Crawford (1994)). This is also the case with other disease states, but HIV and genetic conditions deserve more attention, because society may have the desire or the potential to contain or eradicate these conditions.[6]

The reader is probably familiar with much of the negative discourse that surrounds HIV, such as anxiety around contagion issues, often combined with the fear of the perceived unusual sex practices, or drug-using activities. Monitoring the spread of HIV has always been seen as crucial. This may be partly due to the need to keep the disease contained within the reservoirs where it was first encountered

---

[6] For example, during the Nazi regime in Germany several thousands of individuals from families that carried Huntington's disease were killed (Harper (1992)).

and out of the wider community. Certain risk groups, according to this discourse, are more threatening than others due to their leaky, contaminated, and uncontrollable bodies (women and injecting drug users) (Demas et al. (1995); Lupton (1994)). This has been translated into practices of control in terms of physical exclusion and confinement of people with HIV as seen in Cuba (Scheper-Hughes (1994)), or the promotion of tattooing and visible labelling to identify potential carriers (Watney (1987)). Victims may be outlawed in order to return the community to purity (Douglas and Calvez (1990)) and the lines are re-drawn between the healthy self and unhealthy other (Joffé (1997)).

These representations of HIV-positive individuals may now be moderating somewhat as the disease and its treatment evolves; people with HIV may no longer be seen as AIDS victims or AIDS carriers but as AIDS survivors depending upon how they deport themselves once HIV-positive (Lupton (1999)). Preventing transmission of the virus to others remains a high priority however, to the extent that, in the USA, legislation exists to protect "innocent" individuals from the HIV-positive person where infection might occur through unprotected sexual interactions (Lambda Legal Defense and Education Fund (2000); Sears (2000)). The law also requires statutory notification of new HIV cases under the Public Health Control of Disease Act 1984 and the Public Health (Infectious Diseases) Regulations 1988, SI 1988/1546 (Montgomery (1997)), as indeed it does also for TB and some other infectious or sexually transmitted diseases.

These negative representations of HIV and resultant practices are partly to do with the desire to create a stable and predictable world where sources of pollution are controlled and under surveillance. It has been suggested that this ideal of purity or perfection, as a feature of modernity, is also implicit in the discourse of the new genetics. Part of the discourse is thus about the creation of a stable and predictable world where there is no place for disabling and disfiguring genetic conditions and encompassed within it are ideas about surveillance, social cleansing, quality control of children (Chadwick, 1992; Lippman, 1991) and eugenics .

If individuals ever start to be seen as collections of genes rather than as complex individuals with good quality of life, the scene may be set for a revival of eugenics (Petersen (1998)). To what extent might this now be occurring? In the current climate it is worth noting that eugenics had two features in particular. One was that concern for future people took precedence over the interests, autonomy, and rights of the living. The second was the concept that the interests of mankind as a whole were deemed more important than those of the living individual, or indeed of potential unborn children (Wikler (1999); Wilkie (1993)). Certainly, as a parallel, we can note that there has been rather less in the literature about what it is like to live with a genetic condition, either in prospect or currently present in the family, and that perhaps potential children are being considered without due regard for the rights of the living. Tom Shakespeare makes the point that it is rare to hear the voices of people affected (with notable exceptions such as Richards (1996)) and there is widespread ignorance about what it is like to live with a genetic condition or understanding about how much symptoms affect people's lives (Shakespeare (1999)). Does it then follow that if everybody thinks that genetic disease involves a terrible life and an early death then screening of pregnancies is thought necessary and termination is the only possible response to eradicate such human suffering?

The variation in the actual experiences of people affected with inherited illnesses may be obscured. A public image of CF, for example, suggests that the impairment is dreadful (NIH (1997)) but findings in the ongoing study suggest that the self image and quality of life of adult CF patients (as ascertained by a body chart) is considered by them to be largely positive. Participants' self images were also more positive than the image that was generated by them for a "public view of CF", suggesting that they consider the public to have a poor understanding of what life is like for someone living with CF. An important consideration arising from this concerns the extent to which pre-existing ideas can be changed and whether they inform decision-making in a genetic counselling context.

5. GENETIC IDENTITY

These issues of body image have major implications for those currently living with genetic conditions. Although many of the respondents in the study did support pre-natal testing and termination of affected pregnancies in CF and HD, some had very clear objections to it. The main objection rests on the grounds that terminating a pregnancy where the foetus carries the same genes as a person living with a specific disorder may say something negative about the life of the person currently living with that condition.

These quotations illustrate this point particularly well. The first quotation is from a woman carrier of CF who has one child already affected and who went through IVF treatment to ensure that she didn't have a second CF baby:

> "We have talked about this with John, when we were going through the IVF, because obviously it involved me going down to London quite a lot, being there early for scans and egg collections and what have you. It was quite an issue for him, you know, why is all this happening and he did say at the time, you know what would have happened if you'd known that I'd have had CF when you were pregnant? So yes it's an issue that we've all talked about I think, and John's fairly pragmatic about it and he's said, you know if you could have a baby that doesn't have CF, then that's obviously preferable to having a child that does. But I don't know that he's particularly thought about, that we would have perhaps terminated this pregnancy if it had" (P12: 0074–0084).

The second quotation is from a young woman with CF talking about her parents' decisions:

> "So my dad always said, looking at me now he would never, he would have made the biggest mistake of his life and that's where I think to myself, OK they might have a disorder, CF when they're younger or they see it in the baby, unborn, but medical advances—they could never have looked 20 odd years later and seen me as I am now,

even when I was born they were told I would only live three months. So the advances and stuff like this. I think that everyone has a right—and it's up to them, if they can't cope. I wouldn't want to be brought into this world if I was going to suffer from day 1 and suffer badly you know so, it's again it's a hard question, it's up to the individual. I know that, I'd hope that I wouldn't (terminate a pregnancy) purely from the fact that I know the way I am and obviously . . . my baby carrying the genes of the way I am, I know that she'd think similar with her attitude in life, so I personally probably well I personally wouldn't but I would not ever grudge anyone who would because if people can't cope" (P19: 0191–0202)

Finally, this third quotation is from a man with CF in his 30s:

"So yes I do completely and in some ways, I think that's worse thinking like that because then you feel you can't escape it. And also because I sometimes feel like I'm fundamentally flawed, or at least society thinks I am. And it's very hard not to take that on board and your rational side can keep telling yourself, 'no that's just what they say, you're fine. You're a normal person it's just that you've got two base pairs that are different, etc. etc.' and that everybody has different alleles they just don't all have such drastic consequences. But emotionally sometimes that's hard to remember. If you live in a world where it's still a valid reason for aborting a foetus you know, and I have very mixed feelings about all that. I haven't got an answer, but it affects me very, very deeply, it upsets me deeply to feel that society doesn't want people like me around" (P5: 0052–0061).

In sum, both HIV and certain genetic conditions can be controlled in various different ways and the spread prevented. The case for HIV is relatively straightforward. Although some treatments are available, the disease is ultimately fatal, the symptoms are unpleasant, and it can affect people at any stage in their lives, but often affects predominantly young people. Control is at the level of the individual not of future generations. In the genetic conditions, however, decision-making is complicated further by judgements of perceived quality of life; onset may be sufficiently late in life for an individual to have achieved a relatively full life, or the person may have the potential to live into his or her 40s. We are also talking about future generations, their genetic identity, and what makes a life worth living (Ashcroft (1999)).

6. CONCLUSION

It is clear that genetic conditions and the HIV virus are transmitted to others through different routes, but the discourses can be read in the same way; in both examples we're talking about an ideal world, human perfection and more or less coercion (Newell (2000); Shakespeare (1999); Wikler (1999)). This last section of the chapter will raise one final question. Does the analysis of our DNA result in a unique kind of understanding of our bodies and relationships, and give a distinct kind of knowledge, or does genetic hype overstate the power of genetic knowledge?

We have seen that some of the special facets of genetic testing may not be as unique as is often presumed. However, the final aspect of this kind of knowledge that may be unique relates to the way that it can be used to prevent the transmission of genetic conditions to a future generation. This is not the same in HIV or illness conditions and perhaps is the key area where implications of genetic tests are different. In making decisions about the quality of life of the next generation and their right to exist, we are taking decisions that may change the course of society and have wide-ranging legal ramifications. What, for example, are the legal issues involved in potential wrongful life suits where a child is born with a genetic condition knowing that his or her parents could have tested and terminated that pregnancy and gone on to have a "perfect child"?

These are controversial issues and power and choice can be frightening, particularly when we as a society in general have limited understanding of how genetics works and when we feel we have no control (Murray (1997)). Even for people who have lived with a genetic condition all their lives, the understanding of inheritance and details of genetic processes is obscure as this quotation from one of the respondents with CF illustrates:

> "I think since all the genetic things that have been happening recently, I think people are only beginning to think about that side of things and come to terms with it, and even me, who's had a condition that's genetically related since I was born, I still don't really think that deeply about it" (P20: 0156–0159).

From the evidence above we can also see that each different condition may have to be looked at in its own right. From a social science perspective it makes very little sense to generalise from one or two of the first-discovered genetic conditions to the group as a whole. For some, interventions will be possible and for others, not. For some onset will be early and for others much later in life. Perceptions of quality of life, which are so important in making decisions about the lives of future children (Ashcroft (1999)), also vary considerably.

If those with genetic conditions themselves are only just beginning to consider some of the wider implications of changing discourses of genetics, there may be less chance of these filtering into wider society without the implementation of targeted education programmes. We treat genetic knowledge as special because we consider it to have a special impact on the body, because of issues of confidentiality, and because of the wider implications for others, whereas perhaps we should be treating it as special because of the use to which tests can be put. These issues should be carefully considered at different levels. Consideration is needed at a societal level, in terms of how we use genetic test results for reproductive choices, at an individual level, taking into account how advancing genetic technology has the potential to stigmatise those currently living with genetic conditions, and at a legal level in terms of how we regulate future policies.

REFERENCES

ADAM, S., WIGGINS, S., WHYTE, P. et al., "Five Year Study of Prenatal Testing for Huntington's Disease: Demand, Attitudes, and Psychological Assessment" (1993) 30 *Journal of Medical Genetics* 549.

ARMSTRONG, D. MICHIE, S. and MARTEAU, T., "Revealed Identity: A Study of the Process of Genetic Counselling" (1998) 47 *Social Science and Medicine* (11) 1653.

ASHCROFT, R. E., "Genetic Information and 'Genetic Identity'" in A. K. Thompson and R. Chadwick (eds.), *Genetic Information: Acquisition, Access, and Control* (New York, London, Kluwer Academic/Plenum Press, 1999).

AXWORTHY, D., BROCK, D., BOBROW, M., and MARTEAU, T., "Psychological Impact of Population-based Carrier Testing for Cystic Fibrosis: 3 Year Follow-up" (1996) 347 *The Lancet* 1443.

BAYER, R., "Clinical Progress and the Future of HIV Exceptionalism" (1999) 159 *Archives of Internal Medicine* 1042.

BECK, U., *Risk Society: Towards a New Modernity* (London, Sage, 1992).

BEKKER, H., DENNISS, G., MODELL, M., BOBROW, M., MARTEAU, T., "The Impact of Population Based Screening for Carriers of Cystic Fibrosis" (1994) 31 *Journal of Medical Genetics* 364.

BELL, J., "The New Genetics in Clinical Practice" (1998) 316 *British Medical Journal* 618.

BINEDELL, J., SOLDAN, H. R., SCOURFIELD, J. and HARPER, P. S., "Huntington's Disease Predictive Testing: the Case for an Assessment Approach to Requests from Adolescents" in A. Clarke (ed.), *Genetic Testing of Children* (Oxford, Bios Scientific Publishing, 1997).

BRAUDE, P. R., DE WERT, G. M., EVERS-KIERBOOMS, G., PETTIGREW, R., and GERAEDTS, J., "Non-disclosure Preimplantation Genetic Diagnosis for Huntington's Disease: Practical and Ethical Dilemmas" (1998) 18 *Prenatal Diagnosis* 1422.

BROWN, T. and LANGFELDER-SCHWIND, E., "Update and Review: Cystic Fibrosis" (1999) 8 *Journal of Genetic Counselling* (3) 137.

BURY, M., "The Body, Health and Risk" in M. Bury (ed.), *Health and Illness in a Changing Society* (London and New York, Routledge, 1997).

CHADWICK, R. F., "The Perfect Baby: Introduction" in R. F. Chadwick (ed.), *Ethics, Reproduction and Genetic Control* (revised edn., London, Routledge, 1992).

CHAPMAN, E., "Body Image and HIV: Implications for Support and Care" (1998) 10 *AIDS CARE* (Supplement 2) S179–S189.

—— , "Support and Interaction for People Living with HIV", unpublished doctoral dissertation, University of Cambridge, 1999.

—— , "Conceptualisation of the Body for People Living with HIV: Issues of Touch and Contamination" (2000) 22 *Sociology of Health and Illness* (6) 840.

—— and BILTON, D., "Quality of Life for People Living with Cystic Fibrosis: Implications for Ethical Dilemmas", paper presented at the XIIIth International Cystic Fibrosis Congress, Stockholm, 2000.

COLES, M. and DOUGHTY, R., "The Law and Health-care Workers: Confidentiality, Testing and Treatment" in P. T. Cohen, M. A. Sande and P. A. Volberding (eds.), *The AIDS Knowledge Base* (3rd edn., Philadelphia, Lippincott Williams and Wilkins, 1999).

CONRAD, P. and GABE, J., "Introduction: Sociological Perspectives on the New Genetics: an Overview" (1999) 21 *Sociology of Health and Illness* (5) 505.

COX, S. and MCKELLIN, W., "'There's This Thing in our Family': Predictive Testing and the Construction of Risk for Huntington Disease" (1999) 21(5) *Sociology of Health and Illness* 622.

CRAWFORD, J., LAWLESS, S., and KIPPAX, S., "Positive Women and Heterosexuality: Problems of Disclosure of Serostatus to Sexual Partners" in P. Aggleton (ed.), *AIDS: Activism and Alliances* (London, Taylor and Francis, 1996).

CRAWFORD, R., "The Boundaries of the Self and the Unhealthy Other: Reflections on Health, Culture and AIDS" (1994) 38 *Social Science and Medicine* (10) 1347.

DEMAS, P., SCHOENBAUM, E. E., WILLS, T. A., DOLL, L. S., and KLEIN, R. S., "Stress, Coping and Attitudes toward HIV Treatment in Injecting Drug Users: a Qualitative Study" (1995) 7 *AIDS Education and Prevention* (5) 429.

DOUGLAS, M. and CALVEZ, M., "The Self as Risk Taker: a Cultural Theory of Contagion in Relation to AIDS" (1990) 38 *Sociological Review* 445.

EVERS-KIERBOOMS, G., DENAYER, L., DECRUYENAERE, M., and VAN DEN BERGHE, H., "Community Attitudes Towards Prenatal Testing for Congenital Handicap" (1993) 11 *Journal of Reproductive and Infant Psychology* 21.

GIDDENS, A., *Modernity and Self-Identity: Self and Society in the Late Modern Age* (Stanford University Press, Stanford, 1991).

GIG, *Genetic Testing, Screening and "Eugenics": A Genetic Interest Group Policy Paper* (1999).

GOFFMAN, E., *The Presentation of Self in Everyday Life* (Harmondsworth, Penguin, 1959).

——, *Stigma: Notes on the Management of Spoiled Identity* (London, Penguin Books, 1963).

HALLOWELL, N., "Doing the Right Thing: Genetic Risk and Responsibility" (1999) 21 *Sociology of Health and Illness* 597.

HARPER, P. S., "Huntington's Disease and the Abuse of Genetics" (1992) 50 *American Journal of Human Genetics* 460.

——, *Huntington's Disease* (London, W.B. Saunders Company Ltd., 1996).

——, LIMA, C., and CRAUFURD, D., "Ten Years of Presymptomatic Testing for Huntington's Disease: the Experience of the UK Huntington's Disease Prediction Consortium" (2000) 37 *Journal of Medical Genetics* 567.

HAYDEN, M., "Predictive Testing for Huntington's Disease: the Calm After the Storm" (2000) 356 *The Lancet* 1944.

HEDGECOE, A., "The Popularization of Genetics as Geneticization" (2000) 9 *Public Understanding of Science* 183.

HELMAN, C., *Culture, Health and Illness: An Introduction for Health Professionals* (Oxford, Butterworth Heinemann, 1994).

HILDT, E., "Ethical Aspects of Neural Tissue Transplantation" (1999) 40 *Croatian Medical Journal* (3) 326.

INTERNATIONAL HUNTINGTON ASSOCIATION AND THE WORLD FEDERATION OF NEUROLOGY RESEARCH ON HUNTINGTON'S CHOREA, "Guidelines for the Molecular Genetics Predictive Test in Huntington's Disease", (1994) *Journal of Medical Genetics* (31) 555.

IREDALE, R., "Eugenics and its Relevance to Contemporary Health Care" (2000) 7 *Nursing Ethics* 205.

JOFFÉ, H., "The Relationship Between Representational and Materialist Perspectives: AIDS and 'the Other'" in L. Yardley (ed.), *Material Discourses of Health and Illness* (London and New York, Routledge, 1997).

JUENGST, E. T., "Caught in the Middle Again: Professional Ethical Considerations in Genetic Testing for Health Risks" (1997) 1 *Genetic Testing* 189.

KAVANAGH, A. M. and BROOM, D. H., "Embodied Risk: My Body, Myself" (1998) 46 *Social Science and Medicine* 437.

KING, D. S., "Preimplantation Genetic Diagnosis and the 'New' Eugenics" (1999) 25 *Journal of Medical Ethics* 176.

LAMBDA LEGAL DEFENSE AND EDUCATION FUND, "State Criminal Statutes on HIV Transmission" (Lambda Legal Defense and Education Fund updated by the ACLU National Prison Project, 2000).

LAWLESS, S., KIPPAX, S., and CRAWFORD, J., "Dirty, Diseased and Undeserving: the Positioning of HIV Positive Women" (1996) 43 *Social Science and Medicine* (9) 1371.

Levy, M. and Richard, S., "Attitudes of von Hippel-Lindau Disease Patients Towards Presymptomatic Genetic Diagnosis in Children and Prenatal Diagnosis" (2000) 37 *Journal of Medical Genetics* 476.

Lippman, A., "Prenatal Genetic Testing and Screening: Constructing Needs and Reinforcing Inequities" (1991) (XVII) *American Journal of Law and Medicine* (1 and 2) 15.

—— , "Prenatal Genetic Testing and Screening: Constructing Needs and Reinforcing Inequities" in A. Clarke (ed.), *Genetic Counselling: Practice and Principles* (London, Routledge, 1994).

Lupton, D., *Moral Threats and Dangerous Desires* (London, Taylor and Francis, 1994).

—— , "Archetypes of Infection: People with HIV/AIDS in the Australian Press in the Mid-1990s" (1999) *Sociology of Health and Illness* 21(1) 37.

Modell, B., "Concerted Action on Developing Patient Registers as a Tool for Improving Service Delivery for Haemoglobin Disorders" in G. N. Fracchia and M. Theophilatou (eds.), *Health Services Research* (Amsterdam, IOS Press, 1993).

Montgomery, J., *Health Care Law* (Oxford, Oxford University Press, 1997).

Murray, T. H., "Genetic Exceptionalism and 'Future Diaries': is Genetic Information Different from Other Medical Information?" in M. A. Rothstein (ed.), *Genetic Secrets Protecting Privacy and Confidentiality in the Genetic Era* (New Haven, London, Yale University Press, 1997).

NIH, "Genetic Testing for Cystic Fibrosis" (1997) 15 *NIH Consent Statement Online* (4) 1.

Nerwell, C., "Biomedicine, Genetics and Disability: Reflections on Nursing and a Philosophy of Holism" (2000) 7 *Nursing Ethics* (3) 227.

Petersen, A., "The New Genetics and the Politics of Public Health" (1998) 8 *Critical Public Health* (1) 59.

RADAR, "Genes are Us? Attitudes to Genetics and Disability" (RADAR Survey, London, 1999).

Richards, M., "Daily Life and the New Genetics: Some Personal Stories" in T. Marteau and M. Richards (eds.), *The Troubled Helix: Social and Psychological Implications of the New Human Genetics* (Cambridge, Cambridge University Press, 1996).

Richards, M. P. M., "How Distinctive is Genetic Information?", *Studies in History and Philosophy of Biological and Biomedical Science* (forthcoming, 2001).

Sacks, V., "Women and AIDS: An Analysis of Media Misrepresentations" (1996) 42 *Social Science and Medicine* (1) 59.

Scheper-Hughes, N., "AIDS and the Social Body" (1994) 39 *Social Science and Medicine* (7) 991.

Schiliro, G., Romeo, M. A., and Mollica, F., "Prenatal Diagnosis of Thalassaemia: the Viewpoint of Patients" (1988) 8 *Prenatal Diagnosis* 231.

Schiller, N. G., Crystal, S., and Lewellen, D., "Risky Business: the Cultural Construction of AIDS Risk Groups" (1994) 38 *Social Science and Medicine* (10) 1337.

Sears, B., "Barebacking and HIV Disclosure: What's the Law?" (*Positive Living,* AIDS Project Los Angeles, 2000).

Shakespeare, T., "'Losing the Plot?' Medical and Activist Discourses of Contemporary Genetics and Disability" (1999) 21 *Sociology of Health and Illness* (5) 669.

Sharpe, N. F., "Psychological Aspects of Genetic Counseling: A Legal Perspective" (1994) 50 *American Journal of Medical Genetics* 234.

Simon, P. A., Weber, M., Ford, W. L. et al., "Reasons for HIV Antibody Test Refusal in a Heterosexual Sexually Transmitted Disease Clinic Population" (1996) 10 *AIDS* (13) 1549.

STATHAM, H. and SOLOMOU, W., "Antenatal Screening for Down's Syndrome" (1998) 352 *The Lancet* 1862.
SUPER, M., ABBOTT, J., "Genetic Advances in Cystic Fibrosis: to Screen, to Treat or Both?" (1998) 20 *Disability and Rehabilitation* 202.
TURNER, B. S., *The Body and Society* (London, Sage, 1996).
WALDBY, C., *AIDS and the Body Politic: Biomedicine and Sexual Difference* (London, New York, Routledge, 1996).
WATNEY, S., *Policing Desire: Pornography, AIDS and the Media* (London, Comedia, 1987).
WEITZ, R., *Life with AIDS* (New Brunswick, New Jersey, Rutgers University Press, 1991).
WIKLER, D., "Can We Learn from Eugenics?" (1999) 25 *Journal of Medical Ethics* 183.
WILKIE, A. O. M., "Genetic Prediction: What are the Limits?" *Studies in the History and Philosophy of Biological and Biomedical Sciences* (forthcoming, 2001).
WILKIE, T., *Perilous Knowledge: The Human Genome Project and its Implications* (London, Boston, Faber and Faber, 1993).
ZHANG, L., REAMRATNAM, B. and TENNER-RACZ, K., "Quantifying Residual HIV-1 Replication in Patients Receiving Combination Antiretroviral Therapy" (1999) 340 *The New England Journal of Medicine* (21) 1605.

18

Science, Medicine and Ethical Change

DEREK MORGAN

1. INTRODUCTION

THE TWENTIETH CENTURY has seen unparalleled changes in the scientific basis of medicine and as "medicine became imbued with science, so the limits of its endeavour have changed" (Jacob (1998) p. 22). Medicine is moving from what Jonathan Glover (1977) once called "causing death(s) and saving lives" to what might be seen as "saving deaths and causing lives". Perhaps this is nowhere more aptly illustrated than in the decoding of the structure of the DNA double helix; the discovery by Watson and Crick of the molecular structure of the very foundations of life. With this has come, for medical jurisprudence, a metamorphosis every bit as startling as the scientific and technological changes themselves. Radical scientific changes in what can be achieved, whether through cloning or genetic testing, recovery, storage and use (sometimes posthumously) of gametes, have heralded what we might call a "reconstitution of the body". Whether this comes about as a result of a conspiracy of the scientific and medical professions against the laity to push professional dominance into domains traditionally outside medicine's province, or whether we are witnessing the destabilisation of the boundaries of lay and professional competence in an age of democracy, as Roy Porter (1997) p. 702 has recently argued, falls to be debated elsewhere.

The expansion of the capacity to act "has not been accompanied by a comparable expansion of the capacity to predict, and as a result the prediction of the consequences of scientific action are necessarily less than the action itself" (Porter (1997) p. 9). Of course, I do not want to deny, whatever others may hold, that many of the advances in science, medicine and surgery are real contributions to human well-being; the development of micro-surgery is an obvious example, and there are many others. But that is quite a different point. Science has acquired the power "to define situations beyond what it knows about them" (de Sousa Santos (1995) p. 47), in large part because the interesting, difficult and consequential questions are not scientific ones but social and ethical ones.

But it has also been claimed that there are important changes in the ways in which moral decision-making in medicine has developed, which have no less significant implications for a study of medical law. Boaventura de Sousa Santos (1995) p. 34 has argued that we are living in a state of epistemological turbulence:

"it is as though Durkheim's motto has been reversed. Rather than studying social phenomena as if they were natural phenomena, scientists now study natural phenomena as
if they were social phenomena".

There are indeed suggestions that the very basis of ethical inquiry and the knowledge available to us have changed radically,[1] although Gillian Rose (1996) p. 7 has
roundly denounced these kinds of analyses as evincing "despairing rationalism
without reason". Bruce Jennings (1991) has observed that moral decision-making
within medicine is becoming increasingly institutionalised and subject to for-
malised procedures and constraints. Across the broad landscape of contemporary
medicine, including human subjects research, organ procurement and transplantation, assisted reproduction, the rationing of healthcare and the foregoing of life
sustaining treatment:

> "ethical choice and agency are now embedded as never before in a network of explicit
> rules and formal procedures and processes for making decisions. These rules stipulate
> (within certain limits) what types of decision may be made, how they may be made, by
> whom, and with the assistance of what resources" (Jennings (1991) p. 452).

Science and medicine are increasingly drawn into ethical debates where clashes
between the scientific method and philosophical, metaphysical and ethical questions are inevitable. Ethical choices are increasingly institutionalised; they are
embedded in statutes, regulations, directives, court opinions, administrative man-
dates, and institutional protocols. In decisions regarding terminal care, for example, these rules inform counselling and educational mechanisms, encouraging
individual patients and their families to engage in treatment discussions and to
give prior statements about wanted and unwanted treatments.

This "embedded" quality of decision-making has important relationships with
the kinds of ethical concerns and the ways in which they are expressed. Jennings
(1991) p. 451 argues that there has been an important recent shift away from epistemological questions about the relationship between a rational, knowing subject
and a rationally knowable, objective morality as the primary focus of ethical
theory. He sees a shift towards an approach that aims to understand morality "as
a socially embedded practice", always only meaningful in context. These transformations have important consequences for the ways in which we conceptualise
(and even describe) the setting of a legal framework and the establishment of
ethical standards for regulating scientific and technical societies.

2. ENTER MEDICAL LAW

Medical law is, in large part, a process of naming, blaming, claiming and declaiming (Felstiner, et al. (1980–81)). Each of these issues has important ethical and
philosophical dimensions. Naming—is this person "ill", "chronic", "acute"? and

---

[1]   See, e.g., Lyotard (1979); Gilligan (1982).

so on; blaming—exploring questions of individual and state responsibility for health and healthcare, and our collective responsibility for other nations' health; claiming—what are our entitlements to healthcare, of access to services? and declaiming—about saying who we are and whom we want to become, giving a moral and symbolic emphasis to law.[2] These questions concern, more broadly, our efforts to define the sort of society that we say we are and that we want to become. Each of these questions has important philosophical, ethical, sociological and political dimensions, as well as legal ones.

There is, of course, a different set of questions that could be asked, questions that are predicated on a different understanding of the role and contribution of law. Here, law is seen not just as an autonomous body of knowledge, but as a factor that contributes to—which, indeed, facilitates—the so-called public understanding of science, and which also contributes to the (less well-developed) inquiry of what we might refer to as the "scientific understanding of the public". Is medical law to be seen only as an instrumental response to medical practices? Or are there ideological and symbolic elements to it too? The emergence of medical law has hardly occurred in an intellectual, cultural, scientific or jurisprudential vacuum.

Orlando Figes (1996) pp. 733, 857n, has described the immediate post-revolutionary period in Russia as an "age of optimism in the potential of science to change human life and, paradoxically at the same time, an age of profound doubt and uncertainty about the value of human life itself in the wake of the destruction of the first world war". In the late twentieth century, Western societies have, by contrast, a tendency to view scientific "progress" with a profound scepticism, at least as to the human and economic costs involved. Eric Hobsbawm (1994) p. 11 has called the last half century the "crisis decades" and has argued that, even more obvious than the uncertainties of world economics and world politics, was a social and moral crisis, reflecting the post-1950 upheavals in human life. These decades, he has suggested, have witnessed a crisis of the beliefs and assumptions on which modern society was founded, as deep as any:

> "since the Moderns won their famous battle against the Ancients in the early eighteenth century. This is a crisis of the rationalist and humanist assumptions, shared by liberal capitalism and communism".

The exploration of different values and the values of "difference" are features of what has been called the "risk society" (Beck (1992)). According to Giddens (1999), one of the most remarkable metamorphoses of the twentieth century is the transition from what "nature" could do humankind to what humankind can do and has done to "nature"; risk societies are societies that live "after nature". Allied with this, Giddens argues, is an end of tradition; what ethics is, what it consists in, how it is applied, and to whom and in what ways, is no longer uncontested. To live after the end of tradition, says Giddens, is essentially to be in a world where life is

---

[2] This discussion draws from and builds on Felstiner et al. (1980–81).

no longer lived as fate. Almost any news story, and much modern medical litigation, turns on this very discovery, as claims of entitlement to posthumous use of sperm, whole body cryopreservation and judgements about conjoined twins serve readily to illustrate.

The advent of risk society presumes a new politics because it presumes a re-orientation of values and strategies relevant to pursuing them. For Giddens, this leads to the so-called "third way" in politics. More generally, this is what perhaps gives rise to Hobsbawm's "general concern with ethics" (Hobsbawm (1994) p. 287). Ethics, in the limited sense of a concern with different values, has become the paradigm form of social inclusion in the risk society. Ethics, perhaps more than politics, is becoming the paradigm form of participation. Medical law, in this context, has contributed to a number of remarkable metamorphoses that are leaving a deep imprint on both medicine and law. I want now to explore this land of metamorphoses where, a bit like Gregor Samsa, we can almost no longer be sure what we will wake up to find in the morning.[3]

Martyn Evans (2001) reminds us that the practice of medicine is driven by human values (the relief of suffering prominent among them). This recognition, he argues, should replace an exclusive focus on ethics (hitherto highly dominant in normative analyses of medicine) because the range of human values encompasses more than ethics alone. Indeed, medicine presupposes moral, aesthetic, socio-political, intellectual and epistemological values which together construct what medicine is, what it does and what its aims are. Ethics refers to the first and most obvious category of values, moral values, but in time it might come to be seen as merely a special case of a more general concern.

Illnesses are a fusion of individuals' biological processes and biographical experiences; this is true to some extent of all illnesses but is especially true of chronic illnesses. Thus the treatment of chronic illnesses, in particular, requires a fusion of biological and biographical understandings. Illnesses are "episodes in a narrative from conception to corruption" (Evans (2001) p. 150); the provision of medical care is a response to narrative episodes and, of course, constitutes further such episodes. When we speak of health and illness we, of necessity, address a package of conceptual questions (Boorse (1975)). These include political questions—the role and responsibility of the state in securing, promoting or damaging the health of its citizens, and those whom it affects indirectly, intentionally and accidentally, through the extraterritorial effects of its behaviours;[4] and questions of gender, race and ethnicity. If our understanding of medicine's task is to be driven by our understanding of the human values at stake, the question of what medical (or health-care) law actually is, admits of both descriptive and conceptual answers. Margot Brazier has expressed one voice of concern in precisely this regard: "unless the law can settle upon some coherent and defensible definition of illness, the elasticity of

---

[3] In Franz Kafka's story, Gregor wakes one morning to find himself mysteriously transformed into a large beetle. See *Metamorphosis and Other Stories* (London, Vintage, 1999).

[4] See, e.g., Peter Townsend and Nick Davidson, (eds.), *Inequalities in Health* (Harmondsworth, Penguin, 1972) (The Black Report).

the concepts of illness may snap" (Brazier and Glover (2000) p. 208) and the concept of medical law with it.

Medicine is intimately bound up with our corporeality, involving questions of identity, of what it means to be human; what does it mean to talk of the (embodied) "self"? The body is part of what it is to be me, in some sense it *is* my "self". Into this complex ethical and epistemological arena has stepped the strange case of nucleus substitution.

3. IDENTITY ISSUES: THE CASE OF NUCLEUS SUBSTITUTION

Licences under the Human Fertilisation and Embryology (HFE) Act 1990 may not authorise the nucleus substitution (replacement) of an embryo (section 3(3)(d)). A licence is required for the creation of an embryo outside of the body (sections 3(1)(a) and 1(2)), where an embryo is defined as a live egg that has been fertilised or is in the process of fertilisation (sections 1(1)(a) and (b)). Quite clearly, this prohibits cloning, where the technique involves replacing the nucleus of a cell of an embryo *with a nucleus taken from elsewhere*, such as a person, or another embryo:

> "A licence cannot authorise . . . replacing a nucleus of a cell of an embryo with a nucleus taken from a cell of any person, embryo or subsequent development of an embryo" (section 3(3)(d)).

Until recently, it was assumed that any cloning by nuclear substitution would entail such a replacement of the *nucleus* of an embryo, or replacing the nucleus of an egg with a *nucleus* from an embryonic cell. Indeed Dolly had been preceded at birth by Morag and Megan, but they had been born following the use of an embryonic or fetal cell. The Dolly technique, however, involved nucleus substitution into an *egg* and not an embryo. A donor cell was taken from an adult animal (here, an udder cell) and cultured in a laboratory. A donor *cell* was taken from the culture and "stored" in a medium which kept it just alive; the reason for this was to slow down or shut down the activities of the cell and send it into a period of dormancy (or "quiesence"—scientifically called the G0 or Gap Zero cell stage). The G0 cell was then placed alongside a sheep *egg cell* (oocyte, *not an embryo*) from which the nucleus had been removed. An electric pulse was used to fuse the two cells and activate embryo development, which after 5 to 6 days further development in a laboratory was implanted in the "surrogate" (gestational) ewe, Dolly's "mother". Some 150 days later, to public astonishment and incredulity, Dolly's birth was announced in the scientific literature.[5]

The Dolly technique not only stormed the popular imagination and gave the *Boys from Brazil*[6] their greatest exercise in the last 15 years, but it also appeared to

---

[5] I. Wilmut, (1997).
[6] "The Boys from Brazil" (ITC/Producer Circle, 1978, dir. Martin Richards and Stanley O'Toole).

shake the foundations on which the HFE Act had been built; the scientific rocks on which the legislative house had laid its foundations were being battered by the waves of scientific endeavour and coming increasingly to resemble the shifting sands on which public policy's slippery slopes have their first outing; law was surfing again the turbulent seas of chaos theory.

The Warnock Committee[7] made the assumption that the vast majority of embryos used in research would be spare embryos, created in the course of *in vitro* fertilisation treatment, but no longer required for that purpose. The tiny minority of embryos created specifically for research would have been produced by similar techniques (that is, by mixing sperm and egg in the laboratory to achieve fertilisation outside the body). The creation of embryos by means other than by fertilising an egg with sperm was not possible when the issues were debated by the Warnock Committee and in Parliament.

This gives rise to at least two immediate questions; what are Dolly, Millie, Christa, Alexis, Carrel and Dotcom? At one level, they are respectively, one sheep and five pigs. But, created as they were outwith the established fertilisation boundaries—either naturally or scientifically—sparked into life after an electrical pulse, have they been born from a *new kind of embryo*, morally speaking? Secondly, what is the *legal* status of such creations?

(a) The moral argument

As a matter of moral judgement, is a *new* type of embryonic life created by the process of cell nucleus replacement? Moral philosophers and theologians have long emphasised the significance of fertilisation in the genesis of life. Thus Leon Kass (1992) has argued that:

> "While the egg and the sperm are alive as cells, something new and alive *in a different sense* comes into being with fertilisation . . . there exists a new individual with its unique genetic identity".[8]

This has drawn forth the following from Professor of Molecular Biology, Lee Silver: "All non-religious objections to the cloning of human beings" he has suggested:

> "evaporate when a child is born through the fusion of cloned embryos. Such a child will not be genetically identical to either of her progenitor-parents and thus there cannot be any violation to her so-called 'right to genetic uniqueness'" (1998) p. 305.

Silver's point is a good example of the many *non-sequiturs* that abound in this debate. But it also illustrates the role—the declamatory function—that law might assume in order more clearly to mark out the boundaries of personhood in the wake of technological advance.

---

[7] *Report of the Committee of Inquiry into Human Fertilisation and Embryology* (Cm 9314, 1984) (London, HMSO).

[8] (1992) pp. 98–116, emphasis in original.

It seems to me that the resolution of the moral debate has more than usual significance for the legal regulation of embryo research; to paraphrase Margot Brazier, it is more than just an ethicist's tiff. Suppose that, morally, we conclude that an embryo created following cell nucleus replacement is *not* fundamentally a different *type* of embryo because, like all other embryos, it is (a) undoubtedly human embryonic life and (b) could develop into a human being. A "purposive" (or resulting) moral view of the embryo would lead us to regard these as morally compelling reasons for treating cell nucleus replacement embryos like any other embryo. On this view, the moral status of the embryo is given from what results and not (although some once thought and wrote differently) from the mechanisms or processes—or even some particular point in that mechanism or process—by which it comes into existence. If this moral point is valid, then, contrary to Beyleveld and Pattinson, Brazier and Silver, a legal position based upon a "purposive" interpretation of the 1990 Act is similarly defensible.

Margot Brazier (1999) p. 189 has aired her worries on this particular question; "nuclear substitution challenges our understanding of what a human embryo is and what its moral claims may be". While this is one of the first essays in the United Kingdom in which this moral status has been publicly raised, I suspect that it will not be the last. Brazier reminds us that opposition to embryo research is often based on the view that fertilisation is of primary significance; it is the fusion of egg and sperm that begins a new, genetically unique, human being. But, when the embryo is created by the cell nucleus replacement technique and not from the fusing of sperm and egg—*when fertilisation never takes place*—in what (moral) sense is an embryo as a genetically unique entity created?

The use of cell nuclear replacement to produce human embryos might be thought to create a new form of embryonic life, one that is genetically virtually identical to the donor of the cell nucleus. This prospect goes further than that contemplated by either the Warnock Committee or Parliament when it debated these issues. The creation of embryos in this way is not ruled out under the 1990 Act, provided that any research use to which it is proposed to put the embryo is for one of the five existing purposes. Although these embryos differ in the method of their creation, they are undoubtedly human embryonic life which, given the right conditions, could develop into human beings. But are they the same *type* of embryo, morally speaking, as that which deserves respect as a member of the human species as Warnock originally thought and as the 1990 Act decreed? As Brazier (1999) p. 189 asks, "what is the fundamental nature of cloned cell tissue or organs?"

(b) The legal argument

It is important here immediately to make several observations. First, cell nucleus replacement is not specifically prohibited by the 1990 Act. Secondly, the same is true of "embryo splitting". Embryo splitting occurs naturally at a very early stage of embryonic development in the formation of identical twins. This can also be done *in vitro* in some species at the 8-cell stage and identical "cloned" embryos may develop. The HFEA gave careful consideration to embryo splitting as an additional possible form of infertility treatment in 1994, when its potential use at the 2- or 4-cell embryonic stage was discussed. After considering the social and ethical issues involved, the HFEA decided to ban embryo splitting as a possible fertility treatment and indicated that it would not licence research towards the development of cloning as a form of treatment. However, the Authority did not then make a similar prohibition in respect of cell nuclear replacement research. Thirdly, the so-called Dolly technique, where the nucleus of an egg cell is replaced with a nucleus of a somatic cell taken from an adult, was beyond the bounds of scientific credibility when the 1990 Act was passed.

Somatic cell nuclear transfer raises, at the very least, a new legal question on the ambit of the 1990 Act. As the technique involves nucleus substitution into an egg and not an embryo, and as this is not specifically covered by section 3(3)(d), is it prohibited? As fertilisation is not involved, such that section 3(1)[9] does not apply either, is it regulated at all by the Act?

The Human Genetic Advisory Commission (HGAC) and the Human Fertilisation and Embryology Authority (HFEA), in their consultation paper on cloning and the subsequent report *Cloning Issues in Human Reproduction* (1998), rejected the arguments that would have left cell nucleus substitution outside the regulatory ambit of the Act. Rather, following counsel's advice, they declared that, depending on the method used, cloning is either prohibited, or subject to licensing. The Report observed that while "embryo splitting and the nuclear replacement of eggs are not expressly prohibited . . . both involve the use or creation of embryos outside the body". Hence, they concluded, "they fall within the HFE Act and therefore come under the jurisdiction of the HFEA".[10] Clearly, such a position relies on a "purposive" rather than a "literal" interpretation of the 1990 Act and the meaning assigned to the term "embryo".

The HFEA have made it clear that it will not issue a licence for any research "which has reproductive cloning as its aim".[11] A team of scientists in South Korea reported in 1998 that they had achieved nuclear replacement in a human ovum and then cultivated the fertilised egg to an early embryonic stage, although other scientists doubted the veracity of the report.[12] It is far from settled that the application of the "Dolly technique" to humans would fall within the narrowly drafted provisions of the 1990 Act. At least three objections have so far publicly been registered; from Deryck Beyleveld and Shaun Pattinson, from Margot Brazier and from the All-Parliamentary Pro-Life Group.

First, Beyleveld and Pattinson have insisted that using the Dolly technique does not involve the creation of an embryo at all, because an embryo is defined under the Act as "a live human embryo where *fertilisation* is complete", includ-

---

[9] "No person shall bring about the creation of an embryo . . . except in pursuance of a licence".
[10] HGAC and HFEA, *Cloning Issues in Reproduction, Science and Medicine* (1998), para. 3.4.
[11] *Ibid.*, para. 5.4, p. 11.
[12] *The Guardian*, 17 December 1998.

ing "an egg in the process of *fertilisation*". Indeed, as they aver, Wilmut (2000)[13] has himself suggested that "[t]he oocyte is an egg but it has *not been fertilised* and it *never is fertilised* because the nucleus is transferred to it".[14] Beyleveld and Pattinson (2000) p. 233 add their belief that "in practice, it is very likely that the term 'fertilisation' will be judicially construed to include the nuclear substitution of an egg, especially since the HFEA seems to be acting according to the construction of this term".

Margot Brazier (1999) p. 189 has offered a similar interpretation: "I would contend that nuclear substitution into an egg cell is unregulated in the United Kingdom today". Using the analogy of plant breeding, she avers that cell nucleus substitution constitutes "propagation" but not "fertilisation". Section 3(1), requiring a licence from the HFEA to bring about the creation of an embryo, is subject to the definition of an "embryo" in section 1. It provides that "embryo means a live human embryo" and, if that is all that it said, then cell nucleus replacement would clearly be within the statutory scheme of the 1990 Act.

The All Parliamentary Pro-Life Group has taken up and challenged the interpretation offered by the joint consultation paper issued by the HFEA and the HGAC of April 1998. Repeating the Authority's and the Commission's view that embryo splitting and nuclear replacement of the eggs fall within a "purposive" interpretation of the legislation, the Parliamentary group objects that the HFE Act defines an embryo as "a live human embryo where fertilisation is complete", and observe that:

> "the clear intention of Parliament was to prohibit the creation of cloned human embryos, both for research and reproductive purposes . . . since a cloned embryo has not undergone fertilisation, it might be argued that a cloned embryo is not an embryo for the purposes of the Act. If the courts were to adopt this interpretation, it would follow that the HFEA has no power to regulate the creation or keeping of embryos" (para. 1.3.2–3).[15]

They conclude that it is questionable that "work which would create cloned human beings cannot lawfully be carried out", as the Government had concluded, and call for the Act to be clarified to ensure that such a prohibition was unassailably in place.

Let me add to this my own view. Recall that I have argued that, from a moral point of view, and taking what we might call a "purposive" or result-oriented approach, it may be possible to reconcile the cell nucleus substitution embryo with embryos created *in vitro* in what, astonishingly, we might now call "the ordinary

---

[13] Wilmut is the scientist who created Dolly the sheep.

[14] The emphasis is mine. Beyleveld and Pattinson offer a second example of difficulties with legislative interpretation. The German Embryo Protection Act (Embryonenschutzgesetz) 1990, is clearly intended to prohibit cloning; section 6 renders it an offence to create an embryo that is genetically identical to another embryo, fetus, or any living or dead person; but the Act does not define the term "genetically identical", so it is questionable whether it is wide enough to encompass a clone produced by somatic cell nucleus transfer whose mitochondrial DNA will not be identical to that of the nuclear DNA donor.

[15] Quoted in Morgan (2001) p. 192.

way". It follows, contrary to Brazier and Beyleveld, that there is no particular difficulty in accepting the HFEA's view that the creation of embryos by cell nucleus substitution is *already* brought within the scheme of the HFE Act 1990 by an extended interpretation of section 1.

Section 1 is limited not just in the one way that Beyleveld and Brazier have pointed out, but in an additional way too. Correctly, they have reminded us that an "embryo" in section 1 means "a live human embryo where fertilisation is complete". Where an embryo is created by cell nucleus replacement (CNR), fertilisation never takes place, and it is difficult to accept that an embryo within the meaning of the Act has been created. And herein lies the second difficulty.

Section 1(1)(a) in full states:

"In this Act, *except where otherwise stated* (a) embryo means a live human embryo where fertilisation is complete".

The emphasised words indicate that the legislators could have provided for embryos created other than by *in vitro* fertilisation to be included within the statute, but evidently they did not. To read the statute as providing for embryos created by cell nucleus replacement is to read it as providing that an "embryo" means a live human embryo where fertilisation is complete, *unless the context otherwise requires*. And that, decidedly, the Act does not do.

The fundamental problem with adopting a "purposive" approach to the interpretation of section 1 (commended to the HFEA) is that, as a matter of statutory interpretation practice, the "purposive" approach can only be relied upon where there is an ambiguity produced by a "literal" interpretation of the provision in question. On the face of the Act, there does not appear to be any such ambiguity. However, the way in which a court might be persuaded to approach this difficult question might well depend on *context*.

Imagine two types of cases in which the question of the legal status of the CNR embryo and the ambit of the 1990 Act might come to be argued. First, suppose that an embryologist advised of the "literal" interpretation argument decides that s/he will proceed to create CNR embryos without reference to the HFEA. The embryologist does so, conducts experiments on those embryos without applying to the HFEA for a licence, and is then prosecuted under sections 3(1) and 41(2) for carrying on without a licence an activity for which it is said a licence is necessary. Conviction or indictment on such a charge carries a possible term of imprisonment of up to two years. The usual rule in a criminal prosecution would enable the embryologist to claim the benefit, and here the protection, of the "literal" interpretation of the 1990 Act. A court might be less willing to adopt a sympathetic approach with an embryologist who had kept the CNR embryos (or conducted experiments that entailed keeping the embryos beyond the appearance of the "primitive streak"—the "14 day rule"—as provided for in section 3(3)(a) and (4)). But if the "literal" argument is correct, such experiments would not be unlawful under the 1990 Act. Whether the embryologist might commit an offence under another enactment is a moot point.

Secondly, suppose that a case comes before the High Court by way of an application for judicial review. This would be appropriate if, for example, the HFEA refused to grant a (particular) licence to conduct experiments on CNR embryos, or attached conditions to a licence, providing that CNR embryos are not to be used, or that the embryos are not to be kept beyond the statutory period. Here the embryologist's argument would be that s/he is being unlawfully deprived of a research opportunity by the HFEA which, it is alleged, is acting beyond its powers. The strength of the case for a "literal" rather than a "purposive" interpretation of the Act is far less compelling in this second type of case.

Clearly, then, section 1 of the HFE Act is open to competing interpretations. It is the essence of statutory interpretation that words do not interpret themselves, but that begs the question of how particular interpretations are settled upon. The examples I have given suggest that the interpretation to be settled on might depend on the circumstances in which the case is brought to the court; I believe that this *contextual* argument has some weight of legal experience behind it. [16]

4. LAW, SCIENCE AND PUBLIC POLICY

I suggest that there is a real tension between science and law, in what, respectively, science and law have to contribute to the interpretation of laws seeking to regulate science. It is as well to be clear here about what we mean by what we say, for as Humpty Dumpty recognised: "Words mean what I want them to mean; And the question is, whose in charge". As Mulkay (1997) p. 2 reminds us:

> "The examination of the rights and wrongs of embryo research in Britain during the 1980s was highly unusual in the degree to which it subjected a particular branch of scientific inquiry to sustained, collective appraisal . . . The public debate over embryo research led people to assess the morality of scientific research in its approach to such fundamental concerns as birth, death, disability and respect for human individuals. In the course of the debate, people's hopes and fears about this area of scientific investigation and their conflicting ideas about the place of the life sciences in present day society were publicly formed and displayed as they struggled to respond to the challenge posed by embryo research, and by the associated technology of controlled human reproduction".

As Brazier intimates, the debate signifies more than just a lawyer's tiff—negotiations over moral values in a pluralistic "risk" society are at stake, and consensus is difficult to find. It has been argued, for example, that research aimed at understanding a broad range of diseases, through the extraction of stem cells, treats the embryo as no more than a convenient source of research material, and thus offends morality by removing respect for the embryo as an entity in itself. The moral objection to the use of embryos may be amplified, for some people, if embryos were to be produced in a laboratory for the specific purpose of extracting stem cells for experimental use, even though the ultimate benefit might be the

[16] See *Coventry Waste Disposal v. Solihull Borough Council* [1999] 1 WLR 2093.

understanding of disease or its treatment. Such an approach, some would argue, does not retain any sense of the respect for the embryo, used by the Warnock Committee to justify research on embryos.

A contrary moral view is that, provided the research is necessary to secure bene-fits to human health in the future, the use of embryos at a very early stage in their development is not lacking in respect. Taking this view, it might be argued that the use of embryos to increase understanding of disease does not differ so fundamen-tally from the purposes of currently permitted research, even though conceptually the embryo is more closely associated with the reproductive process. In particular, research leading to potential treatments for major diseases of tissue or organs may not be any less respectful of the embryo's moral status than research on congeni-tal disease, for example. Indeed, if there is greater potential for the research to benefit a wider range of people or treat a wider range of disorders, such research may be more ethically justified.

The current "research purposes" specified in the 1990 Act pertain only to research that could be envisaged at the time the Act was debated. It is, however, difficult to argue that they were based on immutable moral criteria. The existence in the 1990 Act of the power to broaden "research purposes", in due course, sup-ports this view, and indeed that is what has now been achieved by the enactment of the Human Fertilisation and Embryology (Research Purposes) Regulations 2001 (S.I. 2001/188). In all types of embryo research under consideration, it has to be accepted that the embryo cannot itself receive any benefit. It is used instru-mentally—as a means to an end—and will be destroyed. This is, in any event, an inevitable outcome for all spare embryos, whether donated for research under the currently allowed research purposes, or no longer required for treatment. If the arguments of the Warnock Committee are accepted, the issue to be considered is one of balance, whether the research has the potential to lead to significant health benefits for others, and whether the use of embryos at a very early stage of their development in such research is necessary to realise those benefits.

Margot Brazier (1999) p. 167 has commended the British model of regulation as adopted and enacted in the Human Fertilisation and Embryology Act 1990, but cautions that "again and again, as new medical developments emerge, we debate the same issues in different guises". As with the Red Queen in *Alice Through the Looking Glass*, public policy in regulating biotechnology is forever rushing to stay in one place: "you see, it takes all the running you can do, to keep in the same place. If you want to go somewhere else, you must run at least twice as fast as that".[17]

---

[17] "Alice Through the Looking Glass", in M. Gardner (ed.), (1960), p. 210. See also M. Ridley, *The Red Queen: Sex and the Evolution of Human Nature* (Harmondsworth, Penguin, 1994). It is instructive to recall Gardner's (1990) p. 170 exploration of the "end game" in the chess game in which Alice and the Red Queen take part: "Throughout the problem, Alice remains on the queen's file except for her final move when (as queen) she captures the Red Queen to checkmate the dozing Red King. It is amus-ing to note that it is the Red Queen who persuades Alice to advance along her file to the eighth square. The Queen is protecting herself with this advice . . . Of course, in a real chess match, the game would have been up long before, because the White King had earlier been placed in check by the Red Queen without either side taking account of the fact".

With this in mind, we might recall the danger of ignoring an important plea, made by the late German philosopher Hans Jonas, for what he called a "scientific futurology"—a "lengthened foresight"—which will help to disclose what is possibly at stake, what values and traditions we may pass up, what goals and opportunities we ought, in all conscience, to deny ourselves; "what we must avoid at all cost is determined by what we must preserve at all cost".[18]

REFERENCES

BECK, U., *Risk Society: Toward a New Modernity* (London, Sage, 1992).

BEYLEVELD, D. PATTINSON S. and HAKER, H. (eds), *The Ethics of Genetics in Human Procreation* (Ashford, Ashgate, 2000).

BOORSE, C., "On the Distinction Between Health and Disease" (1975) *Philosophy and Public Affairs* 5.

BRAZIER, M., "Regulating the Reproduction Business?" (1999) 7 *Medical Law Review* 166.

—— and GLOVER, N., "Does Medical Law have a Future?" in P. Birks (ed.), *Law's Future(s)* (Oxford, Hart, 2000).

EVANS, M., "Philosophy and the Medical Humanities" in H. M. Evans and I. G. Finlay (eds.), *Medical Humanities* (London, BMJ Books, 2001).

FELSTINER, W., ABEL, R. and SARAT, A., "The Emergence and Transformation of Disputes: Naming, Blaming and Claiming" (1980–81) 15 *Law & Society Review* 631.

FIGES, O., *A People's Tragedy: The Russian Revolution 1891—1924* (London, Pimlico, 1996).

GARDNER, M., *The Annotated Alice* (Harmondsworth, Penguin, 1960).

GIDDENS, A., "Risk and Responsibility" (1999) 62 *Modern Law Review* 1–16.

GILLIGAN, C., *In A Different Voice* (Cambridge, Mass., Harvard University Press, 1982).

GLOVER, J., *Causing Death and Saving Lives* (Harmondsworth, Penguin, 1977).

HOBSBAWM, E., *Age of Extremes: The Short History of the Twentieth Century 1914—1991* (London, Michael Joseph, 1994).

JACOB, J., *Doctors and Rules: A Sociology of Professional Values* (London, Routledge, 1998).

JENNINGS, B., "Possibilities of Consensus: towards Democratic Moral Discourse" (1991) 16 *Journal of Medicine & Philosophy* 447.

JONAS, H., *The Imperative of Responsibility* (Chicago, University of Chicago Press, 1984).

KASS, L., "The Meaning of Life—in the Laboratory" in K. D. Alpern (ed.), *The Ethics of Reproductive Technology* (New York, Oxford University Press, 1992).

LYOTARD, J-F., *The Post Modern Condition: A Report on Knowledge* (Manchester, Manchester UP, 1979).

MORGAN, D., *Issues in Medical Law and Ethics* (London, Cavendish Publishing, 2001).

MULKAY, M., *The Embryo Research Debate: Science and the Politics of Reproduction* (Cambridge, Cambridge University Press, 1997).

PORTER, R., *The Greatest Benefit to Mankind: A Medical History of Humanity from Antiquity to the Present* (London, Harper Collins, 1997).

ROSE, G., *Mourning Becomes the Law: Philosophy and Representation* (Cambridge, Cambridge University Press, 1996).

[18] Jonas (1984) p. 28.

Silver, L., *Remaking Eden* (London, Weidenfeld & Nicoloson, 1998).

de Sousa Santos, B., *Toward a New Common Sense: Law, Science and Politics in the Paradigmatic Transition* (London, Routledge, 1995).

Wilmut, I., "Viable Offspring derived from Foetal and Adult Mammalian Cells," (1997) 385 *Nature* 881.

Wilmut, I., Campbell, K. and Tudge, C., *The Second Creation* (London, Headline, 2000).

Index